ANALYZING INTELLIGENCE

Additional Praise for *Analyzing Intelligence*

"At last . . . a comprehensive compendium of thought and insights on the profession of analysis! A must read for anyone interested in intelligence reform, analytic transformation, and for the fifty percent of intelligence community analysts with less than five years experience."

—TIMOTHY R. SAMPLE, president, Intelligence and National Security Alliance
and former staff director, House Permanent Select Committee on Intelligence

"The most wide-ranging introduction to the vital craft of American intelligence analysis that has ever been published for the general audience of peers, scholars, and students. As editors, George and Bruce both exemplify and advance the professional standards they preach. Readers will find plenty of healthy self-criticism and recognition of problems. Yet readers may end up questioning some preconceptions of their own as they encounter essays that knock down some caricatures and corrosive myths that too often dominate contemporary discussion of intelligence issues."

—PHILIP ZELIKOW, White Burkett Miller Professor of History, University of
Virginia, and executive director of the 9/11 Commission.

"*Analyzing Intelligence* offers a sophisticated overview of the history, performance, and practice of intelligence analysis. The contributors explore why good analysis is extraordinarily difficult and how changing threats, technologies, and expectations are shaping the intelligence profession."

—JAMES J. WIRTZ, Naval Postgraduate School, Monterey, California

ANALYZING INTELLIGENCE

ORIGINS, OBSTACLES, AND INNOVATIONS

ROGER Z. GEORGE
JAMES B. BRUCE
Editors

In cooperation with the Center for Peace and Security Studies
Edmund A. Walsh School of Foreign Service
Georgetown University

Georgetown University Press
Washington, D.C.

Library of Congress Cataloging-in-Publication Data

Analyzing intelligence : origins, obstacles, and innovations / Roger Z. George, James B.
Bruce, editors ; in cooperation with the Center for Peace and Security Studies, Edmund A.
Walsh School of Foreign Service, Georgetown University.
    p. cm.
  Includes bibliographical references and index.
  ISBN-13: 978-1-58901-201-1 (alk. paper)
   1. Intelligence service—United States—Methodology.   2. Military intelligence—United
States.   3. National security—United States.   I. George, Roger Z., 1949–   II. Bruce,
James B.   III. Georgetown University. Center for Peace and Security Studies.
  JK468.I6.A843 2008
  327.1273—dc22

                                            2007031706

15   14   13   12   11   9 8 7 6 5

Printed in the United States of America

To three pathfinders for the profession of intelligence analysis

Sherman Kent

Richards J. Heuer, Jr.

Jack Davis

Contents

Part Four: Diagnosis and Prescription

Part Five: Leading Analytic Change

Part Six: New Frontiers of Analysis

Preface

THIS BOOK PRESENTS an exposition and critique of U.S. intelligence analysis. A single author could not have written it as authoritatively or completely. When we decided to produce this kind of volume on intelligence analysis, we made two critical decisions at the outset: first, to commission new chapters, because what we were seeking was simply not available in the current literature; and second, to recruit the most qualified experts to write these original contributions. We also sought to bring these fresh perspectives together in a way that would yield a whole that is truly greater than the sum of its parts. We hope we have succeeded in these daunting collaborative tasks.

Collaboration is more than cooperation toward a common goal. For this project it has been a career-long sharing of ideas on how to make intelligence analysis a true profession. In a sense, it took more than two decades of contact between the editors to produce this volume, as we constantly crossed paths in our professional lives. Both of us studied international relations theory and political science before joining the intelligence community. Our analytic careers both began at the National Intelligence Council and converged again at the Central Intelligence Agency's (CIA's) Directorate of Intelligence, Office of European Analysis. In these rather different organizations, we became well acquainted with how intelligence analysis is conducted at both the intelligence community and agency levels. Here we were first exposed to the talents of such phenomenal analysts as Hal Ford, a vice chairman of the National Intelligence Council and mentor of national intelligence estimates writers like ourselves. And we also encountered Jack Davis, at the time a national intelligence officer and later a career-long developer and teacher of tradecraft. Later, we were again privileged to serve at the National Intelligence Council, drafting and managing national intelligence estimates, where we were able to see the impressive skills of some of the best analysts in the U.S. government—and some of the frailties of the estimating process.

In these assignments and others, we had our share of triumphs and setbacks, along the way observing how intelligence analysis works in practice and how it might be made to work better. Seasoned by firsthand contact with intelligence at both its best and worst, we could not avoid developing ideas regarding how to improve analysis.

These combined experiences have taught us to be humble but also to be more demanding of intelligence. We came to believe that "lessons learned" must be shared with others; otherwise, changes in the analytic habits of others will not occur. But we could not hope to provide a complete set of important lessons. Thus, the other contributors to this book have multiplied our own insights exponentially in understanding the origins, practices, problems, and prospects of the craft—and aspiring profession—of intelligence analysis. Above all, we aim to improve it.

Such ideas were also nurtured by our working on analytic tradecraft issues while serving in different parts of the CIA. One of us worked on preparing some of the early Alternative Analysis instructional materials for CIA analysts. The other became a student of denial and deception as a factor degrading U.S. intelligence and later served as a senior staff member on the President's Commission on the Capabilities of U.S. Intelligence Regarding Weapons of Mass Destruction (the Silberman-Robb WMD Commission). Most recently, we spent time together at the Sherman Kent School for Intelligence Analysis, where we were deeply involved in preparing new tradecraft primers and monographs to help overcome some of the cognitive biases and other tradecraft errors that played such a destructive role in the intelligence failure concerning Iraqi weapons of mass destruction.

In pursuing this project, we have benefited tremendously from the insights gained in many conversations over the years—not always consensual—with our contributors as well as with other intelligence colleagues and critics. We cannot give enough credit to Richards Heuer, whose ground-breaking book *Psychology of Intelligence Analysis* set the standard for serious consideration of the impact of the cognitive dimensions of intelligence analysis. Likewise, working for and with many of the other contributors to this volume has enriched our professional careers as well as inspired us to try to capture what we have collectively learned about the art and science of analysis.

Both of us owe a debt of gratitude to a number of teaching institutions, two of which especially helped encourage our interest in preparing a book of this nature for future analysts. In particular, Georgetown University's Security Studies Program, where we are currently adjunct professors, has been a leader in graduate-level intelligence studies, both a source of eager and challenging students and an ideal incubator for the ideas found in this book. Likewise, the National War College, where each of us has taught at separate times, sets a high standard for professional education—a model, really, that we believe should be emulated in a future National Intelligence University.

This book would not have been possible without the generous support of Georgetown University's Center for Peace and Security Studies (CPASS), the research arm of its Security Studies Program. Through its director, Daniel Byman, and deputy director, Ellen McHugh, CPASS has provided indispensable resources as well as enthusiasm, advice, and many other forms of steady encouragement throughout our project. Richard Brown of Georgetown University Press has been especially understanding of deadlines along with the added burdens of working with intelligence practitioners, including the inconvenient but necessary "prepublication review" process at the CIA. In that regard, we appreciate the CIA's Publication Review Board's timely review of our manuscript as well as excellent guidance.

We also must thank our wives, Cindy and Penny, for their understanding and support, and also apologize to them for the many lost weekends, evenings, and early mornings, when we were crafting or correcting text and sending copious e-mails back and forth to coordinate research, rewriting, reformatting, and the myriad details associated with our drafting and editing responsibilities. For that, there is no way to repay our patient spouses but with love.

Last, but certainly not least, we thank Matthew Larssen, our able George-town University research assistant, whose careful manuscript preparation, fact checking, and mastery of style guides have made this book not only more presentable but also more sound because of his attention to detail. Perhaps more important, Matt was a sanity check on the themes and ideas contained in this book. And it is for his generation of intelligence analysts that we have written it.

Intelligence Analysis—The Emergence of a Discipline

JAMES B. BRUCE AND ROGER Z. GEORGE

SLIGHTLY MORE than half a century ago, the American scholar and pioneering intelligence analyst Sherman Kent lamented that the U.S. intelligence community lacked a professional literature.[1] Serving as the head of the Central Intelligence Agency's (CIA's) Office of National Estimates, Kent hoped to define and develop a professional intelligence analysis discipline, noting that academic professions could not operate without an understanding of the field or a comparable body of knowledge. Today, though there is surely a large body of general writing on intelligence, most professional intelligence analysts still share Kent's complaint. Indeed, many writers have instead concentrated on the past and current failings of intelligence and policy officials, putting the record "straight" as they see it, or exposing sensational intelligence operations to excite or infuriate the public. However, they have largely neglected defining the discipline of "intelligence analysis" or adding to the collective knowledge on what constitutes good analytic principles and practices.

Defining the Analytic Discipline

Is there a professional discipline known as "intelligence analysis?" Considerable effort has been devoted to defining what is meant by the general term "intelligence," which surely encompasses analysis as one part of a multifaceted process of gaining specific, often secret, information for government use.[2] Analysis is the thinking part of the intelligence process, or as the former career analyst and senior official Douglas MacEachin has phrased it, "Intelligence is a profession of cognition."[3] It is all about monitoring important countries, trends, people, events, and other phenomena and in identifying patterns or anomalies in behavior and cause–effect relationships among key factors that explain past outcomes and might point to future developments with policy implications for the United States. Another key founder of CIA analytic practices and principles has phrased it more succinctly: "The mission of intelligence analysts is to apply in-depth substantive expertise, all-source information, and tough-minded tradecraft to produce assessments that provide distinctive value-added to policy clients' efforts to protect and advance U.S. security interests."[4]

Analysis is but one part, but ultimately in our view the decisive part, of the intelligence process that produces insight for policymaking. The typical diagram of the intelligence cycle found in figure 1 exemplifies how many see the intelligence process. It starts with identifying what the customer needs (requirements) and ends with delivering the intelligence (dissemination) to satisfy those needs.[5] Despite its simplification of what is a very complex process, this conceptualization does underline the analyst's pivotal role in transforming information provided by various collection systems into judgment and insight for the policy customer. Whether that information is good, bad, or somewhere in between, the analyst must put it into a context that is relevant and useful for the policymaker.

This analysis comes in a variety of forms. Traditionally, one thinks of products—so-called finished intelligence analysis—which is printed and distributed to select government users. This definition of analysis conveys, however, a mechanistic and also somewhat linear process, which figure 1 represents. The "production-line" metaphor conjures up an image of analysts writing, reviewing, editing, and publishing an assessment, and then moving onto the next question or task. In reality the cognitive part of analysis is more akin to a computer model that has been collecting and interpreting incoming data and constantly reassessing how new data might change not only the findings but also the computer model being used to organize and interpret the data. The forms that analysis can take, then, are not limited to the printed or even the electronic word or graphic. As often, "analysis" occurs when analysts interact with policymakers over the telephone, via the Internet, during a videoconference, or at a meeting. This form of intelligence support has been referred to as "analytical transactions." Though impossible to quantify, perhaps tens of thousands of such transactions occur yearly.[6] Moreover, the sharing of data, hypotheses, interpretations, and questions among analysts, and other nongovernment experts is possibly

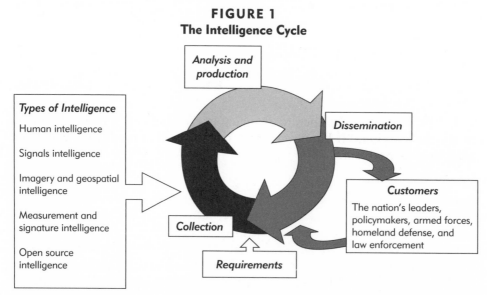

FIGURE 1
The Intelligence Cycle

Source: Adapted from a briefing, *The Intelligence Community,* available at the Director of National Intelligence website (www.dni.gov).

where the most insightful cognition is occurring, rather than on the page of a finished assessment or a PowerPoint slide.

The Complete Analyst

The analytic process, then, must be understood as demanding more than just a well-educated individual who can write concisely. The complete intelligence analyst must combine the skills of historian, journalist, research methodologist, collection manager, and professional skeptic. That is, at a minimum, he or she must demonstrate a very unique skill set:

- mastery of the subject matter as well as related U.S. policies,
- understanding of research methods to organize and evaluate data,
- imagination and scientific rigor to generate as well as test hypotheses,
- understanding of unique intelligence collection methods,
- self-awareness of cognitive biases and other cognitive influences on analysis,
- open-mindedness to contrary views or alternative models that fit the data, and
- self-confidence to admit and learn from analytic errors.

What distinguishes an intelligence analyst from an expert outside the intelligence community, then, are not the first three characteristics, which are shared with many international affairs specialists, although these attributes are especially important in intelligence. Many so-called subject matter experts are well versed in the history, politics, culture, and language of many countries or are technical experts in a wide variety of areas; they may also be very attuned to U.S. policy deliberations and indeed be involved in advising a number of government officials on the correct policies to adopt. And many foreign affairs specialists may have methodological expertise. Where the intelligence analyst distinguishes himself or herself is in having the other four characteristics. The complete analyst must be an expert on how to use intelligence collection capabilities; be both imaginative and rigorous in considering explanations for missing, confusing, and often contradictory data while at the same time being able to be a self-critic of one's own biases and expectations of what the data show; and, most important, be open to changing one's mind and consciously trying to ask the question, "If I'm wrong, how might I need to modify the way I am analyzing the problem?"

Searching for a Literature

As of 2007, the body of scholarly writing on intelligence analysis remains—nearly fifty years after Kent's lament—surprisingly thin. It is true that academics and intelligence professionals have seen a growing literature on intelligence in recent years. Yet with some qualified exceptions, not a single book has exclusively addressed intelligence *analysis* and nothing recent has treated it comprehensively.[7] This is surprising given the importance of the subject and the thousands of professionals who practice the craft daily throughout the sixteen agencies in the U.S. intelligence community. Moreover, the two most recent U.S. intelligence failures—the September 11, 2001, terrorist attacks (failure to "connect the dots") and Iraq's weapons of mass destruction (WMD) (failure to accurately estimate their amount or their complete absence)—are frequently cited, correctly, as failures in analysis. A thorough survey over the past two decades of the literature on U.S. intelligence analysis yields meager results. This book aims to begin to fill that puzzling void.

In the past five years, the intelligence literature has been expanded by multiple investigations into the U.S. intelligence community's performance in the September 11 attacks and the Iraq war. Unfortunately, these reviews have provided us with a rather incomplete picture on how to improve intelligence analysis. The 9/11 Commission Report provides a brilliant recounting of the hijackers' plot and copious recommendations on how to improve intragovernmental information sharing and defensive measures against global terrorism. However, there is scant attention at all devoted to understanding how analysis might have been better and to laying out any game plan for improving intelligence analysis on terrorism. The sound-bites that the U.S. intelligence community "lacked imagination" or "failed to connect the dots" are hardly sufficient insight on why U.S. experts were unable to grasp the audacious nature of the threat.[8] Sadly, professionals learn little from this well-written report other than to acknowledge that agencies should have done better at information sharing, should have been writing more national estimates, and should have been thinking more imaginatively.

The record is better in the reviews conducted on U.S. analysis covering Iraq's WMD programs. In addition to faulting collection efforts, fragmented intelligence community operations, management, and other aspects of the intelligence system, the Silberman-Robb WMD Commission was explicit in critiquing the analytic record as well as the analytic process. The commission's critique was based on an in-depth examination of the analytical process involved in producing both current reporting as well as estimative intelligence on Iraq's suspected WMD programs, and on other cases including Libya, Afghanistan, Iran, North Korea, and terrorism. Overall, from these cases the report found a "lack of rigorous analysis." In particular, it found "finished intelligence that was loosely reasoned, ill-supported, and poorly communicated," and "too many analytical products that obscured how little the intelligence community actually *knew* about an issue and how much their conclusions rested on inferences and assumptions."[9]

Although the WMD Commission noted several analytical successes, such as with some intelligence on Libya and the A. Q. Khan nuclear proliferation network, it also found a preponderance of "serious analytical shortcomings." These included

inadequate Intelligence Community collaboration and cooperation, analysts who do not understand collection, too much focus on current intelligence, inadequate systematic use of outside experts and open source information, . . . and poor capabilities to exploit fully the available data. Perhaps most troubling, we found an

Intelligence Community in which analysts had a difficult time stating their assumptions up front, explicitly explaining their logic, and, in the end, identifying unambiguously for policymakers what they *do not know*. In sum, we found that many of the most basic processes and functions for producing accurate and reliable intelligence are broken and underutilized.[10]

The WMD Commission's major recommendations on analysis focused on improvements in

- management of analysts,
- utilization of nontraditional sources, including open sources,
- understanding of how foreign denial and deception can have an impact on collection and analysis,
- long-term research and strategic thinking, and particularly
- tradecraft (or methodology) through much improved training, especially to produce analysis that is more rigorous and transparent.[11]

We intend to give particular attention in this volume to these issues and to others as well.

Having said all this about what has been written so far on the recent intelligence failures, we believe there is still a notably thin professional literature on intelligence analysis. Part of this glaring absence is the result of management imperatives that are driven by *current intelligence* demands (as opposed to more in-depth research and less time-pressured analysis) and do not permit sufficient time to reflect on the intelligence community's past performance or to record the lessons learned, from which subsequent generations of analysts can benefit. Another part is a justified sensitivity to focusing too exclusively on the intelligence community's past failings—which are easier to document than its many successes.

Indeed, defining successful analysis is itself a complex question. When analysts convincingly warn of a possible threat and policymakers heed this advice, disaster may be averted; then, policymakers may claim that intelligence analysts exaggerated the threat in the first place. In other cases, good analysis helped to shape a policymaker's perspective on an issue early in the decision-making process, leading to successful policy formulation and implementation. Accordingly, the policy question seems relatively unimportant and the international repercussions seem so unimportant that few outsiders can appreciate the counterfactual consequences of flawed analysis that could have driven policy in a different direction and dramatically changed the U.S. stakes in an issue. Little effort, of course, has been made to record these routine "successes" where timely and well-constructed analysis was part of a policy process that went smoothly or did not result in a major crisis or controversy. This is an area where more work remains to be done.

Putting Analysis in a Policy Context

To understand analysis and how to improve it, one must understand how it fits into the actual policymaking process here in the United States. Certain realities must be recognized so that analysis can be better understood. First, policymakers live in an information-rich environment. Second, intelligence provides an important part of the information used to make decisions. Analysis tries to bound the uncertainty inherent in complex international developments and tailor understanding to fit specific government needs.

An Information-Rich Policy Environment

When U.S. national security decision makers deliberate over significant policy issues, information that bears on those decisions is always important and often vital. Whether deciding to negotiate with or coerce another country, whether deciding to intercede in an ethnic conflict to halt genocide, or whether deciding how to stem an insurgency using a mixture of policy tools, the policymaker is relying on a multitude of information sources to determine what course of action the government should take. National security policymakers enjoy access to a broad range of information to help them deliberate such issues and support their decisions. Some of that information will be reliable; some not. Some is biased, calculated to influence. Some is irrelevant or useless. Often it can be controversial. Some is secret or highly sensitive. But much of it comes from open sources such as newspapers, media outlets, the Internet, and scholarly articles and books. Some are opinion pieces in magazines and op-ed pages written mostly in Washington and New York. Still other information comes from personal and professional contacts, other interested U.S. policymakers and stakeholder government agencies, policy advocates, and opponents—or even from select foreign officials or foreign plotters and power seekers, and additional knowledgeable parties who may be interested or disinterested and whose involvement may never be publicly known. And some information for policy decision making comes from the intelligence community.

Using Intelligence Analysis to Bound Uncertainty

Intelligence officials cannot control which sources of information policymakers will use or how they will use them—that is the sole prerogative of policymakers. But intelligence officers do have a unique vantage point compared with those in the policy world to weigh and assess the relative reliability and accuracy of many sources of information available to decision makers. Notably, what intelligence officials *can* control is the quality and quantity of the intelligence information that will be provided to government officials. The better the quality and relevance of the information, the higher the policy impact—or so intelligence officers hope.

The lion's share of intelligence for these policymakers often comes in the form of *analysis*.[12] Such analytical products are referred to as "finished" intelligence because analysts have synthesized raw information collected from multiple sources and have interpreted the meaning of such information in the context of the policymakers' needs. That is analysis. These analytical products are almost always classified "secret" or "top secret" to protect intelligence sources and methods. They can be as short as a paragraph-length article found in the *President's Daily Brief* or as long as hundred-page estimative or "forecasting" studies such as National Intelligence Estimates (NIEs). These analyses can also fall somewhere in the middle in the form of periodic updates or specific "warning" documents designed to alert officials to emerging situations that may require their urgent attention and action. Many times these products are the result of analysts' judgment that an issue needs to be brought to the attention of a policymaker. However, senior policymakers will often request "tailored" analysis for a particular issue, typically quick but sometimes in depth, to help inform their decisions or actions. These results of the analytic process are typically aimed at explaining the facts of a situation, identifying key uncertainties, and projecting a range of possible outcomes based on a rigorous review of the facts as well as the knowable unknowns.

Why Intelligence Matters: The Cuban Missile Crisis Example

In light of the vast array of information at their disposal, it is fair to ask: Why should senior policymakers pay attention to intelligence? This is not a rhetorical question. Given their extremely tight schedules, long hours, and heavy workloads, decision makers have to be quite selective in what they read and who they see. For their part, intelligence analysts can never assume access to senior policymakers or that their written products will even be read by the customer(s) for whom they were expressly prepared. Why should policymakers bother with intelligence?

The short answer is that intelligence, especially finished intelligence—the analytical products and the on-call expertise of the analysts who produce them—bring *value added* to the national security policymaking process. Most policy officials appreciate this. This is more true after September 11, 2001, than before when skeptical policymakers began to grasp the idea that intelligence reporting, for all its shortfalls, was typically as good as or better than the competition. In general, the ability of intelligence analysts to command policymakers' attention is the result of the value added they bring to decision making: intelligence collection, analytical expertise, objectivity, and timeliness. We examine these four aspects found in the 1962 Cuban missile crisis as an illustration of successful intelligence performance.

Collection

Intelligence analysts enjoy a special advantage: Intelligence has special sources of information that are unavailable elsewhere. This is a global and unique resource of the intelligence community. Each year, the U.S. taxpayer spends billions of dollars on classified intelligence collection programs. These include a variety of technical collection means and human sources that are tasked to penetrate adversary governments and organizations such as terrorist groups.[13] Information collected by human intelligence (HUMINT) or technical espionage can be a priceless resource uniquely available to intelligence analysts and, through them (and sometimes directly), to their senior customers in national security decision-making positions. This key attribute of intelligence—the *collection of secret information by secret means*—gives analysts a major edge over the unclassified and open source competition because nearly all this clandestinely acquired information is inaccessible otherwise. Analysts are also often engaged in developing collection requirements, tasking collectors, and redirecting collection efforts, and they sometimes participate in the validation and evaluation of the intelligence collected.

The analysis of such information can make the difference in a complex decision. For example, overhead photography collected by U-2 aircraft revealed emplacements of offensive nuclear-capable missiles covertly deployed by the Soviet Union in Cuba in 1962. Sensitive documents such as the highly classified Soviet SS-4 missile manual provided to CIA by the spy Oleg Penkovskiy enabled analysis that probably extended the decision-making time available to President John Kennedy and his national security team during the heat of crisis. Together, these extraordinary collection successes made a decisive difference in President Kennedy's ability to successfully manage the only direct nuclear confrontation between the United States and the Soviet Union during the cold war.[14] Had we not discovered the secret missile emplacements—and discovered them *before* they became operational—the United States would have faced a significant new strategic disadvantage in the nuclear deterrence equation that had provided bipolar stability since the development of nuclear weapons. Defusing a crisis that brought the superpowers to the nuclear brink shows how intelligence provided uniquely valuable information from special collection sources to U.S. analysts and policymakers that could not have been acquired from any other information provider.

Analysis and Judgment

U.S. intelligence analysts are often regarded as the most authoritative experts in government on many specialized subjects ranging from highly technical issues such as laser or particle physics and virulent pathogens to exotic linguistic groups, rare dialects, and sources of regional instability. Some of the most authoritative experts on particular countries and regions of interest to U.S. national security are found as often in intelligence agencies as in major universities. Intelligence agencies recruit from top graduate schools in most subject areas, and the prevalence of graduate degrees among analysts at "all-source" agencies such as the CIA, Defense Intelligence Agency, and the State Department's Intelligence and Research Bureau is probably the equivalent of most universities and think tanks. Significantly, in-depth expertise in the analytical ranks is also *focused* on issues and problems of direct interest to current policymakers, rather than on historical or other academically interesting subjects of only tangential relevance to U.S. national security.

Just as the Cuban missile crisis illustrates the impact of special collection capabilities that revealed the hidden Soviet missiles, it also demonstrates the power of analysis. The stunning information delivered by the U-2 aircraft from Cuban airspace was not just pictures of land below. It was "raw" imagery that revealed sensitive intelligence to the trained imagery analyst looking for telltale "signatures" that uncovered the presence of offensive missiles with sufficient range to deliver nuclear warheads to targeted cities in the United States. But only the highest-quality analysis could have answered the most pressing question when the missiles were revealed: How much time would the decision makers have before the missiles become operational? (Another way of putting the question is: "How many days are available to manage this crisis before the Soviets could launch the nuclear missiles at U.S. targets?") This high-stakes question required accurate interpretation of U-2 imagery and in-depth analysis of the HUMINT provided by Oleg Penkovskiy. It was through a remarkable exploitation of Soviet classified materials that Penkovskiy provided clandestinely (referred to as Ironbark documents) that highly trained technical analysts were able to estimate—accurately, it turned out—how long it would take to complete the installation: On October 19, 1962, only five days after the missiles were discovered, analysts had concluded that they would be operational by October 27, only thirteen days from their initial discovery—and what turned out to be the final day of the crisis when the Soviets backed down.[15] This significant finding not only bound the president's time frame; it probably extended it by as much as three days, permitting more precious time to manage the crisis before the Soviets would have been able to unleash a nuclear strike at American cities.[16] The role of intelligence in helping policymakers manage this dangerous crisis illustrated (*after* the missiles were discovered) an extraordinary combination of intelligence collection and analysis at its very best.[17] The tense crisis ended as the Soviets agreed to remove the missiles, and they did so under close U.S. monitoring. President Kennedy and his crisis Executive Committee almost certainly could not have enjoyed the same successful outcome without the extraordinary level of intelligence support they received.

Objectivity

A key attribute of intelligence analysis is maintaining policy relevance while assiduously avoiding policy advocacy. This heritage of *policy neutrality* traces directly to Sherman Kent[18] and is nearly hardwired in the culture of analysis. Analysts strive to work problems and issues of high salience to policymakers, but they seldom construct their analytical path in a way that easily suggests a preferred policy outcome. More typically, they seek to enlighten and inform policymakers and to reduce uncertainty about complex and evolving situations but to avert policy prescriptions. They find their satisfaction in helping the policymaker to think through complex issues without specifying what to do about them. Being information providers perhaps to a fault, intelligence analysts are happy to leave the policy choices to the officials responsible for making them.

Again, the Cuban missile crisis makes the point: As the president and his Executive Committee worked their way through a myriad of policy options—from doing nothing and accepting a Soviet fait accompli to launching "surgical" nuclear strikes against the missiles under construction—intelligence analysts played a vital but highly restrictive role in the decision-making process. Their place was to provide information and analysis that could illuminate policy choices and possible consequences but not to advocate or oppose any particular course of action. A particularly significant analytical contribution to the crisis management process included sound estimates on likely Soviet reactions to U.S. measures during the crisis, including the successful blockade (or "quarantine") ultimately selected by the president, and—also accurately—that Soviet reactions would concentrate on "political exploitation" and any Soviet military responses would not occur beyond Cuba itself.[19] Analysts did not advocate one or another policy option, but they successfully illuminated the likely outcomes of the major policy options available to the president and his crisis decision makers.

Of course, this characterization of analysis as policy neutral greatly oversimplifies a more complicated and subtle problem often referred to as the *politicization* of intelligence. Not all policymakers see analysts quite the same way. Seen from the policymakers' trench, intelligence analysis should support policy and is thus not always welcome when it may seem to undermine a preferred policy choice. In this way, providing intelligence is risky in high-stakes policymaking. It does not always help the policymaker accomplish his or her objective. Intelligence is most helpful when the policy-level customer is genuinely searching for understanding and is not committed to a particular policy course of action. Once committed, the policymaker tends to evaluate the usefulness of intelligence in direct proportion to the extent that it advances the favored policy objective. Often, intelligence can have exactly the opposite effect.[20] It is sufficient at this point to establish that the *aim* of intelligence analysis is to advance the policy process through the provision of unique information packaged to enhance understanding and to reduce the uncertainty of policy decisions, not necessarily to influence the selection or support (or rejection or undermining) of any particular policy choice. For the most part, policymakers seem to appreciate the studied objectivity they can generally expect from intelligence analysts.[21]

Timeliness

A fourth value-added aspect of intelligence in policymaking is getting the information to policymakers in time so that they can act on it if immediate action is needed. For example, if the Soviet missiles had been discovered in Cuba *after* they had already become operational—or worse, publicly announced by an emboldened Nikita Khrushchev as a strategic fait accompli with an accompanying ultimatum—American policymakers would have faced a very different and far less favorable set of options. The timeliness attribute is at the heart of *warning* intelligence, where analysis plays every bit as critical a role as collection because *both* must work for warning to succeed. In spite of a flawed estimate in September that failed to anticipate the Soviet gambit, the timely and successful U-2 overflights in October, and the trenchant and accurate analysis that followed show the Cuban missile crisis as an outstanding intelligence warning and crisis-support success.

WMD in Iraq: Confronting Intelligence Failure

As the successful Cuban missile crisis case shows, intelligence can provide unique value added to policymaking through special collection, insightful analysis, strictly objective policy relevance, and timeliness. But failure is also part of the record. If intelligence always worked as effectively as it did during the Cuban missile crisis, there would be no controversy over whether it was worth the billions it costs every year, over the need for or shape of intelligence reform, or especially over its putative value added for policymakers. Intelligence failures are disquieting. They shake the confidence of those who argue that the intelligence community consistently provides the most insightful and most reliable information available to policymakers.

Perhaps the most disturbing recent failure is the erroneous estimates of WMD in Saddam Hussein's Iraq. The now-well-known October 2002 NIE on Iraq made major errors in assessing Iraq's WMD programs. This NIE erroneously judged that Iraq had stockpiled as much as 500 tons of chemical weapons (CW) and had an ongoing CW program; that Iraq had an active biological weapons (BW) program with BW agent stored there, along with mobile BW labs; that Iraq was reconstituting its nuclear weapons program; that Iraq had a program of unmanned aerial vehicles that was probably capable of delivering BW agent to foreign shores, including to U.S. shores; and that Iraq had missiles whose range exceeded permissible limits under UN sanctions.[22] Only the last of the five major judgments (on missiles) proved to be correct. Four were completely wrong. Estimates—correct or not—so closely tied to a U.S. decision to take military action are necessarily in the spotlight, and rightly so. But even if this estimate had not been central to the debate over the Iraq invasion, it would still merit attention because of what it uncovered about the current state of U.S. intelligence analysis.

Why were the key findings so wrong?[23] Briefly, it was a significant *collection* failure, because both human and technical intelligence collectors had failed to penetrate Iraq's WMD programs, and collection had also provided some wrong and misleading information. It was also a significant *analysis* failure. Reviewing the record, we find that analysts were more dependent on faulty collection than they comprehended, failed to question their past assumptions, and drew erroneous conclusions from dated, wrong, and poor information.[24] In short, on two key measures of unique value added—special collection and expert analysis—intelligence failed almost completely. Whether it also failed a third key test, strict objectivity, remains a matter of dispute. Two major inquiries, one by the Senate Select Committee on Intelligence and the other by the Silberman-Robb WMD Commission, have given analysts a clean bill of health. Both concluded that they had found no evidence whatever of politicization; that is, that policymakers had not apparently influenced intelligence judgments favorable to the war decision.[25] But other observers think this is a more complex and nuanced problem and even if there were no obvious arm twisting by policymakers, the omnipresent war preparations surely distorted analysis.[26] As figure 2 illustrates, then, the possibility for analytic errors can occur in three critical areas: where there is poor or missing information, where unchallenged mindsets or assumptions exist, or where bias may interfere with analytic objectivity. These three areas will be explored throughout this book.

FIGURE 2
From Collection to Customer: The Analyst's Pivotal Role

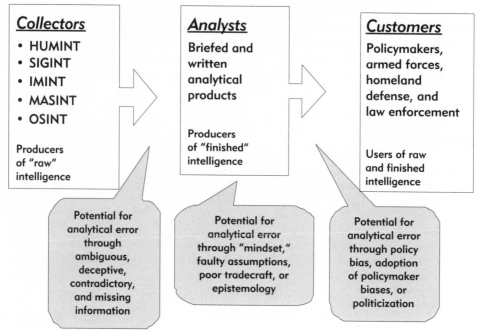

Analyzing Intelligence Analysis

Whether we focus on missiles in Cuba in 1962, on WMD in Iraq forty years later, or on other major successes and failures in the years that preceded or followed these two significant cases, our central goal is to address how the vast amount of intelligence analysis—at its best and at its worst—is produced for senior policy and military customers, and how and why it succeeds or fails in this critical mission.

This book draws on the individual and collective experience of many intelligence experts—most of whom have enjoyed long careers as successful analysts themselves, some as senior managers of analysts, and others who are scholars of the issues we pose here. The book explains how analysis has been conducted and how it can improve. We examine how intelligence analysis has evolved since its origins in the middle of the last century, including attention to its traditions, culture, and track record. We examine how analysis supports the most senior national security and military policymakers; how analysts must deal with the perennial challenges of politicization, analytical bias, and foreign denial and deception; and how they must become masters rather than victims of an ever-changing collection environment. We propose new ways to address perennial issues in warning analysis and emerging analytic issues like homeland defense; and we suggest new forms of analytic collaboration in a global intelligence environment. We introduce specific new ideas for evaluating alternative hypotheses, and for developing self-corrective techniques to improve analytical reliability.

We also consider imperatives for the development of a new profession of intelligence analysts.

If this book can illuminate the less-well-known or poorly understood attributes and issues of the intelligence analytical process and can then point to promising ways to improve it, we believe it can help to raise the quality and reliability of analysis. Simply put, our principal objective in the following chapters is to provide a better understanding of analysis for both the producers and users of intelligence.

Notes

1. Sherman Kent, "The Need for an Intelligence Literature," reprinted in *Sherman Kent and the Board of National Estimates*, ed. Donald Steury (Washington, D.C.: Center for the Study of Intelligence, Central Intelligence Agency, 1994), 14–15.

2. Michael Warner, "Wanted: A Definition of Intelligence," *Studies in Intelligence* 46, no. 1 (2002): 15–22.

3. Douglas MacEachin, "Strategic Analysis," in *Transforming U.S. Intelligence*, ed. Jennifer E. Sims and Burton Gerber (Washington, D.C.: Georgetown University Press, 2006), 117.

4. Jack Davis, "Intelligence Analysts and Policymakers: Benefits and Dangers of Tensions in the Relationship," *Intelligence and National Security* 21, no. 6 (December 2006): 991–1021; the quotation is on 1007.

5. This way of depicting the intelligence process as a cyclical phenomenon greatly oversimplifies how it works in practice. For a critique of this approach, see Rob Johnston, *Analytic Culture in the U.S. Intelligence Community* (Washington, D.C.: Center for the Study of Intelligence, Central Intelligence Agency, 2005), chap. 4; and Mark M. Lowenthal, *Intelligence: From Secrets to Policy* (Washington, D.C.: CQ Press, 2000), 50–51. The depiction of the intelligence cycle in figure 1 omits one of the customary five stages: processing (between collection and analysis).

6. Davis, "Intelligence Analysts and Policymakers," 999.

7. Richards Heuer's seminal *Psychology of Intelligence Analysis* (Washington, D.C.: Center for the Study of Intelligence, Central Intelligence Agency, 1999) addresses the cognitive dimensions of the analytical process. Robert M. Clark provides an excellent practical introduction to analysis that puts the collection target at the center of a modeling approach in *Intelligence Analysis: A Target-Centric Approach*, rev. ed. (Washington, D.C.: CQ Press, 2007). A small number of other books cover more limited aspects of analysis, such as Cynthia Grabo's work on warning, *Anticipating Surprise: Analysis for Strategic Warning* (Washington, D.C.: Joint Military Intelligence College, 2002). On estimates, see Hal Ford, *Estimative Intelligence: The Purposes and Problems of National Intelligence Estimating* (Lanham, Md.: University Press of America, 1993). More specialized works on methods are provided by David A. Schum, *Evidence and Inference for the Intelligence Analyst* (Lanham, Md.: University Press of America, 1987), 2 vols.; and Morgan Jones, *The Thinker's Toolkit: 14 Powerful Techniques for Problem Solving*, rev. ed. (New York: Three Rivers Press, 1998). Rob Johnston has conducted the only ethnographic study of intelligence analysis; see Johnston, *Analytic Culture in the U.S. Intelligence Community*. Two memoirist views of heads of the CIA's analytical directorate are Russell Jack Smith, *The Unknown CIA* (New York: Berkley Books, 1992); and Robert M. Gates, *From the Shadows* (New York: Simon & Schuster, 1996). The remainder of the unclassified literature on intelligence analysis in the past twenty-five years is only article-length and found in periodicals or in anthologies covering topics much broader than analysis itself. See Roger Z. George and Robert D. Kline, eds., *Intelligence and the National Security Strategist: Enduring Issues and Challenges* (Lanham, Md.: Rowman &

Littlefield, 2006), chaps 23–27; and Loch K. Johnson and James J. Wirtz, eds., *Strategic Intelligence: Windows into a Secret World* (Los Angeles: Roxbury, 2004), chaps. 8–13. Except for Clark, the only other book-length treatment of analysis writ large was published nearly thirty years ago; see Roy Godson, ed., *Intelligence Requirements for the 1980s: Analysis and Estimates* (Washington, D.C.: National Strategy Information Center, 1980). Most recently, two highly critical books on the CIA's performance allege major analytic failings, yet neither focuses on analysis or provides what can be considered a comprehensive or balanced assessment of the analytical track record. Richard L. Russell, *Sharpening Strategic Intelligence: Why CIA Gets It Wrong and What Needs to Be Done to Get It Right* (New York: Cambridge University Press, 2007), purports to evaluate the CIA's strategic intelligence performance but sheds little light on the complex reasons behind the failures and does not analyze the successes at all. A more popular book, by Tim Weiner, *Legacy of Ashes: The History of the CIA* (New York: Doubleday, 2007), also claims to be a comprehensive history of the CIA performance, but it also barely mentions analytical issues. Weiner's shallow treatment provides almost no insight into the causes of the many failures he selectively cites, and because he found few successes worth mentioning, he provides little insight into this aspect either.

8. The 9/11 Commission's somewhat cryptic recommendation that the U.S. intelligence community must "bureaucratize imagination" leaves a lot to be desired in the way of practical measures. See *The 9/11 Commission Report*, authorized ed. (New York: W. W. Norton, 2003), 344–48. One interpretation is that the commissioners meant to encourage the development of more analytic units whose sole mission would be to challenge conventional analytic lines held by agency analysts. These units would in a sense regularize the use of "contrarian" thinking techniques (e.g., devil's advocacy or Team A/Team B analysis) or "thinking like the adversary" (so-called red-cell analysis). However, the commission was never very clear about what it meant by the phrases, nor has any commissioner subsequently explained it.

9. Commission on the Intelligence Capabilities of the United States Regarding Weapons of Mass Destruction, *Report to the President of the United States, March 31, 2005* (Washington, D.C.: U.S. Government Printing Office, 2005) (hereafter, *WMD Commission Report*), 12 (emphasis in the original).

10. Ibid., 389; emphasis in the original.

11. *WMD Commission Report*, chap. 8. The findings on Iran and North Korea are not reported in the unclassified volume.

12. Often, "raw" or unanalyzed intelligence from a sensitive human or technical source is provided directly to senior policymakers. This kind of intelligence can be ignored or it may have an impact on policy debates. Sometimes this raw intelligence—provided without context or other analytical evaluation—can be both influential and wrong.

13. Intelligence collection and its relationship to analysis are given expanded treatment in chapter 12 in this volume.

14. See Mary S. McAuliffe, ed., *CIA Documents on the Cuban Missile Crisis, 1962* (Washington, D.C.: History Staff, Central Intelligence Agency, 1992); James G. Blight and David A. Welch eds., *Intelligence and the Cuban Missile Crisis* (London: Frank Cass, 1998); Dino A. Brugioni, *Eyeball to Eyeball: Inside the Cuban Missile Crisis* (New York: Random House, 1991); and Jerrold L. Schecter and Peter S. Deriabin, *The Spy Who Saved the World* (Washington, D.C.: Brassey's, 1995).

15. Raymond L. Garthoff, "US Intelligence in the Cuban Missile Crisis," in *Intelligence and the Cuban Missile Crisis*, ed. Blight and Welch, 27; and Schecter and Deriabin, *Spy Who Saved the World*, 334–35.

16. The three added days are the conclusion of the CIA's Richard Helms, then deputy director for plans (operations). In addition to bounding the decision-making time frame, analysis of the Penkovskiy documents in conjunction with U-2 imagery enabled extremely valuable intelligence judgments on the key information the policymakers needed, e.g., missile range (which U.S. cities could be hit), accuracy (1 to 1.5 miles), warhead size (3000 pounds, or 25 kilotons to 2 megatons), and missile refire rate (5 hours). Schecter and Deriabin, *Spy Who Saved the World*, 334–35, 466.

17. The Cuban crisis also illustrates an important analytical failure, namely, the flawed judgment of an estimate produced less than a month before the missiles were discovered that essentially argued that the Soviets probably would not secretly put offensive nuclear missiles in Cuba. Although DCI John McCone personally disagreed with that judgment, he did pass the estimate on to a concerned President Kennedy as the best thinking in the intelligence community at that time—soon to be refuted by newly discovered facts (SNIE 85-3-62, September 19, 1962). This erroneous estimate, along with other intelligence failures, is discussed in chapter 12 in this volume.

18. Sherman Kent observed some fifty years ago that the most important relationship for analysts, that with the policy officials they seek to inform, does not fall naturally in place but requires careful thought to set right and constant efforts to keep effective; see Sherman Kent, *Strategic Intelligence for National World Policy* (Princeton, N.J.: Princeton University Press, 1949). Kent articulated the basic challenge to effective ties when he observed that "if analysts get too close to their policymaking and action-taking clients, they would be in danger of losing the independence of mind and the substantive depth and analytic expertise that enabled them to make a distinctive professional contribution to national security. Yet if they stay too far apart from those they are charged to serve, they would be cut off from the feedback and other guidance essential for making that contribution." Jack Davis, "Improving CIA Analytic Performance: Analysts and the Policymaking Process," *CIA Sherman Kent School of Intelligence Analysis, Occasional Papers* 1, no. 2 (September 2002).

19. Garthoff, "US Intelligence," 31–32.

20. Gregory F. Treverton, *Reshaping National Intelligence for an Age of Information* (Cambridge: Cambridge University Press, 2003), 183–85. We explore this issue in some depth in chapters 4, 5, and 6 of this volume.

21. See chapter 5 in this volume.

22. National Intelligence Council, *Iraq's Continuing Programs of Weapons of Mass Destruction*, NIE 2002–16HC, October 2002; and Colin L. Powell, "Speech to the U.N. Security Council, New York, Feb. 5, 2003," in *The WMD Mirage*, ed. Craig R. Whitney (New York: PublicAffairs, 2005), 77–106.

23. This failure is discussed more fully in several chapters that follow, especially in 10, 11, 12, and 14.

24. *WMD Commission Report*, 157–76; Jamie Misick, deputy director of intelligence's "State of Analysis Speech," All-Hands Meeting, CIA Auditorium, February 11, 2004.

25. *WMD Commission Report*, 187–91; Senate Select Committee on Intelligence, *U.S. Intelligence Community's Prewar Intelligence Assessments on Iraq*, 108th Congress, 2nd Session, July 9, 2004, chapter 9.

26. Paul Pillar, "Intelligence, Policy, and the War in Iraq," *Foreign Affairs* 85, no. 2 (March/April 2006): 15–28. Similarly, the CIA's Tyler Drumheller argues that Iraq better illustrates a policy failure that sought only supportive intelligence; interview on *Sixty Minutes*, CBS Television, April 23, 2006; he followed with *On the Brink* (New York: Carrol & Graf, 2006). The topic of politicization is dealt with more extensively in chapter 6 by Gregory Treverton.

PART ONE
The Analytic Tradition

TO SET THE FOUNDATION for examining how analysis is changing and must adapt, part one provides a general understanding of how analysis has evolved over its first fifty years, some of the major challenges, and what an intelligence discipline might look like. Each author brings considerable expertise to this discussion.

John H. Hedley traces the changes in the analytic practices, organization, and priorities from the cold war until today, highlighting major changes that were introduced as a result of policy needs and major international events. Analysis, as he notes, began almost as an afterthought or by-product of U.S. decision making in the 1940s and has since become a central feature of the national security process.

Richard J. Kerr, a distinguished senior intelligence official under numerous administrations and presidents, has spent a career experiencing and addressing successes and failures of analysis. In his chapter he provides one practitioner's view that the record has been mixed but creditable. Some remarkably accurate, insightful, and even prescient assessments tempered by periodic failures reveal enduring problems of analytic mindsets, inadequate or misleading information sources, and unrealistic expectations on the part of policymakers for what they can expect from intelligence analysts.

Finally, Rebecca Fisher and Rob Johnston, who are leading the Lessons Learned project in the Central Intelligence Agency's Center for the Study of Intelligence, conclude that intelligence analysis after fifty years is on the way to becoming a formal discipline. Looking at intelligence analysis through the lenses of law, medicine, and library science, certain commonalities emerge, leading the authors to suggest that intelligence analysis can make a similar transition to an authentic professional discipline. Analysis will be significantly enhanced as a result.

CHAPTER 1

The Evolution of Intelligence Analysis

John H. Hedley

THE EVOLUTION of intelligence analysis in the United States parallels the mid-twentieth-century emergence of the American concept of national security. That concept drove the mushrooming transformation of the United States into a national security state in response to World War II and, especially, to the Soviet superpower threat to America's survival that emerged in its aftermath. America's loss of innocence at Pearl Harbor was a watershed, bringing a realization that the United States was vulnerable to attack from a distant foe and that developments anywhere in the world could directly affect U.S. interests—and lives. Pearl Harbor and the dawning of the cold war propelled a change in America's understanding of intelligence and of national security as a term encompassing the complex mix of diplomacy, military strength, and intelligence that now would frame and equip America's central role in international affairs. Global threats to U.S. national security would require global information; intelligence, heretofore thought of essentially in terms of military operations during war, would need to cover not just enemy military forces but also political and economic developments worldwide.

Attempts at having an organization to do intelligence analysis had occurred on only a few earlier occasions in American history, each relating to wars and lasting only briefly. Probably the first all-source intelligence organization—created during the U.S. Civil War—was the Bureau of Military Intelligence, under the auspices of General Joe Hooker, commander of the Union's Army of the Potomac. More than half a century elapsed before President Woodrow Wilson created "the Inquiry," a secret group of specialists to support the president's need for information on the situation in Europe. General Marlborough Churchill, director of military intelligence, then led a team of scholars from the Inquiry and his own Military Intelligence Division to Europe to provide intelligence support to President Wilson at the Versailles Peace Conference. This group of several dozen analysts produced America's first presidential current intelligence product.[1]

The roots of contemporary intelligence analysis did not take hold until World War II but were being planted even before the Japanese attack on the U.S. Pacific Fleet in Hawaii. Whether or not the United States would be drawn militarily into combat in what clearly could be a war of global dimensions, the U.S. intelligence apparatus was conspicuously inadequate. Alone among the great powers,

America had no centralized agency responsible for collecting and analyzing foreign intelligence. As a first step toward creating an integrated service, President Franklin Roosevelt summoned from private legal practice a personal confidant, William J. Donovan—a soldier and statesman who undertook overseas missions as the president's personal envoy to appraise the emerging situation and survey America's anticipated intelligence needs. In July 1940 Donovan traveled to England to assess Britain's capacity to resist a German invasion and its vulnerability to German Fifth Column activities. At the end of 1940 he launched a three-and-a-half month tour of the Mediterranean basin. Donovan—a careful observer of social, political, and military conditions—returned convinced that a regular channel of strategic intelligence information was essential and that political and psychological factors were destined to play a major role in the looming "total" war.[2]

The president agreed, endorsing Donovan's recommendation that there be assembled in Washington a corps of "carefully selected trained minds" with a knowledge of both languages and research techniques. On July 11, 1941, Roosevelt signed an Executive Order creating the civilian Office of the Coordinator of Information, responsible directly to the president and the Joint Chiefs of Staff. Roosevelt named Donovan to the post and instructed him to "collect and analyze all information and data which may bear upon national security."[3] Within the new office, Donovan created a Research and Analysis Branch (R&A), naming the president of Williams College, James Baxter, as its head, with an eminent Harvard historian, William Langer, as deputy. Recognizing that a body of expert knowledge could be found in the nation's universities and research institutions, Donovan, Baxter, and Langer set about recruiting scholars.

Staffing the new venture was not a problem. Professors welcomed the chance to serve the war effort with their academic skills. Recruits for R&A, as the branch was called, came from many fields, especially historians, economists, political scientists, geographers, psychologists, anthropologists, and diplomats. Soon after the Office of Strategic Services (OSS) came into existence in 1942, R&A became its analytic arm, and an Enemy Objectives Unit staffed by R&A economists set up shop in London—the first example of forward-deployed analysts—to support the Allied bombing campaign against Germany by analyzing the vulnerabilities of Nazi industry. More than sixty R&A officers served in London, and more than four hundred would eventually serve in a dozen overseas outposts. R&A would grow to more than nine hundred analysts before the war was over, comprising a "chairborne division" of OSS officers whose intellectual inquiry cast a wide net in support of combat operations and wartime and postwar planning. R&A analysis produced reports on a wide range of issues—for instance, assessing the condition of rail transport on the Russian front, the relation between aggression and business structure during the Weimar Republic, attitudes of the Roman Catholic Church in Hungary, and the political ideas of Charles de Gaulle. Anthropologists studied Japanese films and psychologists listened to the speeches of Joseph Goebbels. R&A regional specialists studied the Communist Party of India, inflation in Burma, guerrillas in the Philippines, trade routes in the Congo, and rival cliques in the Japanese army.[4]

The authorities and duties of the wartime R&A were limited, however. Its analysts were not "all-source" analysts; they had virtually no access to the signals intelligence that proved crucial to the Allied victory. The R&A Branch was not a "centralized" intelligence organization; it had no authority to coordinate intelligence for the president. Finally, the OSS was a war-fighting agency, and Donovan never thought of R&A as being "policy neutral." Victory was the goal, and finished intelligence was only another weapon in the U.S. arsenal.

Truman Takes Charge

When World War II ended, the new president, Harry Truman, promptly dissolved the OSS—in September 1945—but retained its analytical capability, transferring the elements of the R&A Branch to the Department of State. Truman wanted a centralized organization to coordinate intelligence for him, and numerous postmortems on Pearl Harbor had recommended creating a central clearinghouse for all-source intelligence to warn of future threats. R&A's analysts had won many admirers, and even critics of the OSS agreed that R&A had proved that patient research and the collation of mundane information could yield valuable insights for commanders and policymakers.[5] The Executive Order eliminating the OSS established the Interim Research and Intelligence Service as a holding place for R&A, from whose resources Secretary of State James Byrnes was to fashion a new, State Department–based intelligence entity. Truman thus gave State an opportunity to be at the center of what was to become the intelligence community. Instead, a pitched bureaucratic battle broke out. From the outside, the War and Navy departments insisted that State should not be the center of the new intelligence structure. From the inside, equal hostility came from Byrnes's assistant secretary for administration and many Foreign Service officers concerned that State's traditional diplomatic function would be overwhelmed by the intelligence component.[6]

Truman, impatient with the squabbling and bureaucratic paralysis, took matters into his own hands. In February 1946 he established a Central Intelligence Group (CIG) and authorized it to evaluate intelligence from all parts of the government. CIG soon got an independent budget and the authority to hire its own workforce rather than merely accept officers offered by other departments. By the end of 1946, CIG's Office of Reports and Estimates (ORE) had taken on at least three hundred people to correlate and evaluate information and prepare a daily intelligence digest for the president. Although much was in flux, two concepts that have remained key to the U.S. analytic mission were by this time firmly established: Donovan's idea of having smart people work at making sense of all the available intelligence, and Truman's insistence on having a central clearinghouse to correlate intelligence for the president and his advisers.[7]

Gaining recognition for ORE as the central clearinghouse for intelligence was not easy. The White House had authorized CIG's head—titled the director of central intelligence (DCI)—to "centralize" research and analysis in "fields of national security intelligence that are not being presently performed or are not being adequately performed."[8] This mandate helped to make CIG the primary foreign intelligence arm of the U.S. government, but it did not give CIG a controlling role in intelligence analysis. On paper its functions were manifold: to produce national-level intelligence—current, scientific, technical, and economic—and to accomplish interagency coordination of national estimates. The latter proved especially difficult in the face of institutional resistance from established organizations guarding their information and what they saw as their prerogatives. Indeed, the existing intelligence organizations were not about to subordinate their own limited analytical capabilities to the upstart CIG.

The current intelligence mission, conversely, grew in response to the customer with the highest priority: the president himself. On the very day that Truman brought the CIG into existence, he asked it to produce a daily summary of current intelligence. He wanted a single digest to help him make sense of the several departmental summaries crossing his desk. The president received the first Daily Summary within a week and was well pleased with it.[9] This modest publication created the precedent for one of the Central Intelligence Agency's (CIA's) core missions—the provision of strategic warning intelligence to the nation's leadership. Truman's interest, combined with the pressure of events in Europe, focused ORE's efforts on current reporting rather than research or forecasting.[10]

The CIA at the Center

In 1947 President Truman signed the National Security Act, creating the CIA, National Security Council (NSC), and Department of Defense (DoD). The CIA began its existence in September 1947, with Congress (judging from the floor and committee debates over the ratification of the National Security Act) expecting it to provide the NSC—the organization that would coordinate and guide American foreign and defense policies—with the best possible information on developments abroad. Members of Congress said they hoped the new CIA would provide information that was "full, accurate, and skillfully analyzed" as well as "coordinated, adequate" and "sound." Senior military commanders testifying on the bill's behalf used similar adjectives, saying the CIA's information should be "authenticated and evaluated;" "correct," and based on "complete coverage." When the CIA provided such information, it was believed, the NSC would be able to assess accurately the relative strengths and weaknesses of America's overseas posture and adjust policies accordingly.[11]

Congress guaranteed the CIA's independence and its access to files in other government departments to give it the best chance to produce authoritative information for the nation's policymakers. The CIA was to stand outside the policymaking departments of the government, the better to "correlate and evaluate intelligence relating to the national security." Other departments and agencies would continue to handle intelligence of national importance. Indeed, the State Department's Bureau of Intelligence and Research (INR), in terms of personnel, was at its zenith during this period of the late 1940s and the 1950s with a staff of about seven hundred. But the INR's analytic focus was on basic research. Some 40 percent of the INR's budget came from the CIA and supported analysts whose job was writing for the National Intelligence Surveys—comprehensive intelligence community studies whose goal was to include everything a warrior or a warrior-diplomat might need to know to fight against or alongside any country in the world. The INR's access to the secretary of state was limited until Secretary Dean Acheson instituted daily morning briefings as the Korean War brought the INR an analytic transition—as crises invariably do—to an emphasis on current intelligence.[12] But the CIA was the only entity specifically charged by the National Security Act with the duty of producing national intelligence for the president. To accomplish this, the DCI was given the right to "inspect" all foreign intelligence held by other agencies, as well as the right to disseminate it as appropriate. If the DCI happened to be a military officer, then he was to be outside the chain of command of his home service; this would help him to resist any temptation to shade his reports to please his superiors.[13]

The creation of the CIA made possible a significant expansion of the Office of Reports and Estimates from 300 staff employees in late 1946 to 709 by the end of 1950.[14] In the words of the R&A veteran Ray Cline, the future deputy director for intelligence heading analysis at the CIA and later a director of the INR, the expansion of ORE made the CIA "a little bigger than before but not much better."[15] Its analytic ranks were thin on experience and credentials. During the critical year of 1948—which saw Soviet-instigated crises in Europe, including the fall of Czechoslovakia and the blockade of land access to Berlin—ORE's Soviet and East European branch was comprised of only 38 analysts. Their strength was previous exposure to the Soviet Union; 9 had lived there and 12 spoke Russian—both high figures for an era when American knowledge of the USSR was limited, even in academia. But their backgrounds were less impressive in other respects. Only one had a PhD, and 6 had no college degree. Several of those with college experience had studied fields far removed from their work.[16]

Organizing Analysis

Spurring the evolution of intelligence analysis in the United States—and especially enhancing the CIA's role as America's premier all-source analytic agency—was the fallout from Communist North Korea's surprise invasion of South Korea in June 1950. Suddenly the cold war had turned hot less than a year after the Soviets exploded an atomic bomb and China went Communist, and Sino-Soviet collusion against the West seemed undeniable. In the fall of 1950, Truman named a new DCI: Walter Bedell Smith—an army general who had been chief of staff to General Dwight D. Eisenhower in the European theater, and from 1946 to 1949 had served as ambassador to the Soviet Union. Smith was appalled at the slackness of CIA analytical work on Korea, and he soon made sweeping organizational changes. He implemented the recommendations of a 1949 NSC survey report (overseen by OSS veteran and New York attorney Allen Dulles) and divided ORE into three functional offices: the Office of National Estimates (ONE), whose sole task was the production of coordinated "national estimates"; the Office of Research and Reports (ORR), to support ONE and conduct basic research; and the Office of Current Intelligence (OCI), to write summaries and other brief products for policymakers.[17]

ONE had two components: a staff to draft the estimates and a board of "wise men" to review and coordinate them with the other intelligence agencies. ONE initially depended on departmental contributions but would rely increasingly on steadily growing CIA analytic resources. CIA drafts were negotiated with other members of the intelligence community, however, and thus gradually became less "CIA" than interdepartmental products.

ORR, for its part, had the Map and Basic Intelligence divisions, and a newly created Economic Research Area. ORR's Map and Basic Intelligence divisions amassed reference data and integrated it into products like the National Intelligence Surveys as vital "services of common concern" provided for the intelligence community and the U.S. government. The State Department claimed primary jurisdiction in economic as well as political intelligence, but in 1951 it struck a bureaucratic truce with the CIA to allow ORR to analyze the communist economies. The economic arena became the focus of the CIA's research and analysis effort, a development that had a major impact on military and strategic analysis of the Soviet Union.[18]

Current intelligence needed an organizational home but would not fit well in ONE or ORR. President Truman had been an avid reader of daily intelligence since 1946, so it was axiomatic to DCI Smith that the CIA must produce all-source current intelligence and do it well. Smith made the CIA's daily publication an all-source product—for the first time including signals intelligence—and changed its name to the *Current Intelligence Bulletin*. OCI analysts must have been pleased in early 1951 when Truman thanked the DCI for the new publication: "Dear Bedell, I have been reading the intelligence bulletin and am highly impressed with it. I believe you have hit the jackpot with this one."[19]

In January 1952, DCI Smith established the Directorate of Intelligence (DI)—which continues to this day—to formulate strategic intelligence for U.S. policymakers. Within the new directorate, an Office of Current Intelligence produced a daily intelligence publication for the president and senior policymakers, and an Office of National Estimates drafted and coordinated longer-term national estimates. An Office of Scientific Intelligence conducted weapons-related research—despite opposition from the military services, which saw that as their exclusive domain. An Office of Research and Reports did basic research—much of it economic and related to Soviet war potential——and gradually introduced political research, despite the State Department's opposition.[20]

Setting Standards

Sherman Kent, who became head of the Office of National Estimates in 1952, helped set the tone for that organization for its next decade and a half. A veteran of the OSS's Research and Analysis Branch, a former professor, and an intelligence analyst for more than three decades, Kent would leave a legacy as perhaps

America's foremost practitioner of the analytic craft. His 1949 book, *Strategic Intelligence for American World Policy*, explained analysis and the intelligence process in ways that continue to inform intelligence professionals today. His concepts of right and wrong in intelligence estimating were rigorous: no policy direction, no shading evidence or slanting analysis to reach a desired conclusion, no slipshod writing or shortcuts.[21]

The Korean War generated pressures for information that spurred a rapid expansion of the CIA's DI into the major center of national intelligence analysis. Government-wide demands for reporting and strategic assessments of communist intentions led to dramatic growth that brought the number of DI personnel to 3,338 by the end of 1953.[22] And the DI was responding to more and more tasks—especially producing current intelligence and providing the analytical underpinning to products of the Office of National Estimates—as its capabilities in economic and scientific analysis continued to grow. The DI's OCI developed into something of an empire during the years Allen Dulles was DCI, with its own courier service, its own print shop, and even its own security (justified by the fact that the signals intelligence in its products needed special handling). Contemporaries recall the OCI turning out "a flood of the best written, most carefully analyzed intelligence reporting ever to hit Washington desks," a fact Dulles duly appreciated and used in meetings with President Eisenhower and the NSC.[23]

Dulles's years as DCI marked a change in the way the CIA conceived its analytical functions and duties. In the beginning, its leaders and their counterparts in other intelligence agencies wondered if it should be doing analysis at all—perhaps it should only provide current intelligence summaries and various reference services. The long debates in Washington over Soviet strategic forces during the 1950s, however, changed this perspective. No single policy department had the means or the will to penetrate the crucial mysteries shrouding the Soviet defense industries, ballistic missiles, and nuclear weapons, and the DI (aided by advances in collection, particularly the imagery obtained by U-2 aircraft) stepped in to provide this vital service. Having built the essential expertise to do so, moreover, DI analysts discovered that their work held another virtue: It offered a policy neutrality—and, thus, objectivity—that could transcend the policy pressures that might color departmental analyses. The growing size of the DI and the expansion of its assignments, combined with its independence, central role, and direct access to the president, made it increasingly Washington's most prominent and influential concentration of analysts.

At the same time, the cold war saw other analytic cadres, primarily in the State and Defense departments, continuing to play key roles as both competitors and contributors. The makers of foreign and defense policy—primarily the secretaries of state and defense—are key intelligence consumers with different intelligence needs reflecting their unique operational responsibilities. Each maintains his or her own analytic components to ensure that their specific operational intelligence needs are served. These components in most cases were working the same strategic issues as the DI, but from the perspective of departmental roles and information needs in support of specific tactical requirements. The fact that their work overlapped resulted in a duplication of efforts, but by design that duplication has been tolerated—indeed encouraged—in the American system as a way of providing checks and balances in the form of competitive or alternative analysis.

The 1960s: Technology and Bureaucracy

The decade of the 1960s saw a major revolution in collection technology with often significant analytical challenges and organizational changes. In 1960, a whole new dimension of intelligence collection had begun coming from the skies when the first photo-reconnaissance satellite, code named Corona, detected the first operational Soviet intercontinental ballistic missiles. The volume of Corona images gave rise in 1961 to the creation of the National Photographic Interpretation Center (NPIC), an ancestor of today's National Geospatial-Intelligence Agency. The CIA's DI operated the NPIC as a joint effort with the Pentagon. All-source analysts saw a flood of new source material.

Analytically, the decade featured the Cuban missile crisis, which in 1962 brought the United States the closest it ever came to global nuclear war, then Vietnam, which became America's longest war—delivered by television into America's living rooms and deeply embroiled in U.S. politics. Although estimators did not believe beforehand that the Soviets would deploy offensive missiles in Cuba, CIA analysts guided the U-2 reconnaissance flights that confirmed the Soviet missile deployment. CIA analytic components played prominent roles in briefings at the White House for several weeks. This high-profile monitoring of progress at the missile emplacements underscored the analysts' value throughout the crisis in providing intelligence support to policymaking. The Cuban missile crisis also advanced the CIA's capacity to engage in military analysis. DCI John McCone, with encouragement from Secretary of Defense Robert McNamara, won regular access to data on U.S. strategic planning, which further enhanced the CIA's role in strategic research. McCone also won formal recognition from DoD that the CIA could do military-economic intelligence and studies of the cost and resource impact of foreign military and space programs. Essentially, DoD endorsed what the agency had been doing for over a decade.[24]

Vietnam carried the CIA's analytical role even further, as CIA analysts looking at the bleak realities of the war waged an uphill battle against the optimism of U.S. policy. The CIA's strategic political-military perspective and the use of sophisticated analytic techniques convinced Defense Secretary Robert McNamara in 1966 to bypass DoD analysts and ask CIA analysts to produce a comprehensive assessment of the war—a "Red Team" assessment titled "The Vietnamese Communists' Will to Persist."[25] The CIA's Vietnam analysis came against a backdrop of McNamara's creation of the Defense Intelligence Agency (DIA) in 1961, seen by many observers as reflecting a desire to eliminate the duplication involved in having separate Army, Navy, and Air Force intelligence organizations.

The DIA Joins the Mix

The creation of the DIA owed at least as much to a bureaucratic tug of war within DoD as to the idea of centralizing military intelligence to reduce duplication and parochialism. The years following creation of DoD (and the CIA) by the National Security Act of 1947 saw a succession of amendments and DoD reorganizations aimed at shifting the balance of power in the Pentagon away from the separate armed services and toward the secretary of defense and the collective Joint Chiefs of Staff.[26] But the military services were allowed to maintain control of their individual intelligence organizations in recognition of their need for specialized tactical intelligence for combat commanders. Autonomous military intelligence components—the services argued—facilitated flexibility and responsiveness to the disparate intelligence requirements of different service missions.[27]

President John F. Kennedy, impressed with the concept of a strong single manager, which was the dominant organizational paradigm in business and industry in the early 1960s, chose the foremost practitioner of the new technique as his secretary of defense. Robert McNamara quickly became convinced of the need to eliminate service bias from strategic intelligence and threat assessments, and he hoped to accomplish this by removing the evaluative capabilities from the individual services. They would handle only the collection of raw intelligence and some processing, while analytic production and dissemination would occur at higher levels—preferably under the direction of the Office of the Secretary of Defense. He saw the creation of a consolidated military intelligence agency as his primary means of achieving the National Intelligence Estimates that would be so essential to his strategic reassessment. "I believed," McNamara wrote, "that removing the preparation of intelligence estimates from the *control* of the military services would reduce the *risk* that service biases—*unconscious* though they might be—would color the estimates" (emphasis his own).[28]

As originally conceived by McNamara, the DIA would serve the strategic, national intelligence needs of the secretary of defense rather than the narrow, tactical intelligence needs of the Joint Chiefs of Staff. But it was not that simple; by the spring of 1961 there was open conflict between the military services, represented by the Joint Chiefs, and McNamara and his civilian analysts over the future of military intelligence. To end the internecine strife, McNamara agreed—in a significant departure from his previous position—to let the DIA report to him *through* the Joint Chiefs rather than directly.[29] In the end, the DIA's activation in the early autumn of 1961 as a combat support agency carried the day for the Joint Chiefs and the armed services.

In the decades that followed, DIA's analytic mission has grown exponentially. Its director, a three-star general, now serves as the principal adviser on substantive intelligence both to the secretary of defense and the chairman of the Joint Chiefs. The DIA's all-source, defense-related analysis encompasses current and estimative intelligence production. Its analytic ranks—comprising a significant segment of the DIA workforce, which has grown to a total of some seven thousand—contribute to intelligence community coverage of the proliferation of weapons of mass destruction, international terrorism, international narcotics trafficking, and defense-related foreign political, economic, industrial, geographic, and medical and health issues.[30] Like the State Department's INR, the DIA began providing departmental intelligence uniquely supporting the mission of its department's role in making and implementing policy. At the same time, the INR and DIA would critique, coordinate, and contribute their own perspective to the national intelligence produced at CIA. During the cold war this was especially the case in the preparation of National Intelligence Estimates, and most especially the case in estimating the military capabilities and the strategic threat posed by the Soviet Union.

Colby's Innovations

William Colby became director of central intelligence in 1973 believing that the Office of National Estimates had lapsed into an "ivory-tower mentality" detached from the needs and concerns of policymakers. He replaced it with a group of national intelligence officers (NIOs), each to be responsible for coordinating estimates on a particular region or subject. The NIOs were to range "throughout the intelligence community and the academic world to bring to me [Colby] the best ideas and to press the different disciplines to integrate their efforts."[31] Although the NIOs were to assign the drafting of each estimate to the intelligence community's best analysts on the particular subject, CIA officers filled many of the NIO positions, and CIA analysts did most of the drafting.

One of Colby's short-lived innovations was a new, high-level daily publication in newspaper format. He reasoned that senior policymakers were newspaper readers and that an intelligence "newspaper" with a very restricted circulation would create interest and ensure that the latest intelligence reached policymakers directly (instead of being screened by their staffs).[32] The DI expanded its twenty-four-hour staffing to make the new *National Intelligence Daily* (which replaced the *Current Intelligence Bulletin*) as timely as possible. Most material was drafted during normal working hours, but each drafting component had someone staying late for updates. Six days a week, teams of two editors each worked shifts of noon to 10 p.m., or 9 p.m. to 7 a.m., to edit drafts and decide on their placement in what was usually a four-page publication slightly smaller than a regular newspaper page. The editors wrote the headlines, gave a final review to the pages pasted onto a light table layout, and waited while a full-scale offset press in an adjacent room rumbled with the morning's edition as dawn was breaking. The *President's Daily Brief* (PDB) still went to the White House, while the new *National Intelligence Daily* served others at the top levels of the national security community—a key reader being National Security Adviser Henry Kissinger.

Colby also introduced Vice President Gerald Ford to the *PDB*—the most sensitive of daily analytic products—inadvertently paving the way for the CIA later to gain daily access to the Oval Office. Having invited Ford to visit the CIA in 1974, Colby innocently mentioned the *PDB*—which, it turned out, Vice President Ford had never seen! Only then did President Richard Nixon authorize him to receive it, and the CIA sent a senior DI officer to take the *PDB* and other pertinent items to Ford early each morning at his residence. When Nixon resigned later in 1974 and Ford became President, Ford continued the practice of having a CIA officer deliver the *PDB*—now to the Oval Office—and discuss items with him.

Ford's second DCI, George H. W. Bush, adopted this practice when he became vice president. He was an advocate and avid reader of the *PDB* throughout the administration of Ronald Reagan, when a CIA officer with the *PDB* would sit down at the beginning of each day separately with the vice president, the president's national security adviser, the secretaries of state and defense, and an added recipient, the chairman of the Joint Chiefs of Staff. When he became president, George H. W. Bush made the *PDB* his first order of daily business in the Oval Office—a practice his son, George W. Bush, chose to continue.

Rebuilding Analysis

Under President Ronald Reagan's choice as DCI, William Casey, the CIA's analytic directorate was revamped along geographic rather than functional lines, both to more closely align it with the State Department's regional bureaus and to integrate political, economic, and military experts into offices analyzing the Soviet Union, Europe, Africa, Latin America, the Near East, South Asia, and East Asia. A new Office of Global Issues would tackle "transnational" topics. Analysts suffered a rough period of sorting out responsibilities and space while maintaining the quality and quantity of their work. Hundreds of analysts had to move and learn to work with different colleagues. They adjusted, and the restructuring succeeded in enhancing interdisciplinary research and analysis.

The geographic structure meant that the CIA's country analysts now worked together, but the attention required to cover transnational problems such as terrorism soon exceeded the capabilities of a single Office of Global Issues. Collectors needed regional and country analysis in order to target operations more effectively. Further innovation was needed to integrate analysis with fast-moving law enforcement issues. The answer came in the creation of "centers," each focused on a single transnational issue and including representatives from other intelligence community organizations. The centers brought analysts of various academic disciplines and area expertise to work side by side with collectors, operations officers, and representatives of law enforcement. The new Counterterrorism Center's success at using this integrated team approach in the mid-1980s became a model for additional centers. It was followed in 1989 with the Counternarcotics Center (it was later expanded to the Crime and Narcotics Center) and other DCI centers addressing counterintelligence, proliferation, arms control, and environmental concerns.[33]

The 1980s saw not only reorganization but also the first wave of a revolution in office technology that would eventually transform the analysts' working environment. By then every analyst had a secure telephone. Manual typewriters gave way to electric typewriters and then first-generation word processors. Vast resources were devoted to the enormous task of giving each analyst a main-frame-supported personal computer on his or her desk. By 1985, analysts throughout the intelligence community had gained the capability to read, store, and retrieve classified cables and documents electronically. In the late 1980s, analysts and databases were linked into local area networks, eventually reaping rewards from greater speed and flexibility but along the way suffering the inevitable headaches of pioneering new information systems. At the same time, CIA analytic resources were further stretched by the addition of military support missions brought on by the Persian Gulf War, the Balkan conflicts, and other peacekeeping missions.[34]

Restoring Relevance and Rigor

The reordering of priorities to which CIA analysts—still the largest collection of civilian all-source analysts in the intelligence community—responded put actionable intelligence at the top. This applied not only to support for the military but also to law enforcement and the CIA's own clandestine operations. Expectations intensified for analysts throughout the community—not just at the CIA—to warn of looming threats, to target collection and operations, and to give U.S. officials greater leverage in international negotiations. "Opportunity analysis" was to identify actions or events that could be turned to the U.S. advantage. Analytic products reflected the new emphasis, and increasing numbers of analysts went on rotational assignments to the various centers, policy agencies, and overseas.

New intelligence priorities placed further emphasis on education in and about intelligence. The long-standing recognition of the importance of training and education was reflected in the DIA's Defense Intelligence School, which was renamed the Joint Military Intelligence College (JMIC) in 1993.[35] By 1997, the JMIC achieved the ability to grant an accredited bachelor of science in intelligence degree. The JMIC's broad-based curriculum encompasses a program leading to a master of science in strategic intelligence degree and includes funding student and faculty research and providing publication opportunities.[36] At the CIA, John McLaughlin, as deputy director of intelligence from 1997 to 2000, established the Sherman Kent School of Intelligence Analysis, the CIA's most intensive effort to teach the tradecraft of analysis and learn from the lessons of the past.[37] Officers with extensive analytic experience run its Career Analyst Program, through which new analysts spend four months honing their analytic thinking, writing, and briefing skills. Interim assignments enable them to apply themselves in various jobs. While adding courses for journeyman analysts and for supervisors, McLaughlin also established a Senior Analyst Service to provide a career track by which analysts could advance to senior grades on the basis of expertise and performance alone, rather than by opting for staff and managerial assignments.

Underlying all these efforts are debates over issues that probably never will be resolved, such as how best to organize analytic components, the proper balance between current intelligence and in-depth research, and whether analysts should tell policymakers what issues are important—or the other way around. During much of the cold war, long-term research on the relatively stable Soviet target was a necessary focus of analytic assessments. Since then, the organizational pendulum has swung toward closer involvement of analysts in support of collection, operations, and policy objectives. On September 11, 2001, counterterrorism took top priority for the indefinite future. The attacks that day on the World Trade Center in New York and the Pentagon in Washington underscored the growing challenges to intelligence in an era of international terrorism in which small groups of individuals can inflict destruction once wielded only by nation-states.

America's terrorist tragedy in 2001 led to a scramble—in a presidential election year—to enact the Intelligence Reform and Terrorism Prevention Act of 2004, legislation that created the position of the director of national intelligence as a supposed institutional corrective for the fact that the vast U.S. national intelligence apparatus did not somehow prevent the terrible events of September 11. The reorganization followed the completion of various inquiries and studies into what went wrong and what might be done about it.[38] The overriding conclusions of these inquiries with respect to intelligence analysis were that there had been a failure of imagination—that analytic assessments had become too risk averse and more concerned with avoiding mistakes than with imagining surprises—and that there was insufficient integration of analytic efforts across the now sixteen-member U.S. intelligence community. The putative solution was to establish the Office of the Director of National Intelligence, which now is at pains to emphasize integration and collaboration in intelligence analysis and to provide central direction aimed at rising above the bureaucratic fiefdoms that can prevent the sharing of sources and analytic perspectives.

Today, under the deputy director of national intelligence for analysis, competitive all-source analytic centers—predominantly the CIA's DI, the DIA's Intelligence Directorate, and the INR, but including the National Security Agency, the National Geospatial-Intelligence Agency and, increasingly, the National Counterterrorism Center and other intelligence community agencies—not only help override purely parochial views but also achieve a practical continuum of alternative analysis. The National Intelligence Council—already a recognized center of strategic analysis producing national intelligence estimates and other intelligence community assessments—is placing increased emphasis on peer review and the use of outside experts. Multiple analytic agencies produce Competitive Analysis but at the same time coordinate and contribute to the preparation of a range of community products, including items for the *PDB*—once the exclusive preserve of the CIA.

Continuing Challenges

Today's analytic community is filled with new faces, its ranks having expanded rapidly to fill new positions approved by Congress to help fight the war on terrorism while still providing coverage of events, issues, and trends worldwide. New developments and capabilities in information technology enable analysts to work in new ways within a classified environment that struggles to keep up with the ever-accelerating pace of available technology. The global war on terrorism, and especially U.S. combat operations in Iraq and Afghanistan, also put current intelligence back in the forefront, again raising questions of emphasis in comparison with longer-term, in-depth research.

The grist for the analysts' intellectual mill is, as ever, a mix of usually incomplete and frequently contradictory fragments of information—from a near vacuum in vital areas during the early years to an overwhelming volume today. Yet the challenge and excitement felt by the analytic community assembled on the eve of World War II is doubtless felt every bit as keenly in facing the challenges of the twenty-first century. Analysts have a unique opportunity to learn about and strive to understand what is happening in the world. They know that as they can help illuminate complex issues, detect patterns, and identify targets, they can increase the U.S. government's understanding and effective response with respect to far-flung developments. Their performance and prospects—strengths and weaknesses, successes and failures, pitfalls and possibilities—are examined in the chapters that follow.

Notes

1. "Significant Dates in DI History," unpublished, compiled in 2001 by Frans Bax, first dean of the Sherman Kent School of Intelligence Analysis, Central Intelligence Agency.

2. Barry M. Katz, *Foreign Intelligence: Research and Analysis in the Office of Strategic Services, 1942–1945* (Cambridge, Mass.: Harvard University Press, 1989), 2.

3. William J. Donovan to Franklin D. Roosevelt, "Memorandum of Establishment of Service of Strategic Information," June 10, 1941, in *Donovan and the CIA: A History of the Establishment of the Central Intelligence Agency*, by Thomas F. Troy (Frederick, Md.: University Publications of America, 1984), 420.

4. Katz, *Foreign Intelligence*, 18.

5. Dean Acheson, *Present at the Creation: My Years in the State Department* (New York: W. W. Norton, 1969), 157–63.

6. Mark Stout and Dorothy Avery, "The Bureau of Intelligence and Research at Fifty," *Studies in Intelligence* 42, no. 2 (1998): 18–19.

7. John H. Hedley, "The DI: A History of Service," in *The Directorate of Intelligence: Fifty Years of Informing Policy: 1952–2002* (Washington, D.C.: Central Intelligence Agency, 2002), 3. This chapter draws heavily on the content of the author's essay in that commemorative volume.

8. National Intelligence Authority Directive number 5, July 8, 1946, reprinted in *Central Intelligence: Origin and Evolution*, ed. Michael Warner (Washington, D.C.: Central Intelligence Agency, 2001), 24.

9. Harry S. Truman, *Memoirs*, vol. 2, *Years of Trial and Hope* (Garden City, N.Y.: Doubleday, 1956), 58. See also Arthur B. Darling, *The Central Intelligence Agency: An Instrument of Government to 1950* (University Park: Pennsylvania State University Press, 1990), 81–82. The *Daily Summary* did not include signals intelligence, but by the end of 1946 the editors were able to check draft articles against signals intelligence reports. See Russell Jack Smith, *The Unknown CIA: My Three Decades with the Agency* (McLean, Va.: Pergamon-Brassey's, 1989), 34–35.

10. Much of the publicly available information on the organizational history of CIA analysis appears in a 1975 history produced by staffer Anne Karalekas for the Senate Select Committee to Study Governmental Operations. Her draft was based in part on histories written

by CIA's history staff, and it was reprinted under the title "History of the Central Intelligence Agency" in *The Central Intelligence Agency: History and Documents*, ed. William M. Leary (University: University of Alabama Press, 1984), 10, 26.

11. Lyle Miller, "Legislative History of the Central Intelligence Agency—National Security Act of 1947," declassified draft, Office of Legislative Counsel, Central Intelligence Agency, July 25, 1967, 40, 45, 47, 48, 50.

12. Stout and Avery, *The Bureau*, 17, 19.

13. See section 102 of the National Security Act of 1947, which is reproduced in Warner, *Central Intelligence*, 30.

14. A table of organization with these figures, dated December 20, 1950, is cited in *Assessing the Soviet Threat: The Early Cold War Years*, ed. Woodrow J. Kuhns (Washington, D.C.: Central Intelligence Agency, 1997), 12.

15. Ray S. Cline, *Secrets, Spies and Scholars* (Washington, D.C.: Acropolis Books, 1976), 92.

16. Kuhns, *Assessing the Soviet Threat*, 1.

17. Karalekas, *History of the Central Intelligence Agency*, 28–34.

18. Ibid., 90.

19. Harry Truman's letter to DCI Smith, March 8, 1951, quoted by John L. Helgerson, *CIA Briefings of Presidential Candidates, 1952–1992* (Washington, D.C.: Central Intelligence Agency, 1996), 27.

20. Ludwell Lee Montague, *General Walter Bedell Smith as Director of Central Intelligence* (University Park: Pennsylvania State University Press, 1992), 92–95.

21. Smith, *Unknown CIA*, 75–76.

22. Karalekas, *History*, 35.

23. Cline, *Secrets, Spies and Scholars*, 146, 151–53.

24. Karalekas, *History*, 93.

25. For a brief but excellent overview, see Daniel W. Wagner, "Analysis in the Vietnam War," in *Fifty Years of Informing Policy*, expanded edition containing classified documents (Washington, D.C.: Directorate of Intelligence, 2002), 131–36.

26. Keith C. Clark and Lawrence J. Legere, eds., *The President and Management of National Security* (New York: Praeger, 1969), 175.

27. Walter Laqueur, *A World of Secrets: The Uses and Limits of Intelligence* (New York: Basic Books, 1985), 33, quoted by Patrick Neil Mescall, "A Creature of Compromise: The Establishment of the DIA," *International Journal of Intelligence and Counterintelligence* 7, no. 3 (Fall 1994): 253.

28. Quoted from personal correspondence with Mescall, ibid., 263.

29. Ibid., 265–66.

30. Defense Intelligence Agency, www.dia.mil.

31. William Colby and Peter Forbath, *Honorable Men: My Life in the CIA* (New York: Simon & Schuster, 1978), 351–53.

32. Ibid., 354.

33. Office of Public Affairs, Central Intelligence Agency, *Consumer's Guide to Intelligence* (Collingdale, Pa.: DIANE Publishing Co., 2000), 13–14.

34. President Bill Clinton in 1995 issued an order—Presidential Decision Directive 35—making the intelligence community's first priority "the intelligence needs of our military during an operation," as he explained in a speech at CIA Headquarters on July 14, 1995.

35. This was renamed the National Defense Intelligence College in 2007 and is now a fully accredited program.

36. Defense Intelligence Agency, www.dia.mil/college.

37. In 2000, following the collapse of the Soviet Union, the then–deputy director of intelligence, Douglas MacEachin, initiated the first major analytic training program throughout CIA's analytic corps. The so-called Tradecraft 2000 workshops were two weeks long and became the basis for later development of so-called Alternative Analysis courses, which

34 | John H. Hedley

employed structured analytic techniques designed to expose key (often termed "Linchpin") assumptions. See Roger Z. George, "Fixing the Problem of Analytical Mindsets," in *Intelligence and the National Security Strategist*, ed. Roger Z. George and Robert D. Kline (Washington: National Defense University, 2005), 315–16.

38. E.g., see *9/11 Commission Report: Final Report of the National Commission on Terrorist Attacks upon the United States* (New York: Barnes & Noble, 2004), and *Report of the Commission on the Intelligence Capabilities of the United States Regarding Weapons of Mass Destruction* (Washington, D.C.: U.S. Government Printing Office, 2005). See also Richard A. Posner, *Preventing Surprise Attacks: Intelligence Reform in the Wake of 9/11* (Lanham, Md.: Rowman & Littlefield, 2005); and Richard A. Posner, *Uncertain Shield: The U.S. Intelligence System in the Throes of Reform* (Lanham, Md.: Rowman & Littlefield, 2006).

CHAPTER 2

The Track Record: CIA Analysis from 1950 to 2000

RICHARD J. KERR

OUTSIDE SCHOLARS' EFFORTS to evaluate the intelligence community's (IC) performance are inevitably complicated by the secret nature of the IC's activities and by an understandable unfamiliarity with the cultures, art forms, and work practices used by intelligence analysts. Moreover, as Richards Heuer points out in chapter 16 of this volume, we all suffer—both critics and defenders—from hindsight biases, which one certainly must acknowledge. Indeed, a career professional like me can suffer as much from too much familiarity with the topic based on more than thirty years of practicing and managing analysis.[1] Moreover, I can only hope to give the reader a sense of what the Central Intelligence Agency's (CIA's) performance has been, based on my own direct experience as well as official duties as an independent consultant and reviewer of controversial intelligence problems, some of which are popularly referred to as "intelligence failures." Trying to assess the strengths and weaknesses of the CIA's analytic effort—much less those of the entire intelligence community—over a fifty-year period is daunting.

As John Hedley notes in chapter 1, the CIA and IC have undergone huge organizational as well as personnel changes during this period to reflect the shifting demands from the policy community. One must consider not only the array of thorny intelligence problems but also the many surrounding factors that may have caused analysis to stay on track or go astray. Predictably, the expectations of policymakers have always exceeded intelligence agencies' ability to provide information, insight, and warning.

Moreover, the magnitude and diversity of issues addressed by intelligence over this eventful half century is staggering. International events of interest to those involved in national security come like waves on the shore—constant but mixed with frequent storms and an occasional hurricane. There were few lulls in U.S. interests, and developments worldwide were constant and demanding.

The fifty-year period under review witnessed numerous coups or coup attempts, major revolutions or minor rebellions, and countless major terrorist incidents. In any year during this period, there are literally dozens of major events that demanded policymakers' attention. Moreover, just since 1990 nearly one-third of all developing states have experienced serious societal unrest. During the past half century, decolonization and democratization have more than doubled the number of states—many of which remain unstable. Add to this dynamic nation-building process the rise of other global issues like energy needs, weapons proliferation, global financial discontinuities, international terrorism, and insurgencies fueled by tribal and interethnic conflicts, and one can see just how daunting the task of assessing major world developments can become for a global intelligence service.

Some of these problems and topics had no end and others went on for weeks, months, and often years. Finally, the CIA also provided intelligence support to a wide range of international negotiations from the vital (e.g., American–Soviet arms control talks, multilateral disarmament conferences, or the law of the sea negotiations) to many virtually unknown forums (e.g., the allocation of radio frequencies). The plate was full.

How to Measure Performance?

To assess the overall performance of the CIA, one must begin with a reasonable set of objectives or standards. Other chapters cover analytic roles in greater detail, but it is important to keep in mind what analysis actually does:

- Assess the significance of new developments as they relate to U.S. policy. Identifying opportunities for U.S. policy is also part of this job.
- Provide warning of dangerous situations to policymakers, perhaps the most difficult task of the intelligence analyst.
- Develop longer-term assessments of major political, military, economic, and technical trends, a core mission of intelligence. Research is like an intellectual savings account that provides the capital that accumulates and builds knowledge.

In fact, research—the foundation of expertise—underlies all analytic tasks. It not only benefits intelligence consumers but also serves to train and build a knowledge base for analysts. Research can also, but does not always, force analysts and consumers to stretch their minds, challenge preexisting mindsets, and imagine alternative outcomes.

The Record: From Cold War to Terrorism

Characterizing fifty years of analysis on the myriad intelligence topics covered can only be done with the benefit of hindsight. Using the clarity that time provides, we can see that U.S. intelligence, especially when compared with foreign intelligence services, has provided American presidents and their foreign affairs teams with the broadest and most comprehensive information of any government on the planet. This historical record has witnessed many failures, but far more successes, which are seldom heralded or not recognized because they seem—after the fact—so commonplace. But most important, no president can afford to be without intelligence analysis, nor can he or she afford to ignore the

CIA and other agencies' analysis without risking even greater missteps. What the record shows is that CIA's analysis has helped to reduce the inherent uncertainty surrounding many foreign events, raise the level of understanding of the policy debates conducted by national security teams, and alert decision makers to many critical issues that they would otherwise have missed or judged unimportant.

The Rise and Fall of the Soviet Union

Clearly, the struggle with the Soviet Union was the most pressing challenge to intelligence analysts for most of the post-1945 period. Though there was no direct fighting between the military forces of the United States and the USSR, many international crises and brushfire or proxy wars across the world had their roots in the cold war, and nearly all were assessed in the context of the struggle with the Soviets.

The major effort of intelligence during the cold war was to assess Soviet strategic and conventional military forces and to provide judgments about doctrine, tactics, capabilities, and intentions. Very little was known about the secretive Soviet Union in the 1950s, and early CIA officials characterized the challenge as making an "inventory of ignorance."[2] For analysts to do their job, it was necessary to build an entire suite of systems to collect human, photographic, communications, and electronic signals, as well as other data. Analysts who knew what data were needed and who understood the systems' strengths and weaknesses gradually built up a knowledge base on the Soviet Union that was impressive and without equal in the Free World.[3]

Over the years there has been severe criticism of intelligence produced on the Soviet Union's military power. But looking at the fifty-year scope of activity, it is clear that the CIA's work was impressive in scope and often prescient. There were few major weapon systems—out of the hundreds of strategic missile, tactical missile, submarine, aircraft, and air defense systems—that were not identified and had their capabilities assessed in considerable detail. The size of the strategic and conventional forces was well documented, as was information on tactics, strategy, and doctrine. CIA analysts—using satellite collection programs—were responsible for dispelling the notion of a "missile gap" and later for the discovery of the Soviet missiles covertly placed in Cuba in 1962. In the 1970s, new space-borne verification systems and an analytic understanding of Soviet nuclear programs made it possible to engage in vital arms control negotiations that dramatically reduced the size of the Soviet nuclear inventory, which could be reliably monitored by the CIA and IC analysts.

CIA analysts largely concluded throughout the 1960s and 1970s that the Soviets were bent on achieving strategic parity with the United States so as to avoid the humiliation they suffered in Cuba and to negate U.S. strategic advantages in the future. Debates raged throughout this period on whether the Soviet leadership would contemplate nuclear "war fighting" or largely accepted American concepts of deterrence—all of which highlighted the challenges of deriving intentions and motivations from intelligence on military programs and capabilities.

Accordingly, over the years CIA and IC estimates of Soviet strategic nuclear programs and plans were also frequently subject to review and criticism. On the whole, the record shows that the CIA was able to track those developments reasonably well. There were no significant strategic surprises. Our estimates in the late 1960s and early 1970s were somewhat low, while our 1980s estimates erred on the high side. Accordingly, the CIA also adjusted its methodologies and acknowledged discrepancies from what analysts expected to observe. For example, in a declassified self-evaluation conducted in 1989, the CIA acknowledged the ups and downs in its strategic assessments:

> The high and low projections made from 1970 to 1977 successfully bracketed the actual number of nuclear weapons in the Soviet force. . . . The accuracy of the record in the early 1970s was due to a combination of correct estimates of MIRVs [multiple independently targeted reentry vehicles] on ICBMs [intercontinental ballistic missiles] and of the rate at which these missiles would be deployed. . . . [The] tendency to substantially overestimate the rate of force modernization occurred in every National Intelligence Estimate (NIE) published from 1974 through 1986, and it was true for every projected force—whether it assumed high, moderate, or low levels of effort.[4]

During this period, CIA analysts endured official reviews—the most well known being the "Team A/Team B" exercise of 1976 established by the President's Foreign Intelligence Advisory Board. This study accused drafters of national intelligence estimates on Soviet strategic modernization of systematic bias and a misunderstanding of Soviet military objectives.[5] Sadly, the exercise in what has become known now as "Competitive Analysis" achieved far less than was expected. It did lead to some technical changes in the way subsequent estimates were produced, but mostly it led to charges and countercharges of politicization. Some former arms control advocates asserted the Team B claims were just as biased and off base as any CIA assessments.[6] Senate committee investigations concluded from this experience that the NIE process could be improved—particularly in drawing on expertise outside the government—but chided the way the Team B was made up of outspoken critics of the CIA and U.S. strategic policies that had predetermined the exercise's outcome.[7] Ironically, George H. W. Bush, who presided over the Team A/Team B exercise while director of central intelligence (DCI), subsequently relied heavily on the CIA's strategic analysis and came to be one of the agency's strongest supporters.

Obviously, policymakers were interested in more than the Soviet military. Consequently, there was a major effort to collect and analyze information necessary to understand internal policy and leadership developments, the defense-dominated economy, and Soviet attempts to expand their worldwide reach and alter the balance of power with the United States. Perhaps the most challenging and least satisfactory analytical efforts have been assessments of how Soviet policymakers would calculate risks and opportunities they faced during the cold war. A major strategic surprise was the deployment of nuclear missiles in Cuba during the fall of 1962 in what was the most dangerous moment in Soviet brinksmanship directed specifically at the United States. In a September 1962 estimate, analysts incorrectly presumed that the Kremlin understood the risks it would face, should it confront the John Kennedy administration with a strategic challenge in the Western Hemisphere. Similarly, a later generation of analysts would find themselves also underestimating a different Soviet leadership's willingness to launch a major military invasion into Afghanistan in 1979—partly as a result of the prevailing analytic judgment that the Kremlin would not jeopardize Soviet–American détente nor undertake a risky and possibly disastrous occupation of Afghanistan.[8] Throughout the cold war, intelligence analysts tried to put themselves in the position of Soviet—as well as other autocratic—leaders and imagine how they might assess the risks and gains of taking political or military steps that challenged U.S. interests. Not surprisingly, although American analysts have struggled to "think like the enemy," they frequently failed to understand fully how those decision makers could miscalculate or reason differently than Western analysts. In a sense, analysts were expected to know the plans of enemies who had not yet fully developed them.

The CIA's record on the Soviet economy was consistently better and far more methodologically sophisticated than anything available to analysts of Soviet political and leadership issues. Since the early 1950s, the CIA largely created the discipline of economic analysis on centrally planned economies. The CIA had its critics—both those claiming underestimates and overestimates of the size of the Soviet economy and the burden of related military spending—but it remained the gold standard of economic analysis.[9] In annual presentations to the congressional Joint Economic Committee starting in the early 1970s, the CIA reliably reported on the failings of that economy and its implications for Soviet military spending. To be sure, a panel of outside economic experts did find flaws in CIA economic models and methods, but as noted in a report to a congressional oversight committee in 1991: "We find it hard to believe that anyone who has read the CIA's annual public reports on the state of the Soviet economy since 1975 could possibly interpret them as saying that the Soviet economy was booming. On the contrary, these reports regularly reported the steady decline in the Soviet growth rate and called attention to the deep and structural problems that pointed to continued decline and possibly to stagnation."[10]

This leads us, of course, to consider the repeated charge that the CIA missed the crisis and eventual breakup of the Soviet Union. There is no question that information on political developments in the USSR and its Warsaw Pact allies always presented a difficult problem. However, CIA analysis was remarkably good in following crucial leadership changes in the 1980s as well as the democratic revolutions that swept Eastern Europe. Indeed, the course of "reform," the breakup of the Warsaw Pact, and disintegration of the Soviet Union probably were better assessed by the CIA than by those Soviet officials who were directly involved. The failings of the Soviet system were repeatedly and clearly documented in a steady stream of assessments (see box 2.1). Critics of the CIA forget that President Mikhail Gorbachev himself did not know how the story would end, nor did he intend to bring down the system in the way he did. Again, analysts were confronted with the problem of assessing how well or poorly Soviet leaders might manage the risks they faced or could misunderstand the forces they had set in motion. No Soviet leader had a plan—nor was there a secret directive that could be stolen and analyzed—which laid out the end of the Soviet Union.

BOX 2.1
CIA Assessments on the Soviet Union: The Failing System

June 1979: "Our analysis of Soviet economic developments has reinforced our conclusion that we see every reason to believe that a continued decline in the rate of growth of the Soviet Union is inevitable through most of the 1980s."

August 1985: "Gorbachev's attempt to bolster popular support for the regime carries political risk. His direct appeal to the public could generate concern within key bureaucracies that they are being circumvented, and generate popular expectations that he may not be able to satisfy. . . . Unlike Brezhnev, Gorbachev appears to view attempts to maintain the status quo as more destabilizing than attempts to change the situation."

April 1986: "Soviet leaders will face continuing problems throughout the 1980s and beyond. . . . Overall, however, we believe Gorbachev's political position will remain strong and the USSR under his dynamic leadership is likely to see some improvement in system performance over the next few years. . . . It seems unlikely, however, that Gorbachev will be able to introduce reforms significant enough to arrest long-range negative trends in Soviet society."

July 1987: "Gorbachev has already asked the military and the population to curb their appetites in return for more later. . . . The risks in a more radical reform and a rewrite of the social contract are that confusion, economic disruption and worker discontent will give potential opponents a platform on which to stand. . . . If it suspects that this process is getting out of control, the party could well execute an abrupt about-face, discarding Gorbachev along the way."

September 1988: "Given the depth of divisions in the Politburo, however, there are increasing prospects that conflict will come to a head. . . . We believe there is a greater chance that events will move toward a dramatic resolution. . . . There is a good chance that [Politburo members] will move against Gorbachev or that Gorbachev himself will risk a preemptive move to consolidate his power."

April 1991: "Economic crisis, independence aspirations, and anti-Communist forces are breaking down the Soviet empire and system of governance. . . . [A] premeditated organized attempt to restore a full-fledged dictatorship would be the most fateful in that it would try to roll back newly acquired freedoms and be inherently destabilizing in the long term. Unfortunately, preparations for dictatorial rule have begun."

Note: This summary is excerpted from declassified documents found in *CIA's Analysis of the Soviet Union 1947–1991,* ed. Gerald Haines and Robert E. Leggett (Washington, D.C.: Center for the Study of Intelligence, Central Intelligence Agency, 2001).

Given that this was more a mystery than a secret,[11] then, the absence of violence associated with the breakup of the Warsaw Pact and the Soviet Union is good evidence of the success of U.S. policy and the intelligence upon which it was based. Former national security adviser Brent Scowcroft, who was a principal customer, has said he felt well served by the intelligence community during this tumultuous period, noting that "its purpose is to inform and narrow the range of uncertainty within which a decision must be made . . . and keep policy within reasonable bounds."[12] In my view this is one of those examples where intelligence does not get much publicity, because it was integrated seamlessly into good policy.

If the "tipping point" for the Soviet Union came during the late years of the Ronald Reagan administration and culminated in the administration of George H. W. Bush, it was set in motion by (1) containing Soviet adventurism beyond Europe, (2) eroding Soviet control of Eastern Europe through steady American pressure for many decades, and (3) pressing their defense spending limits. This resolute action by both Democratic and Republican administrations naturally led from one crisis to another. Inside the Warsaw Pact some of the most significant developments were the suppression of the Hungarian Revolution in 1956, the Soviet invasion of Czechoslovakia in 1968, and the Polish crisis in 1980 and 1981. U.S. intelligence analysts not only closely monitored each of these crises but also, particularly in the case of Czechoslovakia, provided detailed warning to U.S. policymakers about Soviet intentions to use force to curtail liberalization. In the 1980 Polish case, analysts were aided by incredibly sensitive human intelligence regarding Soviet intentions and plans. Despite reporting on a day-to-day basis, analysts never flatly predicted when martial law might be imposed. However, U.S. policymakers also failed to act on information they had available, or publicize what they knew of Soviet intentions, which might have altered Polish or Soviet calculations.

To draw, then, a bottom line on the CIA's record on the Soviet Union, one has to conclude that analysts came to understand that system and its strengths and weaknesses better than any other intelligence service. That said, neither the CIA nor even the key Kremlin players themselves could fully grasp the degree to which the Communist Party, the economy, and the political system in general were becoming dysfunctional in the late 1980s. The continuing Soviet investment in strategic military forces and Soviet troublemaking throughout the world preoccupied intelligence analysts more than it should have. Moreover, early signs of civil unrest identified by some American analysts were initially dismissed because of what other experts expected would be Soviet ability to "muddle through" by quelling unrest, arresting dissidents, or otherwise appeasing the Soviet public.[13] But from 1987 until 1989, CIA reports documented the steep rise of a few dozen strikes to more than five hundred, involving hundreds of thousands of workers.

Given the importance and centrality of the Soviet challenge, there was recurring tension throughout the cold war between CIA analysts and virtually every U.S. administration. Some policymakers saw a Soviet hand behind every event that ran against U.S. interests. Attempts by intelligence to assess Soviet action from the Soviet perspective often were seen as "soft." President Richard Nixon and Secretary of State Henry Kissinger, for example, were often critical of CIA analysis that did not support their defense objectives, which would have been aided by more alarming assessments of Soviet anti–ballistic missile defenses. President Jimmy Carter was not pleased by repeated assessments of Soviet misbehavior in Poland and Afghanistan, which complicated his own détente policies. DCI Bill Casey and other Reagan advisers also never agreed with the CIA's insistence that Soviet oil pipeline deals with Europe were unstoppable or that there was no evidence of a Soviet hand in the 1981 papal assassination attempt. And toward the end of the Soviet period, President George H. W. Bush's advisers were not eager to hear senior CIA officers' views on Gorbachev's declining influence in the face of an increasingly popular Boris Yeltsin. Yet, throughout this period, the analysts' job was to understand the strengths and weaknesses of an adversary, not paint a picture that policymakers expected to see.

Watching the Chinese Dragon

The vast U.S. intelligence complex created to follow the Soviet Union also had direct application to other emerging challenges, such as Communist China. China's rise as a world power was closely monitored by CIA intelligence. Like the Soviet problem, analysts struggled to master an understanding of a Soviet-style Politburo, on which there was next to no hard information. As a longtime CIA China watcher has described it, in the early period "intelligence analysts enjoyed few advantages over their academic and journalistic counterparts on the question of the inner workings of the Communist Chinese Party."[14] Despite this collection problem, agency analysts were able to provide policymakers with solid assessments of Mao Zedong's hold on power, the internal Chinese Communist Party struggles, and the slowly emerging Sino–Soviet split for which the CIA was far ahead in forecasting. A Soviet military analyst in the CIA was one of the first to detect the growing tensions between China and the Soviet Union in the early 1960s. The CIA did a creditable job on assessing China's disastrous economic program (the Great Leap Forward) and later the equally destructive political chaos (the Cultural Revolution) that Mao introduced toward the end of his rule.

Analysts also spent much of their time and attention on the emerging Chinese military threat and its direct challenge to Taiwan. The Taiwan Straits crises in the 1950s seem quaint today, but they were major crises, which analysts regarded as possibly going nuclear if not carefully managed (e.g., President Dwight D. Eisenhower's 1954 threat to use tactical nuclear weapons if China attacked the island of Quemoy). The China–Taiwan issue remains a major warning issue into the twenty-first century, as it bears directly on whether U.S. defense commitments might embroil Washington in an Asian conflict. Intelligence assessments consistently judged that China would pursue its goal of recovering Taiwan and would continually test Taiwanese and American resolve. But they saw little evidence that the Chinese would attack Taiwan so long as it risked drawing in the United States. Similarly, agency analysts could provide policymakers some reassurance that, overall, Chinese military objectives remained largely defensive in character throughout much of the cold war. Analysts correctly predicted a Chinese nuclear program would emerge in the early 1960s, but it advanced even more rapidly than some expected. Equally challenging was a good understanding of where it might then lead. As analysts noted in a 1967 NIE, "There is little evidence on Chinese thinking with respect to the role of nuclear weapons in [its] overall strategy."[15] However, they correctly judged that Beijing had no interest or expectation of achieving a Soviet-style "strategic parity" with the United States but rather settled on a very modest nuclear arsenal more aimed at prestige and deterrence than actual war fighting.

CIA military analysts did report on the internal pressures and disagreements inside the Chinese leadership and were quick to develop the story about the attempted defection of Lin Pao to the Soviet Union in 1972. Once Mao's death and various leadership changes occurred, analytic attention turned increasingly toward growing capabilities of the Chinese military (the People's Liberation Army) and China's emergence as an economic power. As economic modernization advanced and political reforms did not, analysts pondered the question of whether internal disorder might result. The tough response of the Chinese leadership to Tiananmen Square protests in 1990 was anticipated, if not the student unrest itself. Intelligence carefully monitored the replacement of unreliable troops in Beijing and the crackdown on protesters. CIA analysts of the post-Mao leadership, reporting on its conviction not to make the mistakes that Gorbachev had in combining economic reforms with political reforms, have also been largely on the mark. This remains a key intelligence question—namely, how China will manage economic modernization and its sociopolitical ramifications.

Not surprisingly, as China's political, economic, and military rise has continued, so too has the attention given to the CIA's analysis and the question of whether it too is "politically biased."[16] Congressional criticism has also been leveled against the CIA for soft-pedaling the Chinese military threat, and in 2000 a congressionally mandated commission (known as the China Futures Group) headed by former army general John Tilleli spent a year examining the CIA's record. There also have been calls—so far unsuccessful—to develop alternative analysis centers at the Department of Defense that would take a more "tough-minded" approach to China. In fact agency analysis has been rigorously following the steady Chinese military modernization effort, and analytic resources on China have steadily grown as a reflection of the importance this subject will hold for future U.S. policymakers. To make the point, open CIA congressional testimony in 2004 is typical of the "tough-minded" analysis that the CIA has been conducting:

Our gravest concern continues to be China's military build-up, which continues to accelerate. . . . China's announced annual defense budget has grown from some $7 billion ten years ago to over $25 billion today. Moreover, we assess the announced figure accounts for less than half of China's actual defense spending. . . . China is downsizing and restructuring its military forces with an eye toward enhancing its capabilities for the modern battlefield. All of these steps will over time make China a formidable challenger if Beijing perceived that its interests were being thwarted in the region.[17]

Truth Telling on Vietnam

Although a distant memory to today's generation, Vietnam occupied CIA analysts' attention for over fifteen years during the very height of the cold war. The record was remarkably good, but it is also a testimony to the difficulty policymakers have in accepting bad news. Early on, DCI John McCone pressed Sherman Kent and his estimators to accept a more benign view of the political scene held by diplomats and generals, but over time even this cold warrior came to view the war as unwinnable. His eventual successor, Richard Helms, recalls that from "the onset, the intelligence directorate and the Office of National Estimates held a pessimistic view of the military developments."[18] Moreover, CIA assessments of the weak South Vietnamese governments and the comparatively resolute North Vietnamese intentions and capabilities were equally pessimistic as well as generally accurate.

After the commitment of major U.S. ground forces in the 1960s, CIA assessments of the war challenged administration assertions that the U.S. and South Vietnamese military strategies could succeed, judging that time and resolution were on the side of North Vietnam. Debates between CIA estimators and General William Westmoreland's military command in Saigon (MACV) over the North Vietnamese order of battle—which became a measure for whether U.S. military actions were winning the war—became very confrontational. CIA analysts, using a broader category of armed combatants, argued that the forces were far higher than MACV was crediting, a prospect that the Lyndon Johnson administration did not wish to explain to a skeptical Congress and public. The debate raged throughout 1966 and 1967, until the CIA agreed not to press the issue.[19] To many analysts, this episode constituted a clear case of caving in to political pressures; to Director Helms and others, it was a recognition that the CIA had made its perspective well known to senior officials and an acknowledgment that the military was ultimately responsible for establishing the strength of an opponent's forces.[20]

Although the CIA assessed the deteriorating political and military situation accurately, it did not forecast the surprise Tet (New Year) Offensive that occurred in 1968. Indeed, even as the CIA correctly declared the Tet Offensive to be a military defeat for the North Vietnamese, Hanoi succeeded in convincing the American public that it was a major Communist victory that only deepened skepticism about the war. The CIA was dead wrong in its assessment that Cambodia was not a principal route for arms entering Vietnam, and it hung onto that judgment in the face of some rather persuasive evidence.

North Korea: The Black Hole

North Korea has been and remains one of the toughest collection and analytic challenges that U.S. intelligence has faced since the end of World War II. Ever since the 1950 surprise attack on South Korea, analysts have been wary of forecasting events in North Korea with high confidence. The North Korean decision to launch an attack southward in June 1950 was judged unlikely because analysts believed Pyongyang was part of the Soviet-controlled sphere of influence and that Moscow had no interest in a war on the peninsula that might spark a global conflict. However, North Korean leaders proved to be as independent minded as Mao, Tito, and other break-away communist regimes. Despite ample evidence of mounting war preparations in early 1950, analysts judged it unlikely that Kim Il Sung would act independently of Moscow.[21]

Since then, analysts have been more wary of ruling out unprovoked aggression on the peninsula, and periodically a crisis has emerged that demanded intelligence to monitor the Demilitarized Zone or other hot spots. For example, in the mid-1970s analysts tracked the North Korean seizure of the USS Pueblo, the shooting down of a U.S. reconnaissance aircraft, and the attack by North Korea on Seoul's presidential palace (the so-called Blue House)—just a few examples of chronic troublemaking that challenged intelligence. U.S. military analysts are still regularly involved in assessing warning indicators of a possible surprise attack against the South and North Korea's growing military capabilities.

The latest analytical preoccupation with North Korea has been its development of a nuclear weapons program. There was persistent speculation in the 1980s and early 1990s as to whether North Korea had developed nuclear weapons or merely had the capacity to do so. U.S. assessments had been heavily "caveated" but left open the real possibility that North Korea might have enough highly enriched plutonium to make a small number of nuclear weapons. In the mid-1990s, this concern led the Bill Clinton administration to press the North Koreans to halt their program in exchange for pledges to supply reactors incapable of producing weapons-grade plutonium and some say to contemplate strikes on the North's nuclear facilities. Pyongyang then averted a confrontation by accepting the 1994 Agreed Framework, but suspicions remained about how much the North Koreans were adhering to those agreements. Most recently, intelligence analysis provided convincing evidence that North Korea had developed a covert program to circumvent those earlier agreements. And in August 2003, the CIA judged that "North Korea has produced one or two simple fission-type nuclear weapons."[22] Moreover, in October 2006 CIA analysts warned of a possible atomic test, which has been subsequently confirmed to be a low-yield detonation of a nuclear device.[23]

The other major North Korean intelligence challenge has been forecasting the development of North Korea's ballistic missile capabilities, which would be needed to deliver a nuclear weapon. In early 1990s estimates of the global foreign ballistic missile threat looking out to 2010, analysts concluded that none of the prospective nuclear states (Iran, Iraq, Libya, North Korea, etc.) likely would have fielded an intercontinental range ballistic missile. These estimates encountered severe criticism, causing Congress to establish special review commissions and ask for annual reports from the intelligence community. The 1995 NIE and subsequent reports came in for special criticism from the so-called Rumsfeld Commission, which declared that the NIE methodology and approach resulted in a playing down of the growing ballistic missile threat.[24] This criticism seemed to have merit, when North Korea surprised defense and intelligence officials by launching a Taepodong-1 missile in 1998, demonstrating that Pyongyang's ballistic missile program had progressed far faster than most analysts believed possible. Since then, senior intelligence officials have acknowledged mistakes and claimed that CIA analysts have responded to most of the criticisms and have sought to characterize uncertainties, alternative scenarios, and warnings in a more forthcoming manner.[25] At this juncture analysts must be prepared to assume the worst and almost plan to be surprised by North Korea's seemingly different strategic logic and way of approaching the West.

South Asia: Monitoring a Powder Keg

Perhaps an unsung success for CIA analysts is the quiet role they played in alerting policymakers in the late 1980s and early 1990s to advancing nuclear plans and military exercises involving Pakistan and India that brought those countries to the brink of war and possible use of nuclear weapons. Those governments' possession of nuclear weapons—not to mention their outright war in 1971—was reason enough for U.S. intelligence to warn policymakers in time to conduct effective mediation efforts. In May 1990 President George H. W. Bush dispatched to both capitals a senior envoy, who used alarming intelligence reports of Pakistani–Indian conventional buildups to bring both sides to their senses. Another key intelligence question in the late 1980s was whether or not Pakistan had nuclear weapons. Intelligence was clear that Pakistan had an aggressive program by 1987 to develop such a capability. However, administration officials tried hard to avoid acknowledging this, as it would trigger a break in U.S. foreign aid to Pakistan, which was critical to American efforts to drive the Russians out of Afghanistan. By then, analysts were confident that both South Asian powers had nuclear weapons and were intent on developing mature programs with delivery systems, making a "balance of terror" on the subcontinent all the more serious.

When India surprised Washington with its May 1998 nuclear tests, and Pakistan quickly followed suit, Clinton administration officials were shocked by a new Indian government's flaunting of international opinion and blamed CIA analysts for not alerting them to the real possibility of a test. The commission formed under Retired Admiral David Jeremiah to investigate this intelligence failure concurred in finding that analysts had misjudged the newly elected Indian government's eagerness to test, even though its election campaigning promised precisely that. What was left unsaid, however, was that analysts had all along acknowledged India's technical ability to test at any moment and had warned the Clinton administration; moreover, successful efforts to dissuade India from testing previously had also forced U.S. diplomats to share imagery with New Delhi to convince them not to test. These demarches ultimately enabled Indian scientists to avoid past testing practices, which had tipped off U.S. analysts in the past to test preparations. That said, the Jeremiah Commission's advocacy of more "Red Teaming" and "Alternative Analysis" was a useful and necessary impetus for the CIA to reestablish more analytic tradecraft training as well as review South Asian intelligence priorities that had taken a back seat to the administration's focus on the Balkans crises, North Korea, Iraq, and counterterrorism priorities.

The Middle East: From Wars to Weapons

Three major wars occurred between Israel and what it referred to as the "confrontational" Arab states. The United States did not support the early British, French, and Israeli adventures in the Suez during the 1950s. But in subsequent wars in 1967 and 1973, Israel received significant U.S. support. Consequently, U.S. intelligence was deeply involved in providing warning of the attacks and daily "situational reporting." The 1967 Six-Day War is a case study of how U.S. intelligence "got it right." Analysts correctly assessed the building pressure on Arab leaders to regain the losses they had sustained in the first two wars against Israel. Gamal Abdel Nasser and his generals had plans to launch joint attacks with Syria, Jordan, and other Arabs. Analysts were alerting the Johnson administration to these worrying trends and ultimately told the president that if Israel decided to preempt the Arabs, the war might last no more than six days.[26]

But if getting it right in 1967 was a sign of analysts understanding the Arab mind, they quickly learned not to become complacent. Intelligence accumulated in the early 1970s, which showed in detail what the Egyptian and Syrian forces were intent on doing to restore their lands and reputations. Ironically, in the face of such overwhelming evidence, analysts failed to recognize that Arabs might launch a war they had no prospect of winning militarily. Thus, analysts as well as policymakers dismissed the signs of hostilities, believing that Israel and other moderate Arab states knew better than they that Egypt and Syria would not dare to try again without a great deal more equipment, preparation, and support. CIA analysts were not alone in holding this mindset and indeed were misled by the confident Israeli assessments that Anwar el-Sadat was bluffing and would not dare take on the Israeli Defense Forces. This Yom Kippur "surprise" war caused Israeli intelligence to institute more Competitive Analysis as well as a dedicated "Devil's Advocate" to challenge conventional wisdom and ensure that no such surprise would ever happen again.

The 1979 fall of the shah of Iran and the rise of Islam in Iran may be one of the most dramatic changes in the past fifty years. The analytic group that followed Iran in the 1970s was competent and experienced. Its analysis foreshadowed some of the developments that were to occur. The shah had alienated the religious base, confiscated lands, and secularized many aspects of the country's life. The military and intelligence services were outwardly strong but had feet of clay and crumbled at the first sign of trouble. The problem for intelligence was that much of the reporting on Iran came from people too close to the regime—the U.S. diplomats, intelligence and military officers, and other "insiders." Little attention was directed toward what was happening in the street or being said in the morning prayers. Analysts in those days had little understanding of the force of the religious movement in politics. In particular, Americans had little or no understanding of the impact that an old—and seemingly unimpressive to us— Ayatollah Khomeni would have on Iran and the world.

Once burned, the CIA was more careful to follow the rise of Islamic extremism in the region. Accordingly, the CIA warned the Reagan administration of the precariousness of Sadat's regime and even suggested in some oral briefings that an assassination attempt could not be ruled out.[27] His murder at the hands of the Egyptian Islamic Jihad in 1981 also drove many political pundits and journalists to predict the early demise of his successor, Hosni Mubarak, but the CIA judged that Cairo would weather those challenges, a judgment that has proved to be accurate, at least as of this writing.

Although the CIA missed the Iranian revolution, it did not miss the signs of growing Iraq/Iran conflict and provided adequate if not early warning of the 1980 war, which lasted for eight years. This war partly conditioned analysts to believe Iraq was too war weary to take on another regional war. So, when Saddam Hussein began his military buildup vis-à-vis Kuwait, many analysts—not to mention Iraq's neighbors—initially suspected a classic bluff aimed at economic blackmail. At that time, a major controversy had broken out on the quality of intelligence prior to the invasion of Iraq. The IC monitored and reported the Iraqi buildup throughout the summer of 1990. At least two weeks before the Iraqi invasion of Kuwait, good intelligence reporting and analysis raised the warning flag almost daily until the invasion. But allies in the area, the U.S. ambassador, and others were not convinced that the Iraqis would take such a dramatic step. Even if there had been total agreement on the likelihood that Iraq would invade, time was at a premium, and there was perhaps too little of it to work toward a policy solution.

The background of U.S. intelligence support for the Gulf War is well documented in other places. The U.S. military planners were unhappy that the CIA did not have the detailed level of intelligence they needed when the decision was made to force Iraq out of Kuwait. As in other cases when U.S. forces have gone to war, the CIA often was expected to produce tactical as well as strategic intelligence—not its primary mission. Some of the other complaints have proven to be ill founded, including those that claimed Central Command bomb damage assessments were better than the CIA's. Suffice it to say, senior military commanders complained that the CIA was not providing sufficient support to the war fighter, even though the Pentagon controlled nearly 80 percent of intelligence resources within its own department.[28] Accepting some of these criticisms, the CIA since 1992 has substantially improved support to the war fighter by beefing up analytic support to the various commands and by creating a CIA unit whose sole mission is supporting Defense Department customers.[29]

Problems with intelligence on Iraq's weapons of mass destruction (WMD) in 2002 now dominate the discussion of intelligence problems. The Iraq WMD Commission report did a creditable job of highlighting the collection shortfalls, flawed analytic tradecraft, and management problems of this case. Clearly, the collection of information and rigorous analysis of that information were not well done. Much of the analysis rested on information that had been collected as much as five years before the war. Assumptions about the status of weapons programs were not challenged. It is explainable and understandable how analysts came to the conclusions they did about the status of Iraq's weapons programs, but they were wrong. Often forgotten, however, is the intelligence produced about the consequences of a war with Iraq, which was often on the mark. But senior officials largely ignored those judgments, which partly explain the challenges the United States now faces. As I and other colleagues reported in an unclassified July 2005 report, the IC's performance was uneven: Analysis on WMD was wide of the mark and must be acknowledged if lessons are to be learned.[30] However, analysis produced prior to the war on a wide range of other issues accurately addressed topics on how the war would develop, how Iraqi forces would fight, the limited Iraqi links to al-Qaeda, the war's impact on the international oil market, and indeed assessments on post-Saddam Iraq.[31]

Latin and Central America: Watching the Neighborhood

Policymakers' interest in Latin America was most intense during the Kennedy and Reagan administrations, when Fidel Castro's Cuba in the 1960s and later Nicaragua and the Contras in the 1980s posed the most direct challenges to U.S. regional policies. The recent rise of Hugo Chávez in Venezuela may presage a similar increase in intelligence analysis of the region. Overall, the analytic record is sound; there were few major warning issues that could match the dramatic 1962 Cuban missile crisis, yet American analysts found themselves going beyond regional and country analysis to take on major transnational issues like narcotics trafficking and instability brought on by drug warlords who were challenging state authority in Central American nations.

Cuba remained a constant focus of intelligence attention, because Castro worked to extend his brand of communism throughout the region and later to covertly support Marxist guerrillas in Angola during the 1960s and 1970s. After the Portuguese withdrew from Angola in 1975, Castro dispatched tens of thousands of Cuban troops to Angola, and they were soon decisive in bringing the guerillas they supported to power. Long-term analysis on Cuba, however, was severely hampered by Cuban counterintelligence successes in doubling supposedly reliable U.S. human sources, in clever deception operations, and through extensive use of a high-level mole in the U.S. intelligence community who was uncovered only in the past few years.

In the 1980s, the Reagan administration's commitment to the overthrow of the Sandinistas in Nicaragua and its support for the Contras proved to be a challenging test of the objectivity of intelligence analysis, not an unusual situation when it came to U.S. policy in South America. CIA operations officers were running the Contra program while at the same time CIA analysts were assessing the effectiveness of the effort. This tension within the CIA was exacerbated by the enthusiasm that CIA director Casey and others in the administration had for the Contras' effort to defeat the Sandinistas. Caught between congressional opponents of the war and administration supporters, Latin American analysts walked a difficult tight wire in reporting. There was good evidence that some of the reporting from the field was less than objective. CIA analysis clearly judged that the Contras could not win a military victory, but Agency experts remained uncertain whether a political victory was possible.

The Tide toward Terrorism Analysis

Barrels of ink have been used to describe the CIA's failure in the September 11, 2001, terrorist attacks. But there has been little attention to its work on terrorism before it reached U.S. shores—given that then, as today, foreign rather than domestic intelligence is the CIA's responsibility. Terrorism abroad has been a fact of life for most of the period being addressed. Though it was centered in the Middle East, it is important to remember that Britain had the Irish Republican Army bombings and killings for years, Germany was tracking the Bader-Meinhof gang, the Red Brigades regularly kidnapped Italian politicians, and Hezbollah was attacking French targets. State-sponsored terrorism was a reality—Iran, Iraq, Syria, and Libya were training and funding terrorist activity aimed at the United States, other Western powers, and their own countries. Commercial aircraft were a favorite target during the 1970s and 1980s. CIA analysis was clear in its judgment that the objective of most Middle East terrorism was ending the U.S. presence in the Middle East and radicalizing governments in the area. In the mid-1980s DCI Casey moved analysts together with operators into a Counter-Terrorism Center. That center had some impressive success together with foreign intelligence organizations in preempting terrorist attacks. Although it took considerable time, the bombing of the Pan American plane over Scotland was traced back to Libya in an impressive intelligence investigation benefiting from a critical clandestine source.

As reported elsewhere, the CIA helped to thwart terrorist attacks against a variety of international organizations, U.S. embassies, airports, and other government facilities over the years. It organized the Afghan opposition to bring down the Taliban and has helped to capture more than a thousand al-Qaeda operatives worldwide. None of this would have been possible without competent analysts who could identify, monitor, and target suspects for arrest and renditions. The details of the attacks on the African embassies (1998), the *USS Cole* (2000) and World Trade Center (1993 and 2001) also suggest that the CIA's analytic role was only part of a much larger story of government-wide failings to collect, analyze, and respond to potential terrorist operations. This is not an excuse as much as an explanation for how hard it can be for analysts of foreign intelligence activities to see the complete picture, when many of those activities are the purview of other U.S. domestic, diplomatic, or military organizations.

In the hunt for Osama bin Laden, it is a fact that the CIA was the one organization that early on was attempting to develop a campaign against the Saudi-based al-Qaeda. It used all sources of intelligence and close cooperation with other intelligence collection agencies to monitor his activities and target him. As one of two people asked by the CIA's director of operations to assess that program, we said at the time that the activity was impressive and a good example of interagency cooperation and innovative use of operational assets and intelligence analysis.

What Can We Learn?

Reviewing the past fifty years of CIA analysis can help us recognize some of the inherent limitations of analysis and develop realistic expectations for what intelligence can provide to U.S. decision makers. Appreciating these limitations should help us in moving ahead in developing better analytic techniques and systems. Drawing a bottom line to the CIA's half decade of analysis shows challenges involving warning, politicization, information gaps, mindsets, and expertise building. Let us look briefly at each.

Warning remains the most difficult challenge that analysts face. Getting it right in some cases is no guarantee that future surprises will not occur. In some cases the CIA got it right and effectively warned policymakers; however, in other cases, it monitored developments but did not recognize them for what they were or did not sufficiently underline to policymakers the implications of an adversary's moves to convince them that action was needed. In the end, flawed mindsets, inadequate warning mechanisms, and poor intelligence–policymaker relationships were at the heart of such failures. These challenges deserve constant attention and are addressed elsewhere in this volume. Suffice it to say, warning remains the principal rationale for having an intelligence community and therefore deserves regular attention in the U.S. intelligence community's training and education programs.

Politicization, though a constant concern for analysts, turns out to be a fairly rare occurrence—but one that often grabs the headlines during any major policy dispute. Logically, intelligence analysis should serve as the basis for major judgments on the most important matters of state; hence, it is no surprise that policymakers often wish to construe intelligence in the most positive light possible. That said, in my own career I have seen little to be terribly alarmed about this. A professional analyst should have no problem turning down any blatant policy request that he or she tailor the analysis to suit a policy preference. And, clearly, I never had any problem and believe that analytic integrity is the single most important attribute of solid analysis. Although I personally could not agree with every judgment reached by CIA analysts in my thirty-two years of service, there was never a time when I felt we had compromised our integrity.

Information gaps, partly the result of poor analytic understanding of what they mean, lie at the heart of nearly every major intelligence failure. Whether it is the Cuban missile crisis, the 1990 Gulf War, or September 11, analysts must constantly be asking whether there is missing information, whether deception and denial are occurring, or whether their judgments must be qualified based on the paucity or poor quality of the information available. Analysts do not have the luxury of *not* reaching judgments, when incomplete or ambiguous information is all they have to go with. This is what distinguishes the better analysts with an understanding of the collection environment from those who merely observe and report only what they see.

Mindsets that prevent analysts from asking the right questions often result when poor information forces them to rely on an adversary's past behavior or on what they previously judged to be an intelligence target's most likely course of action. Not asking the right question about the motivations that drove the Soviets in Cuba, the Egyptians in the Sinai, or the Iraqis in the Gulf was the result of previously held views about how "risk adverse" America's opponents might be or how they might make calculations "just like us." The rigorous challenging of conventional wisdom through the regular use of better and more transparent analytic tradecraft can reduce—if not totally eliminate—the hazards of unconscious mindsets.

Expertise building cannot be achieved quickly or easily. Analysis is fundamentally a "people business," which requires hiring, training, and leading the best thinkers one can find. Throughout the CIA's history, it has sought out the people with the area expertise, technical training, and linguistic skills that would provide the most complete knowledge of important security issues. But these were always Americans, raised in a distinctly American culture and habits of mind. Realistically, security requirements still prevent us from hiring those non-Americans with local knowledge of the Middle East, cultural sensitivity about Asian societies, and the "street smarts" about drugs and thugs. To compensate for this, the CIA must conduct deep research, which encompasses networking with nongovernment and non-American experts outside the organization, regular conference attendance, independent study, and overseas assignments. A more adept mining of open sources and use of new technologies must also be part of the research agenda. Incentives to develop such expertise-building skills and experiences must be encouraged through proper resources and made available to as many analysts as wish to have them.

At the end of the day, policymakers will be the ultimate judges of whether intelligence analysis has served them well or poorly. That said, analysts and their leaders must strive to educate the policy world about some of the limitations they work under and help those in the executive and legislative branches of government to become more sophisticated consumers of intelligence analysis. Demonstrating that analysis can inform policy but not guarantee its success is a realistic goal for the CIA and the broader intelligence community. Policymakers should expect no less, but they should also demand no more.

Notes

The author thanks Roger George, Martha Kessler, Brian Latell, and Tom Wolfe, among others, for providing insights and suggestions to enrich this chapter.

1. Hindsight bias can work in at least two different ways. For outsiders reviewing the IC's past performance, they often forget that not as much was known or appreciated at the time of an assessment as is later known, which then inadvertently shapes the critics' reviews; conversely, intelligence analysts can often recall their past reporting as being more accurate than it actually was or as containing more prescient statements than were, in fact, appreciated at the time by policymakers or themselves.

2. This is attributed to Max Millikan, the founding director of the Office of Research and Reports in 1951–52, and was found in *Soviet Defense Spending: A History of CIA Estimates, 1950–1990*, by Noel E. Firth and James H. Noren (College Station: Texas A&M University Press, 1998), 13.

3. Chapter 12 in this volume examines the importance of the analyst–collector relationship, demonstrating how analysts must direct collectors toward the kinds of data needed.

4. "Intelligence Forecasts of Soviet Intercontinental Attack Forces: An Evaluation of the Record, April 1989," in *CIA's Analysis of the Soviet Union 1947–1991*, ed. Gerald Haines and Robert E. Leggett (Washington, D.C.: Center for the Study of Intelligence, Central Intelligence Agency, 2001), 290–91. This volume contains key estimates and CIA assessments, which illustrate the scope and depth of CIA's work during the cold war.

5. Illustrative of the kinds of critiques was an article written by Albert Wohlstetter, "Is There a Strategic Arms Race?" *Foreign Policy* 15 (Summer 1974): 3–20.

6. Ann Cahn, *Killing Détente: The Right Attacks* (University Park: Pennsylvania State University Press, 1998).

7. See U.S. Congress, Senate, Report of the Senate Select Committee on Intelligence, Sub-committee on Collection, Production, and Quality, *The National Intelligence Estimates A-B Team Episode Concerning Soviet Strategic Capability and Objectives* (Washington, D.C.: U.S. Government Printing Office, 1978), 1–12. Team B was composed of handpicked critics of CIA estimates and, as the Senate committee concluded, "reflected the views of only one segment of the spectrum of opinion."

8. CIA analysts were reporting a steady buildup of forces on the border of Afghanistan and warned that Moscow might introduce small numbers of forces but did not expect a major military campaign that would lead to long-term occupation of the country. See Douglas MacEachin and Janne E. Nolan, "The Soviet Invasion of Afghanistan in 1979: Failure of Intelligence or Policy Process?" Institute for the Study of Diplomacy Working Group Report 111, September 26, 2005, 4.

9. Well-known critics included Franklyn D. Holzman and William T. Lee. Holzman accused CIA of gross overestimates, while Lee claimed the CIA was underestimating Soviet military spending. See Franklyn D. Holzman, "Politics and Guesswork: CIA and DIA Estimates of Soviet military Spending," *International Security* 14 (Fall 1989): 101–31; and William T. Lee, *The Estimation of Soviet Defense Expenditures 1955–75: An Unconventional Approach* (New York: Praeger, 1977).

10. Dan M. Berkowitz, "An Evaluation of CIA's Analysis of Soviet Economic Performance 1970–1990," *Comparative Economic Studies* 35, no. 2 (Summer 1993): 35.

11. As Joseph Nye, former chairman of the National Intelligence Council, points out: "Mysteries are things which it doesn't do you any good to steal, because the people you're stealing from don't know the answer." See Joseph Nye, "Peering into the Future," *Foreign Affairs* 73, no. 4 (July/August 1994): 82.

12. Brent Scowcroft, "Letter to the Editor," *Washington Post*, January 12, 2000.

13. A prescient paper on this theme was a National Intelligence Council assessment titled "Dimensions of Civil Unrest in the Soviet Union," published in April 1983. It documented rising levels of labor strikes, food riots, and other forms of public disturbances that signaled the growing systemic failures that were to become evident under Gorbachev's leadership; now declassified. See Peter Schweizer, *Reagan's War* (New York: Knopf, 2002), 196–97.

14. See John K. Allen, John Carver, and Tom Elmore, eds., *Tracking the Dragon: National Intelligence Estimates on China during the Era of Mao 1948–1976* (Washington, D.C.: Central Intelligence Agency, 2004), xii. This volume contains declassified NIEs on Chinese leadership, politics, economics, and military programs.

15. Allen, Carver, and Elmore, *Tracking the Dragon*, xii.

16. Bill Gertz and Rowan Scarborough, "Inside the Ring: NSC Predicament," *Washington Times*, November 3, 2005. E.g., these reporters claim that a senior CIA China analyst had been advocating "conciliatory" positions toward China and had discouraged analyses that were critical of China's human rights record or warned of China's rising military power.

17. This is an excerpt from the unclassified *DCI Worldwide Threat Brief*, March 9, 2004, 17.

18. Richard Helms, *A Look over My Shoulder: A Life in the Central Intelligence Agency* (New York: Random House, 2003), 311.

19. Sam Adams, the leading Vietnam military analyst at the time, became notorious for challenging MACV figures based on captured enemy documents. His book *War of Numbers: An Intelligence Memoir* (South Royalton, Vt.: Steerforth Press, 1998) became part of the legend of CIA confrontation with the military. Harold Ford, a longtime CIA Asian expert, also recounts the CIA's long history of challenging presidential optimism in his article "Why CIA Analysts Were So Doubtful about Vietnam," *Studies in Intelligence* 5 (1997): 85–95.

20. See Helms, *A Look over My Shoulder*, 328. For another view on the order-of-battle problem, see James J. Wirtz, "Intelligence to Please: The Order of Battle Controversy during

the Vietnam War," in *Strategic Intelligence: Windows into a Secret World: An Anthology*, ed. Loch Johnson and James J. Wirtz (Los Angeles: Roxbury, 2003), 183–97.

21. See P. R. Rose, "Two Strategic Intelligence Mistakes in Korea 1950," *Studies in Intelligence* 11 (Fall/Winter 2001): 57–65. See also Richard A. Mobley, "North Korea's Surprise Attack: Weak U.S. Analysis," *International Journal of Intelligence and Counterintelligence* 13, no. 4 (2000): 490–514. Mobley quotes Ray Cline, then deputy director of intelligence, as saying that the "CIA had written some warnings about the possibility of North Korean attack . . . but they were insufficiently emphatic to capture the NSC audience they should have reached."

22. CIA statement to Congress, August 18, 2003. See Larry A. Niksch, "Korea: U.S.-Korean Relations—Issues for Congress," *Congressional Research Service Issue Brief*, April 14, 2006, 2–3.

23. Statement by DNI, Ambassador John Negroponte, October 18, 2006. See "U.S. Intelligence: Air Samples Confirm N. Korea Nuke Test," *USA Today*, October 16, 2006.

24. "Emerging Missile Threats to North America during the Next 15 Years," Director of Central Intelligence, NIE 95–19, November 1995, forecast that "no country, other than the major declared nuclear powers, will develop or otherwise acquire a ballistic missile in the next 15 years that could threaten the contiguous 48 states and Canada. An Independent Panel (led by former DCI Robert Gates and a group of senior military, diplomatic, and scientific experts) concluded that the NIE—although not "politicized"—failed to adequately address the motives and objectives of governments developing missile programs. In 1998, the Rumsfeld Commission also concluded that "the threat to the U.S. posed by these emerging capabilities is broader, more mature and evolving more rapidly than has been reported in estimates and reports by the Intelligence Community. See *Report of the U.S. Commission to Assess the Ballistic Missile Threat to the United States*, Executive Summary, July 15, 1998.

25. Robert Walpole (national intelligence officer for strategic and nuclear programs), "North Korea's Taepo Dong Launch and Some Implications on the Ballistic Missile Threat to the United States," speech delivered to the Center for Strategic and International Studies, Washington, December 8, 1998.

26. Richard Helms recounts that President Johnson invited the DCI to attend future policy discussions after this episode. See Helms, *A Look over My Shoulder*, 298–305.

27. See John Helgerson, *Getting to Know the President: CIA Briefings of Presidential Candidates 1952–1992* (Washington, D.C.: Center for the Study of Intelligence, Central Intelligence Agency, 1996), chap. 6.

28. Michael Gordon and Bernard Trainor, *The Generals' War: The Inside Story of the Conflict in the Gulf* (New York: Little, Brown, 1995).

29. National Intelligence Support Teams are now routinely deployed with U.S. forces throughout the world. The Office of Military Support within the CIA has the mission of working closely with the Department of Defense to ensure its requirements are met by CIA operators and analysts.

30. Richard Kerr, Thomas Wolfe, Rebecca Donegan, and Aris Pappas, "Issues for the U.S. Intelligence Community: Collection and Analysis on Iraq," *Studies in Intelligence* 49, no. 3 (Fall 2005): 1–9.

31. For explanation of what analysis was prepared on postinvasion Iraq, see Paul Pillar, "The Right Stuff," *The National Interest*, September/October 2007, 53–59.

CHAPTER 3

Is Intelligence Analysis a Discipline?

REBECCA FISHER AND ROB JOHNSTON

AMONG THE MANY EFFORTS to improve analysis, there has been a long-standing desire to transform intelligence analysis into a full-fledged discipline. Indeed, the intent of this book is to advance the state of knowledge about analysis and promote further "professionalization" of analysis along the lines that Sherman Kent had suggested as much as half a century ago. Though many practitioners have espoused the goal of creating a more rigorous discipline, few have considered what a discipline actually requires. The steps toward creating a discipline, however, should be informed by what such a goal actually entails, and upon closer inspection practitioners will be heartened to see that such a goal is not as distant as some might assume.

What Is a Discipline?

Disciplines emerge as systems for maintaining order, routinizing methods, and codifying actions. They are found in communities that recognize and seek to minimize the extent to which the welfare of persons or groups of people is put at risk because of the actions of individuals. The development of professional standards, best practices, consensus statements, and practice guidelines is the logical result of this risk mitigation. We need not look far to find examples of how disciplines such as law, medicine, and library science have evolved to the level of their present-day sophistication and development from what were once largely unregulated practices performed ad hoc.

Though closely associated, the words "profession" and "discipline" convey a nuanced but significant difference in meaning. A profession is widely regarded as a life's work that requires specialized knowledge and often long and intensive vocational or academic preparation. For our purposes, we shall define the word "discipline" as a type of profession, but one in which specialized knowledge and rigorous preparation are operationalized by the introduction of formal or informal governing bodies that are responsible for developing rules of a mandatory or voluntary nature that serve to guide, inform, and ensure the highest possible quality professional conduct and activity. Disciplines are professions that retain the collective wisdom of practitioners and establish standards for archiving and accessing that knowledge. Disciplines distinguish themselves by externally and internally derived licensing and credentialing practices, ethical standards, and continuing education requirements. Insofar as "intelligence analysis" lacks these attributes, the answer to the question "Is intelligence analysis a discipline?" would have to be "no." But perhaps the better question is "Should it be?" This chapter looks to other professions-turned-disciplines and makes the case for an affirmative answer to that question.

The Legal Profession

The American legal profession as we know it began to take shape in the nineteenth century, only recently in our country's history. Prior to the 1870s, practicing law was the domain of the upper class, set apart and venerable; the philosopher Alexis de Tocqueville wrote in 1835: "In America . . . lawyers . . . form the highest political class and the most cultivated circle of society."[1] But around midcentury, a backlash against the elitism associated with the profession, together with the country's burgeoning growth and increasing demand for legal services, democratized the profession, making it much more accessible. What had been a profession of the privileged few was suddenly open to many. Requirements for becoming a lawyer grew arbitrary and, in some jurisdictions, practically nonexistent.[2]

To suggest that the American legal profession was in disarray by the latter half of the nineteenth century would be to understate the extent to which its ranks had fallen: Widespread corruption underscored hosts of other unseemly conduct such as unruly behavior and indecorous speech and dress in the courtroom. In its report to the Bar of the City of New York, the Committee on the Admission to the Bar wrote, "The general standard of professional learning and obligation was high during the first forty years of the nineteenth century. About 1840, it began to decline, and its tendency was steadily downward until about 1870, when it reached its lowest ebb, when even the Bench was invaded by corruption and found support in a portion of the bar."[3]

The first milestone in the restoration of law to its present status as a profession of the educated and regulated was the creation of bar associations. The first of these, the Bar of the City of New York, instituted "rigorous scrutiny of qualifications for membership . . . to maintain the honor and dignity of the professions,"[4] with the overarching goal of assuring the expeditious administration of justice. This turning point was the first of many more bar alliances, most notably the formation of the American Bar Association (ABA) in 1878. The ABA appeared on the American scene at a time when "no uniform code of ethics governed [lawyers'] conduct [and] few institutions for common effort were available,"[5] but by the turn of the twentieth century, the organization had successfully drafted legislation, set standards for law reform, and—most notably for our purposes—established the requirements for legal education in America. By the late nineteenth century, 176 more bar associations had formed. Changes in the way law was taught and the publication of textbooks on specialized topics such as negligence law, taxation, and personal property followed. Each innovation represented a layer of oversight and governance that would transform the profession of law into a discipline.

In keeping with the implementation of educational standards was the systematization of the profession's shared knowledge, establishing the body of case law that came to characterize Western jurisprudence as possibly the world's first "knowledge management" system. Each case generates a unique record of participants, proceedings, and decisions upon which every subsequent case will be based, argued, or rendered null, forming a body of scholarship accessible to any and all. But at its lowest ebb, the legal profession had no uniform and organized system for researching this scholarship; the American Digest System and the National Reporter System, now available in various electronic and print permutations, did not exist. These resources emerged on the American scene in 1872 with the foresighted and entrepreneurial work of John B. West. West's Key Number system, an indexing method still in use, utilizes seven general categories (persons, property, contracts, torts, crimes, remedies, and government)—further divided into 400 major topics (e.g., civil rights, securities, criminal law), and divided further still into nearly 100,000 subtopics—to enable researchers to surface relevant, accurate information out of a confusing tangle of data.

The systematization of legal knowledge and the development of methods for retrieving it marked another passage in the transformation of the legal profession from dilettantism to discipline. One of the major advantages of West's system was its ability to accommodate the ever-evolving status of case law. The system's foundation—a dynamic, adaptable taxonomy—allowed the inclusion of new terms and technologies as they emerged. Another benefit was the product's ability to be updated; printed updates that easily slipped into and out of three-ring binders assured that practitioners' legal references would always reflect the current disposition of the law under study. Over the years West's product, eventually called the *National Reporter*, became known as "the authoritative source of case law, legislation, and most things jurisprudential."[6]

Parallels to intelligence are abundant in law. Substitute the words "intelligence" for "law" and "analysts" for "students" in the excerpt below and you have a more than adequate impression of the current state of U.S. intelligence:

> The law is, after all, a complicated web of interrelated doctrines and often contradictory interpretative texts. First year law students frequently lack the contextual understanding necessary to discover and evaluate all the extant decisions necessary to develop a full analysis of the issues presented to them. In addition to trying to acquire this broad overview of the law and the way it works, they must simultaneously grapple with a multiplicity of challenges: unfamiliar surroundings, a curriculum seemingly designed to keep them off-balance, new ways of thinking, and teachers speaking a new language or, at the very least, a dialect of English with which they are unfamiliar. And, of course, each student is located at a different point along a skills continuum. Legal research is a demanding discipline requiring excellent legal researchers to be curious, persistent, flexible people and these attributes are not universal even, or especially, among lawyers or law students.[7]

Perhaps the most relevant aspect of such a comparison is the notion that, though intelligence community members may indeed be overwhelmed in confronting a "multiplicity of challenges" in a world seemingly designed to "keep them off balance," the urgent call for systematizing both resources and methods persists if intelligence analysis is to achieve "discipline" status with all the rigor, tenacity, and high standards such a designation connotes.

In law, organized resources and systematic research methods, governing bodies that established professional standards and ethical guidelines, and boards impaneled to assure that appropriate levels of education and competence preceded admission to the bar earned the profession its modern-day stature: a discipline—Law, writ large—ultimately emerged, with the benefit being homogeneity and predictability in the manner in which state, federal, and international law is administered and practiced in the United States.

The Medical Profession

The medical community's parallel to intelligence analysis may be more apt owing to the temporal nature—often an urgency—with which members of each group must confront difficult challenges of decision making in life or death and high-risk situations. Reliance upon years of training, individual experience, and consultation with colleagues has prevailed for centuries in medical decision making, an "apprenticeship" learning model of the highest order, forming a pattern of acquiring expertise and finding support for one's decisions that is remarkably similar to what goes on in the intelligence community.

Training, individual experience, and the advice of one's peers, no matter how well intentioned or informed, do not equal evidence. Ferreting out the hard data that should drive the decisions that ultimately bear on whether a patient lives or dies was not always the norm in medicine, any more than it is in intelligence analysis. Here, as in the case of the legal profession, we see that one of the planks of professionalism—as it becomes a discipline—is access to and proper use of a rich body of scholarship.

As with case law, it was not as though medical scholarship did not exist. Pamphlets, reports, and books shaped the practice of medicine from the time of Hippocrates. But a modern-day data repository only began to emerge in 1818, when Joseph Lovell, the first surgeon general of the Army, began collecting books and journals to serve as a reference library for the army surgeons under his command. His collection seeded what was to become the National Library of Medicine (NLM), a collection of millions of journal article references (also known as citations), monographs, audiovisual materials, and specialized collections on topics such as toxicology, environmental health, and molecular biology. Today, the NLM serves health professionals, scientists, librarians, and the public, its servers hosting over 750 million literature searches every year on an annual budget of approximately $330 million.

Medline forms the bulk of the NLM's online repository and provides access to over 16 million citations from the medical literature. Each citation, or "document surrogate," represents an article published in a medical journal. Citations are indexed by human beings who use the Medical Subject Heading (MeSH) system—a taxonomy of medical terms (not unlike West's Key Number system)—to efficiently route users to relevant citations. MeSH terms number nearly

23,000 and permit searching on varying levels of specificity; the MeSH taxonomy is updated annually to reflect changes and advances in medical discovery.

Still, a profession's literature—that is, the mere fact of its existence—does not automatically mean its aggregate membership comprises a discipline. Pressure arising from within its own ranks to improve methods and outcomes is also an integral part of any profession's progression toward becoming a discipline. This type of internal agitation appeared in medicine, as it had in law, in the form of widespread demand for improvements and standardization in education and credentialing. Remarking on this groundswell, Paul Starr, the Pulitzer Prize–winning author of *The Social Transformation of American Medicine*, observes, "In the eyes of reform-minded American educators . . . medicine epitomized both the backward state of higher education and the degraded state of professions in America."[8] He notes that deficiencies in medical education had existed for decades—that in 1875 anyone with a high school diploma could attend medical school, and that the two years' coursework could be completed in any order the student preferred: new knowledge was not, by design, mandatorily built on previous knowledge, which would have ensured a more vertical understanding of medical phenomena and techniques.

The lack of governing boards and credentialing systems common to both late-nineteenth-century medicine and present-day intelligence is not where their similarities end: Starr observes that the most significant failure of the apprenticeship model—the fact that the "medical faculty had no control over preceptors"—resonates in an intelligence environment where subject matter experts face serious constraints in their efforts to train novices in the secrets of "tradecraft" while performing their regular work, the demands of which are in constant flux and various states of urgency. In intelligence, governing bodies and oversight systems—for example, peer review and "tradecraft" specialists whose principal duties focused on analytical skills and training issues—would compensate for some of the gaps and weaknesses in the apprenticeship model by producing consensus statements, practice guidelines, or even informal feedback loops, and their absence only exacerbates an already-vexing problem.

But medicine did begin to close these gaps and fortify the apprenticeship model as early as 1901, with the formation of the American Medical Association's Council on Medical Education. At its first meeting, the council produced standardized education requirements and set about developing the "ideal medical curriculum."[9] Several years later the "Flexner Report" was issued, the product of Abraham Flexner's rigorous tour of 155 medical schools over the course of eighteen months. In his final report, Flexner remarked that, while American medical practitioners were not inferior to their European counterparts, there was "probably no other country in the world in which there is so great a distance and so fatal a difference between the best, the average, and the worst."[10] As Flexner's recommendations were implemented in the form of codified processes of training, credentialing, and board certifying physicians and the body of shared medical knowledge grew in the form of books, papers, and monographs, the medical profession's metamorphosis to "discipline" stature had begun in earnest.

Yet training, credentialing, or board certification alone and access to the profession's collective knowledge (while absent at various times in their histories from both medicine and law) fail to address the danger of resting on one's proverbial laurels in an ever-evolving world of discovery and innovation.[11] In the case of medicine, the manner in which important clinical information (e.g., that contained in Medline and on the shelves of countless medical libraries across the country) was acquired, used, and shared became the hallmark of a discipline, beginning with the realization that evidence rather than opinion needs to gird medical decision making. Before the dawn of evidence-based practice,

> the idea was that when a physician faced a patient, by some fundamentally human process called the "art of medicine" or "clinical judgment," the physician would synthesize all of the important information about the patient, relevant research, and experiences with previous patients to determine the best course of action. "Medical decision-making" as a field worthy of study did not exist. Analytical methods and mathematical models were limited to research projects. Guidelines were merely a way for experts to pass occasional pieces of advice to non-experts. Coverage and medical necessity were defined tautologically; if the majority of physicians were doing it, it was medically necessary and should be covered. Diseases did not require any management beyond what physicians were already providing, and performance was taken for granted.[12]

The terms "art of medicine" and "clinical judgment" are every bit as nebulous here as the term "tradecraft" is among analysts in the intelligence community. What is good tradecraft, exactly? How is it measured? Can it be taught? Or is it so arbitrary that "you only know it when you see it"? These are questions the medical community was forced to ask itself when the British obstetrician and epidemiologist Archie Cochrane published his landmark 1972 book *Effectiveness and Efficiency: Random Reflections on Health Services*.[13] In the bold, outspoken style for which he was known, Cochrane questioned the very manner in which medicine was practiced and called for the rigorous evaluation of *effectiveness* (whether treatments actually work) and *efficiency* (whether treatments represent the optimal use of available resources). This could be accomplished, Cochrane said, by conducting and using results from randomized, controlled clinical trials. Treatment decisions, he held, must always be made consonant with *evidence* rather than on the basis of hearsay, imagined efficacy, or the "standard operating procedure" mentality that so often fails to consider alternative scenarios, derogatory side effects, long-term damage, and blatantly contradictory information. Evidence, here defined as "any empirical observation about the apparent relationship between events"[14] stored in a systematic manner, allows higher-order cognitive processes to build on "givens" like training and access to sage advice. The use of statistical rather than solely anecdotal information supplies a better picture of an entire disease spectrum or process, an increased familiarity with the array of treatment or surgical interventions that might be warranted, and a broadening of the researcher's scope of inquiry—to include possibilities that may otherwise have been overlooked. Cochrane's book marked the emergence of the Evidence-Based Medicine (EBM) movement. A discipline-within-the-discipline of medicine, EBM uses strict criteria to determine the validity and quality of medical research and encompasses:

- *types of studies* (e.g., randomized controlled trials, clinical trials, meta-analyses);
- *publications and repositories* (BMJ's *Evidence-Based Medicine for Primary Care and Internal Medicine* journal, and Cochrane's *Central Register of Controlled Trials* and *Database of Systematic Reviews*, to name a few);
- *study groups* (e.g., journal clubs and the Cochrane Collaboration, a network of practitioners from around the world who share an interest in developing evidence-based resources on particular medical topics); and
- *research methodologies* (specific bibliographic research techniques used to surface authoritative, high-quality medical information).

A corollary to all the above that applies to intelligence analysis would be the creation of an "intelligence literature," which Sherman Kent described in 1955 as "dedicated to the analysis of our many-sided calling and produced by its most knowledgeable devotees."[15] Kent, a professor of history at Yale prior to joining the Central Intelligence Agency (CIA), envisioned the stepwise building of such an evidence-based literature, such that "Major X [would] write an essay on the theory of indicators and print it and have it circulated. . . . A Mr. B [would] brood over this essay and write a review of it, . . . [and] a Commander C reading both the preceding documents and reviewing them both" would provide insights that would enable yet "another man coming forward to produce an original synthesis of all that has gone before."[16] Kent's "systematic literature of intelligence" would be, he acknowledged, "ponderous and a drain on time." However, he also defended the value of precisely such an investment when he wrote, "Taking Mr. X off the current task and giving him the time to sort out his thoughts and commit them to paper will more than repay the sacrifice if what Mr. X puts down turns out to be an original and permanent contribution."[17] In this sense, Mr. X's contribution to the intelligence literature must be viewed as something more than another briefing, paper, or estimate; it is a distillation of his own unique wisdom, filtered through experience, discourse, and debate.

In medicine as in law, organized resources and systematic research methods coupled with professional standards, ethical guidelines, and accomplished senior practitioners—whose job it is to see that appropriate training, demonstrated competence, and access to the entire profession's aggregate knowledge precede a physician's appearance at any bedside—have earned the profession its much deserved "discipline" designation.

Library Services

Acquiring and organizing resources and employing systematic research methods in order to fully exploit them are at the root of every library's raison d'être. Twenty-first-century practitioners of "library science" are members of a discipline whose professional standards and ethos reflect postgraduate education, training, internships, credentialing, and often membership in a variety of professional associations. The 136,660 librarians at work today in America's 117,341 libraries are generally proponents of ubiquitous access to knowledge and outspoken opponents of censorship.[18] Frequently among the most judicious, discerning, and skeptical consumers of information as well, a good librarian is often a patron's best hope of finding exactly what he or she needs in a sea of information where quality, value, and accessibility are often unknown variables.

This role—based on the ability to efficiently deliver high-quality information to information seekers who are less familiar (or completely unfamiliar) with the organization of information—evolved over centuries, achieving its present, democratized iteration only late in the nineteenth century. The earliest libraries existed for the use of rulers and the literate elite. The Alexandrian Library, for example, founded in the third century B.C. and considered the greatest library the world had known prior to the invention of the Gutenberg printing press in 1447, was staffed by highly educated scientists, mathematicians, and astronomers whose access to and familiarity with the library's extensive holdings was—whether intentionally or not—analogous with power and control. As recently as the mid–nineteenth century, to be a librarian—what Ralph Waldo Emerson called a "professor of books"—remained a type of investiture, available to those whose ability to preserve the "library's service to high culture" was assured by their own classical education, training, and superior knowledge.[19] As such, the air of mystery that came to characterize the role of librarians as keepers of wisdom (and others' access to it) endowed them with a certain ideological authority—the validity of which, like "tradecraft" or the "art of medicine"—was impossible to prove or disprove. Librarianship was the realm of experts, with expertise deriving from extensive reading and schooling rather than demonstrated facility with systematic methods in approaching a body of scholarship.

Though the underlying causes are beyond the scope of this chapter, it is perhaps no small coincidence that the late nineteenth century saw dramatic changes in the professionalization of not only law and medicine but also librarianship. Agitation for change reached critical mass with the appearance of the Dewey Decimal Classification System (DDC) in 1873. Known as the "Father of Modern Librarianship," Melvil Dewey transformed librarianship from a divining to a disciplined activity when he developed a system for organizing knowledge. Today, more than a century later, the DDC is still the most widely used classification taxonomy in the world. But this transformation was neither instantaneously achieved nor initially well received. A class of librarian scholars who espoused a more bibliographic approach to the literatures—that is, continually producing definitive reading lists of the "best books" on any given topic to guide public access and consumption, with themselves as final arbiters—vehemently resisted his approach. The flashpoint at which the two factions' ideologies ignited was the American Library Association Conference of 1886, where William Fletcher of Amherst maligned the Dewey system as "an attempt to substitute machinery for brains."[20] But Dewey persisted in what he called his "world work," a lifelong aspiration to "achieve his goal of educating the masses toward improvement [which entailed] the efficient operation of free public libraries properly stocked with 'good reading,' "[21] starting with taking the mystery out of locating and acquiring information.

With the deployment of DDC, librarianship went from the exclusive domain of the elite and abundantly well-read to the purview of anyone who could demonstrate expertise in using systematic procedures. Like West and Cochrane, Dewey's sentinel work made it possible to find, locate, and evaluate information from an infinite number of resources. Similar to the West system and evidence-based medicine techniques, the DDC is constantly refined to accommodate new knowledge: every year Library of Congress specialists classify materials using over 110,000 DDC numbers.[22] West's Key Number system and the NLM's MeSH taxonomy are maintained under a single authority; similarly, control of the DDC resides under the auspices of the Library of Congress. Expanding and amending these essential taxonomies is performed regularly, based upon the consensus of subject matter experts.

Modern libraries—filled with books, serials, audio and video files, and an infinite and ever-increasing number of Web pages—provide support for the psychologist George Kelly's 1963 observation that "all our present interpretations of the universe are subject to revision"[23]—and, in fact, modern libraries are the places most likely to contain *both* the original interpretations *and* their revisions. Today's libraries—chronologically and technologically descended from the Alexandrian Library and its 700,000 scrolls—represent not only access to but transferability and portability of an inexhaustible supply of information. Today's librarians confront the same inexhaustible supply of information as every other user, but they are equipped with schemas that enable the codification of data and methods for surfacing relevance expeditiously. Developing aptitude for making the best possible use of all available information resources is a discipline, rooted in systems and replicable methods, but also in graduate level training, credentialing, and subspecialty pursuit.

"Learning Organizations" as a Discipline

Another way to define a discipline—be it legal, medical, library services, or intelligence analysis—is to think of it as a "learning organization." Whether informal or formal, an effective discipline must be capable of knowledge management, sense making, and what might be called "mindfulness." Along with other established disciplines, intelligence analysis must strive in this direction, and some intelligence organizations are beginning to recognize the significance of these features.

Knowledge management as a system of organizing principles existed in libraries long before it appeared in law, medicine, or intelligence analysis. But it is only relatively recently that "knowledge management" as a pillar of best business practice has arisen, rooted in the work of Karl-Erik Sveiby and Peter Senge in the late 1980s and early 1990s. Sveiby coined the phrase "knowledge management," building on ideas he set forth in his 1986 book *Managing Know-how*. He had come to realize that his scholarly work no longer depended on "formal structures [in which] managers were in control and output was visible" but rather on "substantial invisible knowledge-based assets"—subject matter experts whose knowledge was, in reality, the company's most valuable asset. He recognized that a traditional industrial, "command-and-control" mentality was difficult if not impossible to sustain in a knowledge-dependent environment, where the product itself arises from access to information that is constantly changing. His early work sought an answer to problems confronted by business leaders who "lack explicit tools [and] manage intuitively, by gut feeling . . . traveling in uncharted territory, and [lacking] even a basic theory of knowledge—an epistemology, as philosophers call it."[24]

Senge's 1990 book *The Fifth Discipline: The Art and Practice of the Learning Organization* expanded the knowledge management concept beyond simply a way to capture, organize, and store information to talk in terms of "learning organizations." He defined learning organizations as environments in which "people continually expand their capacity to create the results they truly desire, where new and expansive patterns of thinking are nurtured, where collective aspiration is set free, and where people are continually learning to see the whole together."[25]

Now widely known as knowledge management, this organizational phenomenon encompasses a spectrum of practices and technologies that range from converting tacit knowledge into explicit, codified knowledge to establishing systems for knowledge capture in real time and providing after-action review capabilities. But however they are developed, knowledge management systems—now ubiquitous in many major corporations—support learning organizations by enabling members to literally *make sense.*

Sense making is in fact a type of discipline.[26] In the 1970s, Brenda Dervin is credited with introducing the term "sense making" as a by-product of communication.[27] Around the same time, Karl Weick began to develop the term in the organizational literature to describe how organizations can prepare to react to unexpected challenges. Weick writes, "The unexpected doesn't take the form of a major crisis [but is instead] triggered by a deceptively simple sequence in organizational life: A person or unit has an intention, takes action, misunderstands the world; actual events fail to coincide with the intended sequence; and there is an unexpected outcome."[28]

The value of being a learning organization for analytical agencies is undeniable. Unexpected outcomes are just as unacceptable in the realm of national security as they are in business sectors. To avoid surprises, organizations—and their experts—must continually free themselves from the machinery of preconception and rote by moving with resolve in the direction Weick calls "mindfulness." For him, mindfulness is a type of mental functioning that is "distinguished by continuous updating and deepening of increasingly plausible interpretations" of context, problems, and remedies. For our purposes, *mindfulness* is arguably the most important difference between a pastime or hobby—or a job—and a discipline. The practice of mindfulness as a way of pursuing one's craft—be it law, medicine, research, or intelligence analysis—is a type of investiture, a skill rooted in both cognition and affect, and a lifelong commitment to perfecting that skill by using all of the tools at one's disposal, including the stated or unstated expectations and standards of one's professional peer group. To become a learning organization, then, intelligence analysis must not only embrace better management of the tacit knowledge held by analysts but must also create the conditions that encourage continuous learning, exposure to new ideas, and more flexible business practices that can accommodate unconventional thinking styles and forms of collaboration.

Intelligence Analysis as a Discipline

The examples of law, medicine, and library science are but a handful of professions in which constantly evolving methods and guidelines for utilizing *data* (observations and measurements), *information* (organized data that has been classified, indexed, and/or placed in context), and *knowledge* (analyzed and understood information)[29] have transformed basic aptitudes into formalized, systematized disciplines. The idea that intelligence analysis, closely tied as it is to U.S. national security and public policy, has not yet undergone that transformation is a matter of continuing concern and scrutiny. A number of recent calls for change have coalesced, taking the form of greater demand for increased knowledge sharing, better access to information across components and agencies, and greater accountability.[30] To the extent that intelligence analysis has remained idiosyncratic and lacks oversight mechanisms by which all its practitioners systematically acquire, share, and produce knowledge, it is not yet recognizable as a full-fledged discipline.

Encouragingly, however, intelligence analysis does share many characteristics in common with law, medicine, and library science as these others have evolved into disciplines. For example, academic credentialing in intelligence or intelligence-related studies is available from many private-sector universities. In addition, mentoring, case-based curricula, historical studies, basic and applied research, and a growing literature also characterize work in intelligence analysis in much the same way such channels serve the disciplines of law, medicine, and library science. Elements of a learning organization have also begun to emerge in the world of intelligence analysis. To give just one example, one can cite the work of the CIA's Global Futures Partnership, whose mandate has been to bring innovation experts and unconventional perspectives into the agency in order to challenge current business practices and promote greater sense making.

Specific Steps Going Forward

Thomas Kuhn, describing the now-common concept of paradigm shifts in scientific revolutions, believed that such shifts are tied to cultural and social constructionist models, and that the groups themselves not only organize knowledge but also create reality iteratively vis-à-vis social interaction and relationship.[31] For intelligence analysis to become a discipline in the sense that other professions have, *the practitioners themselves* need to design, develop, and test a system of heuristics and ultimately arrive by rough consensus at something resembling a controlled vocabulary—a taxonomy of terms that enables users to not only cali-brate their thinking but also zero in quickly on relevant sources of information. In the same way that West's Key Number system, the NLM's MeSH, or libraries' DDC make very specific information available to their practitioners, intelligence analysts must construct their own vocabulary, terminology, and way of commu-nicating analytic principles and practices. A standardized nomenclature serves as a platform for the development of a common language—in this case, a univer-sally accessible intelligence vernacular. The very existence of such a nomencla-ture can also serve as a platform for dialogue, discussion, and debate among very diverse communities of interest and practice.

There is a wealth of intelligence scholarship already available in the form of journal articles, monographs, books, and best practice studies. After taxonomic terms are developed, they should be assigned (either manually or by latent semantic indexing) to the writings that already exist so these materials are readily available to all community members. Future materials should be simi-larly indexed and tagged as they are added to a centralized database repository. In addition, the most experienced intelligence analysts and methodologists should be commissioned to regularly gather, collaborate, and write on topics that are of enduring interest to the entire community, with the goal of producing review articles that store the wisdom of their years. Another logical first step is to establish—concurrently with the development of a nomenclature—an over-arching, ubiquitous community of practice. Rather than a rigid, highly regu-lated, and controlled information environment, this would be what Norm Archer calls "a self-organizing network of individuals with ad hoc relationships and no formal ties . . . a loosely organized and informal network that has no central management authority or sponsor [in which] membership is voluntary, and there is little explicit commitment. Members may choose to join or leave as they wish. Most such networks operate virtually, so communication strategy is primarily based on knowledge codification."[32] It is impossible to miss the need for codification in an undertaking of this type, if for no other reason than to allow participants to conceptualize community and build it together as they proceed.

Disciplines are responses to a shared sense of need and the collective agitation for systemic improvement. Generally speaking, disciplines do not develop by mandate (although mandates often do arise as standards, social conventions, and consensus appear). As demonstrated by the examples of law, medicine, and library science, disciplines emerge where groups of people combine their lived experiences and learning with that of others, establishing performance standards and searchable repositories of aggregate knowledge. They adopt "best practice" methodologies used to access these vast repositories of knowledge, whether tacit or explicit, which remain "best" only until better information, experience, or methods become available. Therefore, transforming intelligence analysis from a series of ad hoc activities into a highly intellectualized discipline must be seen as an ongoing process rather than a once-and-for-all solution. An intelligence community literature—supported by an agile and extensive taxonomy and an overarching "community of practice" designed to shelter smaller communities of interest, practice, and expertise—can serve as a rich seedbed for the growth of shared mental models and a shared vision and would represent a first step toward making the best sense of the myriad tasks diligently performed by individuals, teams, agency components, and the entire intelligence apparatus.

Notes

1. Alexis de Tocqueville, *Democracy in America* (London: Longmans, Green, 1889; Washington, D.C.: Regnery, 2002), 221. The citation refers to the Regnery edition.

2. Harry J. Lambeth, "Practicing Law in 1878," *American Bar Association Journal* 64 (July 1978): 1016.

3. Quoted in Lambeth, "Practicing Law," 1016. In 1850, all that was necessary to practice law in Indiana, for instance, was "good moral character" and registration to vote.

4. Ibid., 1018.

5. Whitney North Seymour, "The First Century of the American Bar Association," *American Bar Association Journal* 64 (July 1978): 1040.

6. Jason Krause, "Towering Titans," *ABA Journal* 90 (May 2004): 50.

7. Ian Gallacher, "Forty-Two: The Hitchhiker's Guide to Teaching Legal Research to the Google Generation," ExpressO Preprint Series, September 6, 2005, http://law.bepress.com/expresso/eps/701.

8. Paul Starr, *The Social Transformation of American Medicine* (New York: Basic Books, 1982), 113.

9. Andrew H. Beck, "The Flexner Report and the Standardization of American Medical Education," *Journal of the American Medical Association* 291 (May 5, 2004): 2139.

10. Beck, "Flexner Report," 2140.

11. E.g., see Stephen P. Marrin and Jonathan D. Clemente, "Improving Intelligence Analysis by Looking to the Medical Profession," *International Journal of Intelligence and Counterintelligence* 18 (Winter 2005): 707; and Stephen P. Marrin and Jonathan D. Clemente, "Modeling an Intelligence Analysis Profession on Medicine," *International Journal of Intelligence and Counterintelligence*, no. 19 (Winter 2006): 642.

12. David M. Eddy, "Evidence-Based Medicine: A Unified Approach," *Health Affairs* 24 (January–February 2005): 9.

13. See A. L. Cochrane, *Effectiveness and Efficiency: Random Reflections on Health Service* (London: Nuffield Provincial Hospitals Trust, 1972).

14. G. H. Guyatt, R. B. Haynes, R. Z. Jaeschke, D. J. Cook, L. Green, C. D. Naylor, M. C. Wilson, and W. S. Richardson, "Users' Guides to the Medical Literature: XXV—Evidence-Based Medicine: Principles for Applying the Users' Guides to Patient Care; Evidence-Based Medicine Working Group," *Journal of the American Medical Association* 284 (September 13, 2000): 1290.

15. Sherman Kent, "The Need for an Intelligence Literature," *Studies in Intelligence* 1 (Fall 1955): 3.

16. Ibid., 7.

17. Ibid., 10.

18. "ALA Library Fact Sheet 1: Number of Libraries in the United States," American Library Association, 2006; www.ala.org/ala/alalibrary/libraryfactsheet/alalibraryfactsheet1.htm.

19. Bernd Frohmann, "'Best Books' and Excited Readers: Discursive Tensions in the Writings of Melvil Dewey," *Libraries & Culture* 32 (Summer 1997): 349.

20. Ibid., 352.

21. Wayne A. Wiegand, *Irrepressible Reformer: A Biography of Melvil Dewey* (Chicago: American Library Association, 1996), 33.

22. "Introduction to Dewey Decimal Classification," OCLC [Online Computer Library Center], www.oclc.org/dewey/versions/ddc22print/intro.pdf.

23. George A. Kelly, *A Theory of Personality: The Psychology of Personal Constructs* (New York: W. W. Norton, 1963), 15.

24. Karl Erik Sveiby, *The New Organizational Wealth: Managing & Measuring Knowledge-Based Assets* (San Francisco: Berrett Koehler, 1997), x.

25. Peter M. Senge, *The Fifth Discipline: Mastering the Five Practices of the Learning Organization* (New York: Doubleday, 1990), 3.

26. Warren Fishbein and Gregory Treverton, "Making Sense of Transnational Threats," *Sherman Kent Center for Intelligence Analysis, Occasional Papers* 3, no. 1.

27. Though unwieldy, Dervin's definition of "sense-making" is useful insofar as it captures the enormity of the task and implications of that enormity for workplaces: "Sense-Making is an approach to thinking about and implementing communication research and practice and the design of communication-based systems and activities. It consists of a set of philosophical assumptions, substantive propositions, methodological framings, and methods. It has been applied in myriad settings (e.g., libraries, information systems, media systems, web sites, public information campaigns, classrooms, counseling services, and so on), at myriad levels (e.g., intrapersonal, interpersonal, small group, organizational, mass, national, global), and within myriad perspectives (e.g., constructivist, critical, cultural, feminist, postmodern, communitarian)." Brenda Dervin, "Sense-Making Methodology Site," http://communication.sbs.ohio-state.edu/sense-making.

28. Karl Weick, *Managing the Unexpected: Assuring High Performance in an Age of Complexity* (New York: Jossey-Bass, 2001), 2.

29. For this rendition of the three components of intelligence, see Edward Waltz and his important work on knowledge management in the intelligence and military communities, specifically Edward Waltz, *Knowledge Management in the Intelligence Enterprise* (Boston: Artech House, 2003); and Edward Waltz, *Information Warfare: Principles and Operations* (Boston: Artech House, 1998).

30. Various works on the topic of improving intelligence analysis have appeared in the past two years, notable among them are Jeffrey Cooper, *Curing Analytic Pathologies: Pathways to Improved Intelligence Analysis* (Washington, D.C.: Center for the Study of Intelligence, 2005); Steven Rieber and Neil Thomason, "Toward Improving Intelligence Analysis: Creation of a National Institute for Analytic Methods," *Studies in Intelligence* 49 (2005): 71; and Stephen P. Marrin and Jonathan D. Clemente, "Improving Intelligence Analysis by Looking to the Medical Profession," *International Journal of Intelligence and Counterintelligence* 18 (Winter 2005): 707.

31. Thomas Kuhn, *The Structure of Scientific Revolutions* (Chicago: University of Chicago Press, 1970), 182.

32. Norm Archer, "A Classification of Communities of Practice," in *Encyclopedia of Communities of Practice in Information and Knowledge Management*, ed. Elayne Coakes and Steve Clarke (Hershey, Pa.: Idea Group Reference, 2006), 24.

PART TWO

The Policy–Analyst Relationship

PART TWO lays out the continuing challenge of meeting the policy-maker's high hopes for unerring analysis. Inevitably, the different perspectives of decision makers and intelligence analysts collide or perhaps entirely miss each other like ships in the night. John McLaughlin and James B. Steinberg provide contrasting views of the eternally complicated relationship between analysts and policymakers.

As a longtime analyst and former deputy director of central intelligence, McLaughlin notes that nothing can replace close contact with policymakers to ensure a better understanding of the customer's needs. He also suggests that greater training and "rotational" opportunities are the best remedies for a poor understanding of the policymaker's needs.

Steinberg has reviewed intelligence products as both a former analyst and deputy national security adviser in a pressure-cooker policy environment. He offers the view that the relationship can be improved if intelligence analysts make their tradecraft more transparent and explain to the policymaker the strengths and weaknesses of the intelligence they provide. He also suggests some structural changes in the intelligence–policy relationship to improve communication and understanding.

Finally, Gregory F. Treverton, a RAND specialist and former vice chairman of the National Intelligence Council, tries to capture the complex nature and shades of politicization. Though he offers no single cure and suggests that some degree of politicization is the price of remaining relevant to the policymaking process, he introduces some ideas for what can limit the dangers of what has become a commonplace concern within the analytic community.

CHAPTER 4

Serving the National Policymaker

JOHN McLAUGHLIN

> There is no phase of the intelligence business that is more important than the proper relationship between intelligence itself and the people who use its product. Oddly enough, this relationship, which one would expect to establish itself automatically, does not do this. It is established as a result of a great deal of persistent conscious effort, and it is likely to disappear when the effort is relaxed.
>
> —Sherman Kent, 1949[1]

IF IT IS TRUE, as I believe it is, that analysis is where all aspects of the intelligence profession come together, then it is equally true that dealing with the policymaker is where all the components of analysis come together. It is at the nexus between intelligence and policy that we test everything from the substantive merit of the product to the quality of our tradecraft to our effectiveness in training and managing analysts. And it is also where an analytic profession that strives for objectivity, civility, thoroughness, and balance is likely to meet up with the more jarring qualities—urgency, impatience with nuance or equivocation, and, yes, sometimes even politics. But if this relationship turns sour—if the policymaker does not feel the need for the analytic product—then there is no reason for doing analysis at all. It goes without saying, then, that it is worth thinking about what makes the relationship work and what renders it dysfunctional.[2]

The first thing that must be said is that the relationship between intelligence analysis and the national policymaker is a complex one. Many elements are at play: the very different "cultures" of intelligence and policy, the expectations policymakers bring to the table regarding intelligence capabilities, the analyst's degree of insight into the policy process, the receptivity of both sides to different points of view, the intangible factors of personality and presence that influence all that happens in Washington.[3]

The Policy Culture Versus the Intelligence Culture

The different cultures of policy and intelligence hold the potential to inject a great deal of misunderstanding and tension into the relationship. The culture of the policy world is marked by elements of realism but is essentially—and necessarily—a culture of optimism. Policymaking is a contentious business marked by lots of competing ideas and frequently by heavy intellectual combat. A lot of bureaucratic blood is often on the ground once a particular course of action wins out.

Alternatively, a given policy is often in place mainly because an election has affirmed—or can be portrayed as affirming—the central idea. Indeed, policymakers live in a world heavily influenced by political considerations, and intelligence is only one factor weighing in their decision calculus, as Sherman Kent years ago reminded analysts who thought their views were being discarded.[4] In any event, once a given policy course is set, its advocates earnestly want to achieve its objectives, and they work hard to ensure that they do. They are not blind to obstacles, but their first instinct is to work hard to overcome them, and they are almost always optimistic that they can. It is not that policymakers never question the course they are on—it is that a higher value is assigned to keeping on course and getting to the finish line.

In my thirty years in the intelligence business, I encountered many types of intelligence consumers in the policy world. They fell into two broad categories: those who knew how to interpret and use intelligence; and those who did not or would not, despite considerable understanding of the craft.

Policymakers who knew how to use intelligence generally had a realistic view of what it could and could not do. They understood, for example, that intelligence is almost always more helpful in detecting trends than in predicting specific events. They knew how to ask questions that forced intelligence specialists to separate what they actually knew from what they thought. They were not intimidated by intelligence that ran counter to the prevailing policy but saw it as a useful jog to thinking about their courses of action.

Policymakers who used intelligence less effectively are a more diverse and complicated lot. I dealt with one very senior State Department official some years ago who thought, often justifiably, that he had a more comprehensive and sophisticated understanding of the issues than intelligence specialists. The result was that he almost never requested intelligence support and was content with just an occasional briefing from a trusted senior intelligence officer. To give such policymakers their due, it is likely that their disinterest resulted from some disappointing past experience with intelligence that regrettably closed them off to further use of it.

Other policymakers I dealt with simply could not abide analysis or reporting that ran counter to their own view. I once told an eminent Russian specialist who had simply dismissed assessments of growing corruption in Russia that he ought to consider the analysis "his friend" rather than the "enemy" that he obviously perceived it to be. My point was that his violent disagreement with it at least sharpened his understanding of his own point of view and his ability to argue it effectively—in effect, the analysis laid out the opposing argument. Finally, when the news was bad, policymaker concerns deepened, particularly in the White House or the National Security Council, when we wrote it down in formal intelligence assessments; the concern, common to administrations over the years headed by both parties, was that bad news would leak, causing embarrassment and lending ammunition to those who preferred a different course.

In one case, for example, senior administration officials argued strenuously over the words we chose to use in describing the status of a particular missile system by a developing country; if we termed it "deployed" and if that leaked, the administration fear was that it would have been used by critics to argue that the United States should impose sanctions on an important country whose cooperation was important on other matters. Intelligence officers, of course, can never yield to such entreaties—and we did not in that instance—but this is one of many factors that can heighten tensions in the policy–intelligence relationship.

Such potential frictions are compounded by the culture of the intelligence world. In contrast to the fundamentally optimistic thrust of the policy culture, the culture of the intelligence world is marked by skepticism. The requirement to warn of dangers—and the heavy criticism when warning fails—encourages a darker view than is ever instinctively the case in the policy world. A former director of central intelligence used to define an intelligence analyst as someone who "smells flowers . . . and then looks for the coffin." In short, analysts are trained, and indeed are required, to look for trouble—regrettably often at the expense of opportunity—and are thought to have failed when they do not detect it.

To be sure, there is often contentiousness in the analytic world equal to that in the policy arena, with similar quantities of bureaucratic or intellectual "blood on the floor." But unlike the variegated inputs to policy—everything from domestic politics to personal relationships with foreign leaders—the contention over analytic conclusions is entirely about substantive matters—over what is confidently known, what is not, and what it all portends. In short, the battles in the analytic world always center on what things mean and not—as in the policy world—on what to do.

I saw the results of this frequently as I conveyed intelligence to policymakers. A senior State Department official once complained to me about our assessment of the prospects for progress in negotiations to settle a long-running dispute between two countries over their rights in a third country—a dispute that had involved military operations and had shown few signs of easing through ten years of talks. He said, "All you do is interpret the data, lay out the problems, and tell me that the situation is bleak. I know that. What I need from you is some assessment of what my leverage is with these guys—of what I should do!" Below, I will discuss ways for intelligence officers to be helpful in such circumstances while still observing the prohibition against prescribing policy.

Given such dynamics, the chances are high that analysts and policymakers will bring many misconceptions to the table—or at least high potential for misunderstanding. Policymakers, for example, can interpret the analysts' hesitation to weigh in on policy as evidence that they live in an ivory tower world. And when policymakers make their choices on some basis other than the intelligence assessment, analysts can conclude that policy counterparts either are not interested or are simply ignoring the intelligence.

Bridging the Divide

The potential for these kinds of problems suggests that it is worth having deliberate strategies to avoid them—ways through which analysts can gain a greater understanding of what makes analysis helpful to policymakers and what does not. And for the policymaker, ways must be developed to give them a better appreciation of what analysis is and is not, what it can reasonably be expected to deliver and what it cannot. In this effort, the larger burden must fall on the analyst community. Just as any producer of product in the private sector must take the initiative to understand the consumer, so the analyst as the provider of service has the responsibility to understand what is needed and the most effective way to present it. This can be done in any number of ways, ranging from surveys of recipients, to formal processes for sleeping requirements, to exit interviews with departing policymakers.

In my personal experience, however, the most effective way for analysts to understand what policymakers need is to live and work among them for a period of time. It pays enormous dividends in mutual understanding to deploy some portion of the analyst workforce on temporary rotational assignments into the policy community. These can range from assignments of several months' duration supporting an overseas embassy to a year-long stint in one of the executive branch agencies.

My conviction about this comes from direct experience. During Robert Gates's tenure as deputy director for intelligence (the analytic wing of the Central Intelligence Agency, or CIA) in the early 1980s, he insisted that anyone who wanted to compete for a senior-level promotion ought to have a tour in the policy community. As part of this program, I was deployed to the State Department for an extended tour. While serving there as a special assistant to a senior officer in the Bureau of European Affairs, I had an inside look at how the CIA's work was received on a wide range of issues. I heard our work both praised and scorned and sought to understand why it sometimes elicited the latter reaction. It seldom had to do with the narrow substance of the message.

Such negative reactions more often had to do with other problems. For instance, the State Department officer had already read the raw reporting on which the analysis was based and found little new in what we wrote. Or a particular assessment was simply too long and complicated for a harried policy officer to absorb. Or the analysis was written without a clue as to what policymakers were thinking or doing about the problem and therefore appeared naive, abstract, or uninformed. Or the analyst had pointed out all the problems surrounding an issue but paid no attention to what points of leverage or opportunities the United States might have.

There were obvious learning points in all this. To succeed, the analysis had to be timely, digestible, and informed about the policy context while stopping short of pandering to or prescribing the policy, and it needed to help policymakers in their search for leverage. Ideally, analysts serving in positions like the one I held should not be in policymaking positions but instead serve as onsite analytic resources for policymakers, with the capacity and authority to reach back into the intelligence agencies for analytic support. Analysts who have this experience gain a keen appreciation for the qualities that their work must possess in order to be taken seriously and have an impact. As will be discussed below, these qualities range from accuracy to timeliness to clarity about what is confidently known and what is not.

Efforts also should be made to educate policymakers—particularly new people in an incoming administration—about intelligence capabilities. This has frequently been discussed, but incoming senior officials are usually so overwhelmed with requirements and material—drinking from the proverbial "fire hose," so to speak—that it is very hard to ensure that "education on intelligence" is a priority.

That said, the intelligence community should offer a course on what to expect of intelligence and how to use it to incoming officials at the assistant secretary level and above—along the lines of the orientation Congress offers its newly elected members on congressional rules and procedures. This could be devised and administered by the director of national intelligence or by one of the agencies' institutions, such as the CIA's Center for the Study of Intelligence or the Sherman Kent School of Intelligence Analysis. In the meantime, analysts and their leaders must seize whatever opportunities their work presents to help policymakers understand how the intelligence system works and what they can reasonably expect from it.

Hitting the Target

What must the analyst produce to effectively serve the national policymaker? The key thing is that such support is always about informing policy, not prescribing policy. And it takes many forms. Obviously, the product will be delivered in a variety of publications, but it might also come as a briefing, a response to a specific question, or a telephone call. Essentially, we are talking about the interaction between analysts and policymakers, and in the real world this takes place in all these channels. First and at the most general level, what analysts produce should help policy officials think through the issues and the choices facing them. This is especially true at this moment and will, in all likelihood, continue to be true well into the twenty-first century.

Over the years, I have attended probably hundreds of meetings in the White House Situation Room at the Deputies and Principals levels,[5] and I can attest that the challenges facing policymakers—and the intelligence officers supporting them—have become steadily more complex. To be sure, the period of competition and confrontation with the Soviet Union had its share of life-and-death situations, controversies, and, of course, existential threat to the United States and its allies. But it also allowed most things to be viewed through the prism of our concerns about the Soviet Union. Some connection to the Soviet threat was what got intelligence questions to the front burner, both as requirements and as subjects for assessment.

In the post-Soviet, post–September 11 world, countries and issues have to be dealt with for what they are in and of themselves, and so the range of issues to which both policymakers and analysts must be attentive has grown in scope and complexity. Policymakers' questions and concerns today and for the foreseeable future are likely to involve not just countries in the aggregate but also issues associated with cultures, regions, tribes, ethnic groups, and other particularistic aspects of foreign affairs.

This trend began to emerge in the early 1990s with the growing importance of nonstate actors (terrorists, organized crime, and the like) and accelerated throughout the decade as the post–cold war thaw yielded problems such as Bosnia or Kosovo. This period also saw shifting alliance patterns, the growing prominence of rising powers such as China and India, and the blurring effect that September 11 had on the traditional foreign/domestic distinctions for intelligence—all against a backdrop of technological revolution and globalization. It takes little study to appreciate that in dealing with current issues such as the proliferation of dangerous weapons, terrorism, and specific troubled regions and countries—the Middle East, South Asia, North Korea, Iran, Syria, Iraq, China, and Russia—policymakers today do not have many clear-cut choices or obvious options, nor is there a national consensus about priorities and policy choices.

Analysts can take a number of steps, well short of prescribing policy, to help policymakers think through choices. First, analysts can use a series of conceptual approaches to help policymakers think through complex problems, for example:

- *Test the case*. This involves marshalling data to test whether the policymaker's theory of the case corresponds to reality as it appears to the analyst. If policymakers are considering an effort to alter country A's behavior through economic sanctions, what do intelligence analysts know about the practical impact of the sanctions on the economy of that country? What do they know about the past effectiveness of sanctions in altering the behavior of that country or a comparable one? What do they know about the preparedness and capability of other countries to enforce the sanctions?
- *Provide pointers*. In the example above, if analysts conclude that sanctions would not alter a country's course, they can delineate areas of greater salience for a country's behavior—such as the diplomatic influence of neighboring states, the country's strong desire for security guarantees, and how internal dissent may alter the country's path.
- *Assess underlying forces*. When the future direction of a country or an evolving issue is particularly cloudy—say, just before a major leadership transition—analysts can lay out the forces at work beneath the surface that will constrain or buoy future leaders and have a strong bearing on how a fluid situation is likely to break. What is known, for example, about public opinion, strengths, or weaknesses in the economy that may foreclose some options, or about friction with a neighboring country that may tie down the new leadership?[6]

These and other analytic approaches allow policymakers to map issues, grasp context, and see the problems they are wrestling with from multiple angles.

The second step that analysts can take to help policymakers think through choices, it goes without saying, is to effectively warn of impending dangers.

There is of course a formal intelligence community warning process, complete with a national intelligence officer to oversee the effort. I am concerned here less with that effort and more with every analyst's duty day in and day out to be thinking about dangers that need to be brought front and center for consumers in the policy world. This obviously places a heavy burden on intelligence analysts—but one that has been part of the job since the day President Harry Truman decided that guarding against another Pearl Harbor required a centralized national intelligence system. Because it is impossible to warn of every significant shift on every problem, the analytic community has to establish some formula for "cannot miss" priorities.

It would be safe to assume that anything that threatens the lives of our citizens, threatens to engage or harm our military forces, or threatens the physical security of the United States would be at the top of any policymaker's list. That obviously involves an intense focus on issues such as terrorism, foreign weapons systems and their proliferation, unconventional weapons, and the possible conjunction of these realms. But beyond these obvious focal points for warning and the heavy emphasis it places on detecting danger, every analyst on every issue needs to bear in mind that what policymakers hate most is surprise. If they are surprised about key foreign developments, even when they do not involve life-and-death issues, it forces them into a more improvisational posture and increases the potential for policy error.

Serving policymakers on this dimension means therefore that analysts must constantly ask themselves what is changing in their area of responsibility. It is easy, especially when dealing with something like the fluid politics of a newly emerging democracy, to fall into the trap of thinking that a clear and digestible description of the current situation is analysis. It is—up to a point—and even that is not always easy. But to serve national decision makers, the analyst must focus equally on incremental changes that could gradually become trends and eventually achieve a critical mass likely to generate surprise. In intelligence, surprise—another term for intelligence failure—is almost never the result of an easy-to-detect precipitate shift. It almost always creeps up on you. When analysts are not attuned to this, the result is something like the surprise that resulted from the fall of the shah of Iran in late 1978.[7] An example of success in detecting pivotal trends is the prescient CIA analysis in 1989–91 that pointed to the likelihood of a coup against Mikhail Gorbachev and the probability that it would fail.[8]

In bringing such trends to the attention of the policy consumer, the intelligence officer must build in an explicit statement of his or her underlying assumptions. Assume that the analyst has been arguing that country X is highly stable. The analyst should understand explicitly what combination of evidence and logic leads him or her to this view and make that clear in the assessments that reach the policymaker. A judgment projecting stability, for example, might rest mainly on the iron control exercised by a country's leader, a high rate of economic growth, the absence of a charismatic and effective opposition, or some combination of these. As the analyst detects changes on these dimensions, they should be brought to the attention of the policy customer with explicit judgments about the likely implications for stability in country X. Policymakers want always to be several steps ahead of potentially surprising changes in the area for which they are responsible. It is the intelligence officer's highest duty to ensure that they are.

The third step that analysts can take to help policymakers think through choices is to point out opportunities. As important as it is for the analyst to detect key changes and warn of dangers, chances are that policymakers will stop paying attention if the analyst never does anything but warn. This is the point my State Department contact was making in his complaint about our bleak assessment of negotiation prospects in the mid-1980s. He was basically asking that we alert him to opportunities that might not have been apparent to officials caught up in the hectic game of implementing policy. For instance, a policymaker is grappling with ways to end a costly military conflict, achieve an arms control breakthrough, or end a humanitarian emergency and is frustrated by the obstinacy of the parties. If the analyst's expertise leads him or her to discern what it would take to move one side or the other to compromise—a particular concession, intervention by a third party, or rephrasing of some document—it is perfectly legitimate to advance this view. This could be cast in terms of how the country would react to a range of actions by the United States. Such an approach falls well short of prescribing policy and is one of the analytic achievements that policymakers appreciate most. In other words, policymakers appreciate and need more than warning. Otherwise, they begin to experience what might be called "warning fatigue."

In serving the policymaker in these three ways, the analyst's work should have certain characteristics to be most helpful and achieve the maximum impact. Most senior policymakers live in an extraordinarily hectic world. They do not have a lot of time to absorb information or to reflect on it at length. They often do not have the luxury of avoiding or postponing decisions. Analysts must be mindful of all of this as they prepare assessments. This imposes certain analytic standards on the analytic community for accuracy, clarity, timeliness, revising judgments, and alternative views. Let us look briefly at each.

Accuracy. The first requirement, of course, is for accuracy. I mean this largely in an epistemological sense. That is, beyond simply knowing and conveying the facts, the analyst must think about the limits and validity of what is actually "known." Are the "facts" reported ironclad, observable, and not open to challenge (e.g., a foreign leader said something, and it is recorded on television or in a published speech)? Or are they derived from an intercept where there is no question about what was said but where the context may be obscure? Does the information come from a human source whose motivation might be questionable? Does something seen in imagery from space represent reality, or is it being staged for purposes of deception?

I recall once cautioning a senior policymaker not to refer in a public speech to certain things as "facts," even though they were derived from a series of seemingly credible intelligence reports. Though I did not at the time have strong doubts about the basic thrust of the intelligence, I did have in mind the very high standard that must always be used when characterizing intelligence reporting from a range of diverse sources as "factual."

Clarity. A corollary requirement for the analyst is clarity about the uncertainties and what is unknown. Being explicit about this is critical to the policymaker's understanding of how much weight to place on the analysis among the various factors bearing on a decision. A lack of clarity on the uncertainties carries risks for both the policymaker and the analyst; the former may make faulty decisions based on an unwarranted degree of confidence in the analysis, and the latter runs the risk of ultimately being charged with being misleading or, worse, with "intelligence failure" if he or she has left the impression of greater confidence than the available information warrants.

Timeliness. It is equally critical that the analysis is prepared and arrives in a timely manner. The windows of opportunity for senior policymakers to absorb information and make decisions are often very small. Because analysts are almost always dealing with incomplete information, there is a natural tendency and desire to wait for the latest data. But often this is a classic case of the "perfect being the enemy of the good." An assessment that is correct and complete in every way but arrives too late to affect the policymakers' decision is one of the most regrettable outcomes in the analytic profession.

The tension between the need for timeliness and the requirement to spell out uncertainties does not excuse the analyst from telling the policymaker what he or she thinks—providing a bottom line, even if it must be qualified. Otherwise the work will simply be ignored, except in those rare instances where all concerned recognize that a situation is too fluid for anything other than sheer reportage; in other words, the classic "situation report." On the way to a bottom-line judgment, however, it is critical for the analyst to distinguish between what he or she knows and does not know and then to spell out what he or she thinks in light of that.

Revising judgments. The policymakers' desire for bottom lines does not excuse the analyst from another ingredient crucial to the success of policy support efforts: letting the policymaker know when the analyst's view has changed and, equally important, why. Especially when new data become available and alter an assessment, the analyst needs to be quite explicit about it. Policymakers for their part need to understand that intelligence assessments are highly susceptible to change, because they are almost always based on incomplete data from an information stream that the intelligence community is constantly seeking to enlarge. This is a crucial part of the "intelligence education" that has to be delivered to the policy community. That intelligence assessments will change seems obvious, but to people outside the daily ebb and flow of the intelligence business, it may not be. On a number of occasions when an important assessment changed, senior policymakers have accused me of "moving the goalposts." In fact, all we were doing was factoring in new data.

Alternative views. While responding to the policymakers' desire for a bottom line, the analyst also needs to give some evidence that he or she has examined all the alternative interpretations of the situation. It is seldom the case that intelligence evidence is so complete and clear as to point convincingly to only one outcome. Policymakers deal with such fluid situations that they instinctively understand this, and analysts should at least evince awareness that there are alternative interpretations of the data, especially when there are significant differences among intelligence professionals about how to interpret them.

It is always best to alert policymakers to these differences and why they exist. Generally policymakers appreciate knowing this and often find the analysis more interesting if they understand the differences on the intelligence side. Ideally, though, a description of such differences should not be presented in an "on the one hand, on the other hand" manner or in a way that suggests "anything can happen." This will not be seen as helpful, and as when afflicted with "warning fatigue," policymakers will simply turn off.

Finally, when analysts are generally confident of conclusions and are in a warning posture, it is important that what they present be persuasive. An analytic colleague told me years ago that, confronted with charges of intelligence failure, she said to a former secretary of state that she had indeed told him in advance of an impending war, to which he replied: "You told me, but you didn't persuade me." This at first might seem like a dodge on the policymaker's part, but the remark contains an important point: Analysts must do more than merely state their opinions. Their conclusions have to be laid out in a way that gives the policymaker transparency on many of the factors discussed above: how the evidence and logic are connected, what are the alternative explanations and why have the analysts discarded them, how much of the conclusion is derived from firm evidence and how much from reasoning, and what is the role of precedent and why does it apply or not apply in this case. All these things contribute to the persuasive quality of the argument the analyst hands the policymaker. Without them, the analyst risks having the policymaker dismiss his or her conclusions as mere hunch or intuition that may not have any more value or authority than what he or she reads in the morning paper.[9]

This brief checklist underlines the enormous challenges faced by today's intelligence analysts. A summary way to say all this is that successful support to the national policymaker requires the analyst to:

- Understand the policymaker's world better than the policymaker will typically understand the intelligence world.
- Deal with enormously complex subjects in a highly sophisticated manner, even when given only limited time, space, and data.

Few intellectual tasks in the intelligence business are more demanding than effectively serving national policymakers. But few pursuits are more important, because what ultimately hangs in the balance is the worth of the intelligence support to policymakers as well as the relevance of the intelligence community to the security policies of the United States.

Notes

1. Sherman Kent, *Strategic Intelligence for American World Policy* (Princeton, N.J.: Princeton University Press, 1949), 180.

2. For a broader discussion of intelligence support to policy, see Roger Z. George and Robert D. Kline, eds., *Intelligence and the National Security Strategist: Enduring Issues and Challenges* (New York: Rowman and Littlefield, 2006), 417–47.

3. For our purposes, national policymakers will include the president, the vice president, Cabinet officers, and those who support them in senior positions—undersecretaries, assistant secretaries, deputy assistant secretaries, senior directors, and directors at the National Security Council. At any one time, this amounts to some three to four hundred people. These are the primary executive branch recipients of major intelligence analytic products and the primary requestors of analysis, although clearly hundreds of other officials—office directors and desk officers in various departments, for example—also have access to large amounts of analytic product and levy tasks on the intelligence community. In addition, Congress in recent years has become a heavy consumer of intelligence, particularly members of the Senate and House intelligence oversight committees and the armed services and foreign relations committees. In a typical year, congressional requestors receive well over a thousand briefings from members of the intelligence community.

4. Sherman Kent, "Estimates and Influence," in *Sherman Kent and Board of National Estimates: Collected Essays*, ed. Donald P. Steury (Washington, D.C.: Center for the Study of Intelligence, Central Intelligence Agency, 1994), 33–42.

5. National Security Council meetings involving the deputy secretaries of state and defense, the deputy national security adviser, and the vice chairman of the Joint Chiefs of Staff, along with others, were called Deputies Meetings; the Principals Meetings involved the secretaries of state and defense, the national security adviser, the chairman of the Joint Chiefs of Staff, and often the vice president.

6. This discussion of techniques analysts can employ to help policymakers think through issues and choices benefited from a presentation on this subject by James Steinberg, deputy national security adviser in the Bill Clinton administration, at a conference on "The Role of Intelligence in the Policymaking Process" convened by the Ditchley Foundation in the United Kingdom, January 28–30, 2005.

7. For a discussion of this, see Gregory F. Treverton and Richard Haass, "The Fall of the Shah of Iran," Kennedy School of Government Case Study Program, C16–88–794.0, 1998.

8. Bruce D. Berkowitz and Jeffery T. Richelson, "The CIA Vindicated," *The National Interest* 41 (Fall 1995): 42–43. Berkowitz and Richelson cited declassified analyses to argue against the oft-repeated view that the CIA simply missed the fall of the Soviet Union. This point is also made in chapter 2, on the CIA's record, by Richard Kerr.

9. For discussions of the qualities that contribute to effective analysis, see Mark M. Lowenthal, *Intelligence: From Secrets to Policy*, 2nd ed. (Washington, D.C.: CQ Press, 2003), 108–9; and *Tradecraft Review* 1, no. 1 (August 2004), published by the Directorate of Intelligence, Central Intelligence Agency.

CHAPTER 5

The Policymaker's Perspective: Transparency and Partnership

JAMES B. STEINBERG

POLICYMAKERS CRAVE good intelligence. Why? Because they believe it can and should make the crucial difference between success and failure, at both the policy and personal levels. This should be the recipe for a match made in heaven between the intelligence analyst and the policymaker. Yet the reality, as many of the contributors to this volume show, is often quite different. Analysts typically feel underappreciated, ignored, or misused by policymakers, while policymakers in turn often feel misled or underserved by intelligence.

Why Is There a Problem?

This chronic tension has flared into the public spotlight in the past six years as a result of the September 11, 2001, terrorist attacks and the Iraq war. Why, ask the policymakers—and the public—did the intelligence community fail to warn us about the possibility that terrorists would use airliners as flying bombs? Why did they overestimate Saddam Hussein's capability for weapons of mass destruction (WMD)? Why, ask the analysts, did the policymakers ignore our warning about the risks and dangers of an occupation of Iraq? Why did they set up alternative analytic units to hunt for links between Saddam and al-Qaeda when the established intelligence community repeatedly concluded that none existed?[1]

The result of these two deeply unsettling experiences has led to a rash of proposals for reform of the intelligence community, some welcome and overdue, some merely solving yesterday's problems but of questionable value in meeting the yet unknown problems of the future. Yet few of these efforts have focused on the complex interaction between the policymaker and the analyst. For example, the Silberman-Robb WMD Commission's mandate explicitly excluded the question of how the policymakers used—or misused—the intelligence with which they were provided.[2] And the 9/11 Commission treaded lightly on the question of why the national security adviser could claim—with all sincerity—that no one had warned her about the possibility of terrorist attacks by airplanes, when the Central Intelligence Agency itself had been threatened with just such an attack only six years earlier.[3]

To some extent, the reluctance to delve into these uncomfortable questions comes from a healthy desire to avoid the "blame game." Given the enormous consequences of the evident breakdowns apparent both in the September 11 and Iraq events, however, it is vital that practitioners on both sides try to understand the challenges inherent in the policy–intelligence interaction and how to overcome the gulf and suspicion that haunts this critical relationship. In the previous chapter, John McLaughlin, one of the consummate intelligence professionals during the Bill Clinton and George W. Bush presidencies, gives us vital insights from one side of the divide.[4] In this chapter, I try to complement his analysis and recommendations from the perspective of someone who has served in both the intelligence and the policy communities.

Sources of the Problem

There are a number of reasons for the disaffection between policymakers and intelligence analysts. To an important degree, the problem arises because policymakers want something that intelligence analysis cannot provide: certainty. But the disaffection is also a product of each community's failure to understand what the other has to offer and to work as an organic whole, rather than as two opposing teams volleying a ball back and forth over a high and opaque wall. Helping each side understand the other's needs, capabilities, and limitations is critical to assuring that intelligence analysis can play its rightful, important place in policymaking.

As mentioned above, policymakers crave certainty and abhor surprise. They come to office with more or less defined policy objectives that they hope to attain. They want to work on their priority agenda, not be sidetracked or deflected by unanticipated events. They look to the permanent civil service bureaucracy of government, including the intelligence community, to help them achieve those goals and feel let down that they do not get more help. Why? There are three main reasons.

First, and most important, policymakers harbor unrealistic expectations. There is a tendency among some policymakers to hold the intelligence community to a standard of omniscience and to be let down if the answer is "I don't know." They believe that the enormous sums of money the nation invests in technical and human intelligence collection and in an army of analysts should produce strong, reliable results, and they fault managers and analysts when they do not do so, rather than looking to the inherent limitations of what can be known. At the same time, policymakers are equally vexed if the analyst expresses confidence but his or her judgment is subsequently proven to be wrong.

Second, there is a perception by policymakers that the analytic community views its role as one of cautioner (or worse, naysayer) rather than a support to policy. McLaughlin refers to this as the policymakers' culture of optimism versus the analysts' culture of skepticism. Another way of thinking about this is that policymakers rarely have the luxury of throwing up their hands and saying "too hard" or deferring decisions until the intelligence becomes clearer; often they must act even if the choices are muddy and the consequences are unpredictable.

Policymakers look to the intelligence community to uncover the facts that will help them achieve their goals. Contrary to the views of some critics, most policymakers do not resist bad news if it is reliable and timely, because they know they cannot succeed by sticking their heads in the sand and pretending that adverse developments will go away if they simply ignore or dismiss them. But often policymakers feel that the intelligence community views its mission as solely being the bearer of bad news or "warning"—that is, telling the policy community about all the obstacles to achieving their objectives, rather than identifying opportunities and how to make the best of the situation to achieve them. Yet for many analysts, such a role is tantamount to "supporting" the policy and thus violating the most sacred canon of analytic objectivity and policy neutrality.

Third, policymakers often sense that the analytic community is too insulated from the "on the ground" reality that provides the context for policy. These officials live in the world that they are trying to shape; they meet with leaders of foreign countries and other important actors, travel to trouble spots to observe challenges with their own eyes, and confer with experts in and out of government. Many have also built a considerable body of experience and expertise from their work before assuming office. They believe they have important insights that can inform the analytic process and assess the reliability of other intelligence inputs. By contrast, many intelligence community analysts have had little or no firsthand experience with the problems and people at issue, a product of the recruitment and retention policies in the intelligence community and fears of compromising security.[5] Yet policymakers believe that analysts and intelligence managers resist incorporating their views into the estimative process for fear of "tainting" the product.

No Panaceas

There are no surefire cures for these difficulties. Many are inherent in the nature of policymaking, yet there are a number of things that both the policy community and the intelligence community can do to reduce the frictions and build a more constructive, collaborative relationship that preserves the integrity of the analytic process while enhancing its utility. Let us look briefly at four main things that can be done in this vein.

First, the policymaker needs, and is entitled to, the intelligence community's best judgment. Most policymakers understand that many things are hard to know, and some things are inherently unknowable. Even policymakers know (or can be educated to know) the difference between a puzzle and a mystery.[6] But what is important for policymakers to understand is the degree and nature of uncertainty and, where possible, what steps might be taken to reduce that uncertainty. To take the Cuban missile crisis example discussed in the introduction, the number and state of readiness of the Soviet missiles was a fact that was knowable but difficult to know with absolute certainty. Steps were taken (e.g., overflights, human intelligence) that helped reduce that uncertainty. What Nikita Khrushchev would do in response to various U.S. policy alternatives was inherently unknowable—because it was contingent on actions by others as well as his own assessment of the Soviet Union's interests. Yet even with respect to future intentions, the intelligence community may be in a position to help policymakers—for example, in the case of the Cuban missile crisis, there could have been intercepts of Soviet officials discussing various policy options or prior analogous examples of how Khrushchev had faced other tests of will.

Analysts are often reluctant to venture onto this treacherous ice. To some extent it is a product of their training, which repeatedly emphasizes the uncertainty around the intelligence exercise, a worthy caution. Unfortunately, sometimes it is a product of a desire to escape accountability—making assessments so hedged that they are incapable of being proven wrong. The collective nature of many intelligence "community" judgments tends to further blur assessments, in the effort to achieve consensus at the expense of crispness. Rather than blurring conclusions to achieve broader acceptance or relegating nonmajority views to footnotes, finished analysis should *highlight* the alternative views within the intelligence community (including in executive summaries, which are the products most frequently read by policymakers), and prominently feature the proponents' underlying arguments for their conclusions.

Some try to bound the problem of uncertainty by assigning probabilities to facts or outcomes. I am somewhat skeptical of what I believe is a false sense of concreteness implied in assigning numerical probabilities to individual events, particularly contingent outcomes that depend on choices others have yet to make. But some sense of the degree of confidence (likely, unlikely, hard to judge, etc.) can give a feel for the degree of uncertainty. More helpful is providing some insight into alternative pathways that might be consistent with the data, along with an explication of why the analyst believes one path is more likely than the alternatives.

Second, as other chapters suggest, the policymaker needs and is entitled to analytical transparency from the analyst. Why was the judgment reached? What assumptions lie behind it? What are the sources of uncertainty? This transparency is the necessary complement to the judgment. By providing transparency, the analyst should feel more comfortable with providing a bottom line or best guess, and the policymaker should feel more comfortable in either accepting or challenging it. Although there is constant pressure from policymakers to "keep it short" given the demands on their time, the intelligence community has an obligation not to let this legitimate consideration lead to products that are misleading by omission. Because this approach will lead to better policymaking, I believe that the policy community will be open to somewhat lengthier analytic products.

One important but controversial element of transparency concerns sources. The intelligence community is rightly concerned about protecting intelligence sources and methods. Compromises can destroy the value of enormously expensive technical collection tools and, in the case of human assets, not only wipe out years of patient cultivation but also endanger lives. The policy community is the ultimate loser from leaks, because the loss of the sources will over time lead to less intelligence, and so to less well-informed policy. The track record of protecting such vital sources and methods secrets is unacceptably poor. Although policymakers are responsible for the lion's share of such disclosures, the intelligence community is not without blame. Nonetheless, as the Iraq WMD experience suggests, opaqueness about sources can lead to overreliance on highly questionable sources with their own motivation to "influence" as well as inform. Although the intelligence community should continue to have the primary responsibility for evaluating the reliability of intelligence and the sources that provide it, the policymaker's stake—as well as the insight that the policymakers themselves can bring to assessing the value of sources—requires more transparency than the intelligence community has traditionally been comfortable providing.

Third, the policymaker needs *indicators* from the analysts that will help assess the validity of any judgment going forward. If the judgment is correct, what should we expect to see in the future? More important, what future developments might undermine the validity of the judgment and/or support one of the alternative hypotheses? Disconfirming facts are a far more important, but an often overlooked, part of the analysis process. They are important not only because they have stronger probative value but also because they are the best antidote to the structural problem of wishful thinking or "cherry picking" that infects even the most conscientious policymaker's approach to intelligence. This kind of support is crucial for policymakers to be able to make midcourse corrections or even reverse course if a key assumption turns out to be false.

Fourth, a closely related need is for the analytic community to provide peripheral vision and temporal perspective. How might a U.S. action, which looks well suited to deal with a pending specific problem, affect other U.S. policy actions or foreign actors elsewhere? What will be the likely longer-term effects, the second and third moves by others if the policy is implemented? The stove-piped and time-constrained nature of the policy process too often precludes such examinations. The intelligence community is uniquely well placed to think about linkages and knock-on effects that might change policymakers' calculations about the costs and benefits of different courses of action. This is true of both horizontal and vertical/temporal linkages. In producing finished analysis, the intelligence community can include analysts who specialize in geographical regions other than the area or country that is the obvious focus of the problem at hand, as well as those with a broad range of functional expertise. Ideally, similar efforts to expand the circle would take place in the policy community as well, but for reasons of time and turf, this often proves impracticable. Long-range planning would also benefit from regular meetings between key intelligence community analysts and the leading policy planners in the executive branch.[7]

How Policymakers Can Help

If the relationship is to work successfully, policymakers must take on at least four main types of obligations and responsibilities toward the intelligence community if they expect that community to do a better job of supporting policy.

First, the policy community needs to understand what intelligence can and cannot do. As analysts often say, intelligence is not fortune telling. McLaughlin and other practitioners rightly stress the importance of educating policymakers about the intelligence process. His chapter notes that this is hard to do the moment new officials come into office; however, the intelligence community could do a better job of identifying those who are likely to hold such roles in the future and begin exposing them to these issues even before they come to office. Stronger partnerships with professional schools and graduate programs, as well as outreach to emerging leaders (such as the American Assembly's Next Generation Program) are fertile grounds for such an effort. For current holders of policy jobs, regular briefings on intelligence capabilities and shortfalls are essential.

Second, the policymaking community needs to clearly communicate its goals, priorities, and needs. Analysts are not mind readers; they have limited resources and must make judgments about how to use them most productively. They need to know what is important to the policymaker. A formal requirements process—such as the procedures for identifying and ranking collection priorities that were established by Presidential Decision Directive 35 issued by the Clinton administration—is a useful and important way to align policy and intelligence collection/analysis priorities, but it is not sufficient. These exercises tend to be static and overinclusive, and they sometimes fail to convey what is really on the policymaking community's mind.[8] Of course, the analytic community's work cannot be confined solely to the policymakers' current agenda—there is a need to think about problems and opportunities that have not yet crossed the policymakers' radar screen.

Third, policymakers need to recognize their value to the intelligence community as sources in their own right, and thus keep analysts informed of information and impressions drawn from their own experience. Information sharing is a two-way street. Just as analysts tend to carefully shield their sources from exposure to the policy community, policymakers also tend to fear disclosure of sensitive diplomatic negotiations and other policy maneuvers to the intelligence community. The result is not only inferior analytic product but also one that appears largely irrelevant to a policymaking community, which is working on the basis of a different set of facts and assumptions.

Fourth, and closely related to the third measure, is the need for policymakers to keep intelligence representatives "in the room" when policy is debated. Although analysts rightly take a vow of silence with respect to policy prescriptions, they need to hear the underlying assumptions and beliefs that inform policy, both to correct errors of fact that may creep into policy and to provide policymakers with insights into the factors that might lead them to question or change those assumptions as events unfold. The real danger in the ongoing debate about the danger of "politicizing" intelligence is that both sides will overreact and create a "Chinese wall" that cuts off the analysts from firsthand access to policy debates. McLaughlin suggests one way to achieve this goal—namely, to embed more analysts in policymaking units, not as policymakers themselves but as part of the day-to-day activities of key agencies. For policymakers to gain the benefit of such embedded analysts, they need to appreciate and respect the fact that these analysts are different from other members of the policymaking team and thus should not be subject to the same tests of loyalty or ideological affinity that may be appropriate for "political" appointees—and even more, should not be punished or ignored for putting forth skeptical perspectives or inconvenient truths.

These four suggested measures are even more important in today's national security policy environment, where the challenges are more fluid; the actors, especially nonstate actors, are more diverse and unpredictable; and the sources and quantity of information are growing exponentially. Two key post–September 11 insights—the importance of information sharing, and the need to form flexible, horizontal communities for collaboration that can adapt to fit changing problems—are as relevant to the policymaking–intelligence interaction as they are to the intelligence community itself. In its 2006 report, the Markle Foundation Task Force on National Security in the Information Age (on which I served) stressed the importance of taking into account the needs and unique problems of integrating the policymaker into the newly emerging information-sharing environment mandated by the Intelligence Reform and Terrorism Prevention Act of 2004.[9]

Structural Fixes: Two Modest Proposals

Many of the prescriptions I have offered here are primarily a matter of educating both policymakers and analysts to each other's needs, limitations, and capabilities, and of breaking down the barriers between the two cultures. But two structural reforms that would facilitate a better working relationship are worth adopting. Perhaps most important is the crucial role that the Intelligence Directorate at the National Security Council can and should play to facilitate building the "cross-cultural" community advocated here. Because of the Intelligence Directorate's proximity to key policymakers (including the president) and its ability to participate in all interagency deliberations irrespective of subject matter, it can provide a vital bridging role, thus facilitating the transmission of policymakers' needs to the intelligence community and of intelligence capabilities, limitations, and insights to the policymakers. The directorate can also serve as a translator, particularly in helping policymakers with limited experience in the intelligence world understand the value (and limits) of what the intelligence community has to offer. In recent years, this crucial function has largely been abandoned. The Intelligence Directorate should be given an ongoing seat in the interagency process, not simply be confined to intelligence community matters (e.g., resources, requirements, and covert action).

A second important structural development is one that has begun to be implemented through the National Counterterrorism Center, which is a novel blending of intelligence and policy planning roles that brings both functions into one organization while retaining two distinct reporting lines—to the director of national intelligence for intelligence, and to the president through the Homeland Security Council and the National Security Council for policymaking.[10] This reporting arrangement is uncomfortable to some who fear that it will blur roles and accountability, but it is an appropriate reflection of the need to integrate the policy and analysis function in an area where policy is crucially dependent on both tactical and strategic intelligence.[11]

Minimizing the Risks of Politicization

The approach I have suggested here will seem perilous to some. The traditional arm's-length relationship between policy and intelligence protects against politicization and enhances the protection of sources and methods, but at a high cost of irrelevance, as Gregory Treverton suggests in chapter 6 on politicization. Policymakers need to rigorously engage analysts if they are going to have confidence in their judgments. Analysts, in turn, must be prepared to respond to the probing and challenges raised by policymakers; otherwise, their work can be too easily dismissed as irrelevant or flawed. Strong internal protections within the intelligence community are the best way to minimize the politicization risk, starting with a director of national intelligence, who is seen as a nonpartisan professional with real experience in intelligence and not as someone who is selected by virtue of policy loyalty. Both rigorous oversight by Congress and internal inspector general procedures need to be maintained to protect analysts from the danger of abuse. However, a failure to establish the deep engagement between the two communities would run the even greater danger that we will fail to marshal all the hard-won intelligence and analytic resources available to us as a nation to address the daunting challenges of the future. The cost of this outcome would be less well-informed policymaking when exactly the opposite should be our highest priority.

Notes

1. See Seymour Hersh's discussion of the Office of Special Plans. Seymour M. Hersh, "Selective Intelligence," *The New Yorker*, May 12, 2003, 44.

2. "Second, we were not authorized to investigate how policymakers used the intelligence assessments they received from the intelligence community. Accordingly, while we interviewed a host of current and former policymakers during the course of our investigation, the purpose of those interviews was to learn about how the intelligence community reached and communicated its judgments about Iraq's weapons program—not to review how policymakers subsequently used that information." Commission on the Intelligence Capabilities of the United States Regarding Weapons of Mass Destruction, *Report to the President of the United States*, March 31, 2005, 8. The report does discuss the need to communicate analysis better to policymakers, but this is largely in terms of the format and process of preparation of finished analysis, rather than about the interaction between analysts and policymakers. It also concludes that in the case of Iraq at least, "in no case did political pressure cause [analysts] to skew or alter any of their analytic judgments. That said, it is hard to deny the conclusion that intelligence analysts worked in an environment that did not encourage skepticism about the conventional wisdom." Ibid., 11.

3. See, e.g., the following exchange between National Security Advisor Condoleezza Rice and a reporter: "Q: 'Why shouldn't this be seen as an intelligence failure, that you were unable to predict something happening here?' Dr. Rice: 'Steve, I don't think anybody could have predicted that these people would take an airplane and slam it into the World Trade

Center, take another one and slam it into the Pentagon; that they would try to use an airplane as a missile, a hijacked airplane as a missile.'" White House Press Office, "National Security Advisor Holds Press Briefing," May 16, 2002, www.whitehouse.gov/news/releases/2002/05/20020516–13.html. The 9/11 Commission briefly reviewed the prior intelligence and analysis on the possibility of using an aircraft as a weapon and concluded that the problem was the failure to implement tried and true tested strategies for "detecting then warning of surprise attack." But it fails to answer the question of why the considerable body of information on past plots was never communicated (or at least not effectively communicated) to policymakers. National Commission on Terrorist Attacks Upon the United States, *The 9/11 Commission Report*, July 22, 2004, 344–48.

4. For another thoughtful analysis of the policymaker–intelligence community relationship, see Jack Davis, "Intelligence Analysts and Policymakers: Benefits and Dangers of Tensions in the Relationship," *Intelligence and National Security* 21, no. 6 (December 2006): 999–1021.

5. In my own experience as a negotiator for the United States, I met frequently with senior foreign officials, as well as leaders of all the concerned political parties in the region, and traveled regularly there to meet with community leaders. The available intelligence reporting relied heavily on "secret" information provided by indirect sources, rather than by direct engagement with the key actors themselves.

6. Joseph Nye identifies a mystery as "an abstract puzzle to which no one can be sure of the answer." See Joseph S. Nye Jr., "Peering into the Future," *Foreign Affairs* 73, no. 4 (July/August 1994): 82–93.

7. During the Clinton administration, Joseph Nye, then chairman of the National Intelligence Council, and National Security Advisor Tony Lake established a process involving policy planners at the State Department, NSC senior directors, and the intelligence community to select and analyze key long-term policy issues on regular basis. Although the effort was pointed in the right direction, it depended too heavily on the national security adviser's own involvement, which was difficult to sustain over time. One adaptation that might overcome this difficulty would be to establish a distinctive policy planning office at the NSC, which would participate in this kind of intelligence community–policy community exercise. If the NSC senior director for policy planning then had an automatic seat at the interagency table—just as I suggest for the senior director for intelligence—this perspective could be interjected in the policymaking process in a timely and effective manner.

8. For a critique of the PDD-35 process, see Eleanor Hill (staff director, Joint Inquiry Staff), "Joint Inquiry Staff Statement: Hearing on the Intelligence Community's Response to Past Terrorist Attacks against the United States from February 1993 to September 2001," October 8, 2002, www.fas.org/irp/congress/2002_hr/100802hill.html.

9. See Markle Task Force on National Security in the Information Age, *Mobilizing Information to Prevent Terrorism: Accelerating Development of a Trusted Information Sharing Environment*, Third Report of the Markle Foundation Task Force (New York: Markle Foundation, 2006), 48–49; available at www.markletaskforce.org.

10. See National Counterterrorism Center, "What We Do," www.nctc.gov/about_us/what_we_do.html.

11. In the Clinton administration, this team approach was used with considerable success on policy issues such as Russia and the Middle East.

CHAPTER 6

Intelligence Analysis: Between "Politicization" and Irrelevance

GREGORY F. TREVERTON

MY FIRST EXPERIENCE of being accused of "politicizing" intelligence came soon after I joined the National Intelligence Council (NIC) in the 1990s. As vice chairman, I was responsible for the process of writing National Intelligence Estimates (NIEs), and it was time to do one on cocaine and heroin supplies coming to the United States. We had not yet recruited a national intelligence officer for global issues, so I ran the estimate process myself. The "community" on that issue was large and motley; in addition to the Central Intelligence Agency (CIA), Defense Intelligence Agency, National Security Agency, and the State Department's Bureau of Intelligence and Research, it included smaller agencies like the Border Patrol and Drug Enforcement Administration, which were not the usual suspects when it came to writing and coordinating NIEs.

The motley shape of the drug intelligence community, as it turned out, was paralleled by conceptual slackness. The agencies were quite precise in detailing the quantities of drugs they had eradicated or seized before the drugs reached the United States but professed to have no idea how much they had missed or how much was coming in. That omission was shocking and suggested the need to use wholesale drug prices at entry cities in the United States as a proxy: If those prices generally had been drifting upward, then eradication and interdiction could be thought to be reducing supplies; if, conversely, prices were stable or declining, those policies, however well applied, were not reducing the supplies coming to the United States.

The agency representatives screamed bloody murder, charging that the NIC was politicizing intelligence. They accused me of opposing interdiction and eradication as policy measures, when the criticism was simply that "this is bad analysis."[1] This confusion between challenges to the quality of analysis and its political implications gets to the heart of the politicization problem. Such a personal experience makes for more sympathy for the trial by fire that Robert Gates suffered during his confirmation hearings to be director of central intelligence in 1991, when he was accused, in general, of imposing a hard line on assessments of the Soviet Union and, in particular, of setting in motion a paper that sought to make the strongest possible case that the Soviet Union had been involved in the attempted assassination of Pope John Paul II.[2] Gates was hardly a shrinking violet, and his views of the Soviet Union were quite different from my own, but his critics seemed to have construed hard review of their analytic products as pursuing a policy line—namely, politicization.

Defining the Forms of "Politicization"

This experience and others on the inside of government lead one to be skeptical of "politicization" epithets. Intelligence analysts live and die by their written analyses, and so, hurt feelings and damaged egos being what they are, a reviewer's criticism could easily seem—or be stigmatized as—politicization. As the example of the estimate conducted by the drug intelligence community illustrates, analysts could purport to see a policy agenda behind any criticism of their prose.

In fact, the bigger concern seemed to be politicization's opposite: irrelevance. As Richard Betts puts it in his postmortem on the post–September 11, 2001, reforms of the intelligence community: "The typical problem at the highest levels of government is less often the misuse of intelligence than the non-use."[3] Analysts paid a high price for appearing to "get on the team," "toe the line," or otherwise commit the sin of becoming "politicized." However, they paid no comparable price for being irrelevant. And so, too often, intelligence products seemed to answer questions no one was remotely asking. The questions were either ones that interested the analysts or safe ones. Too often they amounted to "Whither China?" But the policy community virtually never asks "Whither China?" Perhaps it should, especially for the purpose of long-term planning, but that planning is as rare as hen's teeth.

The questions that policy officials ask are usually specific, time sensitive, and operational. And sometimes intelligence analysis seems driven by no question at all. It is akin to all those newspaper op-eds we read, which leave us scratching our heads and asking ourselves: "If that is the answer, just what was the question?" Worse, the more that analysts strive to make analysis relevant, by trying to frame it in terms that will be useful to policymakers, the more they open themselves to charges of politicization.[4]

However, recent events have put the issue of politicization back on the agenda. The most vivid event was the debate about the run-up to the 2003 war in Iraq about whether and how much the erroneous estimates about Iraq's weapons of mass destruction (WMD) capability reflected pressure to which analysts were, or felt, subject to come to a conclusion congenial to the strong policy views of the George W. Bush administration. More generally, on Iraq and other precedents, presidents and their senior colleagues will more and more feel compelled to use intelligence as part of the public case for policies they seek to pursue. That is hardly a new feature of American history—recall Adlai Stevenson showing the UN Security Council those U-2 photos of Soviet missile deployments in Cuba a half century ago.[5] But there are good grounds for thinking the problem will get worse; the temptation will be more prevalent now, as administrations turn to intelligence to give their policies more legitimacy. As a result, intelligence will become more *political* even if it is not more *politicized*.

The starting point is to parse "politicization." In chapter 13 below, John Gannon defines it as "the willful distortion of analysis to satisfy the demands of intelligence bosses or policymakers." This definition might be broadened to encompass "commitments to perspectives or conclusions, in the process of intelligence analysis or interaction with policy, that suppress other evidence or views, or blind people to them." Seen that way, politicization can have at least five different if overlapping meanings. And several forms can be at work at once:

- *Direct pressure* from senior policy officials to come to particular intelligence conclusions, usually ones that accord with those officials' policies or policy preferences.
- A *"house line"* on a particular subject, which shifts the focus of the bias from policy to intelligence. Here, a particular analytic office has a defined view of an issue, and analysts or analyses that suggest heresy are suppressed or ignored.
- *"Cherry picking"* (and sometimes growing some cherries), in which senior officials, usually policy officials, pick their favorites out of a range of assessments.
- *Question asking*, where, as in other areas of inquiry, the nature of the question takes the analysis a good way if not to the answer, then to the frame in which the answer will lie. A related version of this form occurs when policy asks a reasonable question but continues to ask it over and over, which distorts analysis—by depriving it of time and effort to work on other questions—even if it does not directly politicize it.
- A *shared "mindset,"* whereby intelligence and policy share strong presumptions. This is perhaps the limiting case; if it is politicization, it is more self-imposed than policymaker-imposed.

Table 6.1 lays out these forms of politicization and begins to suggest ways to mitigate them.

WMD in Iraq: How Politicized?

The saga of WMD before the Iraq war demonstrated elements of all five forms of politicization, though the limiting case—mindset—was by far both the most important and the hardest to eliminate. By the reports of the WMD Commission and the Senate Select Committee on Intelligence, the first form, *direct pressure* by policy officials, was absent.[6] It is crude, and hence rare, and, besides, analysts would hardly yield or admit to it in any case.[7] It is also fair to report, however, that some intelligence analysts did feel they were under pressure to produce the "right" answer—that Saddam Hussein had WMD. As in all human interactions, the effect is subjective. Policy officials are not likely to order intelligence to heel. Rather, they often have strong policy preferences, ones that intelligence knows, and so the question becomes at what point the growing force of the policy preference amounts to undue pressure on intelligence.

TABLE 6.1
Defining the Forms of Politicization

Type	Description	Ways to Mitigate
Direct pressure from policy	Policy officials intervene directly to affect analytic conclusion	Rare but can be subtle—logic is to insulate intelligence
"House" view	Analytic office has developed strong view over time, heresy discouraged	Changed nature of target helps, along with need for wide variety of methods and alternative analyses. NIE-like process can also help across agencies
"Cherry picking"	Policy officials see a range of assessments and pick their favorite	Better vetting of sources, NIE-like process to confront views
Question asking	How the question is framed, by intelligence or policy, affects the answer	Logic is *closer* relations between intelligence and policy to define question, along with contrarian question-asking by intelligence
Shared "mindset"	Intelligence and policy share strong presumptions	Very hard—requires new evidence or alternative arguments

In the WMD case, the form of the *question* did matter, for it became simply "Does Saddam have WMD?" It was as though the logic train from a single chemical canister to war was visible for all to see; witness Secretary of Defense Donald Rumsfeld's line that the absence of evidence was not necessarily evidence of absence. Intelligence analysis did broaden the question, but issues of how much threat, to whom, and over what time frame got lost in the "Does he?" debate. Moreover, the intelligence community was asked over and over about links between Iraq and al-Qaeda. It stuck to its analytic guns—the link was tenuous at best—but the repeated questions served both to elevate the debate over the issue and to contribute to the community's relative lack of attention to other questions.[8] Question asking had a political effect on intelligence.

So, too, the *house* views inside intelligence played a role. In this case, the fact that intelligence had underestimated Saddam's WMD programs a decade earlier surely contributed to a readiness to err, if at all, in the other direction this time around. David Kay, one of the intelligence community's harshest critiques on Iraq WMD, also admits to having assumed they were there based on his own extensive experiences in tracking down Saddam's stockpiles after the first Gulf War. The other two forms of "politicization," however, were the critical ones in the WMD case. *Cherry picking* is awkward to deal with because having more than one set of analytic eyes on particular evidence and logic usually seems wise. Analysts are cheap by comparison with collection, and so multiple, if not competing, perspectives are often valuable. Indeed, what looks to some—congressional overseers, for instance—like the duplication of analysis can be regarded by others as useful tailoring of analysis to the needs of different consumers.

The presence of multiple perspectives, however, can turn negative in two ways. If multiple views seem pure cacophony, policy officials will rightly say the process is not producing useful intelligence at all. The other negative is permitting cherry picking, especially by senior policy officials. If there are several views among intelligence analysts, and all seem to have about the same status, then why not pick the one most consistent with policy preferences? Not all views are equal, however, and in the WMD case the question being asked in some parts of the government, implicitly if not explicitly, was still narrower than "Does he?" It was "What's the best case that he does?"

Worse, the cherries were not just picked but grown—by a special unit in the policy office of the secretary of defense, labeled the Office of Special Plans. Some of the evidence supporting those cherries was rotten, provided by Ahmed Chalabi and the Iraqi National Congress, which long had been discredited in the eyes of the mainline intelligence agencies.[9] So, it was not a case of multiple sets of eyes looking at the same facts in different ways. The evidence was also different, or judged differently. There is no evidence that the Pentagon operation had a direct effect on the October 2002 NIE, but its perspective became part of broader "intelligence" in the run-up to war, supporting political arguments that the mainline intelligence agencies did not.

In the end, however, the WMD story was one of deeply flawed mindset, one that ran widely across intelligence and policy agencies, and also included key foreign intelligence services whose governments were for the most part opposed to war. If most people believe one thing, arguing for another is hard. It is not just the analysts' fault but, rather, is compounded by having policymakers who share, and even praise, flawed analysis. There is little pressure to rethink the issue, and the few dissenters in intelligence are lost in the wilderness.

This form may be more groupthink than "politicization" in the most common uses of the term. Yet the process occurs not in a vacuum but in the presence of powerful arguments, ones rooted in political agendas or political convenience. For the German invasion of France in 1940, the mindset was "They couldn't attack through the Ardennes."[10] For Pearl Harbor, as for September 11, it was "They wouldn't dare, and anyhow they couldn't." For the 1973 Yom Kippur War, it was "Egypt wouldn't start a war it would lose."[11] For the 1998 Indian nuclear test, it was "They'd be stupid to test, despite their campaign rhetoric."[12] Lest the shortcoming be thought confined to government intelligence, IBM in the 1980s failed to appreciate the implications of personal computers because it assumed the long-term dominance of mainframe technology—a kind of "politicization" stemming from convenience amid the dominance of IBM in mainframes.[13]

Challenging a flawed mindset takes something new, some new evidence or evidence of some new argument. And that is precisely what was *not* available in the WMD case. In that sense, the Iraq failure was as much a collection failure as an analytic failure. As Dennis Gormley puts it, "Intelligence failure is virtually assured when a predisposed analytic mindset is combined with predictable over-head collection systems."[14] Imagery was predictable, signals intelligence was devoted to protecting U.S. and allied pilots patrolling the "no fly" zones, and, with no U.S. official presence in Iraq, traditional espionage, or human intelligence (HUMINT), was limited and catch-can, which made British sources valuable and Iraqi National Congress ones tempting to those with too little experience—or too much agenda. In that sense, analysts both inside and outside government fell back on what *had* been true.

To be sure, in a Bayesian sense, each day the United Nations inspectors did not find evidence of WMD should have shifted the odds a little in the direction of Iraq not having them.[15] (On that score, Rumsfeld was wrong; the accumulating absence of evidence *was* evidence of absence, though not proof.) But it did not. Virtually everyone believed that some evidence would be found. That included intelligence and policy, insiders and outsiders, including those Americans who thought the war a strategic mistake from the start.

In speaking to the WMD Commission, the author used the "perfect storm" metaphor to describe the Iraq WMD case. The commission's report picked up the metaphor but said the Iraq case was not that perfect storm. What the commission meant was that features of it appeared in other cases as well; because two of their five cases remain classified, it is not possible to know for sure, but no doubt the commission is right. What the Iraq case illustrated was a conjunction of pathologies. Mindset was the most important. Because there was so little new collection, nothing challenged that mindset or the inferences from past behavior on which it rested. And Saddam himself tried to convince us that he had what he did not have, or perhaps he did not know he did not have—in any case, the oddest of disinformation campaigns.[16]

Given the storm, and especially the strength of the mindset, it is not at all clear that there was a way to do better. Surely the infamous October 2002 NIE left a lot to be desired; in particular, it was overly technical, without much "Iraq" or political context in it.[17] The Senate Select Committee on Intelligence was scathing about the NIE, concluding: "Most of the major key judgments . . . either overstated, or were not supported by, the underlying intelligence reporting. A series of failures, particularly in analytic tradecraft, led to the mischaracterization of the intelligence."[18] At least, the NIC should have commissioned a Devil's Advocate piece, perhaps ending as a box in the estimate, seeking to make the best case that Saddam did *not* have ongoing WMD programs. Not that the effort would have made the least bit of difference to the debate or the war outcome, for it would not have. But it would have offered greater integrity to the process and therefore some protection to the NIC and to the intelligence community in doing their job.

Addressing Politicization: Innovations in Tradecraft

At the level of the analytic offices themselves, much of the ferment in tradecraft is designed to open up issues, to make sure that alternative or dissenting views are both pursued and heard. In that sense, the nature of today's analytic targets, especially transnational ones like terrorists, makes the challenge of analysis harder but also probably diminishes the force of ideological divides, like those seen over Soviet analysis in the Gates confirmation hearings.

Those transnational targets, like terrorists, differ from traditional state targets in four main ways. First, while America's current terrorist foes are patient, transnational targets are less "bounded" than states. There will be discontinuities in targets and attack modes, and new groups will emerge unpredictably. Second, the new targets deprive intelligence and policy of a shared "story," one that would facilitate analysis and communication. We knew what states were like, even very different states like the Soviet Union. They were geographical, hierarchical, and bureaucratic. There is no comparable story for nonstates, which come in many sizes and shapes.

Third, as a former secretary of defense is said to have quipped about the U.S.–Soviet nuclear competition: "When we build, they build. When we stop, they build." Though we hoped our policies would influence Moscow, as a first approximation intelligence analysts could assume that the Soviet Union would do what it would do. The challenge was figuring out what it would do. The terrorist target, however, is utterly different. It is the ultimate "asymmetric threat," shaping its threat to our vulnerabilities. The September 11 suicide bombers did not hit on their attack plan because they were airline buffs. They had done enough tactical reconnaissance to know it would work. To a great extent, we shape the threat to us, for not just terrorists' intentions or proclivities depend on the seams in our defenses; so, too, do their capabilities. That has the awkward implication for intelligence that it has to understand a lot about *us* in order to understand them.

Finally, given closed foes, cold war intelligence, analysis included, gave pride of place to secrets—information gathered by human and technical means that intelligence itself owned. Terrorists are hardly open, but an avalanche of open data is relevant to them. Because they need to move among us to attack us, they leave a trail in credit cards, reservations, and the like; witness the September 11 hijackers, some of whose true addresses were available in California motor vehicle records. Then, the problem was too little good information; now, it is too much to sift through. Then, intelligence's secrets were deemed reliable; now, the torrents on the Web are a stew of fact, fancy, and disinformation.

The challenges to analytic practice from changing targets—less "boundedness" and more uncertainty, no shared "story," much more contingency on our actions, and too much information of widely varying reliability—hardly guarantee that "house" views of particular issues will not arise in analytic organizations.[19] To be sure, those organizations will be hard-pressed to make sense of what is afoot, and that may tempt analysts to fall back on assumptions or stereotypes. But those do not seem likely to be reified in ideology the way arguments about Soviet intentions were during the cold war, nor, with events moving fast, will analysts have the leisure to polish and repolish their worldviews.

If the cold war analytic process can be caricatured, perhaps not too unfairly, as analysts or small groups framing hypotheses, then looking for information to validate—or, less often, cast doubt on—them, future analysis will be different.

Relatively traditional, hierarchical organizations could then assemble the various puzzle pieces. U.S. intelligence analysts during the cold war did not make much use of formal tools or methods, except in some technical areas.[20] Those analysts tended to operate on the basis of their experience or that of their immediate work unit. Previous assessments or patterns were the point of departure, with analysts tending to look for information that would confirm those patterns—a tendency abetted by time pressure, which drove analysts toward early closure on open issues.

Future intelligence will, by necessity as well as the pressure of overseers, make much more use of machines and formal methods. The whole range of techniques described elsewhere is relevant to that task. They can include "What If?" and Red Teaming, Analysis of Competing Hypotheses, and other forms of what has come to be called "Alternative Analysis"; or scenarios, Delphi-like techniques, factions analysis, and other ways of arriving at and aggregating subjective judgments; or computer software tools to see patterns and retain them or resurrect discarded hypotheses; or finally other new computer-aided techniques for letting analysts "fly through" hundreds of scenarios looking for the effects of changing particular variables.[21]

Better analytic methods alone are no guarantee against politicization, but better analysis is easier to defend against political attacks. After the WMD affair, HUMINT specialists from the CIA's Directorate of Operations now sit in on sessions discussing NIEs to help ensure that the degree of validity of human sources providing information to be used in the NIE is understood, and the process has been extended to other collection disciplines. Scenarios and "What If?" techniques can help ensure that the range of questions asked does not narrow, and that analysis is not too vulnerable to the charge of "You didn't address that." The challenge for intelligence analysis in the uncertain world of transnational threats is to provide more while promising less, for a critical part of doing better will be helping policymakers understand the limitations of analytical tradecraft. Alas, the WMD estimate did just the opposite, for among its "high confidence" judgments, several were plain wrong.

Across agencies, one of the main purposes of the national estimates process is to confront "agency" views, in the hope of ensuring that senior policymakers are not the prisoners of "their" agency views but rather have the benefit of the entire analytic community. For instance, when in the last half of the 1990s we began an estimate on North Korea and its nuclear prospects, the divisions among agencies seemed deeply carved in stone. As one policy observer put it of the State Department view: "Two guys will be standing in an enormous bomb crater, and the guy from State will be saying: 'The North Koreans are trying to send us a subtle and nuanced message.'"

Once into the estimate, however, it turned out that some of the agencies' positions were like trenches dug in World War I. No one could remember quite why they were where they were, or why they had been dug in the first place. As drafting began, there was more flexibility in the other agencies' views than it had seemed (and there was also more to be said for the State Department view than had appeared). The interagency process served as a check on "house" views in various agencies, which might have imprisoned the policy seniors in those agencies.

Addressing Politicization: Types of Intelligence

None of the forms of politicization is easily addressed, but some kinds of intelligence seem more prone to politicization than others. There is a vast difference between intelligence that is providing facts on known topics—for instance, military order of battle, political developments, or economic reforms—and more unknowns that reside in the realm of intentions or as-yet undecided courses of action by an adversary. This continuum—from puzzles to mysteries—is well recognized. For instance, much of intelligence, especially on the battlefield, is puzzle solving and explicitly tactical. The location of the enemy tank column will either be where intelligence says it is or not; intelligence will be either right or wrong, and in most cases the difference will be quickly apparent. That is not to say these tactical puzzles will not sometimes be controversial. During the first war in Iraq in the 1990s, for instance, the commander, General Norman Schwarzkopf, was critical of CIA bomb damage assessments. He had more confidence—misplaced, it turned out—in the assessments of the pilots who flew the missions.

At the other end of a continuum of intelligence types or needs might be deep experts' views of mysteries.[22] But those are just that: expert views. Because they are views on mysteries, matters that are by definition unprovable, they are not likely to be central enough to policymakers' decisions to be subject to intense political pressure. "Sense making" about complexities—issues that are "mysteries-plus," in the sense that they do not arise with history and shape—is still to be accomplished, but it will be a rapid and iterative exercise, a search for some sense in a sea of ever-changing complexity, and so it, too, does not seem to be a likely candidate for politicization.

Rather, it is the needs in the middle of the continuum that seem more problematic. After all, the argument over Iraqi WMD concerned a puzzle, not a mystery, yet it was a puzzle to whose solution the administration had hitched its argument for war. The fault lines in Soviet analysis that exercised the Gates confirmation hearings were not divisions over puzzles, but neither were they over mysteries. They were puzzle-like in that they concerned what was, not what might be. They went to the nature of the Soviet Union, how creative it was and what was driving its actions in what was then called the Third World. Similarly, when in 1976, as director of central intelligence (DCI), George H. W. Bush commissioned outsiders, a "Team B," to assess Soviet strategic objectives, missile accuracy, and air defense in light of official CIA views, Team A, the first set of issues became a major political controversy.[23] That, too, was not an argument over a puzzle, but it *was* an argument over what existed—namely, Soviet objectives—and not what might be.

Rethinking Intelligence–Policy Relations

The issues that are more subject to politicization, not surprisingly, are those that have, or seem to have, obvious policy conclusions. Put differently, they seem, or can be made to seem, to turn policy issues into intelligence ones.[24] For much of recent history, the temptation was most visible for Congress. Especially in eras of divided government, Congress was tempted to make, for instance, sanctions against a particular malefactor contingent on intelligence's conclusions that it had or had not committed some prohibited act. To be sure, this put intelligence in the most awkward of positions, having been given the gun and told to point it at the head of its ostensible masters in the executive branch of government.

Yet the narrowing of the question at issue in the run-up to the Iraq war represented the administration's success at turning a policy question—Should the United States attack Iraq?—into an intelligence one, "Does he or doesn't he?" In this instance, as administration officials admitted later, they believed there were a lot of reasons to invade Iraq, but WMD seemed the best bumper sticker on which to hang the defense of their preferred policy. It was particularly so with regard to one important constituency—namely, Democrats in Congress. For all its recent failures, the intelligence community retains some mystique; at least it is hard for politicians to defend views that are at odds with intelligence. For the October 2002 NIE to argue that "He does" did not settle the question for Democrats but did make it easier for those who were on the fence to side with a then-popular president.

This increased temptation to use intelligence in support of policy seems to argue for insulating intelligence from policy, for repainting the bright white line that many of us have sought to blur. So, too, if policy and intelligence can find new ways of interacting, the line between them will blur and, logically, the risks of politicization would rise. In that sense, both the changes in the politics of foreign policy and the changes in the nature of the intelligence target would seem to argue for new ways to protect intelligence from politicization.

In a fascinating conversation in 2006, George Shultz reflected on different DCIs with whom he had worked, and on the different relations between intelligence and policy they embodied.[25] The contrast was marked between what he called the "Helms approach" and the "Casey approach." Richard Helms, DCI in the Richard Nixon administration, embodied the sharp separation of intelligence officers from policy. When he briefed senior policy meetings, he left the meeting after his briefing. His role was only intelligence. By contrast, William Casey, DCI in the Ronald Reagan administration, actively sought Cabinet status and behaved as a Cabinet officer, mixing intelligence briefing and policy advocacy.

On balance, Shultz, a person of the old school, favored the Helms approach. But he recognized the cost. The approach risked irrelevance, those answers to unasked questions that so troubled me in government. For Shultz, the way to square the circle was to have policy officials, including at the top of government, actively engaged in question asking and probing. Only then would they be well served by intelligence. Put in terms of this chapter, for Vice President Richard

Cheney to journey to Langley to work through CIA analyses of Iraqi WMD programs before the Iraq war would be a good thing, in Shultz's terms, if intelligence hewed to the Helms approach. He did not say it, but Cheney's active engagement with intelligence might risk politicization if intelligence did not feel protected through independence.

Only time will tell whether the changed world of transnational targets, and the need it imposes for intelligence and policy to work more closely, will in fact lead to more risk of politicization. For now, the pressing need seems to be to find new ways of interacting. To the extent that the new cooperation lies in the "sense-making" range of intelligence needs, the risk should be muted by the nature of the task. That task will be rapidly updating assessments in light of new information, all in the midst of enormous uncertainty.

Yet the world of terrorists and other transnational targets will still throw up puzzles or puzzle-like issues on which policies will seem, or can be made to seem, to turn; witness the debate over contacts between Saddam Hussein's government and al-Qaeda. And, in the future as in the past, human nature will tempt policy-makers to seek analyses to suit their policy preference, operators to collect intelligence that validates their actions, and agency officials to present assessments that reinforce their budget requests.

Moreover, for all the hits intelligence and analysis have taken, the temptations of leaders either to try to turn policy issues into intelligence questions or to use intelligence to make the case for their preferred policies seem likely to grow. Intelligence is becoming less special or unusual and more a common feature of American policymaking discussion. And like it or not, it is also becoming more transparent, if not more open. That gradual change has been driven not only by investigative reporting but also by the change in targets; if the campaign against terrorism gives pride of place to intelligence, it also has multiplied the numbers of those who would make claims on intelligence—from foreign cooperators to state and local authorities. In the process the nature of the business is changing, if perhaps too slowly.

If the changed target has changed the intelligence problem, it has also reconfigured the policy problem. The Soviet threat could be *deterred*, but that posed by terrorists cannot, at least not in anywhere near the same degree. The terrorist threat has to be *prevented*, and that requires policies that have an impact far earlier in the chain from adversaries' intentions to their actions. If terrorist foes can act, policy has failed. Thus, prevention puts a premium on intelligence. The rub is not only that the further up that chain, the more "iffy" intelligence will usually be. It is also that administrations will want to use intelligence to justify actions taken in the name of prevention, in advance of pressing, obvious need.

These circumstances require a second look at ideas and institutions to provide intelligence with some insulation from political pressure. The long decline of the congressional intelligence committees and, especially, their slide into sharp partisanship do not seem likely to be reversed before the bitter divisions of their parent bodies are muted.[26] Nor does the 9/11 Commission's recommendation of a single point of oversight for the two houses of Congress seem to have a realistic chance of being implemented. Recentralizing oversight in a single committee in *each* house might be somewhat more thinkable, and it could make the process of oversight somewhat less political by reducing the number of players.

Giving the director of national intelligence (DNI) a set term, like that of the director of the Federal Bureau of Investigation, despite its drawbacks, should be rethought. The argument against a fixed term was that of relevance; if the DCI, now the DNI, was to be the president's principal intelligence adviser, he or she ought to be someone with a good relationship with the president, a person chosen rather than imposed. Now, however, if the circumstances have shifted toward the need for more political insulation, a fixed term for the DNI may not be a bad idea. DNIs would still carefully tend their relationships with the White House, but they would have somewhat more room to tell truth to power in extreme circumstances.

Finally, for all its faults, the risks of politicization over those puzzles or puzzle-like issues underscore the need for a careful process for producing NIEs or something like them. I came away from my time running the NIE process skeptical of both process and product. It was slow and—despite all our efforts to the contrary—both rather disconnected from the policy process and all too likely to produce a hedged and weasel-worded result. My skepticism was about whether the process could produce enough relevance.

Again, however, the changed circumstances shift the argument. As the flawed October 2002 NIE testified, something like the NIE process is no safeguard against the perils of mindset. But the process provides some insulation against "house" views by forcing the houses to argue, and against cherry picking by producing one comprehensive intelligence answer. Innovations in process and tradecraft also could provide some such insulation. Having the collection specialists in the room should help analysts—and customers—better judge sources. More "What If?" and other techniques of Alternative Analysis should broaden the hypotheses that get considered. So should widening the process to consider more information and expertise from outside intelligence and even outside government.

I also came away from my experience with NIEs admiring the British practice of including officials from policy agencies in their Joint Intelligence Committee process. Then, my reason for admiration was relevance; perhaps, with policy officers participating, the results of the process might actually provide an answer to a question someone was actually asking. Now, including policy officials from the start might produce a useful argument over exactly what the question at issue for intelligence really was.

Notes

1. Not to bury the lead, those wholesale prices had generally been declining, but there were some intriguing, suggestive spikes.
2. See James Worthen, "The Gates Hearings: Politicization and Soviet Analysis at the CIA," *Studies in Intelligence* 37 (Spring 1994): 7–20.
3. Richard K. Betts, "The New Politics of Intelligence: Will Reforms Work This Time?" *Foreign Affairs* 83, no. 3 (May/June 2004): 2–8; the quotation is on 7.

4. Betts makes this point nicely, and he also outlines forms of "politicization" akin to those below. See Richard K. Betts, *Enemies of Intelligence* (New York: Columbia University Press, 2007), chap. 4.

5. For this and other historical episodes of intelligence used—or leaked—for policy purposes, see Glenn Hastedt, "Public Intelligence: Leaks as Policy Instruments—The Case of the Iraq War," *Intelligence and National Security* 20, no. 3 (September 2005): 419–39.

6. Formally, this is the Commission on the Intelligence Capabilities of the United States Regarding Weapons of Mass Destruction, *Report to the President of the United States*, March 31, 2004, www.wmd.gov/report/index.html; also see U.S. Senate, Select Committee on Intelligence, *The Report on the U.S. Intelligence Community's Prewar Intelligence Assessments on Iraq*, June 2004, www.fas.org/irp/congress/2004_rpt/index.html.

7. Paul Pillar makes this point in his discussion of intelligence and the Iraq war. See his "Intelligence, Policy, and the War in Iraq," *Foreign Affairs* 85, no. 2 (March/April 2006): 15–28.

8. Ibid.

9. See Kenneth M. Pollack, "Spies, Lies, and Weapons: What Went Wrong," *Atlantic Monthly*, January/February 2004, www.theatlantic.com/doc/200401/pollack; and, esp., Seymour Hersh, "Selective Intelligence," *New Yorker*, May 12, 2003, www.newyorker.com/archive/2003/05/12/030512fa_fact.

10. Ernest R. May, *Strange Victory: Hitler's Conquest of France* (New York: Farrar, Straus and Giroux, 2000).

11. On the 1973 war, see, e.g., William B. Quandt, *Peace Process: American Diplomacy and the Arab-Israeli Conflict since 1967* (Washington, D.C.: Brookings Institution Press, 1990).

12. The postmortem was chaired by former vice chairman of the Joint Chiefs of Staff, Admiral David Jeremiah. The report was never made public, but for reportage on it, see the *Washington Post*, June 3, 1998, and the *New York Times*, June 3, 1998. For the transcript of Jeremiah's briefing on the report, see www.fas.org/irp/cia/product/jeremiah.html.

13. Peter Schwartz, *The Art of the Long View* (New York: Doubleday, 1991), 220.

14. Dennis M. Gormley, "The Limits of Intelligence: Iraq's Lessons," *Survival* 46, no. 3 (Autumn 2004): 10.

15. Bayesian, from Bayes' theorem, describes a process of updating subjective probabilities in light of new evidence.

16. See the Iraq Survey Group, *Comprehensive Report of the Special Advisor to the DCI on Iraq's WMD* (the "Duelfer report"), posted on the CIA website October 6, 2004. An easier-to-download version is at www.lib.umich.edu/govdocs/duelfer.html.

17. The full estimate has not yet been declassified. The Key Judgments are at www.ceip.org/files/projects/npp/pdf/Iraq/declassifiedintellreport.pdf. See also Joseph Cirincione, Jessica Tuchman Mathews, George Perkovich, and Alexis Orton, *WMD in Iraq: Evidence and Implications* (Washington, D.C.: Carnegie Endowment for International Peace, 2004), www.ceip.org/files/projects/npp/resources/iraqintell/home.htm.

18. Select Committee on Intelligence, U.S. Senate, *The Report on the U.S. Intelligence Community's Prewar Intelligence Assessments on Iraq*, June 2004, www.fas.org/irp/congress/2004_rpt/index.html.

19. Elaine C. Kamarck emphasizes uncertainty and information overload. See Elaine C. Kamarck, *Transforming the Intelligence Community: Improving the Collection and Management of Information* (Washington, D.C.: IBM Center for the Business of Government, 2005), 9.

20. For a fascinating assessment by an anthropologist of intelligence's analytic processes, see Rob Johnston, *The Culture of Analytic Tradecraft: An Ethnography of the Intelligence Community* (Washington, D.C.: Center for the Study of Intelligence, Central Intelligence Agency, 2005). See also Gormley, "Limits of Intelligence," 15. The same conclusion ran through a RAND assessment of the analytic community. See Gregory F. Treverton and

C. Bryan Gabbard, *Assessing the Tradecraft of Intelligence Analysis*, TR-293 (Santa Monica, Calif.: RAND Corporation, forthcoming).

21. For a catalogue of alternative analysis techniques, see Warren Fishbein and Gregory F. Treverton, *Making Sense of Transnational Threats*, Kent Center for Analytic Tradecraft Occasional Papers 3 no. 1 (Washington, D.C.: Central Intelligence Agency, 2004), www.cia .gov/cia/publications/Kent_Papers/pdf/OPV3No1.pdf. See also Roger George, "Fixing the Mindset Problem: Alternative Analysis," *International Journal of Intelligence and Counterintelligence* 17, no. 3 (Fall 2004): 385–405.

22. On the distinction between puzzles and mysteries, see Gregory F. Treverton, "Estimating beyond the Cold War," *Defense Intelligence Journal* 3, no. 2 (Fall 1994): 5–20; and Joseph S. Nye Jr., "Peering into the Future," *Foreign Affairs* 77, no. 4 (July/August 1994): 82–93.

23. See Lawrence Freedman, *U.S. Intelligence and the Soviet Strategic Threat*, 2nd ed. (Princeton, N.J.: Princeton University Press, 1986); and John Prados, *The Soviet Estimate: U.S. Intelligence Analysis and Russian Military Strength* (New York: Dial Press, 1982).

24. See Gregory F. Treverton, "Intelligence: Welcome to the American Government," in *A Question of Balance: The President, the Congress and Foreign Policy*, ed. Thomas E. Mann (Washington, D.C.: Brookings Institution Press, 1990).

25. The setting was a conference, and the rendition of Shultz's views is that of the author.

26. The WMD Commission Report lays out a series of recommendations on pp. 337–40, which have not yet been acted on.

PART THREE
Enduring Challenges

THE NATURE of the analytic business has some enduring features, even in this rapidly changing twenty-first century. Part three lays out that landscape for those less familiar with the usual roles and responsibilities of analysts, as well as some of the challenges they face that distinguish their jobs from those of other international affairs specialists.

The coeditor of this volume, Roger Z. George, who has taught national security strategy as well as intelligence analysis, begins with a discussion of how strategy can and should involve intelligence analysis—and its producers—in virtually every stage of the formulation and execution phases. That most outsiders consider the analyst's job as only to "warn" is an oversimplification of the complex set of roles analysts play in promoting good strategy.

The other coeditor, James B. Bruce, along with Michael Bennett—both experienced practitioners in detecting and countering foreign denial and deception—lay out a way to think about this problem as it degrades analysis. For U.S. intelligence to succeed, analysts require a deeper understanding of how intelligence targets act to defeat collection efforts against them. Understanding these dynamics at the root of many analytic failures is necessary to successfully counter foreign denial and deception.

Although this volume is focused on analysis for national security policymakers, a related specialized field for analysts is the even larger field of military intelligence analysis. David Thomas, a career Defense Intelligence Agency officer who has served throughout the intelligence community and worked on many national intelligence projects, provides a comprehensive look at military analysis and the challenges it has faced in the past and new ones it must confront in the future. He also suggests how military analysis needs to improve to face twenty-first-century warfare and a broadening set of military customers.

CHAPTER 7

The Art of Strategy and Intelligence

ROGER Z. GEORGE

If you know the enemy and know yourself, you need not fear the results of
a hundred battles.

—Sun Tzu, *The Art of War*

IN WHAT IS OFTEN regarded as the earliest writings on "strategy,"
the Chinese master Sun Tzu spoke of the need to understand the nature of one's
adversary—his strengths and weaknesses—as well as understanding one's own
abilities in order to fashion an effective way to subdue or defeat an enemy. Sun
Tzu's thirteen chapters on the art of war lay out the commander's skills in knowing all aspects of the battlefield and having his unique collection of "spies" to
obtain critical information on the adversary.[1] Later Western writers on strategy
like Carl von Clausewitz would also write about the need to understand the
adversary, the nature of war, and the political context in which wars were to be
fought if one is to fashion a successful plan of attack or defense.[2] These writings
on strategy underline the integral role that information, insight, and intelligence
play in what we would now call a national security strategy. Unfortunately, few
writings even today go much beyond this general statement to describe or assess
the varied roles that intelligence plays in the formation and execution of current
national security strategy. And yet the effective use of intelligence analysis can
be a critical "enabler" of national security strategies.[3]

Developing a National Security Strategy

Scholars of military strategy have written extensively on what constitutes "strategy"—a debate that will not be resurrected here.[4] However, the essential features
of a national security strategy include the assessment of the international environment in which the United States operates, the identification of principal
threats and opportunities to U.S. national interests, and the formulation and
prioritization of policy objectives and the selection of courses of action (e.g.,
fashioning the means and employing different forms of power) that will be taken
to accomplish the established policy objectives. This seemingly rational and linear process, even if it can be described in a few sentences or in a simple graphic
such as the one provided in figure 7.1, is seldom so simple.

FIGURE 7.1
Paradigm for a Foreign Affairs Strategy

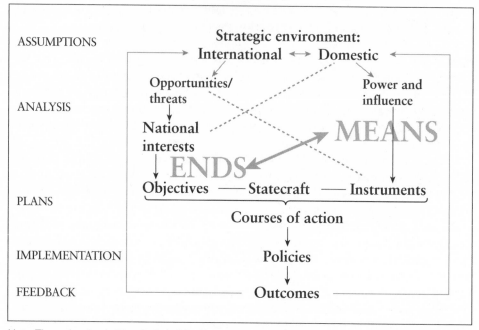

Note: The author thanks Terry Deibel of the National War College for this graphic, which has been used in describing the national security strategy process for many years to the country's future military and civilian leaders. See Terry D. Deibel, *Foreign Affairs Strategy: Logic for American Statecraft* (New York: Cambridge University Press, 2007).

Figure 7.1 shows the rigorous steps a strategist uses to arrive at a well-thought-out strategy. At its core, strategy matches a state's ends (interests) to its means (power). As Sun Tzu notes, the strategist must know oneself as well as the enemy, so that the state can be sure not to misconstrue its true interests or overextend its power. Accordingly, the strategist must develop a clear picture of the domestic and international environment, the threats and opportunities it poses, and the risks and costs of taking different courses of action to achieve one's strategic ends.

Analyst as Enabler

The intelligence analyst, however, also has a key role in enabling the national security strategist to accomplish critical objectives. Though the analyst does not presume to define a national security strategy, he or she must be cognizant of what that national security strategy is, how the current set of decision makers are defining American interests and hence threats and opportunities to it, and the key policy objectives of those decision makers. Today, the analyst has the benefit—and the challenge—of understanding a long list of explicit U.S. strategies on security, homeland defense, counterterrorism, and intelligence that have been drafted in the wake of the September 11, 2001, terrorist attacks.[5] An analyst who has studied the strategic thinking of key policymakers is in a better position to enable those strategists to improve their performance at each step of the decision-making and policy execution process.

Seen in this context, virtually all intelligence analysis is strategic, for it seeks to enable policymakers to achieve their goals with the required means. That is, whether the analyst is describing the general strategic environment, providing warning of some attack, merely describing the details of an adversary's military potential or infrastructure, or providing very tactical targeting information, the endeavor itself is in support of an overall strategy to achieve certain specific ends.

Figure 7.2 displays the distinct and more limited roles that an analyst plays in the strategy formulation and execution process. The strategist brings a worldview or perceptions about the international environment to the strategy-making process. The analyst brings expertise and analytical tradecraft to improve the strategist's understanding of that environment. As the strategist seeks to define the national interest and the principal threats and opportunities posed by the international environment, the key function of the analyst is to identify—that is, "warn" of—events or trends that might constitute such threats or opportunities. As a strategist formulates policy objectives and courses of action, the analyst supports these deliberations by describing the opposing actor's strengths and weaknesses, possible foreign responses to any course of action, and perhaps unforeseen consequences of potential U.S. policy actions—that is, information that relates the real and potential costs and risks of such policy actions.

FIGURE 7.2
Analyst as Enabler: Intelligence and the National Security Strategist

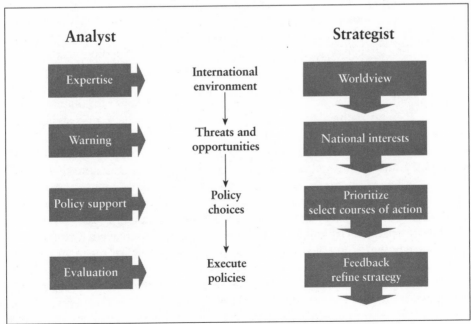

Finally, after policies are implemented, the strategist must reassess the effectiveness of the policies and refine or restructure the overall strategy. At this juncture, the analyst's role is to provide an assessment of how adversaries and allies have reacted to U.S. policies, what intended and unintended consequences those policies might have had, and what future actions foreign state and nonstate actors might contemplate to comply with or oppose U.S. actions.

Deconstructing these four unique ways in which intelligence analysis can enable effective strategy will help to illustrate that intelligence analysis is not a one-size-fits-all proposition. Analysis must be sensitive to the stage at which strategy is being formulated or implemented. Analysis that focuses too much on broad trends when the strategist is already poised to select courses of action or implement specific policy decisions is likely to be disregarded. Likewise, if a decision maker does not share the analytic community's general views of a problem early in the strategy formulation process, then trying to provide policy support can be doubly difficult for the intelligence community.

Shaping the Strategic Context: Analyst Expertise and Tradecraft

The most fundamental goal of both the strategist and analyst must be to comprehend the strategic environment in which the United States and other friendly and adversarial actors are operating. However, the vantage points of strategist and analyst are very different. Whereas the strategist comes to the problem with a well-formed set of values, preconceptions, and policy goals, the analyst must attempt to examine the strategic context from a less explicitly American perspective.

In the cold war, U.S. strategists were both contemptuous toward and alarmed by the communist system. They could see the faults of the system but may have ascribed more ideology to the factors driving Soviet policy than was actually the case. It was the analysts' responsibility to view the Soviet Union in its totality. Understanding its behavior was only partly a function of ideology, as George Kennan pointed out in his groundbreaking "X article" that credited Stalin's actions as much to nationalism and personal paranoia. Also, whereas the strategist might fall prey to a "worse case" view of the Soviet Union's behavior—for example, seeking military superiority, contemplating nuclear first strikes, or exploiting every potential crisis in the world for the benefit of world communism—the analyst was obliged to assess the limits of the Soviet Union's national economic, political, and military power, the importance of Russian self-interest (vis-à-vis other competing communist power centers like China), and understand how interest groups inside the Soviet Union (e.g., the party, the military, the government ministries) might be competing or working at cross-purposes.

An early example of where the intelligence analytic perspective proved far more accurate than that held by some U.S. officials was the intelligence community's early 1960s recognition of the growing Sino–Soviet split. This competition between communist powers was not as clearly recognized by cold warrior strategists, who continued to presume that China was working at the behest of the Soviet Union's goal of world communism. Many scholars now place a great deal of weight on the importance of this misperception in understanding how U.S. strategists concluded that the Soviet Union and China were behind the North Vietnamese war against the United States–backed South Vietnamese government. Only years later would North Vietnamese officials criticize former senior U.S. defense strategists for not understanding that the Vietnamese had been fighting for their independence from China long before they took up arms against the French and then the Americans.[6]

Today, as during the cold war, the analyst must retain a more dispassionate view of the world than the strategist generally brings to the decision-making process. Analysts must consider the world as it exists, not as one wishes it to be. Moreover, analysts must remain consciously more self-critical than strategists, who can ill afford to show doubt about their policies. That is, an analyst does not have the luxury of asserting some judgment merely because he or she holds a PhD in the subject, speaks the language, or has lived in the region. Those credentials are also held by any number of highly educated policymakers. Moreover, the more expert the analyst, the more prone an analyst becomes to the "mindset" trap—that is, believing that his or her view of the problem is the best explanation for all behavior. Yet as many intelligence failures have demonstrated, intelligence experts can become too complacent about their knowledge and too resistant to alternative explanations and thus miss important changes in the international environment or in the attitudes of U.S. adversaries. Hence, the analyst must constantly be challenging his or her views on an intelligence subject and using different analytic techniques to check whether key assumptions are flawed, information is incomplete, misleading, or flatly wrong, or the known facts about an issue could legitimately produce multiple thoughts rather than a single conclusion.[7]

Informing the policymaker qua "strategist" about the changing strategic environment is the most all-encompassing role that the analyst performs daily in many forms. Adding knowledge to the policy debate is what Sherman Kent described as the intelligence analyst's goal of elevating the level of the policy debate. Many policymakers do not always acknowledge this quiet yet pervasive function of intelligence. But it is one that intelligence analysts perform almost unconsciously in their everyday interactions with policymakers via finished analysis, oral briefings, or telephone and face-to-face conversations. Sometimes providing a different perspective to a policymaker can be the most important contribution to a strategy debate if it can put the strategist in the adversary's position or demonstrate that the strategist's perspective on an issue is not the only possible interpretation of the current problem.

Dealing with Threats and Opportunities: The Warning Function

In most cases, intelligence analysts are ultimately—if not always fairly—judged on whether they provided adequate strategic and tactical warning of an impending change in the world. For the national security strategist, however, the challenge is far more difficult. The strategist must first decide what are the enduring American interests that must be protected—a secure homeland, a democratic way of life, a prosperous economy, access to energy supplies, effective alliances and defenses, and the like—and how American hard and soft power will be used to achieve these goals. Defining what are critical national interests at a given moment is not easy, nor is it simple to prioritize, choose among, or balance those interests that might be at times in conflict.[8] If, in fact, U.S. decision makers have difficulty defining what are the most critical U.S. interests worth defending or advancing, then it stands to reason that intelligence analysts will have an equally difficult time determining which issues need to be watched to provide effective warning or—more positively—notification that an opportunity exists to advance an important U.S. interest.

In the post–September 11 world, it is now axiomatic that a central mission of the intelligence community is warning of any terrorist attack. A huge national effort has been launched to create large analytic centers to identify and prevent such threats from materializing. Not only is there a National Counterterrorism Center to which many national intelligence agencies contribute, but there also are separate, departmental counterterrorism activities throughout the government, most especially at the Central Intelligence Agency, the Federal Bureau of Investigation, the Department of Homeland Security, the Defense Intelligence Agency, and the State Department's Bureau of Intelligence and Research. So, in this sense, the analysts' mission is clear. However, there is still a long list of other U.S. national interests that must also be protected and advanced, most of which have not been as clearly enunciated as counterterrorism or counterproliferation. How many analysts also should be following and reporting regularly on international human and drug trafficking, illegal border crossings, and organized crime activity that can threaten and potentially kill U.S. citizens? Moreover, are there senior officials paying attention to these issues, to which analysts might report their concerns?

Analysts—provided they have the necessary resources and information—face two key challenges in providing warning to the strategist. First, does the analyst understand what the strategist believes would be a threat or an opportunity to a key U.S. national interest? At first blush, this might seem a silly question to pose. However, in the past, analytic centers have been established to monitor what senior intelligence community managers considered to be an important challenge to U.S. interests, only to be disbanded when it became clear that senior officials had little or no interest in developing policies against such emergencies. For example, in the late 1990s, the Central Intelligence Agency (CIA) briefly established an "environmental center" whose mission would be to track, monitor, and warn about environmental trends or events (e.g., foreign nuclear reactor accidents like Chernobyl or other naturally occurring events) that might have geopolitical significance. It became clear that a newly elected administration would have little interest in such activities and the resources were reallocated to other priority tasks.

Likewise, the Iraq WMD [weapons of mass destruction] Commission report found that during the middle to late 1990s, when Saddam Hussein was judged to be effectively "contained" by UN sanctions and monitored by UN inspectors, there were few requests for information from the CIA regarding Saddam.

Accordingly, intelligence officials found that other priorities on Iran and North Korea's nuclear programs led to reduced analytical and collection attention on Iraq's WMD programs. When UN inspectors were suddenly expelled in 1998 and U.S. policies shifted toward an active concern about Iraq and its WMD, analysts were in a poor position to answer critical questions regarding the existence and state of those programs, other than to rely on dated reporting and past Iraqi behavior.[9]

The second and related challenge is to convince strategists that they have received a serious warning. In the aftermath of many policy failures, there is a temptation for strategists to claim that strategic or tactical warning was not adequately provided by intelligence analysts. In response, analysts often resort to unearthing past assessments that they believe provided adequate "warning" statements, had the strategist bothered to pay attention. Who is right? Policymakers' claims that the "warning" was not explicit enough and was buried in an assessment are often juxtaposed by the analysts' lament that their frequent assessments were seldom read or dismissed as "crying wolf." In the 9/11 Commission report, controversy swirled around the question of whether "warnings" such as those given to both the Bill Clinton and George W. Bush administrations in the *President's Daily Brief* were in fact explicit enough to be convincing to senior officials (see box 7.1). In part, the problem harks back to the development of the strategic context, which the analyst must understand and shape to prepare key decision makers to recognize a warning when it is indeed being issued. Too often, a strategist can perceive a "warning" as merely a hypothetical, low-probability event and dismiss it as typical intelligence community "worst-case" analysis or "cover yourself" behavior. Only if analysts have put themselves in the mindset of the strategist and properly couched their assessment in a way that connects their conclusions to the strategist's agenda can they expect their customer to recognize a warning when it is intended.

Strategists often accuse the analytic community of waffling about a specific situation or of not making a "warning" sufficiently grave or frequent enough to be compelling. In the heat of national security policymaking, there also is the problem of "noise," which interferes with a strategist actually comprehending the warning that has been provided. Specific warnings might also be diluted by the variety of other inputs—often contradictory—which come from a variety of sources that the strategist has at his or her disposal. Moreover, in what has become a routinely fast-paced, quickly shifting set of policy discussions, a policymaker will have little time to absorb the latest intelligence analysis and determine whether it merits closer inspection. An interruption, a badly summarized staff note on top of cogently written finished intelligence products, or a very lengthy assessment that is put aside for a time when the decision maker has time to read more thoughtfully can all contribute to inattention to a very critical analytic judgment. In responding to an earlier warning provided but unheeded, former national security adviser Henry Kissinger is reputed to have said, "Well, you warned me, but you didn't convince me." Truly, the challenge for analysts is not only to be prescient and take risks in reaching controversial judgments but also to be convincing.

BOX 7.1

Two Warnings: Excerpts from the *President's Daily Brief*

4 December 1998
SUBJECT: Bin Laden Preparing to Hijack US Aircraft and Other Attacks

. . . Bin Laden and his allies are preparing for attacks in the U.S., including an aircraft hijacking to obtain the release of Shaykh 'Umar' Abd al-Rahman, Ramzi Yousef, and Muhammad Sadiq 'Awda. One source quoted a senior member of the Gamaa'at al-Islamiyya (IG) saying that as of late October, the IG had completed planning for an operation in the US on behalf of Bin Ladin, but that the operation was on hold. . . . The Bin Laden organization or its allies are moving closer to implementing anti-US attacks at unspecified locations, but we do not know whether they are related to attacks on aircraft.

6 August 2001
SUBJECT: Bin Laden Determined to Strike in U.S.

Clandestine, foreign government, and media reports indicate bin Laden since 1997 has wanted to conduct terrorist attacks in the U.S. Bin Laden implied in U.S. television interviews in 1997 and 1998 that his followers would follow the example of World Trade Center bomber Ramzi Yousef and "bring the fighting to America." After U.S. missile strikes on his base in Afghanistan in 1998, bin Laden told followers he wanted to retaliate in Washington.

Note: These excerpts from the only two issues of the *President's Daily Brief* so far declassified can be found in the 9/11 Commission Report, *The Final Report of the National Commission on Terrorist Attacks on the United States,* pp. 128–29 and 261; released on July 22, 2004.

Providing Policy Support: The Unseen Role of Analysis

Compared to the "warning" mission of analysts, the job of providing support to policy is far more frequent but far less noticed or appreciated by those outside the decision-making process. Yet, the reality is that strategists spend far more time on the selection and implementation of courses of action—that is, choosing policy instruments and determining how to apply them—than they do on their initial assessment of the strategic context and identification of principal threats. Once strategists believe they understand the international environment and the principal challenges facing the nation, they are concerned primarily about using the military, diplomatic, economic, and other instruments of power at their disposal.

The role of the analyst, then, becomes one of providing analysis that can enable the best application of courses of action—for example, the imposition of sanctions, the offer or cancellation of foreign military assistance, the threat of military intervention, or the use of public diplomacy. Few writers outside the intelligence community, however, recognize the wide range of analytic contributions to this phase in the policy process, which do not fall into the category of a major intelligence warning or prescient reassessment of an important international development. Jack Davis, for example, has written that there are literally thousands of so-called transactions between analyst and policymaker that fall into the category of policy support. These involve the analyst providing bits and pieces of information and insight on a specific policy issue, where the strategist is trying to determine how best to use an instrument like a foreign aid package, or what convincing arguments the policymaker might use in a planned conversation with a foreign counterpart, or what possible countermeasures an adversary might take if the United States were to initiate certain actions designed to increase U.S. influence. Few of these activities are transparent to the outside observer.

For the strategist, however, the real contribution of the intelligence community is precisely in this invisible world of policy support, where he or she can rely on the best information and expertise provided by analysts who will not be constantly second-guessing him or challenging his assumptions or arguing with him over whether a policy is well founded or not. Here is where analysts are at their most objective and least likely to be regarded as undermining current policies with critical analysis. Analysts are being mostly instrumental in providing information, which "supports" current policy objectives, regardless of whether analysts think the policy is correct or likely to succeed. An example of the range of services that can be provided to the strategist is seen in figure 7.3, which illustrates possible analytic contributions to the use of a wide range of policy instruments.

As the figure illustrates, contributions come from military, economic, and political analysts and provide information about how foreign actors may behave or respond to specific U.S. actions. Monitoring key developments like sanctioned regimes or world oil trading patterns, assessing the negotiating positions of important allies or adversaries, and tracking the financial transactions of illicit WMD are part of the daily routine of numerous experts throughout the intelligence community. Moreover, their activities are focused on supporting a specific group of policymakers within the government agencies or in overseas missions. The list of such policy support activities is almost endless and the daily tasking unending. Intelligence community analysts receive such requests or "taskings" at interagency meetings, as a result of a one-to-one briefing, or at the end of an important telephone conversation with a policymaker.

The policy support provided to strategists—if utilized—can be critical to the assessment of the risks and costs of proposed courses of action, which may be selected or are already in train. For example, when considering whether the United States should impose a sanctions regime on a rogue state, analysts will assess the impact such measures might have on weakening the rogue state's ability to acquire or develop weapons of mass destruction, maintain internal control, or threaten its neighbors. At the same time, other analysts are considering the policies and actions of surrounding states, whose compliance with U.S.-sponsored sanctions might impact the effectiveness of the policy. Strategists

FIGURE 7.3
Intelligence as Policy Support "Enabler": Examples from Iraq

Diplomatic power	Economic power	Informational power	Military power
International organizations • Background briefings to P-5 • Demarches on Iraq WMD • Prepare Iraq white papers	*Foreign assistance policies* • Monitor corruption/misuse • Assess impact on development policies • Identify critical shortfalls	*Public diplomacy* • White papers on WMD • Review government's speeches • Monitor/report foreign media coverage	*Coercive actions* • Support interdiction operations • Identify key regime vulnerabilities • Support covert actions
International law • Report atrocities, war crimes • Monitor human rights abuses • Support renditions • Support legal actions against Saddam regime leaders	*Economic sanctions* • Monitor border crossings • Assess regional impact • Report on violations	*Political action* • Pinpoint critical weaknesses of adversaries • Assess receptiveness of foreign audiences to media messages	*Paramilitary action* • Assess insurgency • Support counterinsurgency
Alliances/coalitions • Assess strengths/weaknesses • Monitor government/public attitudes toward Iraq War • Forecast potential actions and contributions	*International trade policies* • Monitor world market • Forecast impact of oil wealth on regime stability	*Intelligence sharing* • Share assessments with IAEA • Joint analysis/collection operations against CT/WMD targets	*Force start of war* • Support intrusive inspection regimes • Support psyops plans/special ops • Identify suspect WMD sites
International negotiations • Assessment of adversaries' negotiation style/posture • Develop U.S. negotiating position	*Humanitarian assistance* • Monitor refugee flows/needs • Forecast economic disruptions caused by war and terrorism	*"Soft power"* • Assess foreign public diplomacy campaigns • Monitor disinformation and propaganda aimed at Western audience	*War plans* • Support OPS plan development • Develop order of battle • Conduct bomb damage assessment

Note: The author has adapted this chart from presentations by Robert Levine of the National War College, who conceptualized the role of intelligence as "enabler" while he was the CIA's faculty representative and was responsible for instructing war college students in the uses of intelligence.

should also consider a policy's costs to include the economic losses suffered by neighboring states to which the United States is allied.[10]

The risks to this course of action are that the sanction regime might not prove to be effective. Intelligence analysts should be assessing the risk that other U.S. adversaries will try to undermine or circumvent the sanctions regime in order to oppose American policies, bolster their own relations with a rogue state, or merely demonstrate their independence from the American superpower. Finally, the intelligence analyst also must consider alerting strategists to the unintended consequences of a course of action. In the case of economic sanctions, analysts would inform decision makers of the possibility that a sanctions regime would create new incentives for organized crime groups to profit in illegal shipments of goods, as well as create new opportunities for the rogue state to undermine U.S. stature by claiming that the "unfair" sanctions regime was hurting the average citizens of the country, which would stir up anti-American sentiments in the region. These types of behaviors were observed in the case of Iraq.

Policy support perhaps is best illustrated as a kind of "scouting" function the analyst can provide to the strategist. In numerous negotiation arenas over the years, strategists have wanted to put themselves into the shoes of the adversary or ally and understand what their negotiating strategy might be. Analysts are often called upon to imagine how the other party will behave in those negotiations, what their bottom lines will be, and what compromises they might be willing to strike. Without suggesting what the U.S. strategist should do, analysts—either as part of a U.S. negotiating team or in written assessments—will often suggest how to play an issue to best American advantage.

Throughout the U.S.–Soviet era of arms control negotiations, CIA analysts were part of the negotiating process, bringing their knowledge of the opposing Soviet delegation and past behavior along with an understanding of Kremlin politics to help shape an effective American strategy. Likewise, today one finds many analysts working to support difficult negotiations vis-à-vis North Korea, Iran, and other states, whose intentions and actions require serious all-source analysis and deep expertise.

Refining the Strategy: The Difficult Job of Evaluation

It would be naïve to assume that a strategy, once set, runs its course "automatically" until it achieves its stated goals. As military commanders often say, "No plan survives first contact with the enemy." Likewise, when developing strategic plans, there is the danger that the strategist will fall into the trap sometimes known as the "fallacy of the first move"—presuming that the adversary will accept the inevitability of an American action and comply in the ways imagined by its creators. Sadly, the world is far more complex and less predictable than this. Numerous times confident strategists proclaim that a stated policy action will be successful and are then shocked by the persistence of an enemy's resistance or an actor's clever response to some U.S. policy action. The analysts' role in the postimplementation phase of strategy formulation is to report back to policymakers on the effectiveness of the courses of action taken in a timely fashion. This role is in addition to the earlier, more predictive role of analytic forecasting; instead, in this case, analysts are required to draw up after-action reporting that strategists can use to reassess or redirect their policies. Not surprisingly, this is a contribution that is needed but seldom welcomed, particularly when it amounts to a failing grade or a less-than-overwhelming success for an American administration. As Richard Kerr has noted elsewhere, "There are no policy failures, only intelligence failures."

Hence, the analyst must read carefully in providing feedback to the strategist if he or she is to maintain the trust of the strategist and survive to provide analysis to policymakers another day. As James Steinberg notes in chapter 5 of this volume, a smart strategist would be foolish to dismiss analytical evaluations of policy simply because they do not conform to his expectations. However, there are examples of where the strategist's expectations and the analyst's assessment of a policy action were widely disputed. The long record of intelligence community evaluations of U.S. military policies in Vietnam and American policymakers dismissing them is recorded by numerous intelligence practitioners and policymakers and mentioned elsewhere in this volume. Intelligence community bomb damage assessments of the first Gulf War, which disputed military claims of destroying nearly all Iraq's Scud missiles, also have been cited as an example where military planners were unwilling to consider the possibility that their air sorties were not nearly as effective as imagined.[11] Likewise, the press heralded a dispute regarding the crisis in the former Yugoslavia in the late 1990s, when the Bill Clinton administration's optimism that Serbian prime minister Slobodan Milosevic would cave after three days of bombings met serious questioning by intelligence analysts.[12]

The current dispute about how successful the war against terrorism has been and whether the Iraq War has contributed to or complicated the U.S. antiterrorism strategy is the most recent example of how analysis aimed at evaluating the effectiveness of policies can become controversial.[13] When analysts provide a reality check that is perceived to challenge the views and assumptions held by policymakers, there is bound to be friction, especially when this becomes a topic of public debate.

An added complication for the strategist is that his or her role is not simply to calculate the costs of adjusting the strategy in terms of the foreign environment. Unlike the analyst who only thinks about how foreign adversaries and allies are reacting to the policy, the strategist must consider the domestic environment in which the strategy has been fashioned. Among these considerations are a strategy's level of congressional, public, and media support; the morale of the American forces fighting overseas; the budgetary pressures; and the overall credibility of U.S. policies. So when intelligence assessments begin to question the logic or effectiveness of a strategy, there is an immediate tendency to resist such inputs. Highlighting the possibility that a strategy needs to be adjusted, because the adversary is not behaving as imagined or because the military or economic tools used were not as effective as predicted, causes major strains in the strategist–analyst relationship. Typically, these frictions probably surfaced earlier in the strategy formulation process, as there likely were disagreements between strategists and analysts in their characterization of the strategic environment, and differences about the likely effectiveness of different courses of action. Most likely, there was some reluctance on the part of strategists to accept the analysts' coaching skills for providing policy support, if they were so skeptical from the beginning of the strategy's underlying logic.

Maintaining the independence of the analytic process is the only real guarantee that strategists will get the unvarnished truth from the intelligence community. Examples of how strategists have not done themselves any favors by hobbling the independence of intelligence services can be seen in the poor advice provided to Stalin or Hitler for fear of retribution. Likewise, it appears that Saddam did not know how weak his military was, or how prepared the United States was to bring about a regime change in Baghdad, because his own security services only told him what he wished to hear. One also can imagine that the North Korean intelligence services have a hard time convincing Kim Jong Il of the seriousness of American counterproliferation concerns or the likely devastating impact of a war on the Korean Peninsula were he to start one.

Improving the Strategist–Analyst Relationship

The model put forward here argues that there should be a close and symbiotic relationship between the strategist and analyst. The reality is that the interactions are anything but smooth and seamless. Too often the strategist and analyst are either working with little appreciation for the other's role or are openly dismissive of the challenges that the other faces in fulfilling their respective responsibilities. The strategist can unintentionally, or sometimes willfully, dismiss the analyst's perspective as uninformed about the policy perspective; worse yet, the strategist may not trust the analyst with knowledge about the true strategy and seek instead to keep intelligence professionals at arms' length for fear that they might jeopardize policy initiatives and are likely to see only the negative consequences of some untried course of action. Analysts, likewise, are sometimes dismissive of the high stakes that strategists face every day. They do not carry the decision-making burden that their policy customers must assume. Analysts can shrug off the uncertainties implicit in their analyses and posit conclusions that are clearly speculative. However, at the end of the day the strategist must arrive at a decision, select a course of action, and face the consequences.

An improved relationship is only likely to come through mutual understanding of the strategist–analyst model. Though every strategist is by nature his or her own analyst, few have actually worked as intelligence professionals or have experienced the challenges of being an analyst. There are no courses on intelligence offered to incoming U.S. government officials to introduce the policymaker to how intelligence works, the strengths and weaknesses of American collection and analysis, or the various analytical methods used by today's professionals.

For the analyst, in turn, there must be a greater appreciation for the complexities facing policymakers and for the "big picture" world in which they live. Too often, the strategist is trying to see how an intelligence briefing or new assessment fits into the broader agenda in which they must operate. Unfortunately, the size and complexity of the intelligence business often results in analysts being responsible for only a "thin slice" of any given intelligence topic. Few analysts are able to give strategists an overriding sense of a specific judgment's impact on the overall strategic landscape they are facing. This narrow account splitting is contrary to the way the strategist views the world. In his or her domain, everything is connected to everything else. Events happening in one country will have consequences somewhere else in the region and the world. They do not have the luxury of inviting an endless line of experts into the office for their piece of the puzzle to be added to the mix. So a start for analysts would be to develop broader and integrative perspectives on their issues, so they can put answers into a context that strategists value. It means real multidisciplinary analysis in each analyst, not just an analytic structure that places narrowly focused military, economic, and political analysts into one unit.

Strategist and analyst must understand each other while maintaining their respective roles. The more we know ourselves, as Sun Tzu noted centuries ago, the more able we are to take full advantage of the knowledge we have developed about our world and America's adversaries.

Notes

1. Quoted from *Sun Tzu, The Art of War*, trans. Lionel Giles, http://classics.mit.edu/tsu-/artwar.html.

2. Michael Howard and Peter Paret, trans., *Clausewitz, On War* (Princeton, N.J.: Everyman's Library, 1993).

3. "Enabler" is used to distinguish intelligence from the traditional forms of "power," which strategists cite as military, political, economic, and informational. Some writers on strategy consider intelligence a means—that is, a type of "informational" power, whereas others argue it is only an enabler of other means.

4. There are excellent studies on strategy, including Robert J. Art, *A Grand Strategy for America* (Ithaca, N.Y.: Cornell University Press, 2003); Colin S. Gray, *Modern Strategy* (New York: Oxford University Press, 1999); and B. D. Liddell Hart, *Strategy* (Westport, Conn.: Praeger, 1954). For an excellent survey of strategic thinking, see Peter Paret and Gordon Craig, eds., *Makers of Modern Strategy: From Machiavelli to the Nuclear Age* (Princeton, N.J.: Princeton University Press, 1986).

5. The recent series of public documents on U.S. national security strategy now include separate "strategies" on national security strategy, homeland security, counterterrorism, weapons of mass destruction, and intelligence.

6. Harold Ford, "Revisiting Vietnam: Thoughts Engendered by Robert McNamera's In Retrospect," *Studies in Intelligence* 39, no. 1 (1996): 95–109, www.cia.gov/csi/studies/96unclass/ford.htm. McNamara made essentially the same points in a talk titled "In Retrospect: The Tragedy and Lessons of Vietnam," April 25, 1995, John F. Kennedy School of Government, Harvard University.

7. See Roger George, "Fixing the Problem of Analytic Mindsets: Alternative Analysis," in *Intelligence and the National Security Strategist: Enduring Issues and Challenges*, ed. Roger Z. George and Robert D. Kline (Lanham, Md.: Rowman & Littlefield, 2005), 311–26.

8. Today, the homeland security debate often focuses on balancing American citizens' right to privacy against their right to feel secure at home. Equally challenging is proper prioritization of domestic well-being in the form of spending on education, health care, or airport security against defense spending or foreign assistance programs designed to avert failing states that can become safe havens for future terrorists.

9. See WMD Commission report, formally known as the *Commission on the Intelligence Capabilities of the United States Regarding Weapons of Mass Destruction*. Its final 600-page report was issued on March 31, 2005.

10. This has occurred on numerous occasions, as when the United States was considering sanctions against Iraq in the early 1990s and Turkey insisted that its losses would be in the billions of dollars. Likewise, analysts were constantly assessing the regional impact of sanctions on Serbia during the Yugoslav conflict, estimating the amount of humanitarian aid needed to support Bosnian refugees, and even trying to assess how weather patterns would impact UN winter relief activities.

11. Richard Russell, "Tug of War: The CIA's Uneasy Relationship with the Military," in *Intelligence and the National Security Strategist*, ed. George and Kline, 479–93.

12. This is found in Allan Little, "Behind the Kosovo Crisis," *BBC News*, March 12, 2000, http://news.bbc.co.uk/1/hi/world/europe/674056.stm.

13. Karen DeYoung, "Spy Agencies Say Iraq War Hurting U.S. Terror Fight," *Washington Post*, September 24, 2006. Similar reporting by the *New York Times* noted that the National Intelligence Council, author of the NIE, had previously concluded that Iraq might become a primary training ground for a next generation of terrorists. See Mark Mazzetti, "Spy Agencies Say Iraq War Worsens Terror Threat," *New York Times*, September 24, 2006.

CHAPTER 8

Foreign Denial and Deception: Analytical Imperatives

James B. Bruce and Michael Bennett

We must significantly reduce our vulnerability to intelligence surprises, mistakes, and omissions caused by the effects of denial and deception (D&D) on collection and analysis.

—President's Commission on the Intelligence Capabilities of the United States Regarding Weapons of Mass Destruction, March 2005

FOREIGN DENIAL and deception (D&D) is a fact of life for every intelligence analyst who has ever worked a "hard target."[1] Such targets are objects of high intelligence interest and are considered to be hard because they defy a wide variety of ordinary collection methods and pose the most difficult analytical challenges. The standard collection activities such as human intelligence (HUMINT), signals intelligence (SIGINT), and imagery intelligence (IMINT) are typically less productive against such targets because the countermeasures these targets take against collection reduce, and sometimes confuse, the factual basis for analytical understanding. During the cold war, the Soviet Union was the exemplary hard target. Today countries like China, North Korea, and Iran offer the best examples, as well as such nonstate actors as international terrorist groups like al-Qaeda and weapons of mass destruction (WMD) proliferation networks.

What Is Denial and Deception?

Highly relevant to national-level policymakers and to war fighters, D&D is defined as *any undertaking (activity or program) by adversaries—state and nonstate actors alike—to influence or deceive policymaking and intelligence communities by reducing collection effectiveness, manipulating information, or otherwise attempting to manage perceptions of intelligence producers and consumers (e.g., policymakers and war fighters).* Those who practice D&D—perhaps a form of asymmetrical warfare—seek to control what intelligence collectors observe and acquire in order to manipulate their perceptions and the content of their products, in an effort to shape the decisions and actions of policymakers and those who can influence them. More specifically:

- *Denial* refers to activities and programs designed to eliminate, impair, degrade, or *neutralize* the effectiveness of intelligence collection within and across any or all collection disciplines, human and technical.
- *Deception* refers to *manipulation* of intelligence collection, analysis, or public opinion by introducing false, misleading, or even true, but tailored, information into intelligence channels with the intent of *influencing* judgments made by intelligence producers, and the consumers of their products.

Effective D&D has the potential to significantly degrade U.S. intelligence capabilities by attacking vulnerabilities in collection and analysis. Such vulnerabilities tend to be costly to the targeted intelligence organization as can be seen in previous U.S. intelligence failures. As shown in chapter 12, of the eight cases of failure examined there, deception was a factor in more than half and denial was a factor in all. That denial is a factor in all these failures suggests that it is not only pervasive but also consequential. Though deception is far less common than denial—it is akin to a silver bullet held in reserve for only the rare but perfect circumstances—its batting average is extraordinarily high, succeeding more than nine times of every ten it is used.[2]

An important historical example of D&D is illustrated in the surprise military attack that Japan conducted against the United States at Pearl Harbor in 1941. The Japanese denial measures successfully concealed the eleven-day transit of a massive naval task force that conducted the attack, killing 2,400 unsuspecting Americans and bringing the United States into World War II. Deception measures were so successful that even Japanese intentions to go to war with the United States were never comprehended by U.S. intelligence, policy, and military officials (see box 8.1).

It is clear from historical cases as well as more recent ones that analysts who underestimate the power of D&D increase their vulnerabilities to its effects, while those who are equipped to understand and counter the techniques that D&D practitioners use will perform better against not only hard targets but any targets no matter their complexity. Successfully countering D&D reduces the probability of getting surprised.

Denial: Foundations for Poor Intelligence

Denial of intelligence collection is a significant impediment to successful analysis. As shown in chapter 12, that denial effectively neutralized collection in major U.S. intelligence failures is one thing. But analysts' failure to understand and correct for successful denial is quite another. In general, analysts need a much better understanding of the impact of intelligence denial on their analysis. Often they may not even be aware that needed information has not been collected, even though it may bear directly on the issue that they are analyzing. When denial measures succeed against the collection disciplines, human and technical, the result is that intelligence sought is intelligence denied. We are thus left with "missing information."

BOX 8.1
Japanese Denial and Deception in the Pearl Harbor Attack

Denial—**intelligence denied through effective operational security:**

- Radio communications between ships in the task force were forbidden beginning on November 10.

- Naval call signs were changed twice between November 1 and December 1 prior to the attacks, slowing any U.S. translations of radio intercepts.

- The northern rendezvous point off Etorufu Island was chosen because it was unlikely to be observed, even by Japanese citizens.

- The military concealed the purchase and attainment of clothing, equipment, and supplies for the rendezvous point and for the northern journey toward Pearl Harbor.

- Dumping of garbage or waste into the water from ships in the task force was forbidden to reduce the likelihood of detection.

- Only top Japanese naval planning officers were aware of the Pearl Harbor plan; military Cabinet secretaries were informed only late in the game, and some Cabinet members were never informed prior to the attack.

- Members of the ships' crews were kept unaware of their destination until after their departure.

- Pilots and crews training for the attack knew nothing of the ultimate purpose of their training.

Deception—**expectations of attack reduced through manipulating information and perceptions:**

- Japan sought to create the illusion that the task force was still in training at Kyushu. The main force in the Inland Sea created massive, deceptive communications to manufacture this ploy. This deception was reinforced by allowing a large number of shore leaves in Tokyo and Yokohama for naval men.

- Japanese military commanders in other theaters such as in Indochina were given false plans for military campaigns other than those actually being planned.

- The Japanese navy issued a war plan on November 5 with full and accurate details of planned attacks on the Philippines and Southeast Asia but omitted any reference to the Pearl Harbor mission whose orders had been communicated verbally.

- The Foreign Office announced that one of its largest ocean liners would sail on December 2 to California and Panama to evacuate Japanese citizens, giving the impression that Japan would not commence hostilities while its liner was at sea.

- The Japanese government and press continued to play up the Japanese–American negotiations prior to the attack.

Sources: Roberta Wohlstetter, *Pearl Harbor: Warning and Decision* (Palo Alto, Calif.: Stanford University Press, 1962), 368–85; and Cynthia Grabo, *Anticipating Surprise: Analysis for Strategic Warning* (Washington, D.C.: Joint Military Intelligence College, Center for Strategic Intelligence Research, 2002), 121–22.

But even when we know that certain missing information is the result of effective denial, the *impact* of that denial on analytical processes and findings is often poorly understood. No one doubts that intelligence findings about any difficult issue (e.g., in terrorism, WMD, or warning) would be different if more and better information had been collected. But the potential impact on analysis of important information that is *not* collected can also distort results. Analytical judgments based on missing information are inherently uncertain; they may also be wrong. Had analysts better identified the impact of missing information on their analysis of Iraqi WMD, a more reliable estimate might have been the result.

Targets of intelligence collection that wish to avert discovery or observation generally have two resources at their disposal: knowledge of their adversary's collection capabilities, and use of countermeasures against the collection activities they aim to degrade such as camouflage against imagery or other direct observation. Good D&D practitioners have countermeasures that work against not only imagery but also human and signals collection efforts. Though much of denial activity is passive, such as practicing good operational security and related nonalerting behavior, and just "staying below the radar," hard targets are notable for their sophisticated denial capabilities, which are not merely passive but also rather actively neutralize intelligence collection methods. Their ability to do this entails an understanding of collection programs that cannot normally be attained at unclassified levels. Sophisticated denial capabilities successfully exploit classified information about collection sources and methods that has been compromised in some way or another, often through spies or through disclosures that may or may not have been authorized. The cumulative effects of many and frequently major disclosures enable D&D practitioners to actively deny U.S. collection efforts.

Effective D&D programs thus require good knowledge of the collection that targets them—it is the bedrock of effective denial. Because all collection disciplines save for open sources are intended to work secretly or clandestinely, their effectiveness depends on the effectiveness of their secrecy. As intelligence is the collection of secret information by secret means, acquiring the target's secrets (e.g., plans for surprise attack) presumes that the most effective collection methods remain a secret.

Secrecy is the opposite of transparency. As an intelligence service's methods become more transparent, its loss of secrecy necessarily impairs its effectiveness. A priority objective of smart intelligence targets is acquiring information that compromises the secrecy of intelligence collection sources and methods. All hard targets conduct priority efforts to learn how to defeat collection. This knowledge can be acquired through both authorized disclosures, such as intelligence sharing or diplomatic demarches, and unauthorized disclosures, such as media leaks that disclose classified information.[3] In particular, media leaks, according to the recent WMD Commission report, "have significantly impaired U.S. intelligence capabilities against the hardest targets."[4] When secret collection capabilities are compromised, analysis is also impaired. Analysts are not only denied information later as a result; they also need to understand the impact of compromises at least as well as the D&D practitioners that defeat transparent collection and thereby degrade analysis.

In general, the effectiveness of denial techniques against collection is often better than it seems. As we come to appreciate the impact of key gaps in our information that result from effective denial, both collectors and analysts need a better understanding about unproductive or unsuccessful collection operations in all disciplines, and why they are not productive. Overcoming key intelligence gaps produced by adversaries' denial activities will require much more effective counterdenial approaches if analysts are to succeed.

Principles of Deception

If denial is the foundation of D&D, then deception is the silver bullet that almost never misses. Dodging the bullet requires an understanding of how deception works. Based on a comprehensive review of the literature on deception, including a large number of historical cases, Bennett and Waltz have described four fundamental principles of deception.[5] These principles can be used as a framework for understanding the deception process by examining the relationship between the deceiver and the target of the deception and why deception is almost always successful. The four principles are:

- *Truth*—all deception works with the context of what is true.
- *Denial*—denying the target access to select aspects of the truth is the prerequisite to all deception.
- *Deceit*—all deception requires and utilizes deceit.
- *Misdirection*—deception depends on manipulating what the target registers.

It might seem odd that *truth* should be a principle of deception. But if deception is to work at all, there must be a foundation of accepted perceptions and beliefs about the world that can be exploited. This first principle is based on the study of deception in nature (e.g., with plants and animals) and the observation that the appearance or actions of one organism are commonly associated with a particular response by another organism.[6] Such systems make deception possible because the deceiver's victim expects a signal to have a reliably expected result. In D&D, the selective use of the truth—supplying the target with real data—establishes the credibility of those channels of communication on which the target depends, such as particular collection disciplines and information collected by them.

Denial, on the other hand, makes deception possible by creating the opportunities the deceiver needs to manipulate the target's perceptions. Denial conceals select aspects of what is true, such as the deceiver's real intentions and capabilities, and denial used alone can have serious consequences even when intentional deception is not a factor. Thus, as the Pearl Harbor example illustrates, denial is also the foundation on which deception is carried out.

Together, truth and denial set the stage for deception methods associated with *deceit*, the most obvious deception principle. Whaley calls deceit in the form of disinformation the "most important single broad category of ruses."[7] Without deliberate deceit, the target is only the victim of misperceptions due to misinformation and/or self-deception, not deception. But when these first three principles are integrated, they allow the deceiver to present the deception target with what appears to be highly desirable, genuine data while reducing or eliminating the real signals that the target needs to form accurate perceptions of the situation. The end result is that the target must rely on data that has been deliberately fashioned so as to manipulate his perceptions to the deceiver's benefit.

With a few notable exceptions, the strategic deception literature generally does not recognize the fourth principle, *misdirection*, as a distinct concept, although numerous authors consider it to be the very foundation of magic.[8] In magic, misdirection diverts the audience's attention toward the magic effect and away from the method that produces it. Likewise, the history of deception is filled with examples where the deceiver either deliberately redirects the target's attention or exploits environmental factors that have the same effect. For example, a feint is perceived as a *real* attack (the truth principle), not a false one; it is used to redirect the adversary's attention away from where the real attack will occur.

Used in concert, these four principles are exercised by the deceiver in such a way as to control what the target of the deception observes, and, as a result, what the target registers and thus what the target perceives. When deception succeeds, it causes the target to act to the deceiver's advantage and to his own disadvantage.

Bias Traps and Analytical Vulnerabilities

The deception principles described above illustrate how deceivers exploit very basic human vulnerabilities at several levels. These vulnerabilities can be attributed to biases—systematic errors in perception, judgment, and reasoning—that fall into three major categories: cultural and personal biases, organizational biases, and cognitive biases.[9]

Cultural and personal biases are the result of interpreting and judging phenomena in terms of the preconceptions and beliefs that are formed by the individual's personal experiences. These are further influenced by the knowledge, beliefs, customs, morals, habits, and cognitive styles that the individual acquires as a member of his or her specific social environment, that is, culture. The preconceptions and beliefs that result can be extremely resistant to change, even in the face of large amounts of discrepant information, and they can thus be exploited by deception planners. Such biases also affect the way analysts interpret events. Cultural biases can also influence how people go about solving problems and analyzing situations, and analytical flaws such as mirror imaging may be the result. Likewise, such personal traits as overconfidence (hubris) can facilitate being deceived. As Godson and Wirtz point out, the successful deceiver "must recognize the target's perceptual context to know what (false) pictures of the world will appear plausible."[10]

Organizational biases are similar to cultural biases and are generally associated with the limitations and weaknesses of large bureaucratic organizations.

These biases are the result of the goals, mores, policies, and traditions that characterize the specific organization in which the individual works, and often appear in the form of barriers to the flow of information within and between organizations. An even more insidious bias appears in the manner in which the very nature of the information about a specific topic changes as it winds up flowing through different channels. Such differences in information across linked organizations such as in the intelligence community are even more extreme when classified information is involved. Barriers to information flows and differences in perception due to the uneven distribution of compartmented information, as shown above, contributed heavily to the United States' failure to anticipate the Japanese attack on Pearl Harbor. Such barriers and differences in perception also played a role in the failure to anticipate the terrorist attacks on September 11, 2001.[11]

Two prominent organizational biases in intelligence agencies are the search for consensus and time pressures. As we have learned in discovering the rationale for Alternative (or "structured") Analysis, if consensus becomes a goal in and of itself, it may deprive decision makers of important information about the basis for the analytical judgments presented, as well as the existence and grounds of alternative views. A second bias, time pressure, is inherent in fast-paced analysis, particularly current intelligence. Analysts have always been under pressure to provide timely intelligence. But the post–September 11 threat environment and congressional pressure for a quick answer, as we saw with Iraqi WMD, may exert added pressure on analysts to make judgments in less and less time. Like the pressure for consensus, time pressures also exacerbate the cognitive biases that increase susceptibility to deception.

Cognitive heuristics represent a wide variety of adaptation mechanisms that help humans to accurately perceive and understand the world around them on a day-to-day basis. They usually help us by reducing the complexity of difficult problems (e.g., assessing probabilities); however, these same processes also make us vulnerable to optical illusions, magician's tricks, con artists, and, of special interest to us, military and political deception. It is impossible to survey the range of cognitive biases that are relevant to denial and deception here.[12] Fortunately, Gilovich provides an excellent framework that is useful for capturing the role these heuristics and biases play in deception. He summarizes much of the social and cognitive psychology research into what he calls *determinants of questionable and erroneous beliefs* and organizes them into categories, three of which are especially relevant to D&D:[13]

- *Too much from too little*—the tendency to form judgments from incomplete or unrepresentative information and to be overconfident about those judgments.
- *Seeing what we expect to see*—the tendency for our expectations, preconceptions, and prior beliefs to influence the interpretation of new information in a way to support our beliefs.
- *Believing what we are told*—the tendency for a good story to seem credible and to bias one's beliefs.

Together, the four principles of deception and Gilovich's determinants of questionable beliefs provide a framework for understanding analysts' vulnerabilities as they apply to D&D. They show how a deceiver can exploit each of the deception principles to gain advantage. For example, from the deception planner's perspective, revealing some truth to the target provides several advantages. In the case of *too much from too little*, selective truth can convince a target of deception, for example, that something exists when it does not. The Allies took advantage of this in World War II when feeding information to the Germans in order to create the false order of battle for FUSAG and other elements of the Fortitude deception plan.[14] The *too much from too little* bias sets the analyst up to misinterpret limited information. Providing truthful information also allows the deceiver to exploit the *believing what we are told* determinant. By incorporating real events, people, organizations, equipment, and information into the deception story, the deceiver can increase the story's immediacy and plausibility, thus making it more believable. This also acts to increase the target's confidence in his sources of information, and it is that confidence in those channels that is critical to the success of deception. The deceiver will use those same channels later, such as a controlled source believed by the target to be reliable to pass false information in order to build up the deception story (the principle of deceit).

Denial has its greatest impact through the *seeing what we expect to see* set of biases. Research studies and real-world events have repeatedly demonstrated that individuals consistently fail to appreciate the limits of the data and information available to them.[15] What is unknown, what is out of sight, is out of mind. Effective denial techniques mean that what little information is available, no matter how ambiguous, may be eagerly grasped and fit to existing expectations and preconceptions. Denial, therefore, is the key to making sure that nothing significant occurs to change the target's mind once the deception plan is put into motion.

Deceit is probably the first thing one thinks of with regard to the relationship between deception and *believing what we are told*. After all, it is deceit in the form of double agents, deception operations like Mincemeat, security "leaks," and exotic camouflage techniques that give deception its historical importance.[16] Analysts and decision makers depend heavily on secondhand information, and this dependence makes them vulnerable to serious biases and errors, especially if those sources are providing false or inaccurate information. More important, deceit exploits the *seeing what we expect to see* bias when analysts readily accept disinformation and fit it to their existing expectations and preconceptions.

Misdirection can be of two general types.[17] One involves physical misdirection, such as a deliberate effort to control the observer's attention. The other is psychological; here the deceiver (e.g., a magician) misdirects the target by attempting to control his or her suspicions. In D&D, real or false objects, phenomena, events, and information are used to achieve either type of misdirection. Movement is a powerful misdirection technique that magicians use to quickly capture the audience's attention. It can have the same effect in deception operations. For example, in World War II, the Allies always made sure to pass information to the Germans about the movement of real and fictional units (i.e., truth and deceit) related to the FUSAG deception to distract their attention from the real buildup in southwest England.

Principles of Counterdeception

To succeed against smart adversaries for whom denial and deception comprise key weapons in their security arsenals, intelligence analysts must master counter-D&D understanding and skills, learn to assess the impact of missing information on their analytical judgments, develop significant expertise in the collection disciplines, and adjust for unwarranted dependency on inadequate information. These imperatives find their practical justification in the experience of poor intelligence community performance against foreign D&D, and their theoretical justification in sound counterdeception principles.

Bennett and Waltz's review of the deception literature produced not only fundamental deception principles but also yielded four *counter*deception principles, all of which point to the analyst's level of knowledge and understanding:

- Know yourself.
- Know your adversary.
- Know your situation.
- Know your channels.

Understanding and acting on these principles is prerequisite to an analytical posture to reduce vulnerability to D&D and mitigate its effects when it succeeds.

Sun Tzu makes it clear that you must know yourself if you wish to have any reasonable hope of success in battle.[18] The same is true for the battle waged between deceiver and target. Whaley has demonstrated how deception can be particularly successful when it exploits the target's expectations and preconceptions (the *seeing what we expect to see* bias). Drawing from the work of Heuer and the cognitive heuristics literature together leads to the first fundamental principle of counterdeception: *Know yourself*. Put succinctly, this principle stresses that the analyst's first defense against D&D is a sound understanding of his or her cognitive vulnerabilities as discussed above.

The *know your adversary* principle should be a constant reminder to analysts and decision makers to consider the means, motives, and culture of their adversary. The means that the adversary has at his or her disposal include doctrine, training, personnel, experience, and technology for concealing or exaggerating intentions, capabilities, and activities. Historically, motives have generally ranged from achieving surprise, bluffing, deterrence, seeking prestige or influence, blackmail, or seeking concessions from the target. Today, specific D&D motives include concealing WMD capabilities and transactions, and planning terrorist attacks. This principle also stresses the need to develop the depth of knowledge of the adversary that makes it possible to begin breaking down ethnocentric biases and come to see things from the adversary's perspective. As Dewar noted, being able to put yourself into the mind of the adversary may be the counterdeception analyst's most effective weapon.[19]

Analysts throughout the intelligence community require a much better under-standing of adversarial D&D capabilities than they routinely exhibit. If they do not understand an adversary's D&D capabilities, they cannot be expected to understand how effective—or how hobbled—their nation's intelligence will be when working against that adversary. Analysts who are assigned a specific coun-try or nonstate actor account should make it their first priority to learn all they can about the D&D capabilities that their assigned target can mount against the specific collection disciplines that produce intelligence on that target.

The third principle, *know your situation*, focuses on the necessity for continu-ally evaluating the environment for cues that indicate that deception should be considered as the adversary is formulating strategies, considering options, mak-ing decisions, or taking action. An important thing to keep in mind is that ana-lysts are confronted by a continuum of deceptive activity and that most of it, like an adversary's routine operational security measures (denial), is normal and likely to occur no matter what the situation is. Because large-scale, sophisticated deception operations are rare, situational factors may offer important cues to the possibility that the adversary is planning or employing more sophisticated deception operations. These situational factors include:

- high-stakes situations;
- asymmetric power relationships between the participants;
- changes in leadership, motives, political goals, military doctrine, or techno-logical capabilities;
- situations involving potential surprise and risk as high-risk/high-gain strategy; and
- events in the international environment that threaten security or provide opportunity.

The fourth counterdeception principle, *know your channels*, is the conscien-tious application of this everyday maxim to the channels of information used by intelligence analysts and policymakers. For the analyst, it means above all else a sound understanding of the collection disciplines—their capabilities and their limitations, and especially their vulnerabilities to denial and deception. In addi-tion, it is critical to understand the extent to which those collection capabilities are known to have been compromised and are thus vulnerable to exploitation by an adversary. An in-depth understanding of collection channels and what the intelligence target knows about them is a vital requirement for effective analysis, particularly against hard targets.

Analysts, as illustrated in chapter 12, require a far better understanding of their *dependency on intelligence collection* than they often demonstrate. Briefly, when collection succeeds, it significantly improves the probability that analysis will also succeed. When collection fails—as it did against al-Qaeda before Sep-tember 11, 2001, and against Iraqi WMD before Operation Iraqi Freedom—it greatly improves the probability that analysis will also fail. Analysts who do not fully understand the broad range of intelligence collection *capabilities* as well as collection *limitations*, nor their enormous dependency on having this special expertise, significantly increase their vulnerabilities to D&D.[20]

Analysts also require a far better understanding of their *dependency on only one or a few key pieces of information.* Sometimes the whole analysis of a complex problem may crumble if a key piece of evidence is removed. If that key datum is unreliable, fabricated, or tenuous—and the analysts are not fully cognizant of its tenuousness or of its potentially exaggerated impact on the analysis—their analysis is likely to be wrong. Their certainty or confidence will also be misplaced. Errors in analysis can sometimes be traced to exaggerated dependence on poor evidence.[21] Just as D&D is a major cause of missing evidence, it is also a potential source of poor or deceptive evidence.

Finally, as we know all too painfully from the pernicious effects of the source "Curveball" on the faulty judgments about Iraq's biological weapons capabilities in 2002, sources of intelligence information require better vetting than ever before. Curveball's impact on the faulty biological weapons analysis in the 2002 WMD National Intelligence Estimate dramatically illustrates the dependency vulnerability discussed just above. The need to apply more rigorous scrutiny to both human *and* technical sourcing is a key requirement for better intelligence adaptability to D&D. Of course, no intelligence service ever takes information at face value from any source. But sophisticated D&D techniques can be subtle and insidious, and reliable intelligence requires even better *counter-*D&D techniques in the vetting of intelligence collection.[22]

Vulnerable Minds and Vulnerable Organizations

Even the most competent analysts and decision makers have found themselves deceived. To make matters worse, they may find themselves accused of incompetence by those blessed with 20/20 hindsight. To say that we are vulnerable to deception is by no means pejorative, because the concept of vulnerability helps to distinguish the important ways that humans and organizations are open to attack or damage by deception. Therefore, understanding our vulnerabilities to deception can act as a guide to actions we can take to mitigate those vulnerabilities.

Such understanding starts by considering the profiles of the vulnerable mind and the vulnerable organization.[23] The *vulnerable mind*—the one least prepared to counter D&D—sees reality unwittingly shaped by its own biases, preconceptions, and expectations. It exaggerates the importance of limited information, and the information it expects to see. It is unduly gullible or influenced by a good story. It tends to be overconfident in understanding complexity. And it lacks accurate, in-depth knowledge of its adversary, including especially the D&D capabilities that adversary may wield. These vulnerabilities represent the end result when the biases discussed earlier meet ambiguous, contradictory, or missing information. This is a formula for successful D&D.

Similarly, the *vulnerable organization* overemphasizes consensus, consistency, and being decisive. It fails to exploit its full collaborative potential, performing with less than the sum of its parts. It has inadequate learning processes and fails to learn from past performance, including its failures, which it tends to repeat.

And it is preoccupied with the present at the expense of the historical or strategic and future perspectives.

With these vulnerabilities as a starting point, we can develop a set of counter-deception analytical imperatives for transforming vulnerable minds and vulnerable organizations into prepared minds and prepared organizations.

The Prepared Mind

Our desired goal is to deliver better, more accurate judgments that will enable the negating or at least mitigation of the effects of denial and deception. The first broad strategy for achieving the goal of reducing the mind's vulnerability to D&D is to improve the analytical process. The *know yourself, know your adversary*, and *know your situation* principles highlight the importance of two interdependent approaches: mitigating cognitive biases, and adopting systematic or "structured" methodologies.[24]

The *know yourself* principle emphasizes continuous awareness of the vulnerable mind's most exploitable weakness: its own preconceptions, expectations, and beliefs. Mitigating cognitive biases is vital to improving analysis; a key corrective technique is the use of the hypothesis. The failure of analysts to generate alternative hypotheses is insufficiently recognized in the intelligence community. This failure can be attributed to the use of a suboptimal heuristic of choosing the first explanation that seems to be the closest fit to the evidence at hand ("satisficing" and jumping to conclusions). A major contribution of Alternative Analysis is that it shows the value of multiple hypotheses.

Just as the failure to generate hypotheses increases vulnerability to deception, so also do confirmation bias and overconfidence. A particularly helpful approach to mitigating confirmation bias and overconfidence is to *restructure the analytical task*. This is aimed at challenging the mindsets that induce confirmation bias and exaggerate confidence. Several methods of restructuring the analytical task can reduce analytical susceptibility to this kind of error. For example:

- Asking analysts to list reasons why their answers to questions might be wrong.
- Instructing analysts to consider the opposite interpretation of a judgment or forecast, or to engage in *any* second explanation task (e.g., explaining a different version of the same outcome).
- Encouraging analysts to generate multiple alternatives or even to better explain a single plausible alternative.
- Asking analysts to "test for fixation," namely, to consider what evidence would be required to convince him or her that the interpretation is wrong, or what evidence could cause the analyst to change his mind or to give up his opinion.[25]
- Asking analysts to assess how far they have "bent the map," that is, monitoring any inconsistencies and discrepancies that have been explained away

(bending the map), which might indicate that other possibilities are being ignored.[26]
- Having analysts monitor "tripwires," events that should not be occurring or levels that should not be exceeded if the favored hypothesis is correct. Finding that too many tripwires are tripped could be an indication that the favored hypothesis is wrong.[27]

The *know yourself* principle emphasizes recognizing the assumptions, preconceptions, and expectations that influence analyst beliefs, while the *know your situation* principle focuses on continually evaluating the environment for the cues that deception may be a factor in the situation under consideration. The use of structured analytical methodologies or "challenge" analysis also provides another way of restructuring problems so that assumptions, preconceptions, and mental models—that is, factors shaping mindsets—are not hidden by making them more explicit so that they can be examined and tested. In particular, such structured methodologies include Analysis of Competing Hypotheses (ACH), argument mapping, and signpost analysis; "challenge analysis" techniques include Devil's Advocacy, What-If Analysis, and High-Impact/Low-Probability Analysis.[28] Using such methodologies can reduce the likelihood that important biases or situational cues are not recognized or ignored.

A prepared mind will make a conscientious effort to see the problem or situation from the adversary's point of view. It will continually test and retest its judgments, update and evaluate all the evidence at hand, and remain alert to cues and anomalies in the environment that something has changed or is missing. It will not ignore its intuition when something does not quite feel right about a complex analytical situation. And it will diligently update and evaluate the credibility of information sources, stay alert to any channels that may have been compromised, and revisit the issue of source vetting and validation.

The Prepared Organization

To conclude, we want to emphasize four things that an intelligence organization can do to facilitate better counter-D&D analysis and to make itself less vulnerable to denial and deception:

- Prioritize an effective counter-D&D analytical capability and ensure that it is well resourced, incentivized, and protected.
- Enable analysts to better collaborate, access, and share sensitive information, and exchange alternative and/or dissenting views.
- Create and encourage a robust analytical learning environment that emphasizes Lessons Learned and structured analytical techniques.
- Emphasize anomaly detection to help ensure that little surprises do not become big surprises.

The prepared organization will be well armed with robust counter-D&D analytical capabilities. Such capabilities can be gauged largely by the strength of the organization's counter-D&D analysis components (or even whether there is one), the quality and stature of the analysts who staff them, the skills of fellow D&D analysts in the hard-target components, and the measure of the training resources that directly support the counter-D&D mission. Though the U.S. IC has seen wide variation in these capabilities in previous decades, they have been perennially short of critical mass.[29]

A positive step toward creating an intelligence community of prepared organizations is the recent effort of the director of national intelligence to create a "culture of collaboration" that emphasizes greater intelligence sharing among analysts.[30] Greater counter-D&D collaboration must also encourage championing alternative views. A more collaborative and sharing environment must continually challenge and update analysts' expectations, mental models, and situational awareness.

Prepared organizations are also learning organizations. For countering D&D, two types of learning are especially required. First, active learning programs that capture and share "lessons learned" to help analysts learn from past performance; these activities should address both previous events and more current issues.[31] The prepared organization will also resist pressures of day-to-day distractions and devote time to learning from unexpected events, knowing that if it fails to do so, it will remain vulnerable to later unexpected events. Another important type of learning will provide analysts practice in situations involving D&D before they encounter it. Both types require more robust intelligence community training programs than are now in place.

Finally, reducing vulnerability to D&D surprises requires paying attention to anomalies, or what Barton Whaley calls "incongruities." Whaley's rule for this is that "when enough evidence is reconsidered in one brief time—in the forefront of the analyst's memory—incongruities, if present, tend to become obvious."[32] Where D&D is concerned, the intelligence community's goal is the same as that in the highly reliable organizations studied by Weick and Sutcliffe, that is, to deal with the small surprises before they become big ones.[33] Analysts should always recall what Cynthia Grabo has taught us about warning failures: "*While not all anomalies lead to crises, all crises are made up of anomalies.*"[34]

In sum, foreign denial and deception pose major threats to successful intelligence analysis. The best counters to the D&D analytical threat begin with an understanding of the principles of deception (truth, denial, deceit, and misdirection), and require a keen awareness of bias traps and cognitive vulnerabilities to being deceived. By knowing yourself, your adversary, your situation, and your channels, you can greatly reduce your susceptibility to D&D-induced faulty analysis. In particular, the prepared mind and the prepared organization together present the best possible assurances of intelligence analysis uncorrupted by foreign denial and deception.

Notes

1. This chapter draws heavily from James B. Bruce, "Denial and Deception in the 21st Century: Adaptation Implications for Western Intelligence," *Defense Intelligence Journal* 15,

no. 2 (2006): 13–27; and Michael Bennett and Edward Waltz, *Counterdeception Principles and Applications for National Security* (Boston: Artech House, 2007).

2. This is based on calculations made by Richards Heuer using two databases starting in 1914 complied by Barton Whaley. One database ($N = 68$) ended in 1968; the other ($N = 93$) in 1972. Both showed a deception success correlation of slightly higher than 0.9. Donald C. F. Daniel, "Denial and Deception," in *Transforming U.S. Intelligence*, ed. Jennifer E. Sims and Burton Gerber (Washington, D.C.: Georgetown University Press, 2005), 138.

3. Commission on the Intelligence Capabilities of the United States Regarding Weapons of Mass Destruction, *Report to the President of the United States, March 31, 2005* (Washington, D.C.: U.S. Government Printing Office, 2005) (hereafter, *WMD Commission Report*), 381.

4. Ibid. See also James B. Bruce, "How Leaks of Classified Intelligence Help U.S. Adversaries: Implications for Laws and Secrecy," in *Intelligence and the National Security Strategist*, ed. Roger Z. George and Robert D. Kline (Lanham, Md.: Rowman & Littlefield, 2006), 399–414.

5. Bennett and Waltz, *Counterdeception Principles and Applications*, 58–66.

6. R. W. Mitchell, "Epilogue," in *Deception Perspectives on Human and Nonhuman Deceit*, ed. R. W. Mitchell and N. S. Thompson (Albany: State University of New York Press, 1986), 358.

7. Barton Whaley, *Strategem: Deception and Surprise in War* (Boston: Artech House, 2007), 17.

8. See J. Lierpoll, Misdirection Resource Center, www.lierpoll.com/misdirection/misdirection.htm.

9. Bennett and Waltz, *Counterdeception Principles and Applications*, 71–88. Richards Heuer pioneered the early work on cognitive bias and how it increases vulnerabilities to deception. See Richards Heuer, *Psychology of Intelligence* (Washington, D.C.: Center for the Study of Intelligence, Central Intelligence Agency, 1999); and chapter 10 in this volume.

10. Roy Godson and James J. Wirtz, "Strategic Denial and Deception," in *Strategic Denial and Deception: The Twenty-First Century Challenge*, ed. Roy Godson and James J. Wirtz (New Brunswick, N.J.: Transaction, 2002), 3.

11. *The 9/11 Commission Report*, authorized ed. (New York: W. W. Norton, 2003), 416–18.

12. For further reading on cognitive biases and deception, see Bennett and Waltz, *Counterdeception Principles and Applications*, chap. 3; and Richards J. Heuer, "Strategic Deception and Counterdeception: A Cognitive Process Approach," *International Studies Quarterly* 25, no. 2 (June 1981). For more on cognitive heuristics and biases, see Daniel Kahneman, Paul Slovic, and Amos Tversky, *Judgment under Uncertainty: Heuristics and Biases* (Cambridge: Cambridge University Press, 1982).

13. T. Gilovich, *How We Know What Isn't So: The Fallibility of Human Reason in Everyday Life* (New York: Free Press, 1991).

14. "FUSAG" refers to General George Patton's First U.S. Army Group, the notional army unit in southern England preparing for the Allied invasion of Pas de Calais—in reality, the deception setting up the Germans for the invasion of Normandy. R. Hesketh, *Fortitude: The D-Day Deception Campaign* (New York: Overlook Press, 2000), 193.

15. Gilovich, *How We Know What Isn't So*, provides a good overview of such research.

16. During World War II, Operation Mincemeat successfully deceived the Germans that Greece and Sardinia were the Allies' next invasion target instead of the island of Sicily, the real target. See Ewen Montagu, *The Man Who Never Was* (New York: Oxford University Press, 1996).

17. P. Lamont and R. Wiseman, *Magic in Theory* (Hatfield: University of Hertfordshire Press, 1999), 36–52.

18. Sun Tzu, *The Art of War*, trans. S. B. Griffith (New York: Oxford University Press, 1963), 84. See also Jennifer E. Sims, "Understanding Ourselves," in *Transforming U.S. Intelligence*, ed. Sims and Gerber, 32–59.

19. M. Dewar, *The Art of Deception in Warfare* (Newton Abbot, U.K.: David & Charles, 1989), 194–203.

20. *WMD Commission Report*, 409–10.

21. Heuer, *Psychology of Intelligence Analysis*, 105–6. Also see the discussion of the Iraq WMD National Intelligence Estimate in chapters 11 and 12.

22. See *WMD Commission Report*, 158–61, 367–72.

23. Bennett and Waltz, *Counterdeception Principles and Applications*, 186–93.

24. Ibid., 200. See also chapters 16 and 17 by Richards Heuer and Tim Smith, respectively.

25. G. Klein, *The Power of Intuition* (New York: Currency Doubleday, 2004), 147–48.

26. Ibid.

27. Ibid.

28. See Davis, chapter 10 in this volume. ACH is discussed by Heuer in chapter 16.

29. James Bruce, "Foreword" to Bennett and Waltz, *Counterdeception Principles and Applications*, ix.

30. Office of the Director of National Intelligence, *United States Intelligence Community, 100-Day Plan for Integration and Collaboration*, 2007, www.dni.gov/100-day-plan/100-day-plan.pdf. See also chapters 15 and 17 in this volume, and CIA, *Strategic Intent: 2007–2011*, available at www.cia.gov.

31. S. Robbins, "Organizational Learning Is No Accident," *Working Knowledge for Business Leaders Newsletter*, Harvard Business School, 2005, http://hbswk.hbs.edu/item.jhtml? id = 3483&t = srobbins.

32. Barton Whaley, "Meinertzhagen's Havesack Exposed: The Consequences for Counterdeception Analysis," unpublished manuscript, 2007.

33. K. E. Weick and K. M Sutcliff, *Managing the Unexpected: Assuring High Performance in an Age of Complexity* (San Francisco: Jossey-Bass, 2001).

34. Cynthia Grabo, *Anticipating Surprise: Analysis for Strategic Warning* (Washington, D.C.: Joint Military Intelligence College, Center for Strategic Intelligence Research, 2002), 31; emphasis in the original.

CHAPTER 9

U.S. Military Intelligence Analysis: Old and New Challenges

DAVID THOMAS

> Moses sent them to spy out the land of Canaan, and said to them: "Go up into the Negev yonder, and go up into the hill country, and see what the land is, and whether the people who dwell in it are strong or weak, whether they are few or many, and whether the land they dwell in is good or bad, and whether the cities that they dwell in are camps or strongholds, and whether the land is rich or poor."
>
> —Numbers 13:17

> Many intelligence reports in war are contradictory; even more are false, and most are uncertain. . . . In short, most intelligence is false.
>
> —Carl von Clausewitz, *On War*, 1873

MILITARY INTELLIGENCE ANALYSIS is as old as warfare itself. From Julius Caesar, Count Belisarius, Salah al-Din, and Ch'i Chi-kuang to the Duke of Wellington, Napoleon Bonaparte, George Washington, and Graf von Moltke, the great commanders originally conducted their own analysis of intelligence obtained from captured documents, prisoners of war, reconnaissance scouts, and spies in order to plan and conduct their campaigns.[1] Military analysis by permanent staffs became a regular activity in the armies of the major European powers in the late nineteenth century.[2] In the case of U.S. military intelligence, the subject of this chapter, analysis did not become a standing function until after World War I, notwithstanding the establishment of the Office of Naval Intelligence (ONI) in 1882, and the War Department Military Intelligence Division (MID) in 1885. Between World War I and World War II, U.S. Army and Navy attaches conducted most of the analysis of German, Japanese, and Soviet strategy, doctrine, tactics, weapon systems, and military capabilities for the MID and ONI.[3]

World War II necessitated the creation of a large, permanent, and powerful U.S. military intelligence structure, including new military intelligence organizations. This structure produced an enormous range of general military, signals, counterintelligence, and scientific and technical intelligence analysis—for the first time in U.S. military history—and became the foundation for the military intelligence community in the cold war. As the result of the 1950–53 Korean Conflict, the Department of Defense (DoD) and the Armed Forces increased the size of the military intelligence community in order to assess Soviet strategic nuclear forces and conventional military capabilities, support strategic and theater nuclear targeting, and provide intelligence threat data on foreign military systems and technologies to U.S. weapons development programs.

In the twenty-first century, the military analysis produced by the Defense Intelligence Components within DoD is an integral element of U.S. military strategy, war planning, weapons development, and joint warfare operations.[4] As often reported, these many organizations now absorb more than 80 percent of the U.S. intelligence community's combined annual spending. As defined in DoD directives, "Defense Intelligence" refers to the integrated departmental intelligence that covers national policy and national security, as well as the intelligence relating to capabilities, intentions, and activities of foreign powers, organizations, or persons, including any foreign military or military-related situation or activity, which is significant to defense policymaking or the planning and conduct of military operations. "Defense Intelligence" includes strategic, operational, and tactical intelligence.[5]

Old and New Challenges

The fundamental challenges to military analysis have not changed since Moses commanded the Israelites to spy on the land of Canaan. They are: Who is the enemy, where is the enemy, and what is the enemy doing at this moment? The advent of permanent military intelligence services and of advanced technical intelligence, surveillance, and reconnaissance systems has aided military intelligence in meeting these basic tasks. These developments also have invalidated, to a large degree, Clausewitz's obiter dictum, that most intelligence in war is false.[6]

The Perennials

Military analysis faces many enduring challenges resulting more from internal factors than from foreign actions. Since World War II, the historical record affirms that personality issues, bureaucratic obstacles, inexperienced analysts, ineffective organizational structures, and leadership misjudgment or incompetence account for most of the warning failures, mis-estimates of enemy strategy and military doctrine, and untimely discoveries of major weapons programs attributable to U.S. military intelligence. These will not be unfamiliar to readers of chapter 10 by Jack Davis, for they afflict analysts wherever and for whomever they work.

Arguably, these obstacles have done as much to debilitate U.S. military analysis as any collection shortfalls or foreign concealment and deception programs, which are directly addressed in chapters 11 and 12 on analyst–collection and deception and denial problems by James Bruce.

Suffice it to say, these challenges are mainly the result of processes or predilections that the United States has created:

- The inattention, inexperience, and obduracy of individual military commanders and political leaders, which can cause them to ignore accurate military intelligence about enemy intentions or capabilities.
- The inflexible, ponderous, and shortsighted bureaucratic behavior of hierarchical military organizations that can impede creative, forward-leaning military analysis and prevent proper dissemination of controversial assessments.
- The predisposition of some civilian decision makers and intelligence officers to ignore or disparage the competence of military intelligence officers and the validity of their judgments.

The Newly Emerging

In the twenty-first century, military intelligence analysis also faces new challenges. These came to the fore during the 1990s. However, their ramifications for DoD, the Armed Forces, and the military intelligence community did not become fully apparent until this century. These challenges are:

- The multipolar world created by the end of the cold war, the rise of China as a global power, the advent of well-armed regional military powers and dangerous nonstate actors, and the proliferation of weapons of mass destruction.
- The difficulty of acquiring, integrating, and using new information technologies to process, analyze, store, retrieve, and disseminate the increasing quantity of technical and open source data needed for servicing the intelligence and operational support requirements created by the additional missions entrusted to DoD and the Armed Forces from the end of the cold war to the present.
- The increasing technological complexity and speed of weapon systems, planning cycles, and military operations, and the demands that they place on military intelligence for real time fusion, analysis, and dissemination of raw data and finished reports to support the U.S. form of joint warfare and operations.
- The expansion of the primary DoD and Armed Forces cold war missions (conventional war and strategic nuclear deterrence) to include counterinsurgency, counterproliferation, counterterrorism, drug interdiction, information operations, maritime interdiction and security, space operations, and peacekeeping missions in coordination with the United Nations.
- The organizational inefficiency and diminished analytical capability within the defense intelligence agencies and service intelligence organizations resulting from repeated internal reorganizations, excessive focus on current intelligence, and the continuing attrition of experienced uniformed and civilian intelligence personnel.

What Is Military Analysis?

Assessing the old and new challenges to military intelligence analysis is difficult without at least a basic understanding of this analysis. That is not as easily accomplished as might be expected, because military intelligence and military analysis are largely neglected subjects in the U.S. intelligence literature and huge misconceptions abound regarding military intelligence. These misconceptions exist despite the size of the military intelligence community; the numerous Joint Chiefs of Staff publications on military intelligence roles, missions, priorities, and techniques; and the 2005 DoD directive that placed the defense intelligence agencies under the authority, direction, and control of a new undersecretary of defense for intelligence, and thus outside the authority of the Office of the Director of National Intelligence (ODNI).[7] The silent status of the huge military intelligence community, a nonexistent definition of military analysis, an early misconception of what it was, and relative disinterest on the part of nonmilitary intelligence officers in the subject all conspire to keep this topic poorly understood.

First, the "silent" status of military intelligence analysis is partly attributable to the paucity of intelligence community, government, and academic publications about modern U.S. military intelligence.[8] Most of the literature on intelligence analysis focuses on issues related to providing intelligence to policymakers.[9] Only two cold war–era books, *The Military Intelligence Community* (1986) and *The CIA and the U.S. Intelligence System* (1986), contain extensive discussions of military analysis.[10] True, the bibliography on military intelligence is substantial and includes books and articles on military intelligence written by former military intelligence officers.[11] Nevertheless, most of the writings on military intelligence discuss historical intelligence operations, signals intelligence, surprise attacks, and counterintelligence activities, rather than assess cognitive, epistemological, and methodological issues in modern military analysis.[12]

To compound the absence of informed writing and commentary on military analysis, recent DoD and U.S. Armed Forces official histories and publications on military operations and military intelligence do not treat analysis in any detail. For instance, the 1998 official history of Army intelligence pays almost no attention to military analysis and estimates.[13] No official history exists of U.S. military intelligence and military analysis comparable to the magisterial four-volume British publication *British Intelligence in the Second World War.*[14]

The National Defense Intelligence College (NDIC), formerly the Joint Military Intelligence College, is the primary defense intelligence organization engaged in academic research and writing on military analysis issues. The NDIC publishes an unclassified journal, *Defense Intelligence*, and open source monographs and books on military intelligence and related analytical issues. The NDIC is making a vital contribution to improving military intelligence and analysis through its academic programs and publications. Nevertheless, it has not yet produced a comprehensive study or instructional monograph that defines and discusses military analysis as a discrete element of military intelligence.[15]

In contrast, there is a superabundance of intelligence community monographs, U.S. government commission studies, congressional reports, memoirs of Central Intelligence Agency (CIA) officials, and scholarly publications about the performance of the CIA and improving analysis for policymakers. These materials focus mainly on current and estimative policy intelligence produced by the CIA, the State Department, and, now, the ODNI. Of the numerous books on U.S. intelligence published since 2000, *Fixing Intelligence for a More Secure*

America (2003), written by a retired military intelligence officer, William Odom, is the only accurate and comprehensive assessment of post–cold war military intelligence organizational and analytical issues.[16]

Second, discussing military intelligence analysis and the challenges confronting it also is complicated by the current lack of intelligence community definitions of "military intelligence" and "military analysis." A standard CIA publication, *A Consumer's Guide to Intelligence* (1996), does not register military intelligence among the five categories of finished intelligence. Furthermore, the glossary of official terms in this guide omits "military intelligence" and "military analysis." Even Joint Chiefs of Staff military publications fail to define military analysis; they define "general military intelligence"[17] and "scientific and technical intelligence,"[18] but not "military analysis" or "military intelligence analysis."[19] In this circumstance, the tendency of U.S. intelligence literature to ignore military analysis is understandable.

Third, the early and misguided view of Sherman Kent, the former head of the Office of National Estimates, that military intelligence is static in nature and tactical in orientation, continues to influence the views of CIA and State Department analysts and academic students of U.S. intelligence.[20] Kent inaccurately saw the scope and role of military intelligence based on his brief and narrow experience in the Office of Strategic Services (OSS) during World War II. However, this experience could not have acquainted him with the total spectrum of U.S. and joint U.S. and British military intelligence analysis.

For example, the War Department, the Joint Chiefs of Staff, and Armed Forces refused to give the OSS analytical elements access to the most important U.S. and British military intelligence data and reporting—specifically, the strategic diplomatic and military signals intelligence obtained by breaking the strategic crypto-systems of Germany and Japan; strategic intelligence estimates prepared by the War Department Joint Intelligence Committee on German, Japanese, and Soviet military capabilities, intentions, and weapon systems; and joint U.S.–British scientific-technical intelligence assessments of German and Japanese weapon systems.[21]

Finally, and as a result of the preceding factors, too many senior civilian policymakers, CIA officials, and academic students of U.S. intelligence consider military intelligence and military analysis to be oxymorons. The historical record of military disasters and associated military intelligence blunders serves to reinforce the private but pervasive view that military analysis at the national level is too important to be left to the military.[22] Under this view, the secretary of defense, the chairman of the Joint Chiefs of Staff, or the director of the Defense Intelligence Agency (DIA) could not advise the president or the National Security Council objectively and competently on military intelligence issues. Doubtless, this belief regarding the value of military intelligence contributes to misconceptions about military intelligence analysis at the national level.

The World of U.S. Military Intelligence Analysis

A detailed explication of the current U.S. defense intelligence organization and its legal authorities, missions, priorities, and roles is beyond the scope of this chapter. Nevertheless, one needs a working understanding of the nature of U.S. military intelligence and analysis to appreciate the ramifications of the old and new challenges facing military intelligence in the twenty-first century.

Briefly, U.S. military intelligence analysis encompasses estimative, analytical, scientific and technical, counterintelligence, counterterrorism, counterproliferation, and counternarcotics, basic, and current reporting in hardcopy and electronic formats. Military analysis also includes developing and maintaining massive hard copy filing systems or electronic databases containing the key elements of general military intelligence, including

- order-of-battle data;
- technical assessments and evaluations of foreign military equipment and weapon systems;
- strategic, theater, and tactical nuclear and conventional weapons targets, and "no strike targets";
- military and civilian infrastructure and lines of communication;
- environmental conditions and cultural features; and
- command, control, communications, and computer (C4) systems.[23]

In aggregate, this enormous body of dynamic analytical reporting and static data addresses the specific strategic, theater, service, tactical, scientific-technical, counterintelligence, and counterterrorism intelligence requirements stipulated by U.S. military strategy, national and joint campaign operational plans, and weapons research, development, and acquisition programs. This reporting and these data also respond to the daily current information needs of the Office of the Secretary of Defense, Joint Chiefs of Staff, Armed Services staffs, national weapons laboratories, and other government departments.

The defense intelligence agencies and service intelligence organizations obtain the bulk of the data used to produce this body of analysis and maintain their databases from national technical means of reconnaissance, foreign open source publications and electronic media, and observations of military attachés. In peacetime, some basic military intelligence data and background information on foreign countries and their militaries can be collected in ways unaffected by foreign military denial and deception programs. In wartime, prisoners of war, deserters, defectors, and captured documents become a major source of intelligence. These same organizations support both unified and joint operations. Their primary peacetime mission is assisting strategic, service, and theater-level operational planning and targeting; weapon system and countermeasures research and development; and assessing foreign military strategies, plans, capabilities, and weapons programs. The most important function of military intelligence analysis is supporting war planning, joint preparation of the battle space, and joint military operations.

Indeed, military intelligence is the basis of operations. Military intelligence analysis undergirds all operational planning, preparation of the battle space, and military deception, counterintelligence, and information operations. For this reason, the organizational structures, finished intelligence products, and databases of the defense intelligence agencies and the service intelligence organizations must be responsive to all existing and contingent requirements of the Joint

Chiefs of Staff, combatant commands, joint force commanders, and staffs at all command levels (see box 9.1).[24]

Finished Products

Military intelligence analysis produces numerous categories of finished intelligence for these ascending levels of operations. For each level, the defense intelligence agencies and service intelligence organizations produce and maintain a specific array of standard finished intelligence products and electronic databases, which they must be able to disseminate in electronic or computerized formats to DoD elements, the Combatant Commands, and operational forces in near real time. Even an incomplete list would include:

- current intelligence reports on recent world events relevant to the Office of the Secretary of Defense, Combatant Commands, and individual Armed Services;
- basic intelligence studies on the geography, topography, weather conditions, military bases, economic resources, communications systems, and lines of communication of potential adversaries;
- order-of-battle data on all major foreign armies;
- estimates of enemy military strategy, plans, and capabilities;

BOX 9.1
Definitions of Military and Intelligence Operations

There are three levels of war—strategic, operational, and tactical—with corresponding intelligence operations: strategic, operational, and tactical:

- The military intelligence community produces strategic military intelligence for the National Command Authority (NCA), the senior military leaders, and the combatant commanders. The NCA uses strategic intelligence to develop national strategy and policy, prepare military plans, determine major weapon systems and force structure requirements, and conduct strategic military operations. Strategic military intelligence supports joint operations across the spectrum of military operations.

- Combatant commanders and subordinate joint forces commands use operational intelligence. Operational intelligence focuses on the capabilities and intentions of adversaries and potential adversaries and supports all phases of military operations.

- Tactical intelligence identifies and assesses the adversary's capabilities, intentions, and vulnerabilities. Commanders use tactical intelligence to plan and conduct battles and engagements. Tactical intelligence seeks to identify when, where, and in what strength the enemy will conduct tactical-level operations.

Sources: Joint Chiefs of Staff, Joint Publication 2–0, *Doctrine for Intelligence Support to Joint Operations* (Washington, D.C.: Joint Chiefs of Staff, 2000), III-1–III-11; Joint Chiefs of Staff, Joint Publication 2–0, *Joint Doctrine for Intelligence Support to Operations* (Washington, D.C.: Joint Chiefs of Staff, 1995), IV-15; and William Odom, *Fixing Intelligence for a More Secure America* (New Haven, Conn.: Yale University Press, 2003), 96–101.

- analyses of enemy military budgets and economic resources;
- scientific and technological assessments and forecasts of enemy weapon systems, military equipment, critical military technologies, physical vulnerability assessments of enemy surface and underground facilities, and analyses of enemy C4 systems and networks;
- operational intelligence (OPINTEL) data and analyses derived primarily from technical systems such as underwater antisubmarine surveillance arrays, early warning satellites, specialized reconnaissance aircraft, and ground-based radars and implanted sensors designed to provide real-time or near-real-time analysis to deployed air, ground, and naval units;[25]
- target intelligence on all categories of enemy military and civilian objectives and infrastructure to support theater and strategic nuclear and conventional strikes by ballistic missiles, cruise missiles, bombers, fighter aircraft, and unmanned aerial vehicles;
- counterintelligence threat assessments related to human, technical, and cyber threats to U.S. weapons programs, military operations, facilities, communications systems, and personnel;
- counterterrorism threat assessment regarding DoD and uniformed military service personnel, facilities, activities, and operations;
- prisoner of war and missing in action assessments; and
- biographies of foreign military personnel.[26]

The finished military intelligence products and databases on basic military subjects such as culture and geography, lines of communication, order-of-battle, C4 systems, and target data intelligence are mainly descriptive rather than analytical. The other categories of military analysis involve analysis, estimation, correlation, synthesis, and validation of all-source intelligence data, including open source materials, as well as foreign military equipment, weapons, and matériel.

Satisfying Customers

The analytical products prepared by the DIA, National Geospatial-Intelligence Agency (NGA), National Security Agency (NSA), and the service intelligence organizations require a higher degree of durability, granularity, and precision than do the current daily and short-term intelligence reports produced by the CIA and the State Department's Bureau of Intelligence and Research for the president, secretary of state, and senior National Security Council officials.[27] Furthermore, the analysis produced by the defense intelligence agencies and the service intelligence organizations differs in two important respects from the mainly current analysis produced by the ODNI, CIA, and State Department for the president, National Security Council, and senior civilian policymakers.

First, military intelligence analysis supports war planning and military operations. Joint Chiefs of Staff and Combatant Command operational planners use military analytical products, as well as information from specialized databases, to develop national-, theater-, and service-level operational plans for a variety of contingencies. Of necessity, the data and analysis incorporated into such plans must remain usable and valid for two years—the standard shelf life of a theater-level operations plan.[28]

Second, military analysis supports the DoD weapons research, development, and acquisition process. Both DoD and the individual military services rely on threat assessments produced by the service scientific-technological centers to develop weapon systems and forces for anticipated future conflicts. Although these scientific-technical assessments receive minimal attention from policymakers, civilian intelligence officials, and academic students of the intelligence community, they determine how DoD spends billions of dollars on weapons programs, advanced technology development efforts, force development, and countermeasures to foreign weapons systems and capabilities.[29]

New Features of Enduring Challenges

As mentioned above, the twenty-first century poses perennial as well as novel problems for U.S. military intelligence analysis. The two fundamental missions—namely, collecting and analyzing data—have not changed. But the challenge of identifying the adversary, assessing intentions and capabilities, locating forces, and assessing the present operational activities is much more challenging in the current environment than it was in the last century; moreover, convincing senior commanders to accept the judgments of military intelligence analysis in planning and conducting operations, and developing weapon systems, becomes correspondingly more difficult.

First, the information requirements and operational speed of U.S. joint forces in high-technology warfare and in facing increased foreign military concealment and deception programs have complicated the ability of military intelligence to accomplish the collection and analysis missions. However, the basic tasks of military intelligence analysis remain the same. The critical difference now is that U.S. military strategies, indications and warning, and target planning for pre-emption, global strike, and deterrence require collection and processing of unprecedented quantities of accurate, precise, and time-sensitive technical, human, and open source intelligence on the infrastructure, facilities, leadership relocation, weapons of mass destruction programs, C4 systems, and war mobilization procedures of potential adversaries.[30] In some cases, the level of detail, or "granularity," demanded by U.S. combatant commands and operational elements from military analytical products and databases on these targets exceeds what current national technical means of reconnaissance and traditional military analytical techniques can deliver.

Second, while advising senior military and civilian leaders remains a central mission, the complexity of operations and degree of Washington micromanaging of the military commanders' jobs has also complicated the military intelligence support mission. U.S. military intelligence analysis must support DoD, the Joint Chiefs of Staff, and Combatant Command decision making at all levels of combat. However, military intelligence officers do not make command decisions; rather, they obey them. Thus, the phenomenon of the overconfident, inattentive, or strong-willed senior military commander or senior DoD official is more present than ever and able to affect the use or misuse of military analysis. Indeed, the historical record includes cases in which hubris or inattention led senior military commanders and political leaders to discard, misunderstand, or fail to act on prescient and timely military analysis.[31]

Third, the U.S. defense intelligence agencies and service intelligence organizations also continue to confront the traditional organizational obstacles posed by the conservative and hierarchical command structures of all military organizations. The most important of these are the inherent reluctance of uniformed and civilian military intelligence officers to challenge the agreed-on strategies, policies, and decisions of senior commanders and defense officials or to circumvent the chain of command to disseminate unorthodox or controversial intelligence assessments—especially warnings about possible surprise attacks or unanticipated enemy courses of action.[32]

The unfolding controversy about DoD planning and senior decision making for Operation Iraqi Freedom and the postwar occupation of Iraq demonstrates the persistent difficulty faced by military intelligence in overcoming the presumptive judgments or skepticism of senior defense policy officials about the accuracy of military intelligence analyses supporting war plans.[33] The debate on prewar decision making and intelligence also illustrates the complexity of convincing both senior defense policy officials and commanders to accept intelligence assessments and judgments that do not support planned or adopted military strategies, policy positions, and command decisions.

The new information requirements for military intelligence analysis are now truly global. At a minimum, they will stretch the analytical abilities, budgetary resources, and organizational capabilities of the military intelligence community to the limit during the coming years. Some of these challenges can be overcome through sophisticated technology, new reconnaissance systems, and more and better collection. Others can be met only through sophisticated organizational reforms and innovative civilian and military personnel policies. And some are probably intractable.

Within the defense intelligence agencies and service intelligence organizations, organizational and personnel policy changes will be needed to rebuild the geographic area, scientific-technical, and counterintelligence expertise lost during the 1990s. This reconstruction effort is essential for reviving in-depth analysis, estimative capability, and national-level scientific-technical threat assessments of foreign technologies and weapons systems. Presently, the military intelligence community devotes the bulk of its analytical resources to current intelligence reporting, basic intelligence products, and elaborate databases. Suffice it to state, the historical record of intelligence and warning failures affirms that excessive focus on current intelligence and short-term analysis is a proven recipe for strategic military and technological surprise,[34] especially with respect to patient, potential adversaries, which act according to long-range national and military strategies, force-building programs, and political-military stratagems instead of domestic election cycles.

The challenge presented by the rise of China as a military and economic global power, the advent of well-armed rogue states like Iran and North Korea,

and the phenomenon of dangerous nonstate actors already is straining the analytical resources and abilities of the entire military intelligence community. During the cold war, military intelligence analysis had the resources and the time
to focus collection, research, and analysis on a single, predictable, and slow-
moving enemy, namely, the former Soviet Union and its Warsaw Pact allies. In
the twenty-first century, no comparable "main adversary" exists. However, the
luxury of time for amassing comprehensive data and nourishing extensive expertise is gone. Moreover, military intelligence and analytical resources are
stretched to service a greater number of diffuse mission areas.

As regards China, military intelligence analysis of the People's Liberation
Army's deployed capabilities, military research and development, and weapons
programs cannot draw on the same level of collection resources and analytical
expertise that the military intelligence community leveraged against the former
Soviet Union. At this time, the defense intelligence agencies and service intelligence organizations almost certainly lack the necessary numbers of language-
capable and well-educated civilian and military sinologists and functional
experts needed to conduct the sophisticated, in-depth research and analysis
required to build a knowledge base and achieve a level of understanding for
China comparable to that amassed on the former Soviet Union. The military
intelligence community had almost fifty years to develop the analytical expertise
needed to assess the military capabilities of the former Soviet Union and the
Warsaw Pact states.[35] In the case of China, Iran, and North Korea, however, no
such gestation period is possible, owing to the press of events, expanded DoD
mission areas, and shortages of potential analysts with the necessary expertise
and experience.

Military intelligence analysis now is faced with the challenge of developing
subject matter expertise while supporting military operations in Iraq and
Afghanistan, and assessing numerous countries and militaries, various fast-
developing issues, and multiple threats to U.S. military strategy and national
security. In contrast, during the cold war, international terrorist groups, criminal
organizations, and insurgent movements were not a major focus of military
analysis. Consequently, the military intelligence community developed minimal
in-depth expertise and institutional knowledge about them. However, in the
1990s, the rise of al-Qaeda, Hezbollah, and narco-cartels and insurgent groups
in Colombia, the Philippines, and elsewhere compelled the defense intelligence
agencies and the service intelligence organizations to divert significant analytical
resources to these nonstate actors.

The military intelligence community is best equipped to support those military missions associated with the complexity of U.S. weapon systems, the high
speed of U.S. military operations, and the integration of new information and
sensor technologies for collecting, processing, and disseminating intelligence for
supporting new mission requirements. Since the end of the cold war, DoD and
the Armed Forces have developed and successfully integrated a spectrum of new
information technology, command, control, communication, computer, intelligence, surveillance, and reconnaissance (C4ISR) capabilities, and new organizational structures and concepts such as the newly established Defense Joint
Intelligence Operational Center. Technological solutions are the strength of DoD

and the Armed Forces. Therefore, the most readily surmountable challenges facing military analysis are those that involve

- developing effective technological solutions to intelligence processing;
- improving dissemination of intelligence data and analysis to planning staffs, joint force commanders, operational units, and weapons platforms; and
- creating information networks capable of ensuring intelligence support to the shortened planning cycles and high-tempo operations mandated by the U.S. style of joint, high-technology warfare.

The new global requirements with expanding military missions combine with the continuing organizational inefficiency and diminished analytical capability to produce the most problematic challenge, with few near-term solutions. In any event, sophisticated information and communication technologies, new collection capabilities, enhanced training, and increased funding for more analysts will enable military analysis to grapple with the new mission areas. Nevertheless, these developments cannot create instant subject matter expertise. They cannot compensate immediately for large numbers of inexperienced uniformed and civilian military analysts. Nor can they rectify the organizational problems caused by the repeated internal reorganizations of the defense intelligence agencies and service intelligence elements, and by the simultaneous creation of new but incompletely staffed defense intelligence management organizations charged with improving the integration of the military intelligence community.

The ongoing expansion of DoD and uniformed service mission areas is stretching the analytical capabilities of the DIA, NSA, NGA, and the service intelligence organizations through repeated secondments of analysts to task forces, overseas assignments, and crisis or special issue working groups. Under these circumstances, the military intelligence community is experiencing difficulty in providing effective training for incoming analysts and developing subject matter expertise among the serving analytical cadre. Yet, without such training and expertise development, military analysis cannot and will not improve in the foreseeable future. Moreover, the new mission areas are complex. Almost every one involves separate and new forms of subject matter expertise, which many uniformed and civilian military analysts hired after the September, 11, 2001, terrorist attacks either do not have or cannot obtain, owing to rotations and reassignments, and incessant demands for current intelligence and short-term reporting.

The broad critique of U.S. intelligence community performance in the Silberman-Robb WMD [weapons of mass destruction] Commission report would indicate that the effects of the above situation on the military intelligence community could be unhappy. For these effects might include the continuing decline in the quality of military analysis, the gathering inability to produce sophisticated assessments and estimates of complex intelligence problems, including those related to the new mission areas, and the failure to anticipate and understand foreign scientific-technical and doctrinal innovations and new forms of future warfare.[36]

Despite the impressive size, funding, and integration of the military intelligence community, the effects of attrition, internal reorganizations, and recent civilian and military employment and promotion policies have reduced the community's overall analytical capability since the end of the cold war. As the report of the Silberman-Robb WMD Commission indicates, these developments are affecting the ability of the military intelligence community to conduct strategic analysis and estimates of foreign strategic offensive and defensive weapons systems, scientific and technological developments, and nuclear, biological, and chemical weapons programs.

Since September 11, the defense intelligence agencies and service intelligence organizations have experienced a sustained attrition of experienced analysts through retirement, private sector competition, and personnel policies designed to replace older subject matter experts with younger generalists and to encourage new analysts to achieve rapid promotion through frequent and varied assignments.[37] In these circumstances, meeting the challenge of rebuilding subject matter expertise and improving military analysis rapidly will necessitate modifying hiring practices in order to emphasize recruitment and retention of experienced military intelligence officers and civilian analysts with advanced degrees primarily in area studies, science, and technology.

The present emphasis in the military intelligence community on current intelligence, and databases threatens to erode the capacity of the defense intelligence agencies and the service intelligence organizations for preparing in-depth analyses and long-range estimates on key countries and major functional issues. Addressing the challenge of improving in-depth military analysis, estimates, and technical assessments of foreign weapons systems, while simultaneously meeting the continual demands for current intelligence and operational support for U.S. forces in Iraq and Afghanistan, almost certainly will require some fundamental organizational changes in the military intelligence community, including

- recreating the DIA Joint Staff Directorate for Intelligence to remove the resource-intensive burden on the DIA's Directorate of Intelligence for producing daily current intelligence for the Joint Staff and the Office of the Secretary of Defense;
- reestablishing formal estimates directorates in the DIA and the service intelligence organizations;
- reinventing the DIA directorate for science and technology, dismantled after the cold war, to provide DoD acquisitions programs with national-level scientific-technical assessments; and
- rebuilding the research, analysis, and estimative capabilities of the service intelligence organizations.

The Future of Military Analysis

The enduring challenges to military analysis are familiar to all students of military history and intelligence. A plethora of recent books, conferences, hearings, and commission reports discusses ways to improve U.S. intelligence analysis. Unfortunately, this professional literature rarely addresses military analysis issues. Thus, it contains no obvious solutions for coping with the status of military analysis, the collection problems caused by foreign denial and deception programs, the misconceptions about the nature of military analysis, and the problem of command and national-level disinterest in the judgments of military intelligence. However, the military intelligence community has a unique strength, which should help it to meet these standing challenges.

Unlike the CIA and the State Department's Bureau of Intelligence and Research, the military intelligence community has a formal, comprehensive intelligence doctrine. This doctrine delineates the specific roles, missions, priorities, and techniques of military intelligence, including analysis and estimates. U.S. military intelligence doctrine is defined clearly and precisely in DoD and Joint Chiefs of Staff directives and publications.[38] The requirements and procedures prescribed by this doctrine contain the essential guidance for making organizational changes and improving analysis to meet the enduring challenges to military analysis in the twenty-first century. To fulfill this doctrine, the U.S. military intelligence community must do what military organizations always have done during difficult periods: follow the manual and go by the book, rather than adopt unproven remedies.

As for the new challenges discussed above, DoD, the Armed Services, and the military intelligence organizations certainly recognize them. Nevertheless, addressing these challenges now will be difficult, because of the demands of the global war on terrorism, the major military operations in Iraq and Afghanistan, and the transformation effort under way in DoD and the U.S. Armed Forces. The defense intelligence agencies and the service intelligence organizations must cope with the new mission areas now, using existing budgets, analytical resources, collection capabilities, and organizational structures.

Of necessity, therefore, the attitude of the military intelligence community is pragmatic rather than visionary. Pursuant to U.S. law, DoD orders, and Joint Chiefs of Staff directives, the defense intelligence agencies and service intelligence organizations must support DoD and Armed Forces planning, joint operations, and matériel and force development at all costs, under any circumstances, and in the face of all challenges—old and new. The military intelligence community cannot pick and choose its own analytical priorities and mission areas or ignore certain externally directed production requirements while it reorganizes and tries to improve its collection and analytical capabilities.

Thus, the military intelligence community does not have the prerogative or the luxury of waiting while the ODNI, defense contractors, or academic experts devise ways to improve military analysis. In this sense, the future of military analysis is today. Any long-range, programmatic improvements to military analysis must be made in increments, during interludes between current conflicts, major crises, and ongoing defense transformation efforts. If military intelligence history is any guide, the most dramatic responses to the challenges facing U.S. military analysis in the twenty-first century will be prompted by the actions of adversaries and the nature of warfare.

Notes

1. See N. J. E. Austin and N. B. Rankov, *Exploratio: Military and Political Intelligence in the Roman World from the Second Punic War to the Battle of Adrianople* (London: Routledge, 1995); and Alexander Rose, *Washington's Spies: The Story of America's First Spy Ring* (New York: Bantam, 2006).

2. See, e.g., Peter Gudgin, *Military Intelligence: The British Story* (New York: Arms and Armour Press, 1989); Douglas Porch, *The French Secret Services: A History of French Intelligence from the Dreyfus Affair to the Gulf War* (New York: Farrar, Straus & Giroux, 1995); and Ye. Primakov and V. Kirpechenko, eds., *Ocherki Istorii Rossisky Vneshney Razvedki* (Moscow: Mezhdunarodniye Otnosheniya, 1996).

3. See Bruce W. Bidwell, *History of the Military Intelligence Division, Department of the Army General Staff: 1775–1941* (Frederick, Md.: University Publications of America, 1986); Jeffery Dorwart, *Conflict of Duty: The U.S. Naval Intelligence Dilemma, 1919–1945* (Annapolis, Md.: Naval Institute Press, 1983); and John Patrick Finnegan, *Military Intelligence* (Washington, D.C.: Center of Military History United States Army, 1998). See also Thomas Mahnken, *Uncovering Ways of War: U.S. Intelligence and Foreign Military Innovation, 1918–1941* (Ithaca, N.Y.: Cornell University Press, 2002); and Leonard Leshuk, *U.S. Intelligence Perceptions of Soviet Power 1921–1946* (London: Routledge, 2002).

4. The term "defense intelligence components" refers to all DoD organizations performing national intelligence, defense intelligence, and intelligence-related functions, including the Defense Intelligence Agency (DIA), National Geospatial-Intelligence Agency (NGA), National Reconnaissance Office (NRO), National Security Agency / Central Security Service (NSA), and intelligence elements of the active and reserve components of the Military Departments. For clarity, this chapter refers to DIA, NGA, NSA, and NRO as the defense intelligence agencies.

5. See Department of Defense Directive 5143.01, November 23, 2005, 14.

6. See Victor Rosello, "Clausewitz's Contempt for Intelligence," in *Intelligence and the National Security Strategist: Enduring Issues and Challenges*, ed. Roger George and Robert Kline (Washington, D.C.: National Defense University Press, 2004), 11–22.

7. Department of Defense Directive 5143.01, November 23, 2005.

8. For bibliography on U.S. military intelligence, see Neil Petersen, *American Intelligence 1775–1990* (Claremont, Calif.: Regina Books, 1992); and Jonathan House, *Military Intelligence, 1870–1991: A Research Guide* (Westport, Conn.: Greenwood Press, 1993).

9. A recent standard intelligence reader—Loch Johnson and James Wirtz, eds., *Strategic Intelligence: Windows into a Secret World: An Anthology* (Los Angeles: Roxbury Publishing, 2004)—has no section or articles on "military intelligence." The discussion of U.S. military intelligence issues concerns mainly estimative errors and warning failures, e.g., the 1941 attack on Pearl Harbor, the 1956–60 "Missile Gap" episode, and the 1967 order of battle controversy involving the Military Assistance Command Vietnam and the CIA. See George Allen, *None So Blind: A Personal Account of the Intelligence Failure in Vietnam* (Chicago: Ivan Dee, 2001); John Hughes-Wilson, *Military Intelligence Blunders* (New York: Carroll and Graf, 1999).

10. Gerald Hopple and Bruce Watson, eds., *The Military Intelligence Community* (Boulder, Colo.: Westview Press, 1986); Scott Breckinridge, *The CIA and the U.S. Intelligence System* (Boulder, Colo.: Westview Press, 1986). See Michael Turner, *Why Secret Intelligence Fails* (Potomac, Md.: Potomac Books, 2005), an otherwise excellent book by a retired CIA analyst that ignores military intelligence analysis.

11. See House, *Military Intelligence, 1870–1991*. Selected books by U.S. uniformed and civilian military intelligence officers include: Phillip Davidson, *Secrets of the Vietnam War* (Novato, Calif.: Presidio, 1990); Jack Dziak, *Chekisty: A History of the KGB* (Lexington, Mass.: Lexington Books, 1988); Cynthia Grabo, *Anticipating Surprise: Analysis for Strategic Warning* (Washington, D.C.: Joint Military Intelligence College, 2002); William Scott and

Harriet Scott, *Soviet Military Doctrine* (Boulder, Colo.: Westview Press, 1988); Joseph McChristian, *The Role of Military Intelligence 1965–1967* (Washington, D.C.: Department of the Army, 1974); William Odom, *The Collapse of the Soviet Military* (New Haven, Conn.: Yale University Press, 1998).

12. The late William Lee, a former CIA and DIA Soviet military analyst and DoD consultant, published scores of detailed articles, monographs, and books on strategic military analytical issues related to Soviet military doctrine, strategic nuclear forces, defense spending, ballistic missile defense, weapons research and development, and strategic and theater nuclear targeting. Lee's publications included *The Estimation of Soviet Defense Expenditures, 1955–1975* (New York: Praeger, 1977); *Soviet Military Policy since World War II* (Stanford, Calif.: Hoover Institution Press, 1986); and *The ABM Treaty Charade: A Study in Elite Illusion and Delusion* (Washington, D.C.: Council for Social and Economic Studies, 1997).

13. John Patrick Finnegan, *Military Intelligence* (Washington, D.C.: Center of Military History United States Army, 1998).

14. See F. H. Hinsley, E. E. Thomas, C. F. G. Ransom, and R. C. Knight, *British Intelligence in the Second World War*: vol. I (London: Her Majesty's Stationary Office, 1979); vol. II (New York: Cambridge: Cambridge University Press, 1981); vol. III, part I (New York: Cambridge University Press, 1984); and vol. III, part II (New York: Cambridge University Press, 1988).

15. Important recent examples of National Defense Intelligence College publications on military intelligence and related analytical issues include *Bringing Intelligence About: Practitioners Reflect on Best Practices* (Washington, D.C.: Joint Military Intelligence College, 2003); and David Moore, *Critical Thinking and Intelligence Analysis*, Occasional Paper 14 (Washington, D.C.: Joint Military Intelligence College, 2006).

16. William Odom, *Fixing Intelligence for a More Secure America* (New Haven, Conn.: Yale University Press, 2003).

17. Joint Chiefs of Staff, Joint Publication 2–0, *Doctrine for Intelligence Support to Joint Operations* (Washington, D.C.: Joint Chiefs of Staff, 2000), p. GL-4, "general military intelligence."

18. Joint Chiefs of Staff, Joint Publication 2–0, *Doctrine for Intelligence Support to Joint Operations* (Washington, D.C.: Joint Chiefs of Staff, 2000), p. GL-8, "scientific and technical intelligence."

19. U.S. Army, FM 34–3, March 1990, *Intelligence Analysis*, does not define "military intelligence analysis." However, chap. 5, p. 2–4, defines tactical-level analysis as "the determination of the significance of the information relative to information and intelligence already known, and drawing deductions about the probable meaning of the evaluated information." Joint Chiefs of Staff Joint Publication 2–01.2, *Joint Tactics, Techniques, and Procedures for Joint Intelligence Preparation of the Battlespace*, p. GL-8, includes a definition of "joint intelligence preparation of the battlespace," which comes the closest to providing a generic definition that is also applicable to the defense intelligence agencies: "The analytical process used by joint intelligence organizations to produce intelligence assessments, estimates, and other intelligence products in support of the joint force commander's decision making process."

20. Sherman Kent, *Strategic Intelligence for American World Policy* (Princeton, N.J.: Princeton University Press, 1948), chap. 7.

21. In reality, the War Department, Joint Chiefs of Staff, Joint Intelligence Committee, Combined Chiefs of Staff Committee, Army and Navy signals intelligence organizations, MID, and ONI, and the G-2 departments and joint centers of the major commands analyzed and disseminated almost all strategic-level, war-fighting intelligence during World War II. Military analysis included SIGINT reports, strategic estimates prepared by the Joint Intelligence Committee, and background information, which the War Department transmitted to the White House Map Room for the president's use. On Joint Intelligence Committee strategic estimates, see Larry Valero, "The American Joint Intelligence Committee and Estimates of the Soviet Union, 1945–1947," *Studies in Intelligence* 9, Summer 2000, 65–80.

22. See Charles Lathrop, *The Literary Spy* (New Haven, Conn.: Yale University Press, 2004), 263, quoting former CIA deputy director of intelligence Bruce Clark, July 1997: "military intelligence analysis at the national level, where the Director of Central Intelligence comes eyeball to eyeball with the needs of the President and the Congress, is too important to be left to the military."

23. See Joint Chiefs of Staff, Joint Publication 6–0, *Doctrine for Command, Control, Communications, and Computer (C4) Systems Support to Joint Operations* (Washington, DC: Joint Chiefs of Staff, 1995).

24. Joint Chiefs of Staff, Joint Publication 2–0, *Doctrine for Intelligence Support to Joint Operations* (Washington, D.C.: Joint Chiefs of Staff, 2000), III-1–III-11. See Gregory Hooker, *Shaping the Plan for Operation Iraqi Freedom: The Role of Military Intelligence Assessments* (Washington, D.C.: Washington Institute for Near East Policy, 2005), for a detailed account of how military intelligence supports the joint planning process at the combatant command level. The author is a Central Command (CENTCOM) intelligence officer.

25. See Christopher Ford and David Rosenberg, *The Admirals' Advantage: U.S. Navy Operational Intelligence in World War II and the Cold War* (Annapolis, Md.: Naval Institute Press, 2005), for U.S. naval OPINTEL from technical sources during the cold war.

26. Joint Chiefs of Staff, Joint Publication 2–0, *Joint Doctrine for Intelligence Support to Operations* (Washington, D.C.: Joint Chiefs of Staff, 1995), GL-7, "general military intelligence."

27. See Robert Gates, "The Use of Intelligence at the White House," *Washington Quarterly* 12, no. 1 (Winter 1989): 35–44, for a concise overview of the types of policy intelligence disseminated to the White House.

28. Joint Chiefs of Staff, Joint Publication 2–0, *Doctrine for Intelligence Support to Joint Operations* (Washington, D.C.: Joint Chiefs of Staff, 2000), III-1–III-11. Hooker, *Shaping the Plan for Operation Iraqi Freedom*, 12–19.

29. Odom, *Fixing Intelligence*, xxiv–xxv, 94–96.

30. Joint Chiefs of Staff, Joint Publication 2–0, *Doctrine for Intelligence Support to Joint Operations* (Washington, D.C.: Joint Chiefs of Staff, 2000), III-1–III-3.

31. See Harold Deutsch, "Commanding Generals and Uses of Intelligence," in *Leaders of Intelligence*, ed. Michael Handel (London: Frank Cass, 1989), 194–260; Ephraim Kam, *Surprise Attack: The Victim's Perspective* (Cambridge, Mass.: Harvard University Press, 2004), chap. 8; and David Murphy, *What Stalin Knew: The Enigma of Barbarossa* (New Haven, Conn.: Yale University Press, 2005).

32. See Kam, *Surprise Attack*, chap. 7, on how this organizational and psychological phenomenon can affect the relationship between decision makers and military intelligence. See also Shlomo Gazit, "Intelligence Estimates and the Decision-Maker," in *Leaders of Intelligence*, ed. Handel, 261–87.

33. See Michael Gordon and Bernard Trainor, *Cobra II: The Inside Story of the Invasion and Occupation of Iraq* (New York: Pantheon, 2006), chaps. 1, 3, 5, 6.

34. See, e.g., Grabo, *Anticipating Surprise*, 5–7; and Kam, *Surprise Attack*, 195–96.

35. See Thomas Garin, "Appraising the Best Practices in Defense Intelligence Analysis," in *Bringing Intelligence About: Practitioners Reflect on Best Practices*, ed. Russell G. Swenson (Washington, D.C.: Joint Military Intelligence College, 2003), 61–93.

36. See Commission on the Intelligence Capabilities of the United States Regarding Weapons of Mass Destruction, *Report to the President of the United States, March 31, 2005* (Washington, D.C.: U.S. Government Printing Office, 2005), esp. chap. 8.

37. See *DIA: Workforce of the Future: Creating the Future of the Defense Intelligence Agency* (New York: Toffler Associates and Dove Consulting, 2003), 92–95.

38. In particular, see Joint Publication 2–02, *National Intelligence Support to Joint Operations*; Joint Publication 2–0, *Doctrine for Intelligence Support to Joint Operations*; and Joint Publication 2–01.3, *Joint Tactics, Techniques, and Procedures for Joint Intelligence Preparation of the Battlespace*.

PART FOUR
Diagnosis and Prescription

THE PERFORMANCE of U.S. intelligence analysis eventually must struggle with the questions of why mistakes are made by experienced analysts. In part four, the contributors take on the question from a number of different angles. The prescriptions are essentially to know oneself better but also to know more about the search for knowledge as well as the search for information.

First, the long-time practitioner and teacher of analysts, Jack Davis, poses the question of how even the best analysts are susceptible to errors. His answers point toward individual, social, and group psychology. In brief, various personal cognitive patterns, interpersonal behaviors inside teams and larger offices, and differences among analysts and managers can conspire against critical thinking and an open mind in ways that cause us to miss new developments. He suggests some practical and effective corrections.

Next, James Bruce offers a glimpse into the world of epistemology—that is, the nature of knowledge. He shows that analyzing intelligence is fundamentally about producing knowledge. There are distinct ways of building knowledge—and therefore building intelligence—and some are more reliable than others. This chapter examines epistemological issues that cause errors in intelligence and highlights implications and recommendations for improving how we should conduct analysis if we wish to make it more reliable.

Finally, Bruce concludes this part with the admonition to "know the collectors," for many analytic failures ultimately lead back to the impact of poor or missing information, which analysts did not sufficiently appreciate. Reinforcing warnings found in previous chapters, he concludes that analysts typically fall back on assumptions—often unwittingly—without fully recognizing their reliance on weak information or failure to see that missing information is distorting their thinking and conclusions.

CHAPTER 10

Why Bad Things Happen to Good Analysts

JACK DAVIS

INTELLIGENCE ANALYSIS—the assessment of complex national security issues shrouded by gaps in authentic and diagnostic information—is essentially a mental and social process. As such, strong psychological influences intrude on how analysts faced with substantive uncertainty reach estimative judgments, coordinate them with colleagues, satisfy organizational norms, and convey the judgments to policy officials. Effective management of the impact of cognitive biases and other psychological challenges to the analytic process is at least as important in ensuring the soundness of assessments on complex issues as the degree of substantive expertise invested in the effort.

An understanding of the psychological barriers to sound intelligence analysis helps answer the question of critics inside and outside the intelligence world: How could experienced analysts have screwed up so badly? Ironically, after the unfolding of events eliminates substantive uncertainty, critics also are psychologically programmed by the so-called hindsight bias to inflate how well they would have handled the analytic challenge under review and to understate the difficulties faced by analysts who had to work their way through ambiguous and otherwise inconclusive information.

An Introduction to Methodology and Definitions

This chapter benefits from numerous discussions the author has had with Richards Heuer about his ground-breaking book on the *Psychology of Intelligence Analysis*, which consolidates his studies during the 1960s and 1970s on the impact of the findings of cognitive psychology on the analytic process.[1] The chapter also takes into account recent reports on what Central Intelligence Agency (CIA) analysts did wrong and how they should transform themselves.[2]

The chapter's insights are essentially consistent with the authorities cited above. But they were independently shaped by my half century of experience at the CIA as practitioner, manager, and teacher of intelligence analysis—and from hallway and classroom discussions with CIA colleagues with their own experiences. Informal case studies presented by analysts in the seminar on intelligence successes and failures—a course the author ran for the CIA from 1983 to 1992—

were particularly valuable.[3] Discussions of intelligence challenges on an early 1980s electronic discussion database called "Friends of Analysis" also were informative.

"Bad things" are defined for this chapter's purpose as well-publicized intelligence failures as well as major errors in analytic judgments generally. As a rule, little is made publicly of the failure of analysts to anticipate favorable developments for U.S. interests, such as the collapse of the East German regime and reunification of Germany, or Slobodan Milosevic's caving in to NATO after more than two months of bombings. But the pathology of misjudgment is much the same as with harmful "surprise" developments; and because the hindsight bias is again at play, sharp criticism from intelligence and policy leaders often ensues.

"Good analysts" are defined as those well-credentialed practitioners of intelligence analysis who have earned seats at the drafting table for assessments on war and peace and the other issues vital to national security—a prerequisite for turning instances of estimative misjudgment into an intelligence failure.

Take, for example, the senior political analyst on Iran who said in August 1978, five months before revolutionary ferment drove the pro-U.S. shah from power, that Iran was "not in a revolutionary or even a 'pre-revolutionary' situation." The analyst had worked on the Iran account for more than twenty years, visited the country several times, read and spoke Farsi, and kept in general contact with the handful of recognized U.S. academic specialists on Iran in the 1970s. More than once in the years before 1979, I had heard CIA leaders wish they had more analysts matching the profile of the senior Iran analyst.[4]

Key Perils of Analysis

This chapter examines the psychological obstacles to sound estimative judgments that good analysts face in four key stages of the analytic process:

- When analysts *make judgments* amid substantive uncertainty and by definition must rely on fallible assumptions and inconclusive evidence.
- When analysts *coordinate judgments* with other analysts and with managers who are ready to defend their own subjective judgments and bureaucratic agendas.
- When analysts, in their efforts to manage substantive uncertainty, *confront organizational norms* that at times are unclear regarding the relative importance of lucid writing and sound analysis.
- When analysts whose ethic calls for substantive judgments uncolored by an administration's foreign and domestic political agendas seek to *assist clients* professionally mandated to advance those agendas.

To be sure, the countless postmortem examinations of intelligence failures conclude that better collection, broader substantive expertise, and more rigorous evaluation of evidence would have made a difference. However, if good analysts are most often held responsible for intelligence failures, then such improvements would be necessary but not sufficient conditions for sounder analytic performance. When dealing with national security issues clouded by complexity, secrecy, and substantive uncertainty, the psychological challenges to sound analysis must also be better understood and better managed.

The emphasis should be placed on substantive uncertainty, inconclusive information, and estimative judgment. To paraphrase a point made recently by the CIA director, Michael Hayden: When the facts speak for themselves, intelligence has done its job and there is no need for analysis.[5] It is when the available facts leave major gaps in understanding that analysts are most useful but also face psychological as well as substantive challenges. And especially on such vital issues as countering terrorism and proliferation of weapons of mass destruction (WMD), U.S. adversaries make every effort to deny analysts the facts they most want to know, especially by exercising tight operational security and by disseminating deceptive information. In short, it is in the crafting of analytic judgments amid substantive uncertainty where most perils to intelligence analysts exist.

Assigning Blame

One does not become an apologist for intelligence analysts if one proposes that an experience-based "scorecard" for analytic failure should generally place the blame on those most responsible for not managing psychological and other obstacles to sound analysis:

- If regularly practiced analytic tradecraft (i.e., "methodology") would have produced a sound estimative judgment but was not employed, . . . blame the analysts.
- If analytic tradecraft was available that would have produced a sound judgment but was not regularly practiced because of competing bureaucratic priorities, . . . blame the managers.
- If analytic tradecraft were available that would have produced a sound judgment but was not employed for political reasons, . . . blame the leaders.
- If no available tradecraft would have produced a sound judgment, . . . blame history.

Psychological Perils at the Work Station

To paraphrase Mark Twain's observation about the weather, everyone talks about the peril of cognitive biases, but no one ever does anything about it. No amount of forewarning about the confirmation bias (belief preservation), the rationality bias (mirror imaging), and other powerful but perilous shortcuts for processing inconclusive evidence that flow from the hardwiring of the brain can prevent even veteran analysts from succumbing to analytic errors. One observer likened cognitive biases to optical illusions; even when an image is so labeled, the observer still sees the illusion.[6]

In explaining Why Bad Things Happen to Good Analysts, cognitive biases—which are essentially unmotivated (i.e., psychologically based) distortions in information processing—have to be distinguished from motivated biases (distortions in information processing driven by worldview, ideology, or political preference). These cognitive biases cluster into the most commonly identified villain in postmortem assessments of intelligence failure: *mindset*. More rigorous analysis of alternatives as an effective counter to cognitive biases will be discussed later in the chapter. Though there is no way of slaying this dragon, analysts can learn ways to live with it at reduced peril.

"Mindset" can be defined as the analyst's mental model or paradigm of how government and group processes usually operate in country "X" or on issue "Y." In the intelligence world, a mindset usually represents "substantive expertise" and is akin to the academic concept of mastery of "normal theory"— judgments based on accumulated knowledge of past precedents, key players, and decision-making processes. Such expertise is sought after and prized.[7] The CIA's Directorate of Intelligence strategic plans invariably call for greater commitment of resources to in-depth research and more frequent tours of duty abroad for analysts—which amounts to building an expert's mindset.[8]

True, a mindset, by definition, biases the way the veteran analyst processes increments of inconclusive information. But analytic processing gets done; and thanks to a well-honed mindset, current and long-term assessments get written despite time and space constraints. In between analytic failures, the overconfidence inherent in relying on mindset for overriding substantive uncertainty is encouraged, or at least accepted, by analysts' managers. And because most of the time precedents and other elements of normal theory prevail—that is, events are moving generally in one direction and continue to do so—the expert's mental model regularly produces satisfactory judgments. More than one observer of CIA analytic processes and the pressures to make judgments surrounded by incomplete information and substantive uncertainty has concluded that mindset is "indispensable." That is to say, an open mind is as dysfunctional as an empty mind.[9]

All analysts can fall prey to the perils of cognitive biases. A case can be made that the greater the individual and collective expertise on an issue, the greater the vulnerability to misjudging indicators of developments that depart from the experts' sense of precedent or rational behavior. In a word, substantive experts have more to unlearn before accepting an exceptional condition or event as part of a development that could undermine their considerable investment in the dominant paradigm or mindset.

To start, the so-called confirmation bias represents the inherent human mental condition of analysts to see more vividly information that supports their mindset and to discount the significance (i.e., diagnostic weight) of information that contradicts what they judge the forces at work are likely to produce.[10] As Carmen Medina also notes in chapter 15 of this volume, "analysis by anecdote" is no substitute for systematic surveys or controlled experiments regarding analyst behavior. But consider this example from one of the CIA's most bureaucratically embarrassing intelligence failures: the assessment informing Secretary of State Henry Kissinger on October 6, 1973, that war between Israel and Egypt and Syria was unlikely—hours after he had learned from other sources that the so-called Yom Kippur War was under way.

CIA analysts were aware of force mobilizations by both Egypt and Syria, but they saw the military activity across from Israeli-held lines as either training exercises or defensive moves against a feared Israeli attack. To simplify the analysts' mental model, shrewd authoritarian leaders such as Egypt's Anwar el-Sadat and Syria's Hafez Assad did not start wars they knew they would lose badly and threaten their hold on power. In particular, before launching an attack, Egypt was assumed to need several years to rebuild its Air Force, which Israel had all but destroyed in the 1967 Six-Day War. And besides, the Israelis who were closest to the scene did not think war was likely until Egypt rebuilt its Air Force.

As it happened, in a masterly deception campaign, it was the Sadat government that had reinforced the argument bought by both U.S. and Israeli intelligence that Egypt could not go to war until it had rebuilt its Air Force. All along, Sadat had planned to use Soviet supplied surface-to-air missiles to counter Israeli battlefield air superiority.[11]

What follows is an anecdotal depiction of the power of the confirmation bias. A decade after the event, the supervisor of Arab-Israeli military analysts gave his explanation of the intelligence failure: "My analysts in 1973 were alert to the possibility of war but we decided not to panic until we saw 'X.' When 'X' happened, we decided not to sound the alarm until we saw 'Y.' When we saw 'Y,' we said let's not get ahead of the Israelis until we see 'Z.' By the time we saw 'Z,' the war was under way."[12]

The "paradox of expertise" explains why the more analysts are invested in a well-developed mindset that helps them assess and anticipate normal developments, the more difficult it is for them to accept still inconclusive evidence of what they believe to be unlikely and exceptional developments. This is illustrated by two additional anecdotes about the Yom Kippur War.

The chairman of the Warning Committee of the intelligence community was concerned about the prospect of war and was ready, in two successive weeks, to sound an alarm in his report to intelligence community leaders on worldwide dangers. Twice he gathered the CIA's Middle East experts to his office to express his alarm, only to bow to their judgment that war was unlikely. After all, he explained, he covered developments all over the world, and only recently was reading with any detail into the Middle East situation. They were the experts long focused on this one issue.[13] Similarly, a top-level official later reported that after surveying traffic selected for him by the CIA "Watch Office," he smelled gun smoke in the air. But when he read the seemingly confident assessment of the responsible analysts to the effect that war was unlikely, he decided, to his regret, to send the report on to Kissinger.[14]

The "paradox of expertise" is also demonstrated through the many remembrances of the those who worked on the September 1962 national estimate on the Soviet military buildup in Cuba, the unpublished 1978 estimate on prospects for the shah of Iran, and the high-level briefings given in 1989 on why the fall of the Berlin Wall was not yet likely. In the latter, less well-known case, a senior analyst who "got it wrong" made a frank observation: "There was among analysts a nearly perfect correlation between the depth of their expertise and the time it took to see what was happening on the streets of Eastern Europe (e.g., collapse of government controls) and what was not happening (e.g., Soviet intervention)." These signs could not trump the logic of the strongly held belief that the issue of German Unification was "not yet on the table."[15] On November 9, 1989, while CIA experts on Soviet and East German politics were briefing President George H. W. Bush on why the Berlin Wall was not likely to come down any time soon, a National Security Council staff member politely entered the Oval Office and urged the president to turn on his television set—to see both East and West Germans battering away at the Wall.[16]

The rationality or coherence bias, also known as "mirror imaging," is another cognitive challenge that helps explain why seasoned analysts can be blindsided by epochal events. Obviously, analysts must understand the modus operandi of the leaders and factions of the countries and nonstate entities that are key to U.S. national security interests, especially regarding adversaries. A great deal of effort is spent on obtaining effective insight into, for example, the intentions, risk calculations, sense of opportunity, and internal constraints of foreign leaders and groups. The effort usually includes tracking speeches and foreign media, reading biographies and histories, parsing human intelligence (HUMINT) reporting, debriefing people with direct experiences meeting such world leaders, and brainstorming with colleagues.

With justification, then, veteran intelligence analysts bridle at charges of "mirror imaging," or of using U.S. values and experience to anticipate actions of foreign leaders and entities. Many of the analysts, for example, who tried to assess the intentions of Soviet leader Nikita Khrushchev in the run-up to the 1962 Cuban missile crisis were accomplished Kremlinologists who had spent years trying to capture the operational codes of behavior exhibited by Khrushchev and other Soviet leaders.[17]

These efforts are usually good enough. But the analysts' psychological drive for coherence often causes them to fill in any gaps in understanding with what they, as American-trained rationalists, think would make sense to the foreign leader or group under assessment. The effect that alternative, egocentric, self-deluding, and self-destructive forms of rationality have on what is usually associated with exceptional events or paradigm shifts only becomes clear to analysts after the failure of collective expert mindset.

CIA analysts, for example, eventually learned that Khrushchev in 1962 thought he faced less risk to his hold on power by ignoring U.S. warnings against placing nuclear weapons in Cuba than he would by rejecting his military's demands that the huge U.S. nuclear advantage be reduced by a crash military production program (that might have destabilized the Soviet economy) or by some other costly means.[18] Similarly, the CIA's Middle East analysts eventually learned that Egypt's Sadat in 1973 was convinced he would lose power if he did not risk war with Israel in hopes of restarting negotiations to regain the Egyptian Sinai lost in 1967.[19] And as CIA analysts learned to their regret, Iraq's Saddam Hussein's deliberate ambiguity regarding possession of WMD in 2002 reflected a seemingly distorted risk calculation that feared Iranian knowledge that he did not have such weapons more than U.S. judgments that he did.[20]

To summarize workstation challenges, when normal circumstances prevail, the hardwired cognitive pathways known as cognitive biases provide formidable benefits to good analysts, and their investment in the development, recognition, and defense of established patterns of behavior underwrites timely and useful support to policy clients. These cognitive biases become psychological obstacles for dealing with the relatively infrequent emergence of exceptional or unprecedented, unexpected, or even unimagined developments. And there is no known theory, practice, or methodological tool for infallible determination of whether a normal or exceptional course of events lies ahead.[21]

Perils of Review and Coordination

On intelligence problems and other complex issues, no matter how accomplished the principal researcher, subsequent review by a well-functioning team of diversified experts generally adds substantially to the soundness of an assessment. And as a rule, even the CIA's often labyrinthine review processes increase the overall quality of assessments, especially by improving poorly argued drafts. That said, psychological phenomena similar to those already discussed—but this time reflecting the interpersonal dimension of intelligence cadres—can and do cause bad things to happen to good analysts. These phenomena include groupthink, boss think, tribal think, and no think.

Groupthink is a phenomenon on which critics of the analytic performance of the intelligence community have leaned heavily as a psychological explanation of flawed assessments. As originally defined, it depicts the dynamic of a cloistered and likeminded small group that highly values consensus and reinforces collective confidence in what can turn out to be a flawed set of assumptions and conclusions.[22] Such groups exist in the intelligence analysis world. But in my direct and indirect experiences with analytic failures, the process most often involved a large number of analysts from diverse bureaucratic offices—many with a penchant for argument, some under orders from their bosses to "fix" the final text so that it conforms to office or agency interests. For example, Sherman Kent, the renowned chief of estimates at the time, observed that at least a thousand intelligence professionals (probably no more than a score of whom he knew personally) contributed directly or indirectly to the flawed 1962 community judgment that the USSR would not install nuclear weapons in Cuba.[23] Thus, the malfunction of analytic groups most often lies in other maladies, such as boss think, tribal think, and no think.

Boss think is not a criticism of the dwindling cadre of CIA gray-haired senior analysts and supervisors who have saved many a junior analyst from flawed assumptions or other analytic errors on an assigned issue. Rather, it occurs when the more senior practitioners who have worked complex substantive issues the longest often act as if they "own" the paradigm through which inconclusive evidence is assessed. Thus, boss think can combine with the paradox of expertise at times in causing delayed recognition of a paradigm shift or a mindset that was built on oversimplified key assumptions. For example, some decades ago, when I was national intelligence officer for Latin America, I delayed the publication of a junior analyst's assessment because it contradicted my view of the country. As it happened, events soon proved me wrong, and, luckily, the assessment was published in time for CIA to garner praise for being on top of the issue.

Tribal think, as well, is not a criticism of the necessary division of responsibility for substantive issues among many analysts within and beyond an analyst's organizational unit. The process of "coordination" allows analysts with different substantive responsibilities and experiences to critique and, as a rule, improve and enrich draft assessments. However, when an analyst tries to deviate from the prevailing paradigm, colleagues heavily invested psychologically in different parts of the issue can be quick to prevent what they see as misinterpretations of events and reports.

One example of tribal think came several months *before* the battering of the Berlin Wall. A CIA analyst circulated a draft assessment that argued that the well-known obstacles to German reunification were no longer strong enough to keep the issue of reunification "off the table." This was a bold and prescient departure from the CIA's prevailing expert opinion. His well-informed and well-intentioned colleagues each asked for "small changes" to avoid an overstatement of the case here and a misinterpretation of the case there. After the coordination process had finished its watering down of the original conclusions by the mending of "small errors," a senior reviewer delivered the coup de grâce by all but eliminating the innovative argument from the paper's key judgments. A reader of the final version of the paper would have to delve deeply into the text to uncover the paradigm-breaking analysis.[24]

In another case, in 1983, eight years before the Soviet Union collapsed, an analyst invested in extensive research and an innovative methodology to conclude that strikes, riots, and other forms of civil unrest were a harbinger of substantial instability. A host of Soviet experts within the CIA strongly resisted this departure from the established position that there was no serious threat to regime stability. The original text was watered down considerably during nearly six months of debate. Even after incorporating numerous changes to accommodate the mindset of the expert critics in the CIA, they refused to be associated with even the watered-down assessment, which was then published by the National Intelligence Council without the formal concurrence of the CIA analysts.[25]

No think, as a psychological barrier to sound analysis, is the analysts' conscious or unmotivated resistance to changing an "agreed-on" assumption or estimative judgment that took hours, if not days, of overcoming tribal think to reach. Even if newly obtained information poses a challenge to prevailing opinions, it can be difficult psychologically for the leading analysts to revisit agreed-on language as long as the body of available information remains ambiguous, contradictory, and otherwise inconclusive. The cost of changing the mindset of one obstinate analyst, much less that of a group of likeminded experts, can be quite high. Rather than calling the consensus view into question, some analysts might prefer not to focus attention on nonconforming information.

Technically specialized experts, considered science and technology analysts, who work on a single aspect of a WMD issue, can be especially vulnerable to a combination of boss think, tribal think, and no think. Once the senior regional analysts or the well-respected national intelligence officers set the broad analytical framework regarding an adversary's intentions, then the science and technology specialists set about assessing the available information; they are probably predisposed to put more weight on the evidence that supports the assumptions set out by the generalists, rather than any disconfirming evidence that would require rethinking or rewriting.

This tendency was singled out for criticism in the several postmortem examinations of the flawed 2002 National Intelligence Estimate on Iraqi WMD. In an interview, one of the CIA's weapons analysts acknowledged accepting as "given" the principal analysts' judgment that the Saddam regime harbored such weapons, and to sifting through the evidence critically, but with the expectation that the case for a particular suspected weapon system was there to be made.[26]

In sum, great deference to the authority of the principal analysts on complex and uncertain issues and their psychological drive to preserve mindset-driven judgments work well in producing reasonably sound assessments under normal circumstances. But the practice is vulnerable to missing exceptional, at times momentous, developments. Perhaps there is an analogy between analysis driven by mindset and nuclear power plants. Both are great for ensuring production—in between meltdowns.

Obstacles in the Organizational Culture

As in any large organization, especially one lacking the discipline of a money-based market, the CIA's norms on what constitutes distinctive value-added analysis to policymakers have not always been made clear. One key to Why Bad Things Happen to Good Analysts has been conflicting organizational signals regarding promotion of overconfidence ("making the call") versus promotion of more rigorous consideration of alternative hypotheses and the quality of information, and thus more guarded judgments for dealing with substantive uncertainty.

Whatever the formal norms regarding the quality of analysis, the operational norms over past decades usually have prized the volume of production over sound tradecraft. Emphasis on volume (as well as on speed and conciseness) of production, in turn, has placed a premium on analytic overconfidence. Put in other terms, informal norms have tended to trivialize the complexity and uncertainty of many national security issues by encouraging analysts to depict and defend a single interpretation of complex events or a single forecast of unknowable future developments.

In part, this institutional overconfidence reflected the aforementioned organizational acceptance of "assessment via mindset"—the experienced analysts' view of how things usually work. In part, it reflected an unacknowledged conflation of lucid writing and sound analysis. An assessment that read well was given credit, deserved or not, for having analyzed events, trends, and prospects effectively. So the "gold standard" for analysis as found in analyst training, as well as in the evaluation of published product, was often assessments with catchy titles and strong topic sentences that "make the call" and marshal compelling albeit selective reporting that supports that judgment.

This forceful and confident-sounding communication style has worked well enough for reporting current "normal" events affecting U.S. interests. It often sufficed when the continuity of trends allowed the experts' mindset to provide informed linear interpretations and projections of events. At other times, however, an understating of the complexity and fluidity of political dynamics in countries of concern to U.S. interests led to woefully inelegant judgments. Twice in my years as an analyst I won recognition by timely prediction of military coups against regimes' policymakers considered a threat to U.S. interests. Unfortunately, my subsequent predictions of when the military would turn power over to duly elected civilian governments were off, in one case by twelve years and in another case by more than twenty years.

As a result of unprecedented criticism of analytic performance over the past several years, leaders of CIA analysis are working assiduously and with promising initial results to change the operational norms to emphasize quality of analysis over quantity of production. As CIA director Michael Hayden has indicated, analysts have to distinguish between the issues on which they can use a laser beam (aimed at the right answer) and the issues on which drawing the sidelines within which policymakers will have to operate would be more suitable.[27]

Policy Bias: The Elephant in the Room

As other contributors to this volume—notably John McLaughlin, James Steinberg, and Gregory Treverton—have pointed out, tensions between intelligence analysts and policymakers are inevitable. Though they point out that many factors are at play, the greatest tensions arise essentially from conflicting professional ethics and objectives. Analysts, as a rule, are charged with assessing events abroad without conscious biasing of conclusions to either support or oppose an administration's foreign policy and domestic political agendas. As a rule, policy officials feel obliged to connect and advance these agendas in any way they can. In most cases, analyst–policymaker tensions prompt both sides to enhance the utility of their contributions to the national interest. But these tensions can contribute to the perception as well as the commission of flawed analytic judgments.

As noted elsewhere in this volume, analysts have to get close enough to policymaking processes to know where clients are on their learning curves and decision cycles, if their substantive expertise and tradecraft are to have an impact on decision making. That means getting close enough to be exposed to, and at times seduced by, the politics of decision making. Policy officials at times challenge the first cut of analysts' judgment and, among other things, ask them to take another look at the evidence, rethink the judgment, or change the question. As Steinberg makes clear in chapter 5, at times policymakers' criticism is levied because of professional concerns about the quality and utility of the analysis. At times, however, the policymaker's goal is political—that is, to use intelligence as leverage against competing policy colleagues or to ensure congressional and public support of departmental or administration initiatives.

Up to a point, as Treverton has suggested in chapter 6, analysts should prefer to be challenged rather than ignored by their clients. Historically, however, analysts and managers at times have resorted to politicization in response to criticism by deliberately distorting a judgment to support, or even oppose, presidential policies.[28]

What is of greater concern for this chapter is the influence of unmotivated (psychologically based) biases in the evaluation of evidence and the calibration of judgments. Whether acknowledged or not, there is often "an elephant in the room" when analysts and their managers know what kind of policy support officials would prefer from their intelligence counterparts. In preparing the 1962 intelligence community assessment on Soviet military intentions in Cuba, for example, the drafters knew that President John Kennedy would welcome conclusions discounting the threat and allowing him to improve relations with the USSR so that he could run for reelection in 1964 as the "peace candidate." In preparing the Iraq WMD estimate some forty years later, the drafters knew that President George W. Bush wanted strong emphasis on the threat that lent support to his decision to invade Iraq.

Analysts in these and similar circumstances admit to the presence of policy pressures but tend to deny that the pressures have an effect on their judgments. Yet there is evidence in postmortem reports and academic studies that analysts in making judgments amid uncertainty at a subconscious level often are influenced by knowledge of the policy preference of either or both the administration and Congress.[29] My own experiences as a producer and observer of analysis on politically sensitive issues would indicate that. Knowledge of what a president or his congressional opposition wants can subtly influence the analytic process, and this accommodation in evaluating incomplete and ambiguous information in part can explain estimative malfunctions by experienced analysts.[30]

Coping Mechanisms: The Rigor of Alternative Analysis

My earlier reference to the similarity in benefits and risks between nuclear power plants and analysis by mindset applies as well to the solutions. Redundant safeguards are funded to reduce the threat of power plant meltdowns. Similarly, redundant safeguards are needed to reduce the threat of analytic meltdowns caused by the limitation of the mental faculties of even the brightest of analysts. To ensure against error in established analytic judgments, the CIA is vigorously promoting Alternative Analysis formats, including forms of challenge analysis (e.g., Devil's Advocacy) and structured analysis (e.g., Analysis of Competing Hypotheses). In a complementary effort, the CIA is promoting more rigorous analysis of alternatives in first reaching judgments on complex and fluid issues— that is, the systematic generation and critical review of alternative hypotheses, as outlined in chapter 11 by James Bruce on epistemology.[31] These are, as previously indicated, promising but only recently instituted initiatives in analytic tradecraft.

Think of the estimative misjudgments touched upon earlier in this chapter. The requirement for deliberate assessment of a range of plausible explanations of events and projections of developments might have shown gaps and contradictions in the assumptions supporting the prevailing mindset, and a need for rigorous scrutiny of the authenticity and "diagnosticity" of available information. As a rule, the more important the intelligence issue and the greater the uncertainty and information gaps, the greater need for incorporating alternative explanations and projections into the text of an assessment. Even a "high confidence" judgment implies enough doubt for the properly skeptical analyst to develop a list of tipping points and signposts for one or more "wild card" developments.

Perhaps the most important contribution managers can make when their analysts present a draft assessment based on a paradigm of an issue the managers were proud to have developed in past years is to ask: (1) What new evidence would make you change your key assumptions? (2) Why not review all the evidence through the optic of those altered assumptions? (3) Why not consider the costs and benefits of including that alternative argument in your assessment?

Externally structured analysis—such as the Analysis of Competing Hypotheses, Argument Mapping, and Signpost Analysis—might have overcome the barriers to sound analysis set up by boss think, tribal think, and no think, as well as by the elephant in the room. As a former practitioner of "analysis by mindset," I bridle at the accusation that my judgments were "intuitive" or not backed by serious thinking. Much deliberative but internalized structuring took place before, during, and after the initial drafting, including via the coordination and review processes. But neither I nor my colleagues could take effective account of hidden and contradictory assumptions and the overweighting and underweighting of individual reports that supported a hypothesis. If I had committed to external structuring, my sleep these days might be less disturbed by recall of my personal collection of poorly argued or overconfident intelligence judgments.

Challenge analysis—such as Devil's Advocacy, What-If Analysis, or High-Impact/Low-Probability Analysis—might have provided analysts and managers with an additional measure of insurance on issues they "couldn't afford to get wrong." Challenge analysis usually is undertaken after the analysts in charge of an issue have reached a strong consensus and are in danger of becoming complacent with their interpretative and forecasting judgments. Challenge analysis is essentially "argument for argument's sake"—that is, a rigorous evaluation of the evidence, including gaps in evidence, from a plausible if seemingly unlikely set of alternative assumptions. As a rule, the primary target audience for challenge analysis is not the policymaker but the analytical community. The primary objective is to test hypotheses and refine judgments or confidence levels, and not necessarily abandon judgments.

Challenge analysis serves well even if the exercise serves only to motivate analysts to reassess their previous line of argumentation before deciding to retain their original judgments—as is usually the case. Challenge analysis provides a distinctive service—as is sometimes the case—when it prompts the responsible analysts to alter collection requirements, analytic methodology, or levels of confidence in existing views. In the end, some combination of the often creative insights of analysis by expert opinion (i.e., mindset) and the insurance against cognitive biases provided by more rigorous and structured consideration of alternatives will best serve the reputation of the community of intelligence analysts, the professional needs of policy clients, and the national interest.

Notes

1. Richards J. Heuer Jr., *Psychology of Intelligence Analysis* (Washington, D.C.: Center for the Study of Intelligence, Central Intelligence Agency, 1999). The present author wrote the "Introduction" to this volume and has a life-long discussion with Richards Heuer regarding this topic.

2. E.g., see Commission on the Intelligence Capabilities of the United States Regarding Weapons of Mass Destruction, *Report to the President of the United States, March 31, 2005* (Washington, D.C.: U.S. Government Printing Office, 2005) (hereafter, *WMD Commission Report*); Rob Johnston, *Analytic Culture in the U.S. Intelligence Community: An Ethnographic Study* (Washington, D.C.: Center for the Study of Intelligence, Central Intelligence Agency, 2005); and Jeffrey Cooper, *Curing Analytic Pathologies: Pathways to Improved Intelligence Analysis* (Washington, D.C.: Central Intelligence Agency, 2005).

3. CIA director William J. Casey (1981–87), who had a low opinion of CIA analysts and averred that at least they should learn from their own mistakes, reportedly requested this course. This story was recounted to the author by an agency training official in 1983.

4. The quoted judgment is cited by Gary Sick, at the time the Iran specialist on the National Security Council staff in Gary Sick, *All Fall Down: America's Tragic Encounter with Iran* (New York: Random House, 1978), 92. Columbia University Professor Robert Jervis, in his unpublished "Analysis of NFAC's Performance on Iran's Domestic Crisis, Mid-1977," November 7, 1978, comments that "the leading political analyst . . . seems to have had as good a general feel for the country as can be expected" (p. 8), released under the Freedome of Information Act in 1995 as CIA-RDP86B00269R00110011003–425X1.

5. Office of Public Affairs Press Release, Central Intelligence Agency, November 30, 2006, www.cia.gov/cia/public_affairs/prress_release/2006/pr11302006.hmtl.

6. For a discussion of the impact of these and other cognitive biases on intelligence analysis, see Heuer, *Psychology of Intelligence Analysis*, 111–72.

7. Jack Davis, "Combating Mind-Set," *Studies in Intelligence* 36, no. 5 (1992): 33–38.

8. See John A. Kringen (director of intelligence), "How We Have Improved Intelligence," *Washington Post*, April 3, 2006.

9. Davis, "Combating Mind-Set," 33.

10. Heuer, *Psychology*, 111.

11. Richard K. Betts, *Surprise Attack: Lessons for Defense Planning* (Washington, D.C.: Brookings Institution Press, 1982), 71. Chaim Herzog, *The War of Atonement: October 1973* (Boston: Little, Brown, 1975), 24–25.

12. Interview with CIA supervisor, 1984.

13. Interview with senior warning officer, 1987.

14. Interview with assistant to former CIA official, 2006.

15. Case study presented in a CIA seminar on intelligence successes and failures, 1990.

16. Case study presented to a CIA seminar on intelligence successes and failures by a senior CIA briefer, 1990.

17. Sherman Kent, "A Crucial Estimate Relived," in *Sherman Kent and the Board of National Estimates: Collected Essays*, ed. Donald P. Steury (Washington, D.C.: Central Intelligence Agency, 1994), 183–84.

18. Fritz Ermarth, reviews of *Essence of Decision: Explaining the Cuban Missile Crisis* by Graham T. Allison, and *Victims of Group Think* by Irving L. Janus, *Studies in Intelligence* 18, no. 1 (Spring 1974): 104 (hereafter, Ermarth, "Book Reviews"). Max Frankel, *High Noon in the Cold War: Kennedy, Khrushchev, and the Cuban Missile Crisis* (New York: Ballantine Books, 2004), 8–10.

19. Herzog, *War of Atonement*, 23. The Insight Team of the London *Sunday Times, The Yom Kippur War* (Garden City, N.Y.: Doubleday, 1974), chap. 3.

20. See the Iraq Survey Group, *Comprehensive Report of the Special Advisor to the DCI on Iraq's WMD, 30 September 2004* (Washington, D.C.: Central Intelligence Agency, 2004), vol. 1, 4–6.

21. Richard Betts, "Warning Dilemmas: Normal Theory vs. Exceptional Theory," *Orbis* (Winter 1981): 38–46, makes a similar point about academic assessments of foreign policy issues.

22. Ermarth, "Book Reviews," 105–6. I am indebted to Fritz Ermarth for "boss think" and other terms used in this section, although my interpretations may differ from his views.

23. Kent, "Crucial Estimate," 175.

24. Presentation to a CIA seminar on intelligence successes and failures by the CIA office director responsible for analysis of East Germany, 1990; interview with the office senior analyst, 2007.

25. Interview with the principal analyst, 2007. A redacted version of the assessment was declassified and cited as an example of the CIA's successful analytic tracking of the pending collapse of the Soviet Union. See Douglas J. MacEachin, *CIA Assessments of the Soviet Union: The Record Versus the Charges—An Intelligence Memorandum* (Washington, D.C: Central Intelligence Agency, 1996), 18.

26. Author's interview with a CIA weapons analyst, 2005. The general point is made in *WMD Commission Report*, 169–71.

27. Kringen, "How We Have Improved Analysis." See also "Opening Statement by Michael V. Hayden before the Senate Select Committee on Intelligence," May 18, 2006, 3; www.globalsecurity.org/intell/library/congress/2006_hr/060518-hayden.htm.

28. Jack Davis, "Intelligence Analysts and Policymakers: Benefits and Dangers of Tensions in the Relationship," *Intelligence and National Security* 21, no.6 (December 2006): 1008.

29. E.g., see Robert Jervis, "Reports. Politics, and Intelligence Failures: The Case of Iraq," *Journal of Strategic Studies* 29, no. 1 (February 2006): 36–38.

30. Davis, "Intelligence Analysts and Policymakers," 1007–9.

31. See chapter 16 below by Richards J. Heuer. See also Roger Z. George, "Fixing the Problem of Analytical Mindsets: Alternative Analysis," *International Journal of Intelligence and Counterintelligence* 17, no. 3 (Fall 2004): 385–404.

CHAPTER 11

Making Analysis More Reliable: Why Epistemology Matters to Intelligence

JAMES B. BRUCE

Another observation I would make concerns what philosophers call epistemological questions: How do we know what we know, and how good is the
information that comprises this knowledge? Is it reliable? Is it true? This is
the core of the intelligence community's problem.

—John J. Hamre, the former deputy secretary of defense, commenting on
the failed National Intelligence Estimate on Iraqi weapons of mass
destruction in *Aviation Week and Space Technology*, September 22,
2003

SINCE INTELLIGENCE seeks to produce a form of knowledge, analysis must be understood as a knowledge-building activity. Improving analysis
thus requires an understanding of epistemology, the branch of philosophy that
deals with the theory, origins, and nature of knowledge. This chapter examines
how understanding epistemology can highlight how knowledge in intelligence is
created, and why some ways of producing it are more reliable than others.
Focusing on an important failed National Intelligence Estimate (NIE), it identifies epistemologically induced sources of error in analysis and possible correctives. It also shows how self-corrective mechanisms can improve reliability and
should become a more integral part of the analytical process.

Knowledge and Intelligence

Intelligence is *knowledge and foreknowledge of the world around us that allows
civilian leaders and military commanders to consider alternative options and
outcomes in making decisions.*[1] If *knowledge* and *foreknowledge* are really what
intelligence agencies are supposed to produce, we should ask, first, what they
are and, second, how agencies actually produce—or should produce—them. A
consideration of epistemology should be a core idea in any discussion of intelligence. It suggests the importance of identifying how different ways of knowing
can have a profound impact on producing intelligence.[2]

Definitions

According to dictionary definitions, *knowledge* refers to "facts, ideas, and understanding, the totality of what is known." A *fact* is a thing known to be true, to have happened. To *know* means "to perceive directly," "to have direct cognition of," "to have understanding of," or "to recognize the nature of." *Foreknowledge* simply means to foresee or to know beforehand.[3] The centrality of both knowledge and foreknowledge to intelligence was long ago explained by the former Central Intelligence Agency (CIA) chief Allen Dulles in his now-classic *The Craft of Intelligence*:

> "In the fifth century B.C., the Chinese sage Sun Tsu wrote that foreknowledge was 'the reason the enlightened prince and the wise general conquer the enemy whenever they move.' In 1955 the Task Force on Intelligence Activities of the Second Herbert Hoover Commission in its advisory report to the government stated that 'intelligence deals with all the things which should be known in advance of initiating a course of action.' Both statements, widely separated as they are in time, have in common the emphasis on the practical use of advance information in its relation to action."[4]

Along with secrecy and espionage, knowledge and foreknowledge are the most durable attributes of the practice of intelligence.

In exploring different knowledge-building techniques and their relevance to intelligence, the basic argument made here is that some of them are inherently better than others and that understanding and acting on this core idea is essential to the analytical process. Because each technique has major implications for the accuracy and reliability of the analysis, analysts should be acutely aware of precisely which knowledge-building techniques they are using when they research, draft, and coordinate analytical products.

Principal Ways of Knowing

There are only a finite number of ways to produce knowledge. This is as true for intelligence as for any other discipline. For the purposes of this discussion, the principal and distinct ways can be reduced to four: authority, habit of thought, rationalism, and empiricism. A fifth way, science, combines important features of rationalism and empiricism.[5] We examine each in turn.

Authority

When someone "knows" something through authority, the basis of knowledge resides in a reference to something more authoritative than the person who claims to know it. For example, if someone claimed to know that U.S. intelligence was engaged in nefarious or illegal acts at home or abroad because he read it in a newspaper or heard it on a television newscast, then the claim to know relies on the authority of the newspaper or network. Ultimately, the validity of that claim will depend on how, for example, the *New York Times* or a CNN news anchor came to know that particular piece of information. The same is true if they learned the information from a professor, parent, poet, or preacher—the validity of the information may vary widely, but the method of knowing it is the same: It is authority dependent.

It should be immediately apparent that this way of knowing depends *completely* on the source of the information. If the authority of the information source is valid, so too is the information. If the authority is weak or wrong, so too is the information. In 2002, for example, President George W. Bush and other senior administration officials claimed to know that Iraq possessed a major program of weapons of mass destruction (WMD). Their claim was based on what the director of central intelligence (DCI) and other authorities in the U.S. intelligence community had told them. The DCI's knowledge, in turn, was based on what the NIE and earlier intelligence products had reported. In this case, the authority was the NIE—the most authoritative intelligence product. We will see below that the various ways of knowing used in the NIE on Iraq WMD also depended heavily on authority. The crippling problem with relying on this way of knowing is that users cannot easily assess any antecedent epistemologies by which the knowledge was created and therefore cannot assess the veracity or sources of possible error. Such antecedent sources of knowledge may lack any internal mechanisms for error discovery and correction.

Habit of Thought

The second method of knowing is best characterized by identifying its two most common forms: prejudice in individuals and conventional wisdom in groups. People often claim to know something because they have "always known it" or because they have always thought something to be true without understanding exactly why. As such, prejudice and conventional wisdom lack specific origins and defy explanation. Stereotypes are a case in point. For example, before World War II, Western intelligence officers commonly believed that Japanese pilots were unskilled and inept and that Japanese military equipment was of poor quality.[6] Of course the experience of Pearl Harbor and later campaigns proved these stereotypes wrong. Similar ethnic and other prejudices and stereotypes are often based only on habit of thought. If asked to explain how they know this, people may cite "evidence," which is typically anecdotal, and they cannot often identify the origins of such information apart from having believed it all along. The source of this knowledge is habitual and based on little else.

Similarly, "conventional wisdom" is collective understanding or knowledge that has no more or less of a basis for being valid than whatever formed such habits of knowing in the first place. Once a collective understanding is reached, no matter the original basis for that understanding, it takes on a life all its own. Conventional wisdom can be a factor in producing knowledge of the physical world as well as intelligence. For example, before the full impact of Copernicus and Galileo, the commonly held belief among the learned and illiterate alike since Ptolemy was that the Earth's position in the universe was fixed and that the sun and stars rotated around this stationary planet. This second-century geocentric view hardened into entrenched knowledge and became an extremely difficult position for the later heliocentric advocates to overturn, notwithstanding observational data and logic.[7]

In intelligence, analogous examples of Ptolemaic conventional wisdom having hardened into knowledge include the consensus that Soviet behavior into the early 1960s was strategically cautious, and that Iranian society into the late 1970s was stable and governed effectively by a strong and capable ruler. Both these examples of knowledge were correct—but only temporarily, because events proved them wrong when the Soviets tried to sneak nuclear missiles into Cuba in October 1962 and the shah's government abruptly fell in 1979. These examples also illustrate how accurate foreknowledge relies on accurate knowledge. Both these intelligence surprises were rooted in habit of thought as a way of knowing. Errors in knowledge ensure errors in foreknowledge.

As a basis for foreknowledge, habit of thought can be a useful predictor of continuity. For warning intelligence, it has proven a reliable—if lazy—way of knowing: The odds generally favor predictions that say tomorrow will look pretty much like today. But this way of knowing inhibits anticipating discontinuity, so major warning failures can be the result.[8] If habit of thought is wrong, its errors must be discovered by some different way of knowing, because it lacks the ability to discover its mistakes by itself.

Rationalism

When knowledge is derived from *reason*, this way of knowing is referred to as rationalism. The great rationalists—Socrates, Plato, Hegel, Descartes, Spinoza, and Kant—differed on methods of reasoning but shared an important attribute: a belief that the human mind can produce knowledge and that knowledge of the physical world is a product of the mind.[9]

Rationalists have devised or identified several *systems of reasoning*, the most important of which are deduction, induction, and abduction.[10] *Deduction* produces inferences or conclusions about particulars that follow from general laws or principles. The best-known example of deductive reasoning is the following syllogism, which illustrates how we can know that Socrates was a mortal:

- *All men are mortals; Socrates was a man; therefore Socrates was a mortal.*

We have learned nothing from this syllogism because the idea proclaiming Socrates' mortality was already fully contained in the premises. This form of reasoning is empty. Its conclusion cannot state more than what is already known in the premises; it can only make it more explicit.[11] Deductive reasoning can, however, assist in the physical sciences because science, unlike intelligence, does have general laws, such as the law of gravity, from which particular kinds of information may be discovered.[12] But its uses in intelligence are more problematic because intelligence lacks general principles with the explanatory power of Newton's laws. It can assist in generating *new* hypotheses, but analysts will generally find little value in deductive reasoning to help them produce reliable intelligence.[13]

In contrast with deduction, *inductive* reasoning searches *for* general principles or more generalized understandings by reasoning from the particulars to the general:

- *Crow 1 is black; crow 2 is black; crow 3 is black . . . Therefore, all crows are black.*

Inductive inference seems to be the dominant choice of reasoning in intelligence analysis. A tool of historians, its intelligence roots are traceable to Sherman Kent.[14] Properly employed, this method can help identify trends, continuity, and change. It helps the analyst make sense of seemingly chaotic data, to see patterns in behavior and events, and to ascertain possible relationships by observing connections among things that might otherwise seem disconnected.

Induction, moreover, can help the analyst to move beyond knowledge to foreknowledge.[15] For example, we may *predict* that after nearly 5 billion years of the sun rising, it is a safe bet that the sun will rise tomorrow morning. We can make this high-confidence prediction based on the sun's unerring track record. Forecasting its arrival tomorrow is foreknowledge we do not have without induction.

But forecasting human events and behavior, such as terrorist attacks and other intelligence issues, invites considerably less certainty than we find in cosmology. And these uncertain future outcomes highlight David Hume's "problem of induction"—namely, that inductive inference is an inherently probabilistic activity and introduces significant vulnerabilities to error. Despite having seen many black crows in the past, we cannot *know* with certainty that all the crows we may see in the future will be black. Unlike deduction, the conclusion is not contained in the premises because it extends to crows yet unobserved. Therefore, the truth of the conclusion cannot be guaranteed.[16] Inductive inference can lead to error.

Intelligence analysts must recognize that analysis often involves inductive inference (often unwitting), so they must better understand the strengths and pitfalls of this reasoning technique. Its most important strengths are its ability to provide tentative explanations for events and outcomes that reveal patterns, to generate testable hypotheses, and to hypothesize future developments.

The most important problem with inductive inference is that different analysts might arrive at different conclusions from the same set of facts or particulars. Another pitfall requires the analyst to fully understand that induction is an inherently probabilistic enterprise: Without a rigorous effort to bound uncertainty, such as through statistical tools, analysts are always at risk of drawing false conclusions about the probability of an occurrence (e.g., the probability of finding a nonblack crow or warning of a terrorist attack).[17] In short, systematic use of induction must be more closely linked with more powerful analytical tools. Otherwise, we cannot improve. As Collier expressed it: Intelligence analysis "seems stuck in the 1950s through the 1960s inductive historical methods advanced by Sherman Kent, instead of adopting the latest social science knowledge."[18] Indeed, a major study of the culture of intelligence analysts found resistance to scientific methods, and even prejudices against them.[19]

Unlike the venerable deduction and induction, *abduction* is a form of reasoning of more recent vintage, developed chiefly by Charles Peirce around the beginning of the twentieth century. Sometimes referred to as the "logic of Sherlock

Holmes," abductive inference seeks to craft the best hypothesis or inference to "fit" otherwise unexplained facts and occurrences:[20]

- *Fact 1, fact 2, fact 3, fact 4 . . . all imply inference A.*

Although it can be expressed as a formal system of logic, abduction is chiefly a qualitative technique applying an investigator's approach to understanding disparate phenomena. Abductive inference is an implicit, if unacknowledged, technique used by intelligence analysts who seek to provide explanations for emerging or ongoing events with a view toward understanding the future. Like other forms of reasoning, although perhaps not an alternative to them, abductive inference excels at generating hypotheses.

A major weakness, like induction, is that different analysts may arrive at different inferences from the same set of facts or give different emphasis to particular facts that lead to different conclusions. Abduction also shares another weakness with both induction and deduction: *Reasoning itself does not make something true; it can only identify a possible truth.* For the scientist, establishing what is true—namely, building knowledge—requires an additional step called *verification* (or falsification). *No rationalist technique, neither authority nor habit of thought, offers this crucial step toward gaining knowledge.* Moreover, when logic makes errors, it has only the capacity to detect the *logic* of its errors but not the factual basis of the premises on which its conclusions are based. The knowledge it produces may sometimes be correct or incorrect, but because its truth depends on the extra-logical content of the facts, knowledge from rationalism alone cannot be trusted as fully reliable. For more reliable knowledge building, we need to turn to the fourth way of knowing: empiricism. It is here that we begin to see the emerging attributes of science, the most reliable knowledge-building technique of all.

Empiricism

The fourth way of knowing represents an important advance in understanding the world. Bacon, Locke, Hume, and Galileo pioneered its early methods. Empiricism is based on what we apprehend from the senses: what we see, hear, touch, taste, and smell. It is about observation, experience, and experimentation. In sharp contrast to the rationalist who believes that knowledge is the product of the human mind, the empiricist insists that "sense observation is the primary source and ultimate judge of knowledge and that it is self-deception to believe the human mind to have direct access to any kind of truth other than logical relations."[21] Rather than dwelling on reason, the empiricist's focus is on observational data. Shifting from an internal mental exercise to externally observable data changes the entire epistemological equation. As Reichenbach explains, the contrast between rationalism and empiricism could not be sharper: "Once empirical observation is abandoned as a source of truth, it is then but a short step to mysticism. If reason can create knowledge, other creations of the human mind may appear as trustworthy as knowledge."[22]

The empirical approach should come easily to the intelligence analyst because the collection disciplines—HUMINT, SIGINT, IMINT, MASINT, and OSINT[23]—are all sensory. The analyst is awash with empirical data. His or her job is to make sense of it, hypothesize about it, draw conclusions from it, write key judgments about it, and convey assessments to customers about what it all means and what it may mean for the future. In producing knowledge and foreknowledge, reliance on collected data makes analysis a fundamentally empirical enterprise.

Critics of empiricism sometimes fault "scientific" methods as inappropriate for intelligence analysis and tout the putatively superior virtues of intuition and reason.[24] Other critics point out, rightly, that facts do not speak for themselves and that not all data are valid. Some things are not what they seem. Discerning intelligence collectors and analysts would agree, but only to a point. Collected data can be misleading, erroneous, distorted, or unrepresentative—and often are. They can be fabricated. Or elusive. But data-free intelligence is not intelligence. A major challenge of intelligence analysts, therefore, is not only to make judgments *from* the data but first to make judgments *about* the data. We will see below that this important step is not always taken or taken carefully.

To summarize, what authority, habit of thought, rationalism, and empiricism all have in common is a demonstrated capacity for producing error as well as truth. But none of the four has the internal capacity to discover when it is wrong or to prescribe the needed correctives for getting it right. In a historically profound development that combines the third and fourth ways of knowing—rationalism and empiricism—the emergence of science produced a new epistemology that presents a powerful new feature to knowledge building: *self-corrective techniques*. Though all five avenues to knowledge can produce error, *only science has the built-in capacity to identify and correct its mistakes*. The implications for intelligence analysis are obvious and irresistible: These self-corrective techniques can markedly reduce the potential for error in analysis and greatly enhance the production of reliable knowledge.[25]

Science

It is the distinctive ability of scientific inquiry to produce sound understanding and reliable knowledge. As a way of knowing, it combines the best attributes of rationalism and empiricism but adds an array of internal procedures that enable it to check itself. Compared with the other four ways of knowing, its capacity for error identification and correction greatly improves its reliability. This feature should make it of particular interest to intelligence analysts. Significantly, a recent study has concluded that developing a science of intelligence analysis would be easier than changing the perceptions of the analysts and managers who oppose it.[26]

This capability of the scientific method for producing reliable knowledge rests on several attributes that other methods lack.[27] Physical and social scientists would generally agree that scientific inquiry must have the following attributes:

- Use of the *hypothesis*. A specific research statement that is falsifiable in principle guides any scientific study. However the hypothesis is initially generated, the investigator is primarily interested in testing how valid or truthful it is. The investigator will collect observable data to test the hypothesis, using rigorous methods to establish whether it is true or false or, more commonly, use inferential statistics to establish the probability that its truthfulness is not a chance or random occurrence. Testing may also identify the conditions under which the hypothesis is most likely to be true or false.
- *Objective methods.* A scientist employs rigorous procedures to ensure that data are collected and analyzed in the most objective manner possible to avoid influencing or distorting the test. Scientists are empiricists. The only data used in the research are those relevant to the hypothesis, but neither the data selection nor the analytical methods should influence the outcome of the study to achieve a particular or desired result, nor should they bias the results.
- *Transparency.* Science is a public activity and its procedures are open to inspection. No study claiming scientific results can shield the methods used to arrive at its findings. Both the findings and the methods used to produce them must be available for public inspection or use. Visibility of methods helps to ensure integrity of the study, as well as its replicability.
- *Replicability.* All scientific investigations must be reproducible by other researchers. If one scientist or group of scientists arrives at any given set of conclusions, another group should be able to repeat the same study, and even possibly using different methods, but still reach the same results. If another group cannot achieve the same results, then the initial hypothesis test may be doubted and the hypothesis remains open to further investigation.
- *Peer review.* New results do not attain the status of knowledge until other knowledgeable researchers either agree or at least concur that the results are consistent with the methods and that the methods were empirically sound. Peer review can sometimes be contentious, but studies that survive the review process are more authoritative than those that do not. Rigorous peer review can impede, prevent, or validate the acceptance of findings.
- *Provisional results.* Scientific findings are always subject to modification as procedures are refined, new results come in, and older ones are superseded. This dynamic feature of scientific inquiry is reinforced by the inherently skeptical attitude of the scientist. This implies an intrinsic readiness to reconsider results when new ideas or information emerge. For the scientist, if ugly facts challenge beautiful theory, facts win.

The upshot of these procedures is vastly improved reliability: When science makes errors—and it sometimes does—it has the inherent capacity to identify and correct them. This self-corrigible capacity was recently demonstrated in the repudiation of two quite public scientific studies: cold fusion in physics and human cloning in biological research.[28] These faulty studies are rare only because they had reached the stage of being announced to the public. Most self-correction in science normally occurs well before findings become headline news.

Errors in Estimating: Undetected and Uncorrected

> The trouble with people is not that they don't know, but that they know so much that ain't so.
>
> —Attributed to Josh Billings (1818–85)

To illustrate the epistemological errors that can occur in analysis, we can now examine the ill-fated October 2002 NIE on Iraq's WMD.[29] It illustrates how all four ways of knowing each contributed to the NIE's flawed judgments, as well as the consequences of failing to incorporate error-detecting and reducing measures.

This NIE produced faulty knowledge. Its three most important key judgments were factually wrong.[30] Two of them that described the chemical weapons (CW) and biological weapons (BW) that Iraq purportedly possessed were wrong with "high confidence." And the key judgment on Iraq's efforts to reconstitute its nuclear program was wrong with "moderate confidence." The capacity of each epistemology to yield error appears to be fully realized in the preparation of this deeply flawed NIE.

Authority

The use of authority as a way of knowing played an important and destructive role in all three judgments. Beginning with CW, the principal question at the time of the NIE was: Does Iraq possess chemical weapons? The NIE said yes. It judged that Iraq had an active CW program involving the production of mustard, sarin, cyclosarin, and VX and had stockpiled as much as 100 to 500 metric tons of them. The NIE also said that Iraq had produced much of its CW in the year prior to the estimate. Contrary to the estimate's conclusions, we now know that Iraq had no CW at all for about ten years before the NIE was published.

Authority played a significant role in this judgment. According to the Silberman-Robb WMD Commission, the most important CW evidence—and most important source of error—was "over-reliance on a single, ambiguous source (Samarra type tanker trucks) to support multiple judgments."[31] Imagery is a specialized collection discipline and the imagery analysts who report its findings to all-source analysts are typically regarded as authoritative. The narrow information on the decontamination trucks at suspect CW sites was far from definitive, and precisely for this reason specialized knowledge gave the impression that the information was stronger than it was. The authoritative nature of imagery analysis—a combination of empirical observation and expert judgment—was accepted as a basis for the CW key judgment in the NIE that we now know was wrong.

The high-confidence BW judgment also was heavily supported by authority, in this case a clandestine human source who claimed insider knowledge of Iraq's

BW programs. The NIE concluded that Iraq had offensive BW weapons, including mobile BW labs. It also said that all key aspects of the BW program were active and that most program elements were larger and more advanced than they were during the Gulf War. Though other information also supported this judgment, none was more authoritative than the reporting that came from the human source code named "Curveball," whose intelligence was disseminated in roughly a hundred detailed reports. The WMD Commission found that the intelligence community (IC) had a "near-total reliance on Curveball for its BW judgments" and that serious problems accompanied this source. The fact that Curveball was later exposed as a fabricator meant that the erroneous BW finding was based heavily on fabricated HUMINT.[32] Reliance on any form of authority that cannot be further verified, as is often the case with sensitive collection, is a major vulnerability of intelligence analysis.

The moderate-confidence judgment in the NIE that Iraq had begun to reconstitute its nuclear weapons program and, if left unchecked, would probably have a nuclear weapon during this decade was also based heavily on authority. Understanding nuclear capabilities requires technical expertise provided, in this case, by two agencies, both of which provided expert judgment that turned out to be wrong. The National Ground Intelligence Center (NGIC) made the crucial judgment about whether certain aluminum tubes procured by Iraq were intended for use in conventional mortars (NGIC's particular expertise) or for use in a nuclear centrifuge. NGIC's expert authority erroneously concluded that the tubes were suitable for use in a nuclear centrifuge rather than in a conventional weapons application, thereby adding significant credibility to the argument that Iraq was reconstituting its nuclear weapons program. Though the Department of Energy (DOE) disagreed with NGIC on this point, DOE did support the key judgment, on other grounds, that Iraq had begun to reconstitute its nuclear weapons program. As the organization with special expertise in nuclear intelligence, DOE was the most authoritative agency on this issue. The combined weight of DOE's and NGIC's expert status lent significant authority to the erroneous nuclear key judgment in the NIE.[33]

In sum, the role of authority in the CW, BW, and nuclear judgments of the Iraq WMD NIE was crucial, its influence perhaps even expanded given the degree of empirical uncertainty surrounding these issues. A twenty-one-day congressional deadline also imposed a major time pressure for resolution of these complex weapons issues; it almost certainly served to exaggerate this way of knowing even beyond what might have occurred under a more relaxed production schedule. That the coordination session ended on a Friday just before the Monday deadline only added to the intensity for closure.

Habit of Thought

Habit of thought as a way of knowing was probably equally influential in the NIE's key judgments discussed here. Like authority, it too helped in meeting a short deadline. Knowledge of Iraq's WMD program was well established after the post–Desert Storm intelligence in 1991 showed that the IC had actually underestimated the program. The IC consensus on Iraq WMD began to build in the early 1990s, and no compelling evidence had surfaced to challenge it. It seems to have hardened into conventional wisdom by the mid-1990s. Saddam Hussein's own behavior reinforced this IC-wide consensus. He conducted a major denial and deception program that both rendered the UN inspection process ineffective and neutralized the effectiveness of U.S. intelligence.[34] This activity only increased Western suspicions that Saddam had weapons he was trying to hide, while a blunted UN inspection system and U.S. intelligence had failed to discover that he had actually eliminated the weapons in the early 1990s.

Habit of thought was effectively admitted by the CIA's deputy director of intelligence (the agency's senior manager of analysts) in a speech to analysts, in which she faulted the practice of "inherited assumptions" that went unquestioned in the NIE process.[35] Many of them were wrong. In its scathing review of the NIE, the Senate Select Committee on Intelligence described this phenomenon as "layering," namely, "the process of building an intelligence assessment primarily using previous judgments without substantial new intelligence reporting" and failing to factor in the cumulative uncertainties through the new assessments.[36]

Overturning a decade of consensus on the weapons would have been a difficult task under the best of circumstances. But analysts lacked good evidence to do so. Worse, to have made the opposite argument—that Iraq had no weapons, which we now know to be the reality—would have stunned policymakers who had been told for years by the IC that Iraq had retained such weapons. The same habit of thought that hobbled intelligence analysts and managers also hobbled the policymakers who had been consuming the erroneous journalistic-style, current intelligence reports on Iraq WMD for years. This particular habit of thought was shared across the intelligence and policy communities.

This habitual way of knowing was not recognized for what it was: a significant barrier to alternative analysis at a time when the impact of authority was also unchecked. Habit of thought, present in all the wrong judgments, was the starting point for an analysis that gave even greater credence to a misguided authority.

Rationalism

The role that reason played in producing erroneous WMD knowledge was probably as strong and error producing as the first two ways of knowing. By inductive inference, analysts built a cumulative picture of CW, BW, and nuclear reconstitution, all adding up to a significant program of WMD. Supported by habit of thought and reinforced by erroneous authority, persuasive reasoning carried the day. Even lacking solid information, analysts concluded that Iraq must have had the weapons even if we were not seeing them. In fact, *not* seeing them seemed to provide evidence that Iraq *had* them. The logic seemed impeccable: We know that Saddam Hussein had them in the past; he is a lying and evil-intentioned dictator; and his pervasive denial and deception efforts explain why we are not seeing them. The logic, therefore, added up to evidence *for* a weapons program, not against it.[37] However persuasive, this argument demonstrates that

as a way of building knowledge, logic is no better than the content of its premises. If the premises contain error, even the soundest reasoning can only repro-
duce error.

Empiricism

In contrast to the above three ways of knowing, empirical observations played
a startlingly minimal role in the NIE on Iraq's WMD: *The IC had no direct
evidence of WMD in Iraq at the time the estimate confidently asserted knowledge of Iraq's weapons programs.* Still, even allowing for the debilitating distortions in the analytical process wrought by the other three ways of knowing, how
could the empirical process break down so badly? The answer seems to be that
what little observable evidence there was of CW, BW, and nuclear reconstitution
was not only overinterpreted but also was not assessed relative to any available
evidence to the contrary. The senior defector's reporting in 1995 that Saddam
had shut down the WMD programs four years earlier was simply disregarded.[38]
Further, aggressive collection efforts in all disciplines kept failing to produce
results. This "negative evidence"—that is, the lack of fresh or convincing observable indicators of Iraq's purported weapons despite the concerted search for
them—was either explained away as denial and deception or discounted because
it did not support the habitual knowledge of a robust and active WMD capability.[39] Called "card stacking" in propaganda, this prosecutor's technique is what
passed for empirical analysis in the NIE.[40] But analysts did not actively consider
the additional hypothesis that the overwhelming lack of evidence on the key
weapons issues might also have meant that Iraq had shut down those programs.
Whatever else it was, this analysis was anything but empirical.

In sum, analysis of Iraq's WMD in the 2002 NIE and the analytical efforts
leading up to it show that when the empirical component of analysis is low, the
impact of other ways of knowing increases, with poor results. It also shows that
the NIE was an epistemological "perfect storm": All four ways of knowing—
authority (faulty), habit of thought (unquestioned), reasoning (flawed), and
empiricism (nearly absent)—failed to produce reliable knowledge. The errors
that each method produced are expected outcomes of epistemologies whose
strengths do not extend to discovering and correcting their own errors. For more
reliable analysis, we need to consider what a more scientific approach might
offer.

Epistemological Lessons for Analysis

To be successful, intelligence analysis must be able to produce knowledge and
foreknowledge that is reliable. The major epistemologies have the potential for
producing error as well as truth, as demonstrated in the errors produced in one
of the most high-visibility and policy-relevant NIEs in years. Because science,
unlike other ways of knowing, possesses unique self-corrective mechanisms

intrinsic to its own procedures, how might we adapt these mechanisms to intelligence analysis? The answer can be found in three parts: the role of the hypothesis, the role of coordination, and a prepublication checklist of epistemological vulnerabilities for analysts and managers.

The Hypothesis

Science is careful to distinguish between *knowledge*, which is true, and a *hypothesis*, which might or might not be true. The distinction is crucial. Before the hypothesis can become knowledge, it must survive rigorous analysis, including systematic efforts to disprove it (discussed below). A nonscientific approach, like the WMD estimate or a determined prosecutor seeking a conviction in a court, will merely try to "prove" something true. In qualitative research, as most intelligence is, this is often not hard to do. The analyst can merely select confirmatory facts and establish an easily reached standard of proof.[41]

In science, the opposite happens. Implementing objectivity rather than trying to prove a point, science actively tries to *prevent* the results from coming out the way the investigator may *want* them to come out. The guiding principle ensuring integrity of results is honest management of the hypothesis under investigation. This process has two parts: hypothesis generation and hypothesis testing.

Hypothesis generation refers to the source of the hypothesis, that is, where it comes from. Hypotheses (statements that can be empirically evaluated) can come from almost anywhere. The most lucrative source of hypotheses is theories and models of behavior (e.g., the behavior of states, groups, and leaders). Apart from explanation, the most important role that theories play is their ability to produce testable hypotheses. This is the test of a good theory. Hypotheses can also be generated by such logical systems as abduction, induction, and deduction (as discussed above). They can also be generated by policymakers, pundits, and assorted advocates who are fertile sources of interesting ideas, even if they advocate them. (Note that while policymakers can play an important role in *generating* hypotheses, their biases soundly disqualify them from any role in *testing* them; that role belongs to intelligence, not policy.) Hypotheses can also be produced by intelligence analysts, especially using such techniques as "brainstorming," "alternative analysis," "structured" analytical techniques, or "challenge" analysis. Examples include Devil's Advocacy, Team A/Team B Analysis, Red Cell exercises, Contingency (or "What-If") Analysis, High-Impact/Low-Probability Analysis, and Scenarios Development.[42] All these analytical approaches are capable of generating hypotheses. None of them, however, can test hypotheses.

Hypothesis *testing* is one of the most important differences between science and nonscientific activity. The whole idea is to make a sound decision about whether a particular research statement is true or false. Hypothesis testing with statistical tools used for quantitative data is, unfortunately, relevant for only a very small number of problems facing the intelligence analyst.[43] The reality is that most intelligence problems are qualitative, not quantitative. This limitation deprives the analyst of powerful statistical tools that can help discriminate between true statements and false ones. Lacking quantitative-like tools for analysis of qualitative issues, can the intelligence analyst still approximate the desired hypothesis-testing steps?

The answer is a qualified no: Present tools for qualitative analysis cannot provide the same level of rigor and, therefore, confidence that we find in quantitative techniques. *But the attributes that provide science with self-corrective mechanisms are still largely within reach.* To date, the social sciences have not yet developed qualitative hypothesis-testing techniques that offer the power of quantitative tests. But recent methodological innovations have brought promising new capabilities that can help the intelligence analyst get closer to this standard.

The Analysis of Competing Hypotheses (ACH), as described in Richards Heuer's *Psychology of Intelligence Analysis*,[44] offers real potential for testing *qualitative* hypotheses. As explained in chapter 16, ACH is now available as software for computer-aided analysis, for collaborative analysis, and in a more technically sophisticated Bayesian approach. Though none of the various ACH versions yet offers a true hypothesis-testing method equivalent to those used in large-N statistical applications, they do provide features that permit a much more rigorous evaluation of qualitative hypotheses than is otherwise possible. ACH "tests" hypotheses by comparing how well each stacks up against the evidence and by trying to *disconfirm* them.[45] It evaluates the *relative* validity of several *competing* hypotheses, that is, alternative explanations for the same observed phenomenon.[46] Referring to the example of the ill-fated WMD estimate discussed above, had ACH been used during the course of this estimate, the likelihood of achieving the same disastrous results would certainly have been lower.

Because ACH requires the comparison of *multiple* hypotheses, analysts would have been forced to examine more than one. But the flawed estimate tried to find evidence to demonstrate only one, that is, that Iraq possessed WMD. Even to have injected a single *alternative* hypothesis into the estimate drafting and coordination process would have improved the analysis. It might, for example, have forced consideration of a senior Iraqi defector's firsthand knowledge, which reported that the weapons programs had been stopped in 1991. Had this hypothesis been allowed to "compete" with the arguments for a weapons program, it would have forced an alternative look at why there was no direct evidence for the weapons. In this circumstance, the discussion might have entertained an idea that was true (Saddam *had* curtailed the programs) and examined the evidence for it. But what turned out be the correct hypothesis apparently never became part of the NIE deliberations.

In addition, ACH would have forced those involved to pay much closer attention to the relationship between the evidence and its role in the NIE's judgments. Even if only one hypothesis had been "tested," a closer scrutiny of the evidence should have undermined the favored view. We now know that the decisive imagery evidence for CW, Curveball's persuasive reporting on BW, and the heavily influential role of the aluminum tubes in nuclear reconstitution did not hold up over time. Conceivably, a much closer examination of the veracity of these three crucial (and we now know fragile) pieces of information to bolster the estimate's weighty findings should have exposed the enormous dependence of these three key judgments on such tenuous "evidence."[47]

In sum, whether or not ACH would have brought us markedly different results, we can be fairly sure that it would not have delivered the same wrong results with the same high levels of confidence.[48] This case vividly illustrates that to improve the reliability of results, the social sciences urgently need to develop qualitative hypothesis-testing techniques for intelligence analysis. Until other techniques arrive, ACH offers the best technique for this crucial step. And it also offers the self-corrective techniques that we find in science, the epistemological role model of choice. Tradecraft tools like ACH ward off "card stacking" and proving favored hypotheses. And the emphasis on generating and testing hypotheses, along with better use of peer review, can help ensure objectivity, transparency, and replicability—all vital self-corrective mechanisms.

Coordination

When analysts meet in a conference room to discuss every sentence and paragraph in an NIE, the often painful process typically results in a better analytical product. *Coordination is the only explicit step in the analytical process that already provides potential self-corrective mechanisms.* But the coordination process, regrettably, is too rarely used for this purpose. For the most part, inter-agency and intra-agency coordination have been corrupted into a linguistic exercise. Analysts and managers seek agreeable prose, *words* that may (or may not) help a policymaker but are crafted to get agreement among the parties in order to publish them. The primacy of finding just the right words to facilitate going to press necessarily subverts an otherwise invaluable epistemological process.

Coordination is the final and critical stage in the analytical process where significant errors can be detected and corrected. But this important feature of self-correction is lost when the focus shifts from epistemology to language. The coordination process needs to be rediscovered for its intended epistemological function to better ensure the reliability of the knowledge and foreknowledge that policymakers get from intelligence.

To incorporate the vital function of self-corrective mechanisms into intelligence, successful coordination should focus on the relationship between evidence and inference, probe for possible error, ask whether all the important hypotheses are being considered, and assess the nature of the evidence and the degree of dependence of the judgments on the quality of the evidence. It should ensure that the distinction between hypothesis and knowledge is clearly noted and that data are assessed by collection specialists as well as by analysts. Some of these functions should occur in ordinary peer review. But a sound coordination should also explicitly identify any judgments that are based on authority or habit of thought. And any judgments based on rationalism must confront the factual basis of the premises of the logic and not just the logic itself.

Epistemology Checklist

For major intelligence products that may have significant policy consequences, such as NIEs issued during war planning, analysts and managers should subject themselves to four tests of knowledge—each asking *how do I know that X is true?*—prior to the publication and release of such products:

1. Is X true because analysts believe in the *authority* of the information that says it is true? *Implications*: If so, be sure to understand the basis of the authority. If that is the principal or only basis for this knowledge, then recognize the enormous dependence of the validity of this knowledge on the soundness of the authority.

2. Is X true because this view is generally believed by most analysts today and it has been *true in the past*? *Implications*: Habit of thought works to a point, but its origins are often unknown and therefore hard to assess, and it is biased toward continuity, resistant to change, and susceptible to blind-side surprise. If this is the principal or only basis for knowing something, then recognize the enormous dependence of the validity of this knowledge on the basis of intellectual inertia. It is often right, but when wrong, it can be very wrong.

3. Is X true because analytical logic produced these conclusions? *Implications*: Because no present method of reasoning alone can produce knowledge, it is best to treat any conclusions derived by logic as only hypotheses that deserve further testing. Rationalist approaches are not only vulnerable to error, they cannot themselves determine whether their conclusions are true or false. Hypothesis testing is an empirical, not logical, operation.

4. Is X true because the *observable data* gathered suggest it is true? *Implications*: You might have gathered different data that would lead you to a different, possibly contradictory, conclusion. If the data gathering is incomplete and key information is missing—in intelligence, it almost always is—you do not have the full story. If it is selective to "prove" a point, it probably will. But the point will be no more valid than the selective techniques that support it. Sound empirical approaches require rigorous testing of multiple hypotheses, not just finding evidence to support a favored one.

As this chapter shows, a better epistemology—science—is available for intelligence analysis. Like the others, it too should be subjected to the prepublication tests of knowledge suggested above. The implications are that this approach to producing intelligence is less error prone because it consciously seeks to identify and correct its errors. If the experience of the October 2002 NIE on Iraq's WMD offers any guide to the selection of epistemologies for intelligence, then future key judgments should meet stricter epistemological standards before being provided to policymakers. Analysis produced using the self-corrective techniques that science offers will greatly improve the probability of getting reliable results.

Notes

The author is indebted to the RAND Corporation for providing time to develop this chapter, and to Roy Kirvan for an extremely valuable critique.

1. Briefing, *The Intelligence Community*, available on the director of national intelligence (DNI) website: www.dni.gov. A similar knowledge-based definition of intelligence predated the establishment of the DNI: "Reduced to its simplest terms, intelligence is knowledge and

foreknowledge of the world around us—the prelude to decision and action by U.S. policy-makers." See Office of Public Affairs, CIA, *A Consumers' Guide to Intelligence* (Washington, D.C.: Central Intelligence Agency, 1999), vii.

2. Epistemology has not been a popular subject in the literature of intelligence, but notable exceptions are Woodrow J. Kuhns, "Intelligence Failures: Forecasting and the Lessons of Epistemology," in *Paradoxes of Strategic Intelligence*, ed. Richard K. Betts and Thomas G. Mahnken (London: Frank Cass, 2003), 80–100; Michael W. Collier, "A Pragmatic Approach to Developing Intelligence Analysis," *Defense Intelligence Journal* 14, no. 3 (2005): 17–35; and Matthew Herbert, "The Intelligence Analyst as Epistemologist," *International Journal of Intelligence and Counterintelligence* 19, no. 4 (Winter 2006): 666–84.

3. Definitions are from the *American Heritage Dictionary* and *Webster's New Collegiate Dictionary*. The more authoritative *Stanford Encyclopedia of Philosophy* defines knowledge as "justified true belief" (JTB). The epistemological standards of this conception of knowledge seem presently beyond reach for most intelligence applications, and my ambitions here are more modest. In JTB terms, the arguments put forth in this chapter are akin to *reliablism*.

4. Allen W. Dulles, *The Craft of Intelligence* (Guilford, Conn.: Lyons Press, 2006), 1; first published in 1963. The author, director of central intelligence 1953–61, was the longest serving DCI in history.

5. These can be found variously in the epistemological literature, but I am indebted to David H. Bayley, formerly of the Graduate School of International Studies, University of Denver, who presented the basic argument made here in his research seminar during my graduate studies there years ago. Michael Collier presents a similar list of seven ways of knowing, adding *faith* and *common sense*, which are implicitly covered here in my discussion of habit of thought below, and *intuition*, which I have combined with rationalism. See Collier, "Pragmatic Approach to Developing Intelligence Analysis," 19.

6. Roberta Wohlstetter, *Pearl Harbor: Warning and Decision* (Palo Alto, Calif.: Stanford University Press, 1962), 337–38.

7. For an explanation of the "paradigm shift" from an earth-centered to a sun-centered understanding of the solar system, see Thomas H. Kuhn, *The Structure of Scientific Revolutions* (Chicago: University of Chicago Press, 1996, 3rd ed.), 67–69, 150–55.

8. For a very small number of cases of abrupt discontinuity such as the Soviet missile emplacement in Cuba and the Iran revolution examples discussed above, habit of thought can be an unreliable basis for warning. These cases are further discussed in chapter 12 of this volume.

9. Hans Reichenbach, *The Rise of Scientific Philosophy* (Berkeley: University of California Press, 1968), chaps. 2–4 and p. 74.

10. A fourth system, dialectical reasoning, was devised by Friedrich Hegel and made famous by Karl Marx but is omitted from discussion here given its limited applicability to intelligence.

11. As Reichenbach explains: "It cannot be overemphasized that logical deduction cannot create independent results. It is merely an instrument of connection; it derives conclusions from given axioms, but cannot inform us about the truth of the axioms." Reichenbach, *Rise of Scientific Philosophy*, 57, and also 37. Also see Kuhns, "Intelligence Failures," 93.

12. E.g., the power of hypothetico-deductive reasoning led to the discovery of the planet Neptune; see Reichenbach, *Rise of Scientific Philosophy*, 100–3.

13. As Kuhns has pointed out, deductive reasoning that helps identify certain consequences that follow from hypotheses, even if such hypotheses are not general laws, can play a useful, if limited, role in intelligence analysis. Kuhns, "Intelligence Failures," 91–92.

14. Kuhns, "Intelligence Failures," 86; the crow example is cited on 89. Also see Collier, "Pragmatic Approach to Developing Intelligence Analysis," 31.

15. "In addition to deduction, the physicist depends on the use of induction, since he starts with observations and foretells future observations. The prediction of future observations is

both his goal and the test of the truth of his hypotheses." Reichenbach, *Rise of Scientific Philosophy*, 114.

16. Ibid., 81–82. This principle is better illustrated if we extend the example from crows to swans: Even after repeated observations of white swans, our temptation to resist the conclusion that all swans are white would be justified with a visit to Australia, where we would find black swans. See Reichenbach, *Rise of Scientific Philosophy*, 242.

17. Inductive logic rests on theories of probability. See Abraham Kaplan, *The Conduct of Inquiry: Methodology for Behavioral Science* (San Francisco: Chandler, 1964), 232–34.

18. Collier, "Pragmatic Approach to Developing Intelligence Analysis," 31. Not all empirically minded analysts agree that the statistical methods used in social sciences are applicable to intelligence analysis. Such skeptics argue that the kinds of variables and relationships studied by intelligence analysts are, more often than not, so specific and complex that they are not easily amenable to classical statistical analysis. See Richards J. Heuer Jr., ed., *Quantitative Approaches to Political Intelligence: The CIA Experience* (Boulder, Colo.: Westview Press, 1978), chap. 1. We return to this issue below.

19. Rob Johnston, *Analytical Culture in the U.S. Intelligence Community* (Washington, D.C., Center for the Study of Intelligence, Central Intelligence Agency, 2005), 19–20.

20. See John R. Josephson and Susan G. Josephson, eds., *Abductive Inference: Computation, Philosophy, Technology* (New York: Cambridge University Press, 1994); and Peter Lipton, *Inference to the Best Explanation* (London: Routledge, 2001).

21. Reichenbach, *Rise of Scientific Philosophy*, 75.

22. Ibid., 32.

23. I.e., producing intelligence from human, signals, imagery, measurement and signatures, and open sources—the collection disciplines.

24. A particularly ill-informed rationalist polemic is made by David Brooks in "The Art of Intelligence," *New York Times*, April, 2, 2005.

25. James B. Bruce, "Dynamic Adaptation: A Twenty-First Century Intelligence Paradigm," winner of a 2004 DCI Galileo Award, 4–5.

26. Johnston, *Analytical Culture*, 19–21.

27. In the vast literature explaining how science works, an excellent primer is Hugh G. Gauch Jr., *Scientific Method in Practice* (New York: Cambridge University Press, 2002). An especially useful adaptation for social science is Kaplan, *Conduct of Inquiry*. Summaries of the applicability of scientific methods to intelligence analysis are in Collier, "A Pragmatic Approach to Developing Intelligence Analysis," and in Johnston, *Analytical Culture*, 19–20.

28. In the physics case, scientists in Utah had claimed the ability to produce nuclear fusion through an unconventional table top process. Subsequent attempts by other physicists to replicate the procedures of "cold fusion" revealed that the original claims could not be upheld by accepted scientific standards. See David Goodstein, "Whatever Happened to Cold Fusion?" *American Scholar* 63, no. 4 (Fall 1994): 527–41. In the human cloning case, a South Korean researcher announced that he had succeeded in cloning human DNA. Hwang Woo-Suk's startling claims were revealed as fraudulent in 2005, as were at least four earlier attempts made by others since 1978. From Wikipedia, www.wikipedia.org.

29. National Intelligence Council, *Iraq's Continuing Programs of Weapons of Mass Destruction*, NIE 2002–16HC, October 2002. Discussion here is based largely on the authoritative Commission on the Intelligence Capabilities of the United States Regarding Weapons of Mass Destruction, *Report to the President of the United States, March 31, 2005* (Washington, D.C.: U.S. Government Printing Office, 2005) (hereafter, *WMD Commission Report*); and on chapter 12.

30. The findings that Saddam Hussein had essentially shut down Iraq's WMD programs in 1991–92—CW, BW, and efforts to reconstitute the nuclear weapons program—are in the study of the Iraq Survey Group (ISG), *Comprehensive Report of the Special Advisor to the DCI on Iraq WMD*, posted on the CIA website October 6, 2004, also referred to as the Duelfer Report; hereafter, *ISG Report*.

31. This has been greatly simplified here; it is fully elaborated in *WMD Commission Report*, 122–24.

32. *WMD Commission Report*, 87–100; the quotation is on 93. Curveball was an Iraqi emigrant source reporting to the German intelligence service that in turn passed his reporting on to DIA's Defense HUMINT Service.

33. See full elaboration in the *WMD Commission Report*, 65–79.

34. *WMD Commission Report*, chaps. 1, 7–8, and pp. 161–62, 169, 352, 372–75.

35. Jamie Miscik, deputy director of intelligence's "State of Analysis Speech," All-Hands Meeting, CIA Auditorium February 11, 2004, 8–9; released March 2004.

36. Senate Select Committee on Intelligence, *U.S. Intelligence Community's Prewar Intelligence Assessments on Iraq*, 108th Congress, 2nd Session, July 9, 2004, 22.

37. *WMD Commission Report*, 169–70. Robert Jervis, "Reports, Politics, and Intelligence Failures: The Case of Iraq," *Journal of Strategic Studies* 29, no. 1 (February 2006): 42–45.

38. This was reporting of Hussein Kamil, Saddam Hussein's son-in-law who defected in 1995. He returned to Iraq three years later only to be killed. See *WMD Commission Report*, 52; *ISG Report* 46, and the Butler Report, formally Committee of Privy Counselors, *Review of Intelligence on Weapons of Mass Destruction* (London: Stationary Office, 2004), 47–48, 51.

39. *WMD Commission Report*, 169–70.

40. For an explanation of how this technique—i.e., using selective evidence to "prove" a favored hypothesis—distorts analysis, see Richards Heuer's reconstruction of how a major Soviet defector was wrongly found to be a KGB penetration instead of a bone fide source. Richards J. Heuer Jr., "Nosenko: Five Paths to Judgment," in *Inside CIA's Private World: Declassified Articles from the Agency's Internal Journal, 1955–1992*, ed. H. Bradford Westerfield (New Haven, Conn.: Yale University Press, 1995).

41. Lawyers can "prove" guilt or innocence. Mathematicians can offer "proofs" for solving certain problems. But science does not try to prove anything. It only seeks to accept a hypothesis as true or reject it as false through reliable methods—and keep the issue open to further investigation.

42. Roger Z. George, "Fixing the Problem of Analytical Mindsets," in *Intelligence and the National Security Strategist: Enduring Issues and Challenges*, ed. Roger Z. George and Robert D. Kline (Lanham, Md.: Rowman & Littlefield, 2006), 318–22. See also chapter 10 of this volume by Jack Davis.

43. In quantitative analysis where the number of cases (or N) is above a certain number (greater than fifty, according to Collier, "Pragmatic Approach to Developing Intelligence Analysis," 26–27), statistical hypothesis testing is a straightforward procedure. Depending on the type of data (nominal, ordinal, or interval), number of cases, and whether the data represent samples or a whole "universe," statistical tests can often reliably determine the probability that a particular hypothesis is true or false. Intelligence questions that lend themselves to quantitative analysis should be treated with appropriate statistical tools for the epistemological benefits of hypothesis testing.

44. Richards J. Heuer Jr., *Psychology of Intelligence Analysis* (Washington, D.C.: Center for the Study of Intelligence, Central Intelligence Agency, 1999); see chap. 8. A PDF file is available at www.cia.gov/csi/books/19104/index.html.

45. Conventional ACH, including the computer-aided version, tests hypotheses by having several of them compete against each other, then the weaker hypotheses, i.e., those with most evidence *against* them, are rejected (instead of concluding that those with most evidence for them have been "proven"). Surviving ones have a stronger claim to being true. This follows Popper's more rigorous test of the principle of falsifiability that requires the disconfirmation of false hypotheses rather than the confirmation of true ones. See Karl Popper, *The Logic of Scientific Discovery* (London: Hutchinson Press, 1959).

46. Unlike most statistical tests, this version of ACH does not measure probabilities with some statistical margin of error. The more advanced Bayesian version does provide a probability calculation for the hypotheses being examined. Because it relies on analysts' expert

judgments about evidence, the resulting data are richer but with the important caveat that the data used are judgmental, not necessarily empirical. See chapter 16 below by Heuer, and *Psychology of Intelligence Analysis* for elaboration.

47. This is an explicit exercise—step 6, the sensitivity check—in ACH. See Heuer, *Psychology of Intelligence Analysis*, 105–6. It is also performed, if by a different route, in the computer-aided version discussed in chapter 16. This step, by whatever means, should be a required activity in the coordination of every key judgment in every NIE.

48. We know that the estimators were facing enormous time pressures to complete the NIE in twenty-one days—which they did. On that timeline, the estimate was in coordination for only three days. We can only speculate whether an added day applying ACH would have justified the probability of getting a better analytical result.

CHAPTER 12

The Missing Link: The Analyst-Collector Relationship

James B. Bruce

ALTHOUGH CONSIDERABLE ATTENTION has been focused on the relationship between the analyst and the policymaker, a key determinant of analytical effectiveness is found at the nexus of the analyst and the collector (see figure 12.1). This chapter explores this critical relationship through a brief examination of eight cases of intelligence failure. It shows that *when collection fails, the probability of analytical failure increases dramatically.* Better analysis can help reduce this vulnerability. A greater appreciation by analysts for their significant dependency on collected intelligence will help illuminate how attentive collectors and analysts can improve the odds for intelligence success.

Intelligence Failure: Eight Instructive Cases

The following case studies of intelligence failure were selected because of their intrinsic importance in intelligence history. They do not constitute a "representative sample" that shows the overall record of intelligence performance over the six-decade period they span, 1941–2002. But they are highly instructive for what they reveal about the important linkage between intelligence collection and analysis. What these cases illustrate, above all, is that collection failures—shown chiefly in the key information that was *not* collected, and in some cases erroneous or misleading information that was—are almost certain to result in analysis failures. Other analytical failures can result from information that is collected but is misinterpreted, especially if denial and deception and a faulty analytical mindset delimit consideration of alternative hypotheses.

From Pearl Harbor to Iraq and a half-dozen major failures between them, we can discern a repetitive pattern of collection shortfalls whose effects can be traced through the analytical process that was itself equally deficient in dealing with them. On the collection side, the single most important factor accounting for failure is the impact of intelligence *denial*—namely, effective countermeasures taken by an intelligence target that prevented successful collection against it. The impact of denial, as nearly all these cases illustrate, is *missing information* needed for analysis. On the analytical side, the failure to correct for the impact of missing information, when combined with a *lack of imagination*, is an almost

191

FIGURE 12.1
The Collection-Analysis Nexus

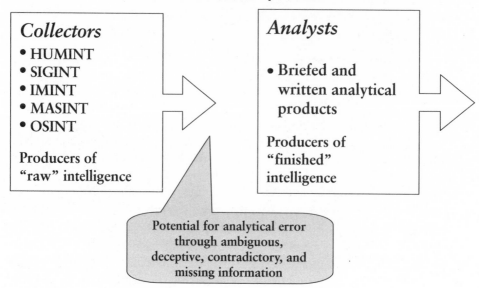

surefire predictor of analytical failure. Other factors, too, such as poor collection requirements, poor information sharing, and the impact of faulty assumptions, also "pile on," helping to ensure intelligence failure.

Pearl Harbor: Failure to Warn of a Surprise Military Attack

The failure to warn U.S. military and political decision makers of the impending Japanese attack in the early morning hours of December 7, 1941, had many roots.[1] On a just-awakening Hawaiian island where a sizable portion of the U.S. naval fleet lay at rest and vulnerable to attack, several hundred Japanese warplanes appeared without warning and, facing negligible air defenses, systematically and methodically sunk or heavily damaged 21 vessels, including 4 battleships. In addition, 164 aircraft were destroyed at four nearby airfields. The capable Japanese bombers and fighters that attacked were launched in darkened skies from 6 aircraft carriers that had steamed from Japan to Hawaii completely unanticipated and undetected by U.S. intelligence. "Secrecy and deception having effectively screened the movements of the Japanese task force," U.S. intelligence had failed to understand Japanese intentions to attack U.S. territory, as well as the place, time, and strength of the attack.[2] Apart from the enormous loss of naval vessels and army aircraft, more than 2,400 Americans were killed in this historic warning failure.

How was this large Japanese flotilla consisting of thirty-three warships and auxiliary craft en route for eleven days missed when the U.S. military should have been alert to its arrival, when both the Army and Navy had, in fact, collected key information that should have warned decision makers? And when—even lacking "smoking gun" evidence that an attack was brewing or imminent—enough information was already in possession of U.S. intelligence that should have forewarned the military about this devastating destruction of American forces and unprecedented loss of life in a single attack?[3]

For our purposes, the answers explaining this failed warning can be summarized in four key facts:

- *Collection degraded by denial and deception (D&D).* The Japanese prepared and conducted this attack in such a way as to neutralize U.S. intelligence. In concealing their intentions to go to war with the United States along with any tactical information that might have tipped off the attack, their successful denial of important information to U.S. collectors enfeebled analysis. They also conducted related deception operations involving naval and other military forces as well as deceptive diplomatic activity that further weakened U.S. intelligence capabilities to anticipate attack.[4]
- *Poor sharing.* What information U.S. intelligence did collect that might have made a difference was not fully exploited, in part because it was not shared between the Army (reading decrypted Japanese diplomatic codes) and the Navy (reading decrypted Japanese naval codes), despite their shared responsibility to warn. Poor sharing of limited collection greatly impeded warning analysis.[5]
- *Signal-to-noise ratio.* Despite the availability of some kinds of information, the signal-to-noise ratio greatly impaired warning: An abundance of marginal or irrelevant information overwhelmed and obscured a few vital pieces that might have enabled successful warning if they had been noticed and properly appreciated for their real worth.[6]
- *Faulty assumptions.* Whatever their capabilities, the Japanese had not revealed any intentions to attack. Analysts not only did not expect a Japanese attack on Pearl Harbor; some actually assumed that it was a very-low-probability event because an attack on Hawaii would mean, according to a key figure at Pearl Harbor, "national suicide" for Japan.[7]

A retrospective look at the Pearl Harbor warning failure suggests that Japanese D&D success against U.S. intelligence was a vital requirement for a successful surprise attack. The failure to collect any information at all on the massive eleven-day transit of the Japanese task force across the Pacific Ocean deprived analysts of the best possible evidence that would have forewarned them of the attack. Distracted by the "noise" of tangential and unrelated information, hobbled by poor sharing of what key information had been collected, and constrained by faulty assumptions, analysts' inability to understand or counter effective Japanese D&D ensured the historic warning failure.

Soviet Missiles in Cuba: Failure to Warn of Covert Emplacements

When the Board of National Estimates considered in September 1962 whether the Soviet Union would attempt to secretly install offensive nuclear missiles in Cuba, just ninety miles off U.S. shores, the resulting special national intelligence estimate essentially concluded that the Soviets would not. Lacking good evidence to show that the Soviet leaders would attempt such a risky military provocation that would dramatically tilt the nuclear balance—and lacking evidence to the contrary—the estimate reasoned that the Soviet leaders would not attempt such a dangerously reckless move that would risk destabilizing the evolving superpower relationship. According to the estimate, a secret missile emplacement in Cuba "would be incompatible with Soviet practice to date and with Soviet policy as we presently estimate it. It would indicate a far greater willingness to increase the level of risk in U.S.–Soviet relations than the USSR has displayed thus far, and consequently would have important policy implications with respect to other areas and other problems in East–West relations."[8]

The analysts who imputed such seemingly rational motives for Soviet restraint were proven wrong when U-2 aerial photography on October 14, 1962, revealed the construction of SS-4 and SS-5 road mobile missile sites about fifty miles from Havana, less than a month after the estimate was issued.

Two factors stand out in explaining why the analysts got it wrong:

- *Collection degraded by D&D.* Key information was missing at the time of the estimate. Effective Soviet D&D prevented U.S. collection from acquiring good evidence earlier that would have better informed analysis.
- *Assumptions misled.* In the absence of good information, that is, empirical evidence, analysts relied on their own assumptions. Thus their reasoning, in this case, was flawed by faulty assumptions.

Soviet D&D efforts to install the missiles undetected were impressive by any measure. The decision-making process and its implementation were heavily compartmented in the Soviet Union. Only a handful of Politburo members and as few as five military officers were cleared into the planning. The cargo being shipped, and its destination and unloading, were heavily concealed to avert U.S. detection. D&D measures to support this operation included "loading from different docks in Soviet ports, false bills of lading, nighttime unloading of missiles in Cuba, and circuitous routes of delivery. These efforts were complemented by the use of public disinformation campaigns, false media reports and high-level, private Soviet denials and 'reassurances' from [Communist Party of the Soviet Union] General Secretary [Nikita] Khrushchev, Foreign Minister Gromyko, and Soviet Ambassador to the United States Anatoly Dobrynin, who acknowledged in his memoirs that he had not been informed of the delivery of offensive missiles in Cuba."[9]

Supporting deception, successful denial took a major toll on analysis. The lack of information on the emplacement of the missiles over a several-month period (until the October discovery by U-2 overflights) severely impaired the analytical process because *failed collection ensured a more prominent role for analysts' assumptions* in preparing the estimate.[10] This matters less when the assumptions are identified, explicitly acknowledged, and correct. But when they are hidden, their impact is insidious; and when they are wrong, as they were in this case, they doomed the estimate to a failed warning forecast.

Analysts might have been able to overcome the impact of failed collection with better tradecraft, such as the use of multiple hypotheses or scenarios to force consideration of more than one outcome.[11] In addition, analysts needed to undertake a vigorous effort to identify their assumptions—in particular, those concerning the putative rationality of the Soviets' propensity for risk aversion and the strategic calculus that led the Soviets to underestimate U.S. resolve to preserve the nuclear status quo.[12] Without identifying such critical assumptions, analysts could not easily assess their impact on steering the analytical process to erroneous conclusions. These important lessons remain for future analytical puzzles, especially those compounded by major D&D.

The Yom Kippur War: Failure to Warn

When Egypt and Syria joined in a surprise military attack against Israel in October 1973, analysts in the U.S. intelligence community—and worse, in Israel—failed to warn of the well-planned Arab invasion. This failure is especially notable given the high state of tension and political hostilities between the belligerents and the general expectations for an outbreak of war since the Israelis had pounded the Arab states and seized so much of their land in the 1967 Six-Day War. Indeed, the alert levels in Israel were high during the autumn of 1973, and the likelihood of an Arab invasion had been hotly debated in the months preceding the attack. It is also notable because, unlike most of the other cases examined here, collection largely succeeded and the failure of analysis cannot be easily blamed on poor collection. In light of the political context, the general expectation for war, and good collection, why did warning fail?

Most students of Yom Kippur agree that Israeli analysts *did* have sufficient information at hand to justify a clear warning of imminent invasion.[13] But the analysts had failed to make the call, partly out of fear of raising false alarms (the "cry wolf" syndrome), and partly because they clung to false assumptions about Arab intentions as well as capabilities. In contrast with most of the other cases examined here, Israeli warning analysts had ample information in their possession, but they either disregarded or misinterpreted what information they had.[14]

To be sure, their warning task was greatly complicated by the deception operations that Egypt and Syria had mounted against the Israelis. The ploy of frequent military exercises amassing troops near the borders was reinforced by public complaints of poor military equipment and maintenance, deceptive statements belying the secret Egyptian–Syrian military agreement, and public posturing for Henry Kissinger's peace initiative just one month before the invasion.[15]

For their part, the Israelis were disadvantaged by an intelligence denial that was good enough to impair their full understanding and support successful deception. They also held to erroneous assumptions about what they called "the Concept," a view that presumed the necessity of Arab air superiority over Israel prior to attack that did not exist at that time. The Concept also relied on the credibility of Israel's deterrent posture to an enemy that was undeterred. Analytically impaired with faulty assumptions, Israeli (and U.S.) analysts did not succeed in understanding the Arab mind, to which the "rationality" of the improbable invasion made perfect sense.[16]

Perhaps the key issue in the Yom Kippur War warning failure is the reliance on unquestioned assumptions. This case dramatically illustrates that when assumptions drive analysis—often unwittingly—analysts need to identify and aggressively challenge them. It is notable that Israeli intelligence formalized an internal procedure of "Devil's Advocacy" following the Yom Kippur warning debacle precisely for this purpose, namely, to ensure that critical but unquestioned assumptions would no longer go unchallenged on important intelligence issues such as warning of a surprise attack.

Revolution in Iran: Unnoticed

The abrupt fall of the once highly popular Shah Mohammad Reza Pahlavi of Iran to the Ayatollah Ruholla Khomeini, a radical Islamic cleric then living in Paris, marked a genuine revolution that shook the foundation of Iranian society and shattered its body politic. In contrast to the countless coups d'état that populate political instability databases everywhere, a genuine revolution like this one only comes along a few times a century. Yet analysts missed this one, not fully comprehending its profound meaning until well after it was over.[17]

How did this happen? Again, this case illustrates a core idea of the collection–analysis nexus: Failed analysis is often only one step behind failed collection. But analysis done smartly—even in the face of poor collection—is not irretrievably doomed to failure if it can learn to develop analytical correctives to collection shortfalls.

Of course the key information that analysts lacked would have characterized the shah's regime as increasingly unpopular, actually hated by growing legions of Islamic radicals, and rapidly losing support among the secular middle classes as well. It would have described a resurgence of Shia Islam in its most fundamentalist strains; and a weak and corrupt system of government whose capacity to govern and political legitimacy were increasingly in question. Above all, it would have revealed a growing, perhaps unbridgeable, chasm between the angry clerics then preaching powerful antigovernment sermons in mosques throughout Iran and a secular and modernizing dictatorship increasingly disconnected from a restive population that it wrongly believed to the end still supported it.

Where was information like this to be found? It was in the "Persian Street," in the mosques and the souks. And it was there for the asking. But U.S. intelligence on Iranian political and societal issues was notably lacking. According to Kenneth Pollack, "The volume of CIA political reporting on Iran in the early 1970s actually dropped below that of the late 1940s, and the U.S. embassy in Tehran had few officers who could speak Farsi or had previously served in Iran."[18] This shortfall was partly by design as the ten CIA case officers had no real presence outside the diplomatic circles in downtown Tehran, and they focused on Soviet requirements or economic and energy issues. Iran's domestic political issues were effectively off limits to U.S. intelligence, largely in deference to the Pahlavi regime. And overdependence on the shah's intelligence service, the SAVAK, to provide the United States with information the shah's regime either did not have or did not want to share was a costly mistake.[19] U.S. human intelligence (HUMINT) collection was blinded to the brewing revolution.

Lacking needed information on the radicalization of Iranian society and the growing subversive power of the clerics, intelligence analysts again were ignorant of reality and comfortable in their assumptions—which were mostly wrong.

In retrospect, the analysts involved seemed addicted to the mindset that the political disturbances in the preceding year were unimportant in the face of a strong and decisive leader who had demonstrated past resiliency and a capacity to take whatever steps were needed to retain control. In fact, this leader was not nearly as strong and decisive as widely believed. Unbeknownst to U.S. analysts (but known to a few French doctors), the leader with a reputation for taking decisive actions against internal unrest was instead terminally ill.[20] Thus a key analytical assumption about the shah's capacity to act was wrong.

In failing to correctly assess a revolution in the making and a declining leader's ability to manage it, this case provides another illustration of the triumph of faulty assumptions over the absence of needed information. This failure, while rooted in poor analyst understanding of limited collection, highlights the dangers of clinging to unquestioned assumptions and the demonstrable lack of analytical imagination.

Indian Nuclear Tests: Surprise on the Subcontinent

The failure to warn U.S. policymakers of impending nuclear tests in the politically volatile South Asia region is also rooted in the debilitating combination of poor collection and poor analysis. But it was aided and abetted by an effective Indian D&D effort that deprived the United States of the kind of information that had successfully tipped analysts to Indian test preparations just three years earlier. Also, deceptive diplomatic statements by India's foreign minister were calculated to reassure Washington that the Indian government had no intentions of testing nuclear weapons.[21]

How did the analysts miss this one? As in the other cases discussed here, the failure begins with successful denial and poor collection. No good intelligence, human or technical, forewarned of imminent testing.[22] But the open press reporting during the elections just months before should have alerted analysts to the campaign intentions of the Bharata Janata Party (BJP), which had just come to power, to make India a full nuclear power. Open source information of decided intelligence interest was either underemphasized or disregarded.[23]

That open press reports did not play a more prominent role in this instance is probably because other collection methods, notably space-borne imagery, had proven so accurate in the past. The attempted 1995 tests had been halted through a forceful U.S. diplomatic demarche that was based on detailed imagery that was also shown—we now know, mistakenly—to the Indians in 1995. This authorized disclosure revealed how U.S. intelligence could detect preparations for testing from space. The lesson was not lost on the Indians, themselves a space power with their own imagery satellites. From this demarche, they learned to prepare their next tests more carefully so as not to repeat their 1995 attempt, which was aborted by outstanding intelligence support to U.S. diplomacy. This time they averted detection by skillfully avoiding satellite observation and by preventing telltale signs beforehand that an imagery satellite might photograph.[24] This adaptation represents sophisticated intelligence denial based on a good understanding of U.S. classified collection capabilities, which the Indians had learned through the backfired demarche process and through damaging press leaks that further disclosed these capabilities.[25]

With previously reliable technical collection now enfeebled and analysts unwitting about these collection limitations, their overdependency on information that never arrived facilitated failure. But it did not guarantee it. Helped along by robust Indian D&D and poor U.S. use of open sources, the failure also relied on invalid assumptions: That the BJP election platform had no greater credibility than any in the United States—an ethnocentric view of how politicians might behave if they acted like Americans, whose fidelity to campaign rhetoric wanes discernibly once the reality of office holding sets in. Not so in this case. Further, the Indians had already demonstrated the technical capability to test just three years earlier. So it is fair to ask why this readiness and capability did not form part of the analysts' understanding of what to expect when a new and hard-line party publicly advocating nuclear weapons had just come to power. This analytical mindset ill served an important warning situation where intelligence collection proved unable to deliver the goods. Better awareness among analysts of their collection dependencies, of the added limitations on collection that effective D&D imposes, and of the potential for surprise when discernible political change is afoot would have mitigated the impact of faulty analytical assumptions.

Soviet Biological Weapons: A Late-Breaking Story

By the time U.S. intelligence analysts began to understand the enormous scope and scale of the Soviets' biological weapons (BW) program built in the 1970s and 1980s, the Soviet system was about to collapse.[26] Yet during the cold war between the two superpowers, the Soviet government had assembled a daunting capability to research, develop, test, and deploy highly lethal bioweapons. Because BW was such a heavily compartmented program inside the Soviet Union, no one in the West had any understanding at all about the magnitude of the effort and the potential menace it posed to the United States. For U.S. intelligence, the issue was all but missing.[27]

This blissful ignorance changed with startling revelations made by two Soviet defectors, Vladimir Pesechnik and Ken Alibek, who had held senior positions in these programs.[28] Alibek disclosed that the Soviet leaders had begun a huge, secret BW program shortly after signing the Biological Weapons Convention in 1972 that outlawed these weapons. By the time that Alibek defected twenty years later, the Soviets had covertly developed and stockpiled hundreds of tons of anthrax and dozens of tons of plague and smallpox for use as weapons. According to this high-level defector, the Soviets had harnessed BW for single-warhead intercontinental ballistic missiles in the 1970s and had begun in 1988 to develop anthrax, plague, and smallpox for use on the multiple-warhead SS-18 missiles for targeting American cities. The Soviets had also conducted research for deployment of BW warheads on cruise missiles.[29] More than 60,000 people in over sixty installations were involved in research, testing, production, and storage of lethal bacterial and viral agents, so how did analysts miss this several-decade military effort?[30]

The pattern is familiar: Poor collection foreshadows analytical failure. In this case, before the defectors there was almost no collection at all. But it was certainly one of the hardest targets in one of the most impenetrable countries because BW ranked among the most secret of all Soviet programs. Even as late as 1990, only four members of the ruling Soviet Politburo were even aware of it. The D&D effort itself was massive. The huge program was cloaked in convincing cover stories, such as pharmaceuticals and genetic research; no discernible evidence could have revealed military involvement; and U.S. inspectors were foiled with elaborate ruses. In one instance of an outbreak of anthrax in Sverdlovsk where over a hundred people had died in a BW accident in 1979, a highly thorough cover-up had masked all possible indications of a BW connection.[31] Like the rest of the world, U.S. intelligence was clueless.

Until the defectors arrived, analysts had no substantial information to analyze. Still, they did not much hypothesize about the threat possibility either, and there appears to have been scant attention given to it in national intelligence estimates or other analytical efforts that might have addressed this significant threat. It does not seem to have generated meaningful collection requirements nor become a worthy analytical issue in the intelligence community.

Apart from the lack of collection that provided no evidence for a BW program, this failure seems equally rooted in an analytical mindset that combined two key attributes. The first was that there was little or no imagination that a strategically significant and well-funded BW program would have been entirely consistent with a massive strategic military machine that sought superiority over U.S. forces in nearly every way that mattered. The second was that analysts are understandably disinclined to entertain beliefs without evidence, especially because outside experts (notably the prominent Harvard biologist Matthew Meselson) heavily discounted a Soviet BW program, and modest U.S. experience with its own BW effort had been shut down in 1969.[32] So why should intelligence analysts expect the Soviet Union to develop BW on a massive scale?

In light of what we now know about this significant Soviet military program, the failure to understand it when it mattered most to U.S. defense planners reveals a disturbing lack of analytical imagination—an inability to generate high-impact if low-probability hypotheses. This analytical disability can only be addressed through concerted tradecraft and better management practices, as well as fully understanding and addressing collection shortfalls. Such approaches could both Red Team and "worst case" yet unimagined scenarios, then mobilize effective analytical strategies to compensate for poor collection—then demand better collection where analytical concerns may justify it. The Silberman-Robb WMD [weapons of mass destruction] Commission report warns of insufficient attention to precisely threats of this kind and the need for substantial analytical capabilities worthy of the threat.[33]

September 11, 2001: Echoes of Pearl Harbor

The "Day of Infamy" that President Franklin Roosevelt called the Japanese attack on Pearl Harbor was repeated sixty years later by the successful execution of a terrorist plot that had seized four U.S. commercial airliners and deployed them as missiles to topple the World Trade Center towers and smash into the Pentagon.[34] When the dust had settled, 3,000 people were dead, overwhelmingly civilians who did not have a clue that their country was so unprepared for this kind of bolt from the blue. Though many will argue whether the terrorist attacks on September 11, 2001, were a strategic warning failure (the character and importance of the terrorist threat were not adequately conveyed to decision makers), others believe that it is at least an open-and-shut case of a tactical warning failure (the event itself was simply not foretold in intelligence). Still others argue that September 11 was not a warnable event. But there is no disagreement that the terrorist warning performance before September 11 will not serve the nation after that fateful date.

In diagnosing the intelligence part of the larger government-wide systemic failure, we can see the same four prominent features of Pearl Harbor repeating themselves in September 11:[35]

- *Collection degraded by D&D.* Al-Qaeda's outstanding operational security was every bit as good as the Japanese had exercised to mask the surprise attack on Pearl Harbor six decades earlier. In successfully denying intelligence collection against the plot—chiefly foiling needed HUMINT and signals intelligence (SIGINT) penetrations—the terrorist plotters left the analysts largely empty handed when better information would have eased the burden of analysis. The key information—attack planning—was missing.[36]
- *Poor sharing.* A major finding of the 9/11 Commission echoed the Pearl Harbor experience that unshared information degrades warning.[37] Just as the Army and the Navy were reluctant to provide each other with intelligence in 1941, largely for bureaucratic reasons, the Federal Bureau of Investigation and Central Intelligence Agency appear to have repeated the pattern in 2000–1. Each had information that would have helped the other—and would have helped the nation—had they opted to share it in time.[38]
- *Signal-to-noise ratio.* As Director of Central Intelligence George Tenet told the 9/11 Commission, the system was "blinking red" during the summer of 2001.[39] Among the countless facts, meaningless chaff, and tidbits of terrorist-related intelligence, there were so few pieces of salient information that pointed to the September 11 planning that they were easily swamped in the surrounding "noise."[40]
- *Faulty assumptions.* The conventional wisdom among most analysts was that terrorist attacks against the United States would most likely occur abroad, not against the U.S. homeland, and that airline hijackings would entail hostage taking. Mass suicide attacks against high-density office buildings in the homeland were not part of the collection or analytical posture.[41]

The convergence of these factors reduced the likelihood of successful warning of September 11 to near-impossible odds. The 9/11 Commission is certainly correct in emphasizing the importance of imagination in analysis, and the lack of it leading up to September 11. But it is misleading at best to characterize the missed warning as a failure "to connect the dots." While they were mired in tens of thousands, perhaps hundreds of thousands, of terrorist threat warnings in 2001,[42] analysts had far too little plot-related intelligence to have specifically warned of the coming catastrophe. The essence of the intelligence problem was less the failure to connect the dots than the overall lack of needed dots—more dots, and better dots—in the first place. To connect the dots, we first need to collect them.

But analysts too have a major responsibility to exercise imagination, to define and direct collection requirements, and to produce more reliable analysis when collection against hard warning problems is likely to come up short. The first crucial step is to notice that collection is coming up short—then act on it.

Iraq's WMD: The Weapons That Were Not There

Despite the high expectations of finding WMD in Iraq in 2003, within several months of launching Operation Iraqi Freedom, U.S. and coalition forces began to face the nettlesome fact that they were coming up dry.[43] A dedicated search team, the Iraq Survey Group, also failed to uncover or locate any WMD anywhere in Iraq. This would not be so significant were it not for the fact that U.S. intelligence, most notably in a national intelligence estimate (NIE) published in October 2002, had claimed that Saddam Hussein's Iraq possessed fairly significant WMD capabilities across a broad spectrum of prohibited weapons, and that the U.S. decision to invade and topple Saddam's regime was predicated on these claims. Intelligence failed.

The 2002 Iraq WMD NIE claimed that[44]

- Iraq had an active chemical weapons (CW) program; that it was producing mustard, sarin, cyclosarin, and VX; and that it had stockpiled as much as 100 to 500 metric tons of CW agents, much of it produced in the year prior to the estimate. This judgment, issued with "high confidence," was wrong.
- Iraq had offensive biological weapons, including mobile BW labs; that all key aspects of the program were active; and that most elements were larger and more advanced than they were during the Gulf War. This judgment, also issued with "high confidence," was wrong.
- Iraq had begun to reconstitute its nuclear weapons program and, if left unchecked, would probably have a nuclear weapon during this decade. This judgment, issued with "moderate confidence," was wrong.
- Iraq was developing an unmanned aerial vehicle capability, probably intended to deliver BW agents, even as far away as the U.S. homeland. This was wrong.
- Iraq had ballistic missiles capable of ranges that exceeded limits allowed under UN sanctions, and it had retained a covert force of up to a few dozen missiles. Wrong on the covert force finding, the NIE's only correct judgment was that the missiles exceeded the UN range limit.

The NIE was wrong on four of the five major WMD issues, so it is fair to ask how analysts had performed so poorly. Looking first at collection, on nearly every measure that counts, U.S. intelligence failed. The combined resources of human, signals, and imagery intelligence had performed miserably against an Iraqi regime that wielded a robust D&D capability against them.[45] None of the three major collection disciplines had been able to produce direct evidence of WMD—or of its absence—at the time of the estimate's preparation in October 2002.[46] Nearly all U.S. collection that characterized Saddam's weapons programs had come much earlier, predating Iraq's covert dismantling of the program in the early 1990s. *All* evidence afterward was spotty and fragmentary, suggestive, and never conclusive. Analysts seemed unaware of this.

An additional dimension of analytical failure is the unwarranted confidence attached to the major NIE judgments when the evidence for them was so tenuous. The judgments on Iraq's BW and CW programs were characterized as "high confidence" and on nuclear reconstitution as "moderate confidence." We now know that the evidence available at the time simply did not support this exaggerated confidence. In the future, analysts will need to do much better at aligning their confidence levels with evidence and conveying their findings to policymakers with greater specification of analytical uncertainty and the basis for their confidence levels on important issues.

In fairness, where analysts lacked good evidence for such programs, they also lacked good evidence demonstrating that none existed. With the notable exception of a single defector's reporting that the nuclear program had been shut down,[47] analysts were hard pressed to identify persuasive evidence to overturn the prevailing intelligence community consensus, built up over the preceding decade, that the Iraqi regime was hell-bent to assemble a significant arsenal of BW, CW, and, soon, nuclear weapons—all the more worrisome in the wake of September 11. Iraq's history and past practices supported this view. Saddam had previously used CW against Iraqi Kurds and neighboring Iran. He conducted a sweeping and effective D&D program that had essentially neutralized U.S. intelligence in Iraq, and he blunted the UN inspection process that had been set up to confirm their destruction—all this conduct reinforced Western suspicions that he must have had something to hide.

As in the previous cases, lacking solid evidence, analysts relied on weaker assumptions—which again were mostly wrong. But their most egregious failing was to insufficiently challenge the evidence. To do this adequately would have required better tradecraft and a better understanding of the collection process, especially its limitations.[48] Some of the evidence for the nuclear reconstitution hypothesis turned out to be based on forged documents (reporting Iraq's intentions to import yellowcake uranium from Niger). Some of the key evidence for CW was based on poor understanding of imagery collection (the periodicity and signatures over Samarra). And the most important evidence for BW was based on fabricated reporting (stories spun by "Curveball" that made their way to the Defense Intelligence Agency from a German liaison).[49]

In hindsight, this all looks so clear. But the pressures of a twenty-one-day deadline to produce the NIE encouraged more superficiality than depth, discouraged more "structured" or systematic tradecraft than deadline-driven journalism, and exposed the typically poor understanding that analysts bring to the collection process. Had the crippling collection limitations been highlighted during—or, preferably, well before—the short-fuse NIE, it is far more likely that analysts would have arrived at more accurate judgments—or at the very least issued the wrong ones with less confidence.

Learning from Failure

Lessons from the cases examined here point to the importance of intelligence collection in the analytical process. The key findings are summarized in the matrix shown in table 12.1.

In all cases, *better collection would have helped analysis*, and in some cases enormously. If only analysts had known of the Japanese carrier task group as it steamed unnoticed toward Pearl Harbor; or that the Soviet Politburo had decided to abruptly overturn the nuclear balance with the United States by sneaking an offensive ballistic missile capability into Cuba; or that Saddam had actually dismantled his WMD program in secret while he used D&D in a policy of calculated ambiguity to hoodwink inspectors, foil intelligence, and deter enemies with weapons he did not really have.[50] If only they knew of bin Laden's plot. With more pertinent and better facts to analyze, analysts are more likely to succeed.

But the reality is that while better collection might have been achievable in some cases, in others it was nearly impossible. The practical difficulties of penetrating the top decision-making circles of closed polities like the former Soviet Union, Saddam's Iraq, or present-day North Korea must be appreciated for what they are. So, too, the penetrability of the top ranks of terrorist groups like al-Qaeda is likely to remain more an aspiration than a reality. Satellites can image a building's roof but cannot look inside, nor read the minds of human targets we seek to understand or change. Better collection requires more effective sources and methods, and far better counter-D&D capabilities than we now have. *Better collection also requires greater analyst engagement and expertise; deeper understanding by analysts of the technical disciplines as well as the human recruitment and vetting process; and better guidance and direction in the requirements process where analysts have major, if often unfulfilled, responsibilities.*

Where much improved collection was just not possible in some of the failure cases examined here (e.g., Soviet BW and the Cuban crisis) or not needed (e.g., in the Yom Kippur War), more caveated judgments and much improved analysis certainly were. How might this have been achieved? The principal correctives for better analysis in the face of major collection deficiencies must begin with a significantly enhanced understanding of the collection process and its limitations. For the most part, however, all-source analysts receive little or no training in collection methods and too few opportunities to learn them on the job. If analysts do not fully comprehend the collection capabilities at their disposal, they cannot fully exploit them. Similarly, if they do not fully understand the collection limitations that impair their analysis, they cannot correct for such impairments in the analyses they produce.

TABLE 12.1
Explaining Failure: Patterns in Eight Cases

Case	Collection				Analysis				
	Key Information Missing	Information Not Shared	Poor Requirements	Denial and Deception*	Poor Imagination	Signal-to-Noise Ratio	Faulty Assumptions	Information Misinterpreted	Uncorrected Impact of Denial
Pearl Harbor		✦	✦	✦✦	✦	✦	✦		✦
Cuban missiles	✦			✦✦	✦		✦		✦
Yom Kippur		✦		✦✦	✦		✦	✦	✦
Iranian Revolution	✦			✦	✦		✦		✦
Soviet biological weapons	✦		✦	✦✦	✦				✦
India nuclear weapons	✦	✦		✦	✦		✦		✦
September 11, 2001, attacks	✦	✦	✦	✦	✦	✦	✦		✦
Iraqi weapons of mass destruction	✦			✦✦	✦		✦	✦	✦

*Note: ✦ = Only denial is present; significant deception is not in evidence. ✦✦ = Both denial and deception are present.

To guard against the pernicious impact of collection limitations, analysts must learn to acknowledge—then correct—an inherent tendency to substitute hidden assumptions for missing information. That this practice is typically unwitting illustrates the importance of identifying hidden assumptions and their effects on analytical results. If the assumptions-to-evidence ratio does not favor evidence, then the tradecraft that analysts use must be good enough to expose and challenge the assumptions that inevitably shape their findings.

Better analytical tradecraft is also a sine qua non for addressing and correcting the inevitable collection shortfalls. Here the recent trend toward a greater use of "alternative analysis" should be reinforced and even accelerated.[51] If the tradecraft of intelligence analysis is no better than a "classified journalism" that reports and interprets fragmentary information superficially—as it typically does in current intelligence and sometimes estimative products, too—then we cannot realistically expect fewer intelligence failures, especially where collection is weak or unproductive against effective denial. "Structured" and rigorous tradecraft (methodologies)—especially those that expose hidden assumptions and feature alternative hypotheses, alternative interpretations, or alternative scenarios—provide needed hedges against analytical failure.

These case studies show that the two most important impairments that analysts need to overcome are the failure to correct for the impact of denial and the failure of analytical imagination—each of which can be successfully addressed through the following techniques. First, correcting for the impact of denial requires that analysts pose the right questions, consider the deception hypothesis, and brainstorm additional hypotheses:

- When assessing hard problems, the analyst must ask: What key information am I missing? Is it missing because the target is thwarting efforts to collect it? Why is collection not better, and if it were, what might I be seeing? What new information would change my assessment, and why am I not seeing it? How good are the target's denial capabilities against collection, and precisely how, where, and why is the target defeating it?
- The analyst should introduce the deception hypothesis, which, more than any other alternative explanation, will invite a cascade of additional questions that will highlight the target's possible objectives and means, and the collection limitations that may keep them hidden.
- The analyst should enlist the help of his or her colleagues in a group exercise to brainstorm additional hypotheses that may highlight further alternative explanations. Outstanding techniques for this are Red Teaming, Contingency "What-If" Analysis, and High-Impact / Low-Probability Analysis.

Second, the best insurance against failures of imagination is to generate alternative hypotheses. In the cases examined here, it seems clear that analysts simply did not imagine that the Japanese intended a surprise attack against Pearl Harbor, how the Soviet Union might secretly place nuclear missiles into Cuba, that weakened Arab states would attack Israel, or that a radical Islamic revolution would topple the shah's government and transform Iran. Nor did they imagine that a new ruling party in India would conduct surprise nuclear weapons tests;

that the Soviets would secretly build a massive BW program after signing a treaty prohibiting them from doing so; that suicidal terrorists would seize U.S. commercial airliners, slam them into office buildings, and kill 3,000 people; or that Saddam Hussein would shut down his WMD programs in secret while thwarting efforts by the UN and Western nations to find that out. There can be no doubt that poor collection greatly elevates the importance of analytical imagination. To achieve it, analysts must significantly increase their use of alternative or structured analysis to generate hypotheses about unlikely but consequential events, even—perhaps especially—if they are otherwise hard to imagine.

The *integral relationship between collection and analysis* is the overarching lesson of the cases examined here. To summarize, when collection fails, it greatly increases the probability that analysis too will fail. The responsibility to produce analytical judgments on the basis of ambiguous, contradictory, and/or missing information is a tall one. Of the three, handling missing information is the most difficult. We currently have no analytical models or tradecraft that address this issue. And most analysts are poorly equipped to deal with effective denial. Like the patients whose terminal disease takes root long before the symptoms are noticed, many analysts do not even know denial when they experience it.

This chapter has focused exclusively on intelligence failures.[52] We can surmise the counterpoint lesson we have learned from failures: When collection improves, or when analysts better appreciate the limited collection on which they are basing their arguments, they will do a better job of assessing the possible outcomes and placing more credible probabilities against a variety of outcomes. We do not know exactly how helpful such efforts can be, but it would be valuable to the intelligence community to invest in a more robust Lessons Learned program that chronicles not just failures but also successes. Such studies should describe an optimal relationship between analyst and collector when things go right. For now, at least, these case studies illustrate that a healthier analytic skepticism about the quality of information being used on most topics would aid our ability to correct collection gaps and bound uncertainty. Analysts should also consider a range of outcomes for analytical problems that are surrounded in secrecy, obscured or distorted by denial and deception, and sometimes muddled by the presence of too much bad or extraneous information (noise) to see the truly important nuggets of truth.

The most important early questions an analyst can ask about his or her assignment or "account" are: How good is collection against my target? Where and how is it weak? What are its major limitations and shortfalls? How can I learn more about these capabilities? What can I do to better exploit them? Can I do anything to help direct or improve them? What D&D countermeasures does my target use to defeat them?

Lacking another collection revolution in the twenty-first century to match the technical breakthroughs that began forty years ago, smart and seasoned analysts and collectors alike will appreciate why much improved collection is not likely to emerge in the foreseeable future. Because analysts will have to live with underperforming collection as far out as we can see, they will be well served to comprehend its implications and prepare themselves for much more challenging analysis that can surmount the collection roots of intelligence failures.

Notes

1. Key sources for this case study are Roberta Wohlstetter, *Pearl Harbor: Warning and Decision* (Palo Alto, Calif.: Stanford University Press, 1962); and John Hughes-Wilson, *Military Intelligence Blunders* (New York: Carroll & Graf, 1999), chap. 4.

2. Cynthia M. Grabo, *Anticipating Surprise: Analysis for Warning Intelligence* (Washington, D.C.: Joint Military Intelligence College, 2002), 123.

3. The example of Pearl Harbor along with the Yom Kippur case below together represent only two of eight cases examined here where there was arguably enough information to have made the call. Of course we only know this in hindsight after a reconstruction of events reveals what the analysts *should* have known. But the cases also illustrate other factors at work (discussed below) that greatly reduced their probability of getting it right.

4. Wohlstetter, *Pearl Harbor*, 121–22; also see box 8.1 in this volume.

5. Ibid., 394.

6. As Wohlstetter explained it in her famous study: "In short, we failed to anticipate Pearl Harbor not for want of the relevant materials, but because of the plethora of irrelevant ones." Wohlstetter, *Pearl Harbor*, 387. Another historian explained it similarly: "The salient fact about the intelligence disaster at Pearl Harbor is that most of the evidence was hidden by a blizzard of other information at the time. . . . Quite simply, the clamor of other voices drowned out the Pearl Harbor material." Hughes-Wilson, *Military Intelligence Blunders*, 73.

7. Admiral Kimel, the senior naval officer at Pearl and commander-in-chief of the Pacific Fleet, quoted in Wohlstetter, *Pearl Harbor*, 55.

8. *The Military Buildup in Cuba*, Special National Intelligence Estimate, No. 85–3-62, 19 September 1962, 2; from declassified excerpts in *CIA Documents on the Cuban Missile Crisis, 1962*, ed. Mary S. McAuliffe (Washington, D.C.: CIA History Staff, 1992), 93. Other sources for this case study include articles in *Intelligence and the Cuban Missile Crisis*, ed. James G. Blight and David A. Welch (London: Frank Cass, 1998), esp. Raymond A. Garthoff, "U.S. Intelligence in the Cuban Missile Crisis," chap. 2; and Sherman Kent, "A Crucial Estimate Relived," *Studies in Intelligence* 8, no. 2 (Spring 1964), www.cia.gov/csi/books/shermankent/9crucial.html.

9. Peter Clement, "The Cuban Missile Crisis," in *The Directorate of Intelligence, Fifty Years of Informing Policy: 1952–2002*, expanded ed. (Washington, D.C.: Center for the Study of Intelligence, Central Intelligence Agency, 2002), 91. See also James H. Hanson, "Soviet Deception in the Cuban Missile Crisis," *Studies in Intelligence* 46, no. 1 (2002), www.cia.gov/csi/studies/vol46no1/article06.html.

10. "There was insufficient evidence to justify a conclusion that Soviet missiles would be (or still less, were being) placed in Cuba. In the absence of clear evidence of deployment, the estimate had to rest on an assessment of Soviet intentions, and the past record tended to support the conclusion that the Soviet leaders would not deploy strategic missiles in Cuba." Garthoff, "U.S. Intelligence," 21.

11. See chap. 16 by Richards Heuer for a discussion of a promising approach to intelligence problems like this one. Also see David T. Moore and William N. Reynolds, "So Many Ways to Lie: The Complexity of Denial and Deception," *Defense Intelligence Journal* 15, no. 2 (2006): 106–11.

12. Significantly, aided by HUMINT and sound hypotheses, analysts did help direct collection, notably by focusing attention on the importance of aerial photography over San Cristobal, which led to the discovery of the missile base construction there. Garthoff, "U.S. Intelligence," 53.

13. E.g., Ephraim Kahana, "Early Warning versus Concept: The Case of the Yom Kippur War 1973," in *Strategic Intelligence: Windows into a Secret World*, ed. Loch K. Johnson and James J. Wirtz (Los Angeles: Roxbury, 2004), 153–65. Other sources used in this case study are Hughes-Wilson, *Military Intelligence Blunders*, chap. 8; Michael I. Handel, "The Yom

Kippur War and the Inevitability of Surprise," *International Studies Quarterly* 21, no. 3 (September 1977): 461–502; and Avi Shlaim, "Failures in National Intelligence Estimates: The Case of the Yom Kippur War," *World Politics* 28, no. 3 (April 1976): 348–80.

14. Shlaim, "Failures in National Intelligence Estimates," 359.

15. Handel, "Yom Kippur War and the Inevitability of Surprise," 497–98; Shlaim, "Failures in National Intelligence Estimates," 356; and Hughes-Wilson, *Military Intelligence Blunders*, 218–59.

16. Kahana, "Early Warning versus Concept," 154–62.

17. Case materials include James A. Bill, *The Eagle and the Lion: The Tragedy of American–Iranian Relations* (New Haven, Conn.: Yale University Press, 1989); Kenneth Pollack, *The Persian Puzzle: The Conflict between Iran and America* (New York: Random House, 2004); and Barry M. Rubin, *Paved with Good Intentions: The American Experience and Iran* (New York: Viking Press, 1981).

18. Pollack, *Persian Puzzle*, 106.

19. Rubin, *Paved with Good Intentions*, 180; Pollack, *Persian Puzzle*, 95, 136–37; Bill, *Eagle and the Lion*, 402.

20. Pollack, *Persian Puzzle*, 136; Bill, *Eagle and the Lion*, 403.

21. Sources for this case study are a press conference of Admiral David Jeremiah, the director of central intelligence's appointee to examine why the intelligence community failed to warn of the tests, at CIA headquarters, June 2, 1998, http://ftp.fas.org/irp/cia/product/jeremiah.html; George N. Sibley, "The Indian Nuclear Test: A Case Study in Political Hindsight Bias," WWS Case Study 3/02, Woodrow Wilson School, August 7, 2002, www.wws.princeton.edu/cases/papers/nucleartest.html; and Evan Thomas, John Barry, and Melinda Liu, "Ground Zero: India's Blasts Dramatize the New Nuclear Age—How Did CIA Miss Them?" *Newsweek*, May 25, 1998, 29–32.

22. Admiral Jeremiah stated at the press conference that India "had an effective denial activity," and later added that "our human intelligence capacity is seriously limited."

23. Note, however, that analysis of campaign promises alone will prove a slender basis for reliable warning and risk more false alarms than accurate forecasts.

24. For an Indian account of how they learned from the 1995 demarche experience to apply D&D countermeasures to beat U.S. intelligence, see Raj Chengappa, *Weapons of Peace: The Secret Story of India's Quest to Be a Nuclear Power* (New Delhi: HarperCollins India, 2000), 403, 413–14, 419–20, 425–28.

25. As Jeremiah noted: "With respect to the disclosures, in part from our Ambassador and in part from press reports, I think that whenever there is an opportunity to look at what someone else is looking at in your territory it gives you some insights into what you would want to do to cover that. . . . We may have disclosed certain kinds of indicators. . . . And, of course, you don't have to show every kind of whole card you have." See also James B. Bruce, "How Leaks of Classified Intelligence Help U.S. Adversaries: Implications for Laws and Secrecy," in *Intelligence and the National Security Strategist*, ed. Roger Z. George and Robert D. Kline (Lanham, Md.: Rowman & Littlefield, 2006), 403, 413; and Thomas, Barry, and Liu, "Ground Zero," 30–31.

26. Principal case study sources are Ken Alibek and Stephen Handelman, *Biohazard* (New York: Random House, 1999); and Judith Miller, Stephen Engelberg, and William Broad, *Germs: Biological Weapons and America's Secret War* (New York, Simon & Schuster, 2001).

27. This significant deficit in U.S. understanding is partly reflected in the major estimates and other intelligence assessments, many now declassified, of Soviet military capabilities that omitted mention of the substantial BW program. See, e.g., Benjamin B. Fischer, ed., *At Cold War's End: U.S. Intelligence on the Soviet Union and Eastern Europe, 1989–1991* (Washington, D.C.: Center for the Study of Intelligence, Central Intelligence Agency, 1999), 341–78; Gerald K. Haines and Robert E. Leggett, eds., *CIA's Analysis of the Soviet Union, 1947–1991: A Documentary Collection* (Washington, D.C.: Center for the Study of Intelligence,

Central Intelligence Agency, 2001), 229–310; and Donald P. Steury, ed., *Intentions and Capabilities: Estimates on Soviet Strategic Forces, 1950–1983* (Washington, D.C.: Center for the Study of Intelligence, Central Intelligence Agency, 1996).

28. Pesechnik headed an important BW institute in Leningrad; he defected while visiting France in 1989. Alibek served for seventeen years in the Soviet BW program, including as deputy director of Biopreparat, the principal BW organization, from 1988 to 1992, when he defected. Biopreparat was established in 1973, a year after the Soviets signed the BW convention, to provide civilian cover for advanced military BW research; at its peak, it employed 30,000 people, half the BW industry. Alibek and Handelman, *Biohazard*, 43, 298.

29. Ibid., x, 5–8, 43, 78, 140–41.

30. Ibid., xii–xiii, 43.

31. Ibid., 70–86.

32. In 1988, nine years after the Sverdlovsk BW accident, a Soviet delegation visiting the United States at the invitation of Meselson persuaded its American audience that the Sverdlovsk deaths were caused by contaminated meats, the official cover story all along. This deception was reported as factual in the April 1988 issue of the authoritative *Science* magazine. Russian president Yeltsin publicly acknowledged the true explanation in a 1993 interview. Ibid., 85–86.

33. Commission on the Intelligence Capabilities of the United States Regarding Weapons of Mass Destruction, *Report to the President of the United States, March 31, 2005* (Washington, D.C.: U.S. Government Printing Office, 2005) (hereafter, *WMD Commission Report*), 503–8.

34. The events of September 11 are best documented in the authoritative National Commission on Terrorist Attacks Upon the United States, *The 9/11 Commission Report*, authorized ed. (New York: W. W. Norton, 2003) (hereafter, *9/11 Commission Report*). The commission discusses the Pearl Harbor and September 11 warning failures on pp. 339 and 346–48.

35. "The most serious weaknesses in agency capabilities were in the domestic arena," notably the FBI, INS, FAA and others. *9/11 Commission Report*, 352.

36. Despite the large number of threats on the radar screen in the summer of 2001, they "contained few specifics regarding time, place, method, or target." *9/11 Commission Report*, 262–63.

37. Ibid., 416–18.

38. In particular, information connecting the domestic and foreign activities of terrorist plotters Midhar, Hamzi, and Khallad. The National Security Agency also had unshared information that could have helped identify Hamzi. *9/11 Commission Report*, 365–66, 417.

39. Ibid., 277.

40. By the spring of 2001, terrorist threat reporting had reached the highest levels since the millennium alert. Threats included attacks against Boston, London, India, U.S. embassies abroad, and the White House. Summer threats focused on Bahrain, Israel, Saudi Arabia, Kuwait, Yemen, Genoa, and Rome. By July, reporting indicated that bin Laden's network was anticipating an attack, something "spectacular." As late as August, most threats suggested attacks that were planned targets overseas; others indicated threats against unspecified U.S. interests. Ibid., 255–63.

41. Ibid., 344–45.

42. According to Richard Clarke, then the top White House official on terrorism, in ibid., 345.

43. This case study is based largely on the authoritative *WMD Commission Report*. The findings that Saddam Hussein had essentially shut down Iraq's WMD programs in 1991–92 are in the study of the Iraq Survey Group, *Comprehensive Report of the Special Advisor to the DCI on Iraq's WMD*, posted on the CIA website October 6, 2004, also referred to as the Duelfer Report after its chairman Charles Duelfer.

44. National Intelligence Council, *Iraq's Continuing Programs of Weapons of Mass Destruction*, NIE 2002–16HC, October 2002. Only the key judgments have been declassified.

45. *WMD Commission Report*, 161–65, 169, 352, 365–84. The effectiveness of Iraqi D&D, notably against UN inspectors after Desert Storm in 1990, was well documented earlier in David Kay, "Denial and Deception: The Lessons of Iraq," in *U.S. Intelligence at the Crossroads*, ed. Roy Godson, Ernest R. May, and Gary Schmidt (Washington, D.C.: Brassey's, 1995), chap. 9; Kay's "Denial and Deception Practices of WMD Proliferators: Iraq and Beyond," *Washington Quarterly* 18, no. 1 (Winter 1995): 85ff; and in Tim Trevan, *Saddam's Secrets: The Hunt for Iraq's Hidden Weapons* (London: HarperCollins, 1999).

46. *WMD Commission Report*, 158–67. A fourth collection discipline, measurement and signatures intelligence (MASINT), possesses unique capabilities against WMD targets but, regrettably, its uses in Iraq were negligible, at least until mid-2000. Still, substantial MASINT reporting over the next two years failed to detect any evidence of WMD. *Ibid.*, 166.

47. Hussein Kamil, Saddam's son-in-law, defected in 1995 and explained that Saddam Hussein had ordered the destruction of the nuclear program in 1991 in an effort to have UN economic sanctions lifted. His statements were not believed.

48. See chapter 16 by Richards Heuer that explains how the Analysis of Competing Hypotheses might have helped with this.

49. *WMD Commission Report*, 75–79 (nuclear), 122–24 (chemical), and 87–108 (biological).

50. Saddam's policy of calculated ambiguity sought to convey contradictory messages to different audiences. He wanted the UN and the West to believe that he had destroyed his prohibited weapons in order to get sanctions lifted. He also sought to purvey doubt to the Iraqi Shias and Kurds and to the Iranians and Israelis that he still possessed a menacing WMD arsenal. His goal to have it both ways failed with the launching of Operation Iraqi Freedom, which cost him his regime, then his life. James B. Bruce, "Denial and Deception in the 21st Century: Adaptation Implications for Western Intelligence," *Defense Intelligence Journal* 15, no. 2 (2006): 18–20.

51. See Roger Z. George, "Fixing the Problem of Analytical Mindsets: Alternative Analysis," in *Intelligence and the National Security Strategist*, ed. George and Kline, 311–27; and chapter 10 in this volume.

52. The study of intelligence successes is beyond the scope of this chapter, but it also represents a significant gap in the intelligence literature more generally. Though attention to failures is necessary to identify pathologies, roots of error, and correctives, attention to successes is necessary to identify "best practices" so they can be repeated with the aim of causing more successes.

PART FIVE

Leading Analytic Change

ANALYSTS DO NOT sit alone at their workstations. They are hired, trained, coached, and evaluated by many others who often are or have been analysts by profession. Part five focuses on these managers and leaders—the ones who can inculcate the analytic standards, values, and commitments that can strengthen the profession but who must also be thinking ahead. To achieve intelligence reform broadly and to introduce some of the analytic techniques and tools suggested in many of the other chapters in this book, there will have to be a managerial revolution of sorts as well.

John Gannon, a longtime manager who rose to become the Central Intelligence Agency's (CIA's) deputy director of intelligence and later chairman of the National Intelligence Council (NIC), speaks with authority as someone who has led analysts both in the CIA and across the intelligence community. Showing his penchant for looking toward the future—as the NIC did under his leadership—he poses some of the new twenty-first-century challenges to managers and suggests that new times require new thinking, including management's updating security practices, outreach efforts, and better use of open sources.

Mark Lowenthal—a former senior official of the State Department's Bureau of Intelligence and Research who has worked in Congress as well as for the last two directors of central intelligence following the September 11, 2001, terrorist attacks—offers some views on what must change in analysis following the tragedy. He, too, suggests that managers must take this as an opportunity to redesign analysis as well as get back to some basics like research to deal with the coming challenges.

For an even more challenging look at what intelligence leaders have to face, Carmen Medina—the former CIA deputy director of intelligence and current director of the Center for the Study of Intelligence—forecasts that analysis must radically change to survive the information revolution. The key metric will no longer be the "finished product" but rather "collaboration"—that is, insight produced through teamwork rather than the efforts of any single analyst. What we recognize as today's analysis will not likely be found in tomorrow's analytic hallways.

CHAPTER 13

Managing Analysis in the Information Age

JOHN C. GANNON

SOME PRACTITIONERS will say that good analysts are born, not made. Though this is true of some colleagues I have known, this book is rightfully focused on improving analysis through practice, study, and better attention to a rigorous tradecraft. However, most intelligence community (IC) analysts do not learn their trade primarily from books, training manuals, or courses but rather "in the heat of the shop floor," under the supervision of experienced managers and mentors. This chapter focuses on explaining the role of managers and suggesting they are an underappreciated resource for improvement in the analytic art. It typically takes several years for an analyst to reach peak performance. It takes even longer to develop a competent IC manager who can function as a substantive and editorial reviewer, an administrator, a teacher, a coach, a mediator, and a troubleshooter constantly on call. In the years ahead, the responsibilities of managers are certain to grow in a more complicated intelligence community and a more dangerous world.

Aware of this, a host of IC managers in recent years—many before the September 11, 2001 terrorist attacks—have boldly led the way in improving analytic tradecraft, in advocating state-of-the-art methodologies, in promoting information technology (including "wiki" applications), in increasing information sharing, and in fostering vital partnerships inside and outside the IC.[1] Their bold efforts should be recognized and applauded. They are on the right side of history.

Nearly six years after September 11, however, the IC's progressive managers are still fighting an uphill battle against a resistant, oversized bureaucracy that continues to make even easy things hard to do. For example, IC initiatives on biosecurity, cybersecurity, information sharing, and homeland security have been hampered by burdensome requirements to coordinate with countless "stakeholders" across the community, when these critical national security missions actually require the unprecedented integration of the best expertise from both inside and outside the IC.

To stress the importance of management, moreover, is not to idealize or romanticize it. Historically, IC management has underperformed if we are to believe multiple congressional and executive branch reports over the years. The bottom line is that immediate supervisors have the greatest impact on the morale and motivation of analysts, who complain most about the managers closest to them. Quality of management, in fact, is a serious retention issue across all the agencies and disciplines of the intelligence community.

Managing intelligence analysts has always been taxing. During the cold war, a team leader or branch chief would normally begin the day early by reading the latest classified and open source information related to the unit's accounts and would then convene or attend sequential "production meetings" with subordinates and seniors on proposals for current production. The manager, tending intermittently to multiple administrative tasks—including training and travel—in support of his or her subordinates, would later review and edit approved pieces and would assist with sometimes contentious IC coordination when required. The chief might squeeze in some time for individual career counseling, or for the preparation of an oral briefing for a high-level policymaker or member of Congress. Membership in an intra- or interagency task force or consultation with bosses, IC counterparts, or consumers might eat up several more hours.

The more conscientious managers would often be found late in the office to review longer drafts or strategic assessments for important consumers—an onerous task that often extended into a weekend. And an inspector general's audit could always be counted on to remind all managers of their broader, overarching responsibilities for teaching and enforcing tradecraft principles, for overseeing relations with internal and external consumers, and for upholding professional ethics in the workplace.

The majority of IC managers today first make their mark as substantive or functional experts. They generally are graded more on their ability to support consumers and defend their team's products and services than on their proficiency in classic management functions or administrative tasks. It also is true that many experienced analysts renowned for their substantive work actually make middling to poor managers of people and process. All this is understandable in an analytic enterprise that performed reasonably well in the IC's first half century. But it will not be acceptable in a future in which other management priorities—such as the active facilitation of internal and external collaboration, the vigorous protection of analytic objectivity, serious attention to budget and finance, flexible resource allocation, and sustained career counseling—will become more important at every level of management. Today's expectations of managers, despite progress on several fronts, simply cannot meet tomorrow's needs. Top leaders will have to enable and empower analysts, whereas all managers will have to lead by calling for more collaborative methodologies and tools and by providing incentives for their analysts to exploit the power of information technologies, the wisdom of outside expertise, and the insight generated by new and rigorous analytical tradecraft.

A series of revolutions is moving the IC toward a more distributed system of intelligence collection and analysis. IC leaders today are challenged: (1) to produce expert analysis, including strategic assessments, in record time on the widest range ever of complex intelligence issues; (2) to exploit an unprecedented glut of open source information, some of it of high intelligence value; (3) to develop issue-based networks of outside experts for ready consultation and collaboration; and (4) to disseminate tailored analytic reports in real time to the broadest base of intelligence consumers in U.S. history. Progress on these goals has been uneven, but the difficulty of achieving them cannot be overstated. To achieve the higher standard that will be required, the IC will have to put much greater stress on management accountability and invest much more in hard-core management training.

This chapter has five objectives. First, it examines these and other challenges facing IC analytic managers today. Second, it assesses in greater depth the drivers of IC reform. Third, it discusses the pros and cons of managing intelligence analysis in the information age. Fourth, it explores two important constants in the intelligence business that will require careful and persistent management attention in the future—the interactive nature of producer–consumer relations, and the distortion of analysis (bias and politicization) in the intelligence process. And fifth, the chapter argues that the diverse and complicated management challenges in the information age require the establishment of a permanent, fully resourced IC training and education institution—a National Intelligence University (NIU).

Key Challenges

Globalization is having a major impact on the intelligence business. It is challenging the IC to boost its capabilities to exploit both open source information and outside expertise while expanding the community's substantive agenda and shrinking the distance between intelligence producer and consumer:

- *Threats are becoming more complicated and more distributed at home and across the globe.* Nation-states and nonstate actors, working alone or together, have greater access to actionable information, global finance, and destructive capabilities—including weapons of mass destruction. New intelligence issues, many related to advances in science and technology, are spawning new subject matter experts and additional consumers. Consumers are more demanding, and more dispersed across all levels of government. Analytic requirements frequently exceed the IC's internal capabilities to meet them, forcing managers to make tough choices.
- *IC security policies on technology, cultural diversity in the workplace, and contacts with outside experts hamper improved performance.* Technology will continue to advance faster than the U.S. government's ability to absorb it, which adds urgency to the need for strong partnership with the outside world. On the inside, the IC needs a more collaborative decision-making process among analytic, security, and counterintelligence stakeholders to govern the hiring, professional development, and outside activities of analysts.
- *The historical interconnectedness of intelligence, policy, and politics is harder to manage in a fast-moving information environment marked by a closer-than-ever IC relationship with policymakers, members of Congress,*

and outside experts. And it is becoming more difficult to counter the bias that permeates the intelligence bureaucracy. Good tradecraft is essential to counter bias and outright politicization. But strong leadership is the only failsafe means to protect analytic objectivity. There is no substitute for responsible and accountable leadership in the hardscrabble intelligence business.

- *Networked consumers increasingly are exploiting alternative sources they find more useful and timely than intelligence products—or are simply "good enough"—to meet their tight deadlines.* At the same time, IC analysts continue to lose comparative advantage on complex national security issues and become more dependent on open source information and on collaboration with outside experts.

- *Career options for analysts are growing in number and appeal outside the intelligence community.* Managers are challenged to motivate and retain a workforce that increasingly sees outside career options and—if current conditions continue—less enticing inside options that limit exploitation of state-of-the-art collaborative technologies, access to the best open source information, and engagement with outside experts.

- *Managers require more and better training to attain the higher management standards needed to prepare and professionalize the IC workforce.* In a fast-action, high-tension working environment, effective management at every level will be essential to orient analysts to an increasingly complicated and regulated business, to smooth coordination in a larger community, to protect analytic objectivity, and to preserve the integrity of the intelligence process. Managers will have to be leaders.

- *A fully resourced IC training and education institution is essential in the era of globalization.* A community that has no institutions—which is the case today—cannot be expected to professionalize its workforce and adapt it to the information age. A "National Intelligence University" would have the mission to incorporate, preserve, and grow the vast body of professional knowledge associated with intelligence. It would not only nourish a common IC identity and commitment. It also would educate all intelligence stakeholders, consumers as well as producers, who influence the process and constitute the "organic whole" of U.S. intelligence. IC reform cannot succeed unless the IC, the White House, and Congress share the same goals and a common strategy to achieve them.

The core message to the IC analytic community, which has been losing its competitive edge in the information age, is not to sound a retreat or to settle into complacency. The call is to strengthen IC management and boost the community's analytical capabilities by aggressively exploiting technology, by substantially increasing investment in human skills and expertise, by improving tradecraft training both locally and in the new IC university, and by forging enduring partnerships with experts outside the community—especially in the scientific world.

The Drivers of IC Transformation

U.S. intelligence analysts are in the midst of an historic transformation, twenty years in the making and with no end in sight. By the mid-1990s, the IC saw the growing interconnectedness of networks moving information, culture, technology, capital, goods, and services with unprecedented speed and efficiency around the world and across the homeland. Globalization was recognized as the defining reality of our age, providing mankind with unprecedented opportunities to do good and with unparalleled capability to do evil.

In a shrinking world of rapid communications, the distinction between foreign and domestic intelligence became blurred, along with the differentiation of national and defense consumers. The community experienced a growing demand for distributed intelligence support, including from military commands and diplomats. IC analysts were challenged to access the best sources of information and expertise, wherever they resided, and to make their operational focus global.

The *geopolitical revolution* swept away the Soviet Union, transformed the face of Europe, and forced the intelligence community to confront a global threat environment in which both state and nonstate actors, acting alone or together, have a much greater potential than in the past to operate against U.S. interests across national borders, including our own. The transnational adversaries include terrorists (employing conventional, chemical, biological, nuclear, radiological, or cyberspace attacks), weapons of mass destruction proliferators, narcotics and human traffickers, and organized criminals.

The IC today is expected to provide expert analysis on nation-states, transnational groups, and regional conflicts, as well as on cyber and bioterrorist threats, humanitarian disasters, migration trends, international financial crises, environmental problems, and infectious diseases. This broad, complex agenda, which stretches the IC way beyond its internal capabilities, demands unprecedented collaboration inside and outside the IC. And on a growing number of these technical issues, the IC has little internal expertise to bring to the table.

The *technology revolution*—including information technology, the rapidly advancing biological sciences, neuroscience, nanotechnology, material sciences, and robotics—has brought good news and "dual-use" bad news for America and mankind. It has been a "wake-up call" to an IC that has seen its comparative advantage in analyzing the Soviet Union dissolve into a heavy dependence on outside experts on the tough issues it faces today, especially those related to science and technology.

The IC, in one generation, passed from an information-scarce environment to an information-glut environment. Major advances in technical collection provided more data than analysts could exploit. Technology promised to save labor for IC managers and analysts, but the opposite occurred. It has made analysts more efficient, customers more demanding, and the workload heavier. To be fair, the intelligence bureaucracy has made serious efforts, many of them successful, to respond to the technological challenge. Analysts today are filtering, searching, and prioritizing massive volumes of information employing link analysis, clustering, times-series analysis, visualization, and automated database population. To be accurate, however, the overall effort—especially with regard to the exploitation of open source information—has fallen short of the mark, according to post–September 11 reports by government watchdog agencies, legislative oversight committees, and both Congressional and Presidential commissions.[2]

Perhaps most telling has been the failure to provide Internet access and comprehensive and effective open source intelligence training to all IC analysts. This is about capability at individual workstations, not at shared terminals or remote centers. It is about training in the use of multiple search engines to include the accessing of databases and commercial imagery. The IC, partly because of security and counterintelligence concerns, has come late to recognize that open source information contains valuable intelligence that it cannot afford to miss—and is missing. It will be for a new generation of IC managers to get their analysts on the web and to expand electronic connectivity and the use of collaborative technologies across the community.

Homeland security is a facet of national security and arguably of the geopolitical revolution. But the enormity of the intelligence challenge it represents justifies treating it separately. The *homeland security challenge* is not just about the alarming proximity of the threat to our neighborhoods, but even more about the new national security stakeholders it brought to the fore, domestic "first-responders" with a legitimate need and justifiable demand for intelligence support.

Since September 11, new legislation and executive orders have stood up the Department of Homeland Security and called for the development of a national intelligence capability, fusing foreign and domestic intelligence. This has accelerated trends toward the integration of foreign and domestic analysis and toward a distributed system of intelligence production to meet the real-time demands of legions of new consumers focused on threat-risk assessment, infrastructure vulnerability and protection, and "all-hazard" preparedness. The challenge is huge. This national intelligence capability is still a distant reality as we approach six years after September 11. IC leaders and managers will be tackling it for years to come.

The September 11 attacks have sharply increased Congressional attention to IC structural and organizational reform. The creation of the Department of Homeland Security, the Office of the Director of National Intelligence, and the National Counterterrorism Center are three prominent examples. These new units are providing stronger focus on priority substantive and management issues. IC managers are working hard to ensure their success. At the same time, today's managers are expected to deal with some of the disruptive and hopefully temporary consequences of the rapid emergence of new structures since September 11: stretched analytic resources, dispersed expertise, cumbersome coordination, a bias towards transnational over regional analysis, military encroachment into the national intelligence domain, a sharply reduced cadre of experienced managers, confused roles and responsibilities among legacy and new intelligence units, and divided accountability. These are serious issues that need to be addressed.

In contrast with an earlier era when analysts were characterized simply as regional or functional analysts, today's intelligence analysts and subject matter experts encompass a vast and growing array of disciplines and labor categories. In addition to new accounts in transnational issues like counterterrorism and counterproliferation, there are freshly minted titles in information technology, biotechnology, nanotechnology, material sciences, the environmental sciences, neuroscience, and robotics. And, of course, there are armies of new consumers for their products and services.

The worldwide computer remediation problem known as Y2K and the September 11 challenges nurtured a generation of cyber and critical infrastructure analysts and threat-risk assessors. Denial-and-deception has become a distinct discipline. Geospatial modeling and animation have emerged as key capabilities. Open source intelligence analysts have appeared widely to help vet and exploit the glut of information available from open sources. Analysis is a growth industry. That's the good news. Production coordination across analytic units has become more complicated than ever. That means more headaches for IC managers and analysts.

Another troubling element of workforce transformation is the growing attrition among analysts. The best analysts, understandably, will seek what they see as the most rewarding professional opportunities and the best compensation for their services. The IC today clearly is providing its analysts with a larger number and wider variety of professional opportunities. At least some analysts, however, bristle at the limited access to advanced technology they encounter in the workplace and at the policies restricting their engagement with outside experts.[3]

Moreover, the community is competing, often at a disadvantage, with private sector or other government employers who have more attractive opportunities or deeper pockets. Shorter IC careers and a more active revolving door will not necessarily constitute a crisis. Sensibly managed, it may actually improve the analytic workforce over time. But it is a given that converting this challenge into an opportunity will require more management attention.

The Pros and Cons of an Intelligence Career

Despite all these challenges, it is hard to beat the kick of the substance and the cut of the people in the U.S. intelligence community. Intelligence can be a challenging and rewarding career and a continuing education, if the analyst is ready to seize exciting opportunities that inevitably will present themselves. They will have ready access to first-rate training to sharpen their technical and professional skills. They will be cleared to receive sensitive, classified information. They will be authorized to put requirements on the IC's global technical and human collection systems. They will brief senior U.S. political, diplomatic, military, and congressional leaders. As senior analysts, they will have access to important policymakers and their "insider" agendas, which analysts will directly support.

Analysts will have the chance to travel internationally, to learn foreign languages, to serve overseas, to develop impressive technical capabilities, and to work closely on important issues with able colleagues from all the intelligence agencies and the policy community. They will rub elbows every day with some of the smartest people in Washington. The policy issues on which they work will be interesting and important to U.S. national security. And analysts covering them generally will have greater impact than they would as academics.

Managers, however, also must explain and enforce policies that restrict the professional activities of analysts. Analysts are not free agents. They work exclusively for the U.S. government—intelligence bosses, policymakers, and increasingly the U.S. Congress. The government sets the priorities and establishes the tight rules of the game. An analyst may challenge bosses or offer personal views on policy internally but has no authority to speak officially in public without prior agency approval. Concepts of academic freedom do not apply. Managers need to help adapt regulations on outside activities to today's requirements—a high priority—but the answer to the perennial question of "For whom do I work?" will not change. And it is a no-brainer that looser regulations on outside activities, which are desirable, will never approach the standards of academic freedom. The management challenge is to get the balance right between the legitimate requirements for security and competent analysis in the information age.

In the years ahead, reformist managers will find their strongest supporters among the new technology-savvy generation of analysts who come to their jobs with advanced information technology skills, intimate familiarity with the web, a sophisticated appreciation for the value of internal and external collaboration—and no corrupting experience in the IC's information-hoarding stovepipes. Anecdotal evidence suggests that this generation is as patriotic as any that came before, and that it appreciates the IC's need for effective security and counterintelligence.

But new analysts also keep aware of other career options and are, at least to some degree, impatient with policies that restrict technology and collaboration to a degree that is counterproductive to today's analytic mission. IC managers today, more than ever, need to listen to the concerns and ideas of the younger generation whose take on the IC's future matters a good deal (see box 13.1).

The Risks of Engagement

Even in the information age, there are important constants in the intelligence business. These include the endemic orientation of the system toward U.S. policy priorities and both the specter of politicization and the pervasiveness of bias in the intelligence process. Managers need to be vigilant in balancing the benefits and risks of the continuous interaction of analysts with collectors, fellow IC producers, policymakers, and sometimes members of Congress, all of whom constitute the indivisible organic whole of U.S. intelligence. In the "warp speed" of the information age, these relationships will be much harder to manage.

The stakes today are often high. Consumers frequently set the priorities and the deadlines, whether or not sufficient data exist to make an empirical assessment. Analysts feel the pressure and often need management support and guidance to deal with it. The president and his national security team demand

BOX 13.1
Questions for Today's Intelligence Managers

These questions should focus management attention on explicit policy changes that would provide positive responses for today's and tomorrow's challenges:

First, why should an analyst want to work in the U.S. intelligence community when managers cannot promise analysts electronic connectivity, state-of-the-art collaborative technologies, or ready access to the Internet and outside experts?[4]

Second, why would an analyst seek an IC career that restricts external professional activities and offers public "scapegoating" of intelligence for their failures?

Third, how will managers hire more analysts with diverse cultural backgrounds and hard language skills and engage outside experts when security and counterintelligence policies stand in the way?

Fourth, how do managers explain the virtues of working in an intelligence community that is without a clearly defined post–cold war mission over other professional opportunities, which do not present the hardships of organizational insularity, outside criticism, and dangers of overseas duties?

Fifth, how will managers deal with an information-savvy customer who questions the intelligence community's role as a center of expertise against the diverse and complicated threats of the twenty-first century?

Note: For perspective, the 1996 strategic plan of CIA's Directorate of Intelligence, *Analysis: Directorate of Intelligence in the 21st Century* (Washington, D.C.: Central Intelligence Agency, Central Intelligence Agency, 1996), set goals for the introduction of technology that ultimately fell way behind schedule. A decade ago, the implications of the information revolution were well understood outside the IC and in pockets within, but community leaders remained biased in favor of clandestine collection and were slow to recognize that the new windfall of open source information contained valuable intelligence.

analytic judgments when they need them, and the meaning of "urgent" has become even starker in the information age. No matter how relevant or incisive, however, IC analysis can be marginalized at times or even ignored in a policy decision-making process that is susceptible to these other influences. And policymakers today have vastly more authoritative information sources available to them that compete with intelligence.

The intelligence community is so big and its customer base so broad and deep that an analyst can always find a comfortable niche working on lower-priority issues with lower-level consumers, where tradecraft can be practiced in its purest form and products are received gratefully without challenge. For those covering high-profile, mainstream accounts, however, even the best practitioners of tradecraft inevitably encounter pressures from consumers and even IC leaders in a policy-driven system not transparent to the outside world. And in the pressure cooker of intelligence, managers always will be needed to lead.

The distortion of analysis has two well-established forms—politicization and analytical bias. Politicization, the willful distortion of analysis to satisfy the demands of intelligence bosses or policymakers, happens in the IC but is relatively rare. It involves the conscious act of a leader, from inside and outside the IC, who directs an analyst to change a judgment—or to decline to make a judgment—for political or policy reasons. This practice cuts at the heart of analytical objectivity, a core value of the IC.

Politicization is a hypersensitive issue among analysts, and a difficult one to manage because the matter demands strong intervention when the offense is clear but can easily lead to stalemate when it is not.[4] A policymaker ordering a change to an analytic judgment may be hard to deal with but the inappropriate action would be transparent. The line often blurs, however, when accusations result from the IC's own review process. Analytic supervisors are charged with substantive review that may appropriately challenge both the assumptions and conclusions of a given draft, which, in turn, may anger the drafter who might then unjustifiably perceive politicization. Managers need to foster open communications with analysts to clarify such cases, and, when deemed useful, encourage their subordinates to consult with the politicization ombudsman now available in some IC analytic agencies.[5]

Bias is a subtle but pervasive influence based on the unconscious exertion of pressure. It is systemic in the IC. The mission of analysis is to inform U.S. policy decisions in support of U.S. interests around the world and to warn against any force that opposes them. This is not a neutral baseline. In the world of intelligence, chronic uncertainty and critical information gaps on major issues invite further bias. Collectors can be enamored of their sources, and analysts are sometimes victims of their own rigid mindset, which causes them to miss signals that their assumptions are wrong. And consumers are frequently invested in their policies and often resistant even to reliable intelligence that challenges their views.

The record is clear. Politicization happens—even U.S. presidents have been guilty of it. As chapter 6 by Gregory Treverton on this topic notes, the dangers of politicization comes with the territory. Pressures to distort analysis are an occupational hazard in the intelligence business, a recurring problem to be managed by rigorous adherence to the best tradecraft, by analytic courage and integrity, and by the timely intervention of responsible managers. Pressures to distort usually surface when intelligence judgments are at odds with entrenched or evolving policy. And, at times, the pressure is against writing at all rather than about what to write.

Tradecraft—including the use of rigorous methodologies, tools, and techniques to challenge assumptions and mindset—is an important factor in promoting and protecting analytic objectivity, but it is clearly not the only one. The Central Intelligence Agency's (CIA's) legendary scholar and foremost analyst, Sherman Kent, published his path-breaking book, *Strategic Intelligence for American World Policy* in 1949, which laid the foundations for analytic rigor and objectivity. Three generations of intelligence officers since then have worked to incorporate increasingly useful methodologies into IC training programs and workplace practices. There is no debate today about the utility of methodologies related to Alternative Analysis, Red Teaming, Competitive Analysis, or the Analysis of Competing Hypotheses (ACH) in reducing uncertainty when information is ambiguous or incomplete.[6] The 9/11 Commission and the WMD [weapons of mass destruction] Commission have added to the pressure on the IC to develop and deploy better tradecraft.[7]

There always has been a gap, however, between the enthusiastic application of methodologies in the classroom and their sparing use in the IC workplace. Analysts in the crush of multiple high-priority tasks with short deadlines rarely have time to develop and assess alternative hypotheses or conduct competitive analyses. Getting this job done depends on strong managers who make time and provide other resources to examine alterative hypotheses. Tradecraft is not just a requirement for analysts. It is a high-order responsibility for managers.

The considerable strength of the IC's "system of checks and balances" depends on people—leadership—not checklists or software. If managers, at every level, do not insist on rigorous tradecraft, on respect for dissent, and on open debate, bias will win in the form of lowest-common-denominator or distorted analysis. If powerful consumers reject or question the need for Competitive Analysis, chances grow that it will not happen. Responsible and accountable managers are indispensable to guide the less experienced, to protect the quality and objectivity of the analytic product, and to uphold the integrity of the production process. In the end, the time-tested and hard-won integrity of U.S. intelligence analysis does not run on automatic. Leadership matters, vitally.

Wanted: A Revolution in Training and Education

The IC manager's responsibilities have grown in the information age, but so has the need for formal training—for collectors, producers, and consumers. Today's analysts face unprecedented challenges in the complexity of the global threats they face; and in the range and depth of requirements they received from national, military, and congressional consumers. Yet, in sharp contrast with our military services and diplomatic corps, no IC training and education institution exists today—even though there are basic issues of analysis and collection that merit a community-wide approach and increasingly complex business issues that demand it. And there is now, more than ever, a need to educate all intelligence stakeholders, consumers as well as producers, who interact in the process.

Most agencies today have their own training programs, but they often are managed or staffed by contractors, and their courses tend to be agency specific.[8] The director of national intelligence (DNI) has attempted to identify a core curriculum for a virtual NIU, but on this, too, progress has been painfully slow. IC training and education, as it is, simply cannot keep pace with changes in the outside world. The DNI's goal to unify and professionalize the intelligence workforce cannot be achieved when even experienced employees know so little about the history of their agencies or important current issues affecting intelligence beyond the narrow limits of their own jobs. Lessons learned over the years should be embedded in the knowledge base that defines the intelligence profession.

The IC needs a National Intelligence University with a permanent central campus, a strong comprehensive curriculum, and a distinguished core faculty.[9]

Its students, in addition to IC professionals, would include a healthy mix of policymakers, military officers, diplomats, and representatives of both the executive and legislative branches—the "organic whole" of U.S. intelligence. The NIU, thus constituted, would develop courses focusing on the organization and mission of the IC; on collection management; language and cultural studies; analytic tradecraft; leadership and resource management; on budget and finance; on IC career development; security; counterintelligence; civil liberties; open source strategies; and on effective policymaker, congressional, and media relations. The university would teach the principles of information sharing, with all its legal and bureaucratic complexities. It would teach professional ethics, with its critical implications for the intelligence business.

The NIU would be a major center for engaging outside experts. It would be an impartial source of competent research, and a credible "institutional memory" for past IC policies and programs. It would look back thoroughly at intelligence successes and failures, and it would look ahead boldly at where geopolitics and technology are likely to take us. And, most important to IC analysts, it would bring professionals from different agencies together to deepen their professional knowledge but also to get to know and respect one another at multiple stages of their careers. For the IC professional, the NIU would be about "us" in the community, not about "me" in my agency.

Notes

1. E.g., this important point is reflected in the ambitious current program of the deputy director of national intelligence for analysis, in the two reports from the National Intelligence Council, *Global Trends 2015* (December 2000, www.dni.gov/nic/nic_2015.html) and *Mapping the Global Future* (December 2004, www.dni.gov/nic/nic_2020_project.html), and in the international Global Futures Forum/Partnership cosponsored by the CIA's Directorate of Intelligence.

2. E.g., see Commission on the Intelligence Capabilities of the United States Regarding Weapons of Mass Destruction, *Report to the President of the United States*, March 31, 2004, 377–80; www.wmd.gov/report/index.html.

3. For one related, critical assessment, see Clive Thompson, "Open Source Spying," *New York Times*, December 3, 2006.

4. A serious study of the issue needs to be integrated into IC training and education. In the author's view, it would reveal an intelligence business that constantly grapples with uncertainty and critical information gaps, and that works (sometimes successfully, sometimes not) to counter "systemic" pressures to distort analysis both from within the IC and from consumers. A fair reading of that history would support the conclusion that credit and blame for the IC's mixed record on both countering distortion pressures and tradecraft failings should be distributed among intelligence collectors, analysts, managers, agency top bosses, policymakers, and Congress. The key variable in improving the quality of analysis for today and tomorrow is leadership.

5. The CIA has had a senior officer assigned as the ombudsman for politicization since the mid-1990s, when Senate hearings focused on this issue. The ombudsman investigates specific cases when charges are brought by CIA officers.

6. The best overall book on analytic tradecraft, which details the ACH process, is Richards J. Heuer Jr., *Psychology of Intelligence Analysis* (Washington, D.C.: Center for the Study of Intelligence, Central Intelligence Agency, 1999). His chapter in this volume elaborates on

one of the powerful analytic techniques that managers must encourage analysts to employ to examine the huge volume of data flooding their inboxes.

7. See Commission on the Intelligence Capabilities of the United States Regarding Weapons of Mass Destruction, www.wmd.gov/report/index.html; and National Commission on Terrorist Attacks, *The 9/11 Commission Report: Final Report of the National Commission on Terrorist Attacks Upon the United States*, July 22, 2004, www.9–11commission.gov/.

8. For example, the CIA University encompasses a series of schools for analysis and operations as well as a "leadership" academy. The instructional cadre is led by staff employees; however, many of the instructors are either annuitants (retired analysts or operators) or contractors hired to teach specific courses. Similar models are to be found in the training institutions found at the National Security Agency, National Geospatial-Intelligence Agency, and the Defense Intelligence Agency. To its credit, the National Defense Intelligence College (previously known as the Joint Defense Intelligence College) has become a fully accredited institution and is open to a wide range of students throughout the U.S. government.

9. The proposal to establish an IC training and education institution was unanimously endorsed by the IC's top analytic managers in 2000. See Assistant Director of Central Intelligence for Analysis and Production, *Strategic Investment Plan for Intelligence Community Analysis* (Washington, D.C.: Central Intelligence Agency, 2000), https://odci.gov/cia/reports/unclass_sip/UnclasSIP.pdf.

CHAPTER 14

Intelligence in Transition: Analysis after September 11 and Iraq

Mark M. Lowenthal

RICHARD HELMS once observed to the staff of the House Intelligence Committee that the Central Intelligence Agency's (CIA's) Directorate of Operations was "where you got into trouble."[1] As Helms put it, the directorate did things overseas—recruiting spies and conducting covert action—that were both risky and illegal in the country where they took place. One of the ironies of intelligence in the early years of the twenty-first century is that analysis has proved to be as risky and controversial as operations. Much of this controversy centers on two issues: intelligence prior to the terrorist attacks of 2001; and the analysis of Iraq's weapons of mass destruction (WMD) programs prior to Operation Iraqi Freedom in 2002.

This chapter looks at where intelligence analysis is and may be going after these two events, focusing on these questions:

- What have we learned—or think we have learned?
- What is different?
- What do we need to do now in intelligence analysis?
- Where do we go from here?

Lessons Learned and Unlearned—Perceived and Real

When asked why we have a CIA, David Kahn,[2] the scholar of intelligence, replied: "It's a two-word answer: Pearl Harbor." It is widely agreed that the attack on Pearl Harbor provided the major impetus for the creation of the intelligence community after World War II. The nation was unwilling to accept another strategic surprise, a view that became more urgent in a world of intercontinental ballistic missiles with nuclear warheads. Judged by this rather stark standard, U.S. intelligence did well during the cold war, providing successive presidents with intelligence to avoid strategic confrontations with the Soviet Union and giving adequate warning (after an initial lapse) of the one near-strategic surprise, Nikita Khrushchev's decision to deploy missiles in Cuba in 1962. This does not mean that there were no surprises across those fifty years, but none of them involved a strategic threat or imminent attack on the United States of the magnitude of Pearl Harbor. For the most part, during the cold war, intelligence succeeded.

The importance of strategic intelligence dwindled with the demise of the Soviet Union in 1991. The decade that followed was somewhat unsettling for the intelligence community as it attempted to find a new focus. Then–CIA director Robert Gates once said that during the height of the cold war, half of all intelligence activities were devoted in some way to the Soviet Union and related issues. Deciding what to focus on in the absence of this overwhelming Soviet issue and in the midst of nearly a decade of severe budget cuts was a daunting managerial challenge. It is difficult to overstate the debilitating effect of these "locust years." George Tenet, half of whose long tenure as CIA director occurred during this period, has said publicly that the intelligence community lost the equivalent of one in four positions—that is, people who were never hired to fill vacancies.[3] Finally, this was also one of those recurring periods of instability at the top of the intelligence community and the CIA. In just under six years (August 1991 to July 1997) there were five directors of central intelligence (DCIs).

Terrorism was not a new issue; it was a recurring one. There had been terrorism largely related to the Middle East in the 1970s and state-supported terrorism in the 1980s. Nor was the hostility of al-Qaeda to the United States a surprise. From the first attack on the World Trade Center in 1993, through the abortive millennium attacks on the eve of 2000, there were several other attacks and some thwarted attacks. The famous *President's Daily Brief* article of August 6, 2001, said that al-Qaeda remained hostile, wanted to attack within the United States, and might use airplanes.[4]

The supposed intelligence analysis "lessons" of September 11 derive primarily from Congress's Joint Inquiry and especially from the 9/11 Commission report. Although the Joint Inquiry noted that the *tactical* intelligence needed to stop the September 11 attacks did not exist, these findings are relevant to analysis:[5]

- a failure to focus information and to appreciate the significance of some intelligence;
- the absence of strategic analysis of al-Qaeda; and
- inadequate funding for counterterrorism, and the related issues of untrained analysts and a dearth of language skills.

Perhaps the lasting contribution of the Joint Inquiry to the future of intelligence analysis was cochairman Senator Richard Shelby's assessment that the intelligence community was unable to "connect the dots." This condescending and demeaning phrase—which equates intelligence analysis with a child's diversion—has entered the common parlance as a pervasive and repeated analytical flaw. But the repeated use of the "connect the dots" phrase has serious implications for the future of intelligence analysis, as will be discussed below.

The 9/11 Commission Report focused more on structural issues but gave these findings or recommendations regarding analysis:[6]

- There was insufficient strategic analysis of al-Qaeda.
- There is a need to institutionalize imagination, to use more red cell analytic groups, and to develop more indicators.
- The report recommended a more issue-center-based organization.

Let us turn to Iraq WMD, which was, compared with September 11, the far more serious issue in terms of intelligence analysis. It was very clear in 2002 that the George W. Bush administration was determined to do something about Saddam Hussein, who was seen as a threat to U.S. security for a variety of reasons. In October 2002, the intelligence community produced an update of its previous National Intelligence Estimate (NIE) on Iraqi WMD, at the request of the Senate Select Committee on Intelligence. The key judgments, as stated in an unclassified version released in July 2003, were that Iraq had continued its WMD programs in defiance of the United Nations; that Iraq had chemical and biological weapons; and that "most analysts assess" that Iraq was reconstituting its nuclear program.[7] Once U.S. and British troops overran Iraq, however, it became apparent that Iraq had very little in the way of a current or near-term WMD capacity.

Like September 11, Iraq WMD engendered a series of investigations and reports. These included two reports by the Senate Intelligence Committee, the WMD Commission, and an analysis led by former deputy DCI Richard Kerr at the request of the assistant director of central intelligence for analysis and production. To these should be added two foreign reports: the Butler Report on British intelligence efforts and the Flood Report on Australian intelligence efforts.[8] The main findings of these various reports pertinent to analysis include:

- Analysis was overly technical in nature, failing to examine the political and cultural contexts for Iraqi actions (WMD Commission, Kerr Group, Flood Report).
- There had been too great a shift away from long-term, in-depth analysis, in favor of short-term products (WMD Commission, Kerr Group).
- There was an uncritical acceptance of established positions and assumptions (Senate, WMD Commission, Kerr Group).
- Analysts indulged in groupthink, that is, analysts too readily came to agree on a position without examining it critically (Senate).
- There were possibly overreactions to previous errors—such as the underestimation of Iraqi WMD capabilities prior to the first Gulf War (Butler Report, WMD Commission).
- There was a "layering" of judgments, that is, using judgments from earlier parts of analysis as the factual basis for later assessments in the NIE (Senate).
- Analysts failed to communicate uncertainties and the nature of intelligence sources (Senate, WMD Commission).
- Analysts were risk-averse (WMD Commission).
- There was no evidence that the analysis had been politicized (Senate, WMD Commission, Butler, Flood).

This was a rather daunting indictment, even if one does not agree with each finding. But one other finding of the Butler Report is also worth considering. The Butler Report doubted that a better intelligence process would have led to a correct conclusion. Certainly more could have been done to make the assessments less stark and more nuanced and to give policymakers a greater sense of the underlying uncertainties. But it remains extremely difficult to describe, in terms of good analytical tradecraft as opposed to a blind leap of faith, how an assessment might have been written that would have come to the conclusion that Saddam was telling the truth and that Iraq did not have WMD in 2002.

One final point about the Iraq NIE is worth noting. It was a singularly unpersuasive and noninfluential document. Although its main points would have been—and almost certainly were—welcomed by policymakers in the Bush administration, it was not written for them and they had little doubt as to the nature of the Iraqi threat. Again, the NIE was written for the Senate, although we know that only a handful of senators bothered to read the estimate, so it had little discernible effect on the 77–23 vote in October 2002 authorizing the use of force if Iraq did not give up its WMD. Finally, much of the same material was used to support Secretary of State Colin Powell at the United Nations but, again, it failed to move any of the nations to change their view and support the use of force against Iraq.

What Is Different?

Like Banquo's ghost at the dinner table in *Macbeth*, the issues of September 11 and Iraq WMD are spectral presences in U.S. intelligence analysis. And it is not clear what will exorcise these issues. In the past, major intelligence failures have been erased by later intelligence successes. For example, President John Kennedy's extremely negative views of the CIA after the Bay of Pigs fiasco were largely erased by its far better performance during the Cuban missile crisis. But hoping for a chance to shine is hardly a strong managerial platform. The true effect of these two issues on analysis is the real or perceived lessons, some of which approach the status of urban legends. Most prominent among these are:

- the importance of and the ability to "connect the dots,"
- the high risk of groupthink, and
- the prevalence of risk aversion.

As with most perceptions and urban legends, the existence of these views is more important than their relationship to reality. There is also a strong undercurrent that holds that not only is the truth out there but that it should be always knowable. This is one of the more insidious implications of "connect the dots," the belief that more depends on following simplistic methodology than good analytic tradecraft.

In terms of the ability to focus and concentrate, the intelligence community remains pretty much where it was after the collapse of the Soviet Union. The war on terrorism is a major issue but arguably does not have the same pride of place as did the Soviet Union. This is not to suggest that the war on terrorism is somehow less important than the cold war. Rather, there are too many other issues that can compete on a more equal basis with terrorism than was the case during the cold war.

This greater equality of priorities carries with it several implications. First, it is more difficult for managers to allocate analytic resources when no single issue is first among equals. Second, it means that there is a wider diversity of skills required among analysts, as well as a greater need to have analysts who are more fungible. There will never be enough analysts to cover every possible issue. When crises break out—especially in areas that were receiving little or no attention—analysts have to be shifted. Here, again, we see the effect of the locust years. Thomas Fingar, the deputy director of national intelligence for analysis, has stated that, in 2006, more than half the analysts in the intelligence community had five or fewer years of experience.[9] This relatively young and inexperienced population goes to the heart of many of the findings of the various Iraq WMD inquiries. They have less analytical expertise and less technical expertise. They are less able to write in-depth or strategic analyses, as opposed to short-term analyses—in large part because they are given fewer opportunities to do so. Also, because of those "missing" 23,000 people from six to sixteen years ago, there are large gaps in the cadres that should now be moving into senior leadership positions.

The intelligence community, following the recommendation of the WMD Commission, has begun moving toward a mission manager approach to organizing analysts.[10] The commission argued that, for certain issues, the community needs a single office that "is responsible for making sure the intelligence community is doing its all to collect and analyze intelligence on a subject." Then–director of national intelligence (DNI) John Negroponte appointed mission managers for North Korea, Iran, Cuba and Venezuela (a single manager for both), counterterrorism, and counterproliferation. Although the mission manager concept may be worthwhile, one can see even in this set of five mission managers inherent problems of coordination. Thus, counterproliferation is a problem in and of itself and specifically in North Korea and Iran. Similarly, Iran's ties to terrorism overlap two mission managers. Which mission manager has the lead in each of these cases? Cooperation and collaboration are necessary and worthwhile goals, but to achieve the mission manager concept *one* manager has to have the lead. Interestingly, the Kerr Group's report argues that issue-based centers will tend to exacerbate the divorce between technical and political analysis that was evident on Iraq WMD.

What Do We Need Now in Analysis?

The main improvements needed to do better analysis are competent analysts. The intelligence community is hiring new analysts in most agencies. Then–CIA director Porter Goss was ordered by President Bush to increase the number of CIA analysts by 50 percent. New analysts are also being hired at the Defense Intelligence Agency and in two of the newest analytic components, the Federal

Bureau of Investigation (FBI) and the Department of Homeland Security. These new analysts represent an opportunity and a challenge.

This new analytical cadre gives the intelligence community the opportunity to do things they have never been done before, primarily in education, training, and career management. Most intelligence components now have some sort of introductory training for new analysts, although the details and contents of each vary. Perhaps that is a good place to start. Now that the DNI has someone directly responsible for community-wide training and education (i.e., an assistant deputy director of national intelligence for education and training, who also serves as the chancellor of the National Intelligence University), it would be a good time to look seriously at the prospect of training all analysts across the community in common curricula and techniques. Even better would be to break the analysts out of the agency stovepipes into which they are put immediately upon being hired and train them in classes that mix together analysts from various agencies. It would be far better to begin inculcating analysts with an intelligence community outlook at the beginning of their careers, rather than waiting for them to be quite senior, as is now the practice. That would go a long way to breaking the agency-based culture that continues to dominate the intelligence community. The military believes very strongly in the concept "Train the way you fight." If the intelligence community truly wants to act like a community, it has to follow this same training concept.

Hand in hand with improved introductory training has to come a serious look at career planning and career management for analysts. There exist at best only vague notions as to the skills and experiences that separate entry-level analysts from those in the middle of their careers and the difference between those in the middle from those who are considered senior. Serious thought has to be given to analyst career paths. How many are there or should there be? Some analysts will need or want to be moved around over the course of their careers. Others, who have developed rare and unique specialties, may stay more within the bounds of their chosen field. There has to be a personnel system that rewards both patterns. Similarly, as analysts become more senior, not all will want to seek or are suited for managerial roles. Again, how should the system deal with these differences in a manner that is equitable and encouraging? The CIA's Senior Analytical Service offers a useful model here, although those analysts do not do enough to serve as mentors (as opposed to managers) for junior analysts. Finally, implementing rather than merely talking about the requirement that analysts have to serve significant assignments in other agencies before they can be promoted to senior ranks should be tried. It would be akin to the Goldwater-Nichols requirement in the military that joint duty assignments are necessary in order to be eligible for promotion to general officer; in intelligence parlance, serving in a policy job would be required before promotion into the Senior Intelligence Service. Too often in the past, this requirement has been given lip service while myriad exceptions were made for too many analysts.

All these recommendations go to two points. First, we have to treat analysts across the intelligence community as a single *professional* cadre. As Rebecca Fisher and Rob Johnston point out in chapter 3, a profession is commonly defined as an occupation that requires specialized training and the mastery of specialized knowledge. Some definitions also include ethical codes and a process of certification or licensing. If, as many of us believe, intelligence analysis is a profession, then we have a ways to go to meet these requirements. We have for too long treated analysis as both art and craft and, though these are important components of the skill set, it is time to professionalize the analytic workforce. The second point is the nature of the workforce. The only way we will erase that experience gap noted by Fingar is if the new analysts stay with their careers. If we fail these new analysts in the structure and management of their careers, they will never become veteran analysts because they will not stay.

Urban Legends and Analytical Challenges

Beyond the workforce issues, significant analytic issues need to be resolved. As stated above, the subtextual message of "connect the dots"—and of several other reductio ad absurdum views of analysis, such as "looking for nuggets"—is that the "truth" of any intelligence problem is ultimately knowable. Put another way, the standard for judging intelligence now appears to be "right or wrong," which is rather stark and wholly unrealistic. The message appears to be that if the analyst just lines up his or her intelligence in the right order, then he or she will know what is coming next, what the answer is. Moreover, the entire burden falls on the analyst—not on the relative availability or paucity of intelligence (or "dots"), or the effort of states to deny or deceive us, or the possibility that more than one answer may emerge. Interestingly, this view actually runs counter to the fears about groupthink, which would seem to advocate—again, often for formulaic reasons—that more than one answer be given.

It will be very difficult, for political reasons, to move away from this "right or wrong" standard. Critics of intelligence analysis will likely see this as an effort to be less rigorous, to duck responsibility, or to invite another September 11 or Iraq WMD. The only way to resolve this issue is to address it head on. There needs to be a debate among the intelligence community, its policy customers, and Congress on what are reasonable standards for intelligence analysis. There is no reason that the press and the public cannot be part of this debate. To be more specific: How often should the intelligence community be correct, and about what issues? It would be fallacious to expect that this debate would result in a specific answer—80 percent, or maybe 75 percent on most issues, but 90 percent on the important ones, and so on. No such answer exists. But it is important—if not crucial—that we arrive at some reasonable criteria by which intelligence analysis can be judged. If we do not, then intelligence analysis will be seen to fail on a consistent basis.

Much depends on how one views the analytical process. Again, if the starting point is "dots" or "nuggets," then intelligence analysis is reduced to finding single-point answers. My own preferred metaphor for analysis is the creation of pearls. It takes between three and six years for a bivalve mollusk to produce a pearl. It is a slow, accretionary process. Similarly, good intelligence rests on knowledge, and this customarily takes years to accumulate. Recall one of the critiques of both September 11 and Iraq: the absence of strategic analysis. Strategic analysis depends on this accumulation over time. The intelligence community spent almost fifty years collecting and assessing intelligence on the Soviet Union. Analysts became steeped in detailed knowledge about Communist Party politics and the workings of various weapons systems. This also depends on analysts developing longer-term careers, again raising those workforce issues.

But this very approach exposes one of the problems in creating analytic standards. The community will tend to do better on smaller issues and run greater risks of "error" on the big issues. The big issues—the events that seem to turn on a dime—are more difficult to assess correctly because they tend to run *counter* to this accumulated knowledge. The idea that the Soviet Union could collapse peacefully, that the Communist Party would quietly give up power, ran counter to the entire course of Soviet history. This was a regime that experienced no limits in its quest for political survival or its willingness to brutalize its own citizens. Given these facts—not intelligence subject to interpretation, but historical facts—what would be the analytical basis for predicting the swift and peaceful demise of the Soviet state? Similarly, what in Saddam Hussein's past behavior—his brutality, his mendacity, his willingness to use chemical weapons against both foreign and domestic targets—leads to an analytical conclusion that he is being truthful when he says Iraq no longer has WMD but he is unwilling to allow inspections to affirm his claim?

The issue of a reasonable standard for analysis also lies at the heart of the risk aversion issue. Analysts are not risk averse. They do not shy away from making difficult judgments. They understand the nature of their work and that they are not being called upon to make predictions. But they are averse to being held to an unreasonable standard, to being liable to be called in front of a congressional committee or investigating commission because they were less than 100 percent right. The fact that some senior analysts have seen fit to buy liability insurance underscores the nature of the problem.

The need to build knowledge is another challenge the analytic community faces. Analysts cannot continually fly by the seat of their pants. They need to know their subjects in some depth so as to be facile with them, to understand trends *and* anomalies, and to have some basis for their conclusions. The trend away from strategic analysis in favor of short-term (or "current" intelligence) reporting has greatly undercut analysts' ability to build knowledge. It becomes a diversion rather than a core value. This is also another result of the locust years. As the analytic cadre decreased, it became more and more difficult to give analysts the time required to build knowledge. The recurring ill-chosen metaphor expressed by managers, about how many analysts they had "in the line," ran directly counter to the building of knowledge. This obsession with the "analytical line" also undercuts opportunities for education, training, travel, or cross-assignments. How can anyone be spared when managers look at their responsibilities as a continuing tactical engagement in which they are always understaffed? That is why the ongoing increase in the number of analysts is an opportunity—if they are managed correctly. If the increased labor power is simply used to buttress "the line," then little will be gained and much lost. But if this expected influx of new analysts is seen as an opportunity to allow a freer use of all analysts, or assign a greater proportion of them to training, then the community will have gained a great deal. Managers should also recognize that not every investment in knowledge building will have an immediate analytical payoff. Some knowledge may not be needed for years; some may never be called upon at all. That is one of the risks of the enterprise.

Hand in hand with a renewed devotion to the building of knowledge and greater emphasis on strategic analysis, some thought should be given to the main vehicle in which this strategic analysis is expressed: the NIE. As the Kerr Group pointed out concerning Iraq, NIEs do not tend to be new, pathbreaking analysis. They are more often compendia and updates of past analysis. It is time, as the Kerr Group argues, to revisit the utility and role of the NIEs. They are too often overly long, flabby documents in which a few estimative judgments are encased within "all the community's knowledge" on a given topic. This heft tends to give added weight to the estimative portions, implying that there is a large body of material supporting the judgments. Often, however, much of the NIE is little more than background and bears no relationship to the estimative judgments. Our British and Australian colleagues produce assessments (their word for estimates) with a maximum of 1,500 words, and very little seems to be lost in the telling.

As the Kerr Group also notes, NIEs tend not to be very influential documents per se, as was the case with the Iraq NIE; they are more often used by this faction or that in the policy community to support their positions, which often requires very artful and selective quotations.

Some will see this recommendation as heresy. After all, NIEs are the intelligence community's considered views, provided by the DNI to the president. One need not abandon that goal when jettisoning NIEs. But as I have written elsewhere, there are also intellectual problems within the NIE process.[11] The fact that the views of *all* agencies are equal is a serious flaw. There is no accounting here for expertise. Take, for example, the issue of Iraq's 81-millimeter aluminum tubes, an issue of tremendous contention in the Iraq NIE. Were the tubes suitable for centrifuges or not? The issue ultimately came down to a judgment by the CIA, which was the drafter, versus the Department of Energy and the State Department's Bureau of Intelligence and Research. Each of these agencies had some legitimate expertise on the issue. However, had the FBI or the National Security Agency decided to weigh in, their stances would have had equal weight, despite their lesser knowledge of the subject. The other intellectual problem is the use of the phrase "most agencies." This is used to show where the main body of opinion lies, but it masks which agencies are involved. Do numbers matter or expertise? Does this mean most of the sixteen agencies that are part of the intelligence community or only a majority of those drafting the estimate? How many is that? Again, the main goal seems to be to give added weight to the judgment. The intelligence community has correctly argued that the Senate's accusation of groupthink on the Iraq estimate is wrong. But the NIE process contributes to this urban legend when it uses the "most agencies" construction.

The intelligence community also faces an important doctrinal issue. The Intelligence Reform and Terrorism Prevention Act that created the DNI gives a new definition to intelligence, which formerly was divided between foreign and domestic. Now there is only national intelligence, which subsumes foreign, domestic, and homeland security intelligence. This third category is still relatively new and undefined. We do not yet have a good working concept for what homeland security intelligence (called HSINT—"his-int"—by some) means. This is not an abstract intellectual issue. If we do not come up with a suitable doctrine for HSINT, we are less likely to be able to stop the next terrorist attack—not that we can stop them all. We still have a significant gap between foreign intelligence and the first responders, whom we tend to flood with every warning of a possible attack. Homeland security needs a working doctrine so it can focus on the things that only homeland security can do and therefore serve as the vital link between foreign and domestic intelligence and the first responders.

Finally, the intelligence community needs to address the issue of politicization. Interestingly, this is not a problem arising from the contents or internal processes of the intelligence work related to September 11 or Iraq. Indeed, as noted, each investigation of the Iraq WMD issue, including the Butler and Flood reports, came to the conclusion that the intelligence was not politicized. But it does stem from how the Iraq intelligence was perceived to have been used.

The Bush administration's decision to fight a preemptive war in Iraq put the intelligence community in the awkward position of serving as the main means of justifying this decision. The controversy surrounding that process and the political division over the ongoing fighting in Iraq have led both political parties to stake out positions on the intelligence community's approach to the "next" issue, Iran's nuclear program. In May 2006, several Democratic senators requested that the intelligence community prepare an estimate on Iran, via a letter to President Bush. Their request made specific reference to the "mistakes made in the run-up to the conflict in Iraq." In June 2006, the Democrats introduced the Iran Intelligence Oversight Act, which would require "an updated national intelligence estimate on Iran with an unclassified summary available to inform debate by Congress and the American people."

In August 2006, the House Intelligence Committee's Intelligence Policy Subcommittee released a staff report, "Recognizing Iran as a Strategic Threat: An Intelligence Challenge for the United States." This report, based on open source materials, concluded that Iran is seeking nuclear weapons, likely has an offensive chemical weapons program, and probably has an offensive biological weapons program—conclusions that were strongly rebutted by the International Atomic Energy Agency the following month.

No matter what the intelligence community produces at this point on Iran, and on most other issues of consequence, it is obvious that the product will be attacked by one political party or the other. This atmosphere is not conducive to thoughtful or useful analysis. The DNI should meet with all concerned senators and representatives and urge them to step back if they truly wish to see intelligence that is objective and may be useful to them, regardless of the final outcome.

Similarly, the September 2006 leak of the April 2006 NIE on trends in global terrorism evidently came from someone seeking to take issue with the Bush administration's policy on Iraq. One paragraph in an NIE of more than thirty pages, according to press reports, was made to represent the entire NIE. Thus it was not surprising that President Bush decided to declassify most of the key judgments to give a more balanced sense of the contents of the NIE. The end result is to turn another NIE into a political shuttlecock. More important, this constant barrage of political intrusion runs the very strong risk of making analysts gun-shy about their work if they fear that it will become an issue for partisan debate shortly after being written.

Where Do We Go From Here?

The years since September 2001 have been as brutal as any for intelligence analysis in the history of the intelligence community. That there has not been a mass exodus of analysts is a testament to their dedication to their profession and to the nation. Morale clearly has suffered, but recruitment numbers remain high—which is reason for optimism.

To repeat, there is an interesting but ephemeral opportunity to make significant changes in intelligence analysis. Some of these will respond to flaws that were evident in September 11 and Iraq WMD. Many would ignore the urban legends that have sprung up concerning those two events.

One of the criticisms of the intelligence community that arose from Iraq was the absence of an institutionalized "lessons learned" capacity. This is quite true. Here is an area where the intelligence community can profit from the military's practice, especially that of the Army. There is much to be gained from a regular lessons learned capability. One learns not only from one's mistakes but also from one's successes—especially those successes that did not follow established doctrine. The DNI's office is actually in the midst of creating such a capability. An obvious place to start would be September 11 and Iraq WMD. The research has been done, although much remains to be done in sifting through the myriad findings, sorting out those that are true or telling from those that are not. But deriving lessons is meaningless unless the lessons are applied and processes are then monitored to ensure that the new lessons are being applied. That is both. the challenge and the opportunity that the intelligence community faces in the post–September 11 and Iraq environment.

Notes

1. Author's notes from a meeting of former director of central intelligence Richard Helms with House Permanent Select Committee on Intelligence staff, May 1995.

2. David Kahn, "The Rise of Intelligence," *Foreign Affairs* 85, no. 5 (September/October 2006): 133.

3. See "Written Statement for the Record of the Director of Central Intelligence before the Joint Inquiry Committee, October 17, 2002," www.cia.gov/cia/public_affairs/speeches /2002/dci_testimony_10172002.html.

4. This *President's Daily Brief* article was released on April 10, 2004. The text can be found at http://www.whitehouse.gov/news/releases/2004/04/20040410-5.html. See also the White House Fact Sheet, April 10, 2004, at http://www.whitehouse.gov/news/releases/2004 /04/20040410-5.html.

5. House Permanent Select Committee on Intelligence and the Senate Select Committee on Intelligence, *Report of the Joint Inquiry into the Terrorist Attacks of September 11, 2001*, December 2002, www.gpoaccess.gov/serialset/creports/911.html. The Joint Inquiry is pointedly silent about Congress's responsibility for inadequate funding and its effects.

6. National Commission on Terrorist Attacks, *The 9/11 Commission Report: Final Report of the National Commission on Terrorist Attacks Upon the United States*, July 22, 2004, available at http://www.9-11commission.gov/.

7. The unclassified version of the Key Judgments of the NIE *Iraq's Weapons of Mass Destruction Programs* can be found at www.gwu.edu/~nsarchiv/NSAEBB/NSAEBB129/nie_first%20release.pdf. The Key Judgments were released at a White House background briefing on July 18, 2003. The text of the briefing can be found at www.fas.org/irp/news/2003/07/wh071803.html.

8. Senate Select Committee on Intelligence, *Report on the U.S. Intelligence Community's Prewar Intelligence Assessments on Iraq*, July 7, 2004, www.gpoaccess.gov/serialset/creports/iraq.html. Senate Select Committee on Intelligence, *Report on Postwar Findings about Iraq's WMD Programs and How They Compare with Prewar Assessments*, September 8, 2006, http://intelligence.senate.gov/phaseiiaccuracy.pdf. Commission on the Intelligence Capabilities of the United States Regarding Weapons of Mass Destruction, *Report to the President of the United States*, March 31, 2004 (hereafter, *WMD Commission Report*), available at www.wmd.gov/report/index.html. Richard Kerr, Thomas Wolfe, Rebecca Donnagan, and Arris Pappas, *Intelligence and Analysis on Iraq: Issues for the Intelligence Community*, July 29, 2004, http://www.gwu.edu/~nsarchiv/news/20051013/kerr_report.pdf. The Butler Report, *Review of Intelligence on Weapons of Mass Destruction*, Report of a Committee of Privy Counsellors, London, July 14, 2004, http://archive2.official-documents.co.uk/documents/dep/hc/hc898/898.pdf. The Flood Report, *Report of the Inquiry into Australian Intelligence Agencies*, July 20, 2004, available at http://www.pmc.gov.au/publications/intelligence_inquiry/index.htm#downloads.

9. Thomas Fingar, speech at the DNI's Information Sharing Conference and Technology Exposition, Denver, August 21, 2006, http://www.odni.gov/speeches/20060821_2_speech.pdf.

10. See *WMD Commission Report*, 317–19.

11. Mark M. Lowenthal, *Intelligence: From Secrets to Policy*, 3rd ed. (Washington, D.C.: CQ Press, 2006), 122–23, 133–35.

CHAPTER 15

The New Analysis

CARMEN A. MEDINA

INTELLIGENCE ANALYSIS is a discipline under scrutiny. When individuals contemplate the intelligence failings associated with the September 11, 2001, terrorist attacks and the fruitless hunt for weapons of mass destruction (WMD) in Iraq, most of the attention is focused on the analytic part of the intelligence profession. In the overview of its report's key conclusions, the WMD Commission, for example, states, "This failure was in large part the result of analytical shortcomings."[1] The paragraph does go on to cite collection issues and problems in communicating with policymakers, but it is analysis that absorbs the first blow. Long before this, former director of central intelligence Stansfield Turner wrote in his 1985 book *Secrecy and Democracy* that "analysis, especially political analysis, is the Achilles' heel of intelligence."[2] Analysts failed to connect the dots in time to prevent September 11, although many recognize that institutional or procedural issues bore considerable responsibility for the failure. In the case of Iraq, analysts are accused of failing to question their assumptions and of building too many arguments on "single-threaded" intelligence reporting that in the end turned out flawed.

Veterans of the intelligence profession and even some less knowledgeable commentators know that this diagnosis simplifies the problem by not adequately considering the role that other parts of the intelligence cycle played—or perhaps more accurately did not play—in these failures, most notably the collectors. As James Bruce argues in chapter 12 of this volume, analysts can only be as good as the information they are analyzing, and in the run-up to both September 11 and the invasion of Iraq, collectors did an inadequate job of preparing the "intelligence battlefield." As the WMD Commission notes, they provided precious little intelligence for analysts to analyze.[3] Even this commentary finesses an important issue—that is, how good are analysts expecting collectors to be, a point examined later in the chapter.

Although collectors have generally escaped the same kind of scrutiny that has befallen analysts, it is important that analysts not use failings in collection as a multiple-use "get out of jail free card." Blaming the collectors overlooks the real reason why we have intelligence analysts: to deal with a world of imperfect information and significant uncertainty. In a world of perfect information, analysts are unnecessary or at least perform tasks, such as filtering or providing context, that are nice to have but not indispensable. Analysts exist because information is imperfect, incomplete, and open to multiple interpretations. If analysts are honest, they would admit to wishing it will always remain so.

These findings of the 9/11 and WMD commissions, the reports of congressional committees, and the extensive commentaries by journalists and academics, however, do not get at the real issue the analytic profession needs to begin tackling. Most of the current critiques of intelligence analysis do not present an existential challenge to the foundational elements and precepts of analytic work. For the most part, they accept the current processes and practices of intelligence analysis and argue that what is needed is better execution. The new ideas that are offered involve the perceived need to make better use of open source information or engage in more collaboration and information sharing, as the deputy director for analysis noted in his speech to the director of national intelligence's (DNI) Information Sharing Conference and Technology Exposition, August 21, 2006.[4] The conventional critique's focus on execution is epitomized by comments often heard from intelligence professionals seeking to diminish the significance of the various commissions' findings. It goes something like this: In the period leading up to September 11, intelligence analysts were accused of not connecting the dots. In the case of Iraq's WMD, they were accused of excessive connecting of dots. You cannot have it both ways, or so they say.

Actually both diagnoses can be correct, and thereby indicative of a more systemic pathology. If intelligence analysts are prone to errors at both ends of the "dot connection" spectrum, the problem may lie in a fundamental failing of the analytic model: in the entire dot connection process or even in the expectation that data—at least the data with which analysts today must work—can be reliably connected by individual analysts. The analytic profession has for some time assumed that its failings were the result of bad behaviors or pathologies, according to some critics.[5] In chapter 10, Jack Davis correctly points out the various psychological barriers to good analysis and that these bad behaviors do contribute to bad outcomes. However, the full diagnosis is more complex. In fact, to speak of a diagnosis is to put too much emphasis on what is wrong with analysis, at the expense of really thinking hard about how analysis needs to be completely different. What is most wrong with intelligence analysis is its essential design, which over the years has failed to adapt to new threats, to new understandings of human and social dynamics, and probably most important to new technologies.

Analysis is at a historic turning point. The intelligence community is entering a new era of analysis, during which it will be discovered that much of what used to be called intelligence analysis was primitive and incomplete. In this new era of analysis, prose prepared by so-called subject matter experts, which today still accounts for the overwhelming majority of analytic product, increasingly will be viewed as not analysis at all but just a form of commentary not unlike that which can be found in *The Economist*, the *New York Times*, or web-log spaces like www.danieldrezner.com. These types of expert commentary certainly have a role in informing national decision making, but commentary should not be considered the same thing as analysis and certainly cannot take its place. Many of the key elements of analysis, such as current intelligence and finished intelligence, will become less and less relevant to the reality of the world, to the needs of policymakers, and probably most important to the search for knowledge and some kind of wisdom.

The argument that intelligence analysis is entering a significant new era is built upon an assessment of how key aspects of the analytic process are changing. In the arenas of information, analytic work practices, and the analyst–consumer/policymaker relationship—defined largely by products and services—the last five years or so have seen critical and accelerated change that looks set to continue for many years to come.

The Data Challenge

The most significant driver changing analysis is the revolutionary explosion in data, both secret and not, that is characterizing the twenty-first century. When baby boomers began their analytic careers about thirty years ago, for the most part they dealt with fairly limited amounts of data. An analyst asked to answer a particular question was almost never able to travel to the areas in question to conduct primary research. He or she could assemble and read all the relevant information, usually in a matter of weeks. Relevant State Department cables and intelligence reports numbered perhaps in the hundreds. Except for a scattering of newspapers and magazines, there were few unclassified sources on foreign affairs. In his speech to the DNI Information Sharing conference, Thomas Fingar, deputy director of national intelligence for analysis, noted that in 1975 he was tasked with compiling a list of Chinese periodical publications. He had seventy-three publications on the list, which he compared to the thousands that would be available today.[6] If the analyst had been hired as a substantive expert on a regional or functional issue, he or she was probably already familiar with the relevant literature on the topic. Access to more current information from foreign, unclassified sources was limited and circumscribed by the effectiveness of the analyst's personal filing system.

Today's circumstances differ radically. The most significant change in intelligence data arguably has been caused by the proliferation of digital media. Although it is increasingly difficult to remember this period, much less information about people and events was captured before the computer era. For those of us who remember, these kinds of data were a nightmare for dissertation candidates and professional researchers to access or process by manual calculations or mainframe computer runs. Back then, the capture of an insurgent leader would uncover some documentary information (perhaps notebooks, but not notebook computers), and nothing like the mother lode struck today. When terrorist networks are disrupted and suspects arrested today, law enforcement and intelligence services often acquire gigabytes if not terabytes of data (a gigabyte is 1 billion bytes of data, and a terabyte is 1 trillion bytes of data), which must be scrutinized not just once but multiple times over long periods to harvest all the useful information and insight from the data. The importance of a list of names, for example, may not become apparent for several years until some new information or development provides critical context with which to interpret the old information. During the 2006 British operation that stopped the plot to bring down as many as a dozen transatlantic jets, deputy police commissioner Peter Clark, the head of Scotland Yard's Antiterrorist Branch, noted that the authorities had found "more than 400 computers, 200 mobile telephones and 8,000 items of removable storage media such as memory sticks, CDs and DVDs," which he estimated at the time contained some 6,000 gigabytes of data.[7]

Open source information, of course, has also exploded. From traditional media to text messaging to YouTube (www.youtube.com), the sheer volume of data overwhelms analysts until they can devise a reliable filtering strategy. In today's increasingly "democratized" information economy, the analyst can no longer depend on authoritative voices to be the primary sources of useful information. The implications of this fundamental change in the nature of information are often overlooked. Whereas during most of the postwar period analysts were dealing with information scarcity, today they also often encounter information overload. Much of this information admittedly is low grade but, as was discovered in hindsight after September 11, critical insights can be derived from the accumulation of large quantities of low-grade information.

The explosion in open source information and the democratization, through the Internet, of the means of production of content is also providing analysts, arguably for the first time ever, with insights into the views and thinking of the average individual. Intelligence collection has long been biased in the direction of elites such as government officials, but in a world of super-empowered common men and women and color-coded revolutions—such as the political upheaval in Ukraine earlier this decade—it is important that analysts have information with which to understand their issues as well.

This explosion of data is leading to a significant change in the nature of analytic activity—what might be termed as a transition from "analog" to "digital analysis." In the world of analog analysis, an individual—the 1960s baby boomer—could reasonably have expected to read relevant information in a defined period of time after which he or she would write a paper that conveyed his or her views on a particular situation or development. Admittedly much analysis today still follows this pattern, but it is increasingly found wanting by consumers. The *Washington Post* columnist David Ignatius reported that many officials at U.S. agencies found that the quality of Central Intelligence Agency (CIA) analysis varies widely, from top-notch to very ordinary.[8] The analysis of the future will increasingly and by necessity be digital. Analysts will be processing huge amounts of data and will be picking up potentially relevant tidbits from any number of sources, both secret and open. For the digital analyst, analytic tools will be essential because the technology of reading will no longer be up to the challenge of processing terabytes and petabytes of data (a terabyte is 1 trillion bytes of data, whereas a petabyte is a quadrillion bytes of data). As Ambassador John Negroponte noted in a 2006 speech at the Woodrow Wilson International Center for Scholars, "The National Security Agency estimates that, by next year, the Internet will carry 647 petabytes of data each day. . . . By way of comparison, the holdings of the Library of Congress represent only 0.02 petabytes."[9]

New Analytic Work Practices

Fundamental changes in the information environment will necessitate significant adjustments in analytic work practices. In contrast to the baby boomer analyst thirty years ago who could expect the information relevant to his or her task to fit on top of a desk, individual analysts today simply do not have the personal capacity to scan, much less analyze, the content that might be relevant to a particular topic. Today's and tomorrow's analytic challenges will require teams of analysts working both sequentially and nonsequentially, co-located and not co-located, just to do an initial exploitation of the data that are often acquired as the result of law enforcement, military, or intelligence operations. And as noted, much of this information will need to be examined repeatedly, over a period of years, as new events and information provide a context with which to interpret old data.

The "lone expert" model will suffice for fewer analytic problems, a development that parallels trends in other knowledge-based fields, such as medicine. The National Institutes of Health's Roadmap for Medical Research—posted on its website in 2002—noted the importance of supporting and removing obstacles to interdisciplinary research teams and initiatives to bring new insights and approaches to health problems.[10] And yet, even some of the most senior intelligence officials, including past CIA directors and DNIs, still frame the issue of expertise as an individual-based attribute rather than emphasizing component or institutional expertise.

The complexity of the world and of the information environment might appear as largely a collectors' problem. However, it will also demand a change in analytic work practices—forcing much greater analyst involvement with collectors to better target and deploy collection assets. Hybrid analysts are already becoming more common—one of the DNI's early initiatives in analysis, for example, has been the establishment of rapid analytic support and expeditionary response teams, which deploy to the field in order to solve difficult analytic problems by working with collectors and engaging in basic survey work.[11] Collectors praise the special something that analysts can provide by discriminating between good data and data appropriately destined for the cutting-room floor and by developing novel approaches and sources for information.

Balancing the demand for analytic talent among these competing requirements will become increasingly difficult. For years, many intelligence analysts and their managers looked down on applications of analytic expertise to help targeting or collectors, viewing this work as somehow "beneath" analysts. Much of this prejudice has dissipated but, as is often the case, the prejudice did reflect at least one legitimate concern: given the choice between fast-paced and exciting fieldwork and the often hard and interminable effort required to generate unique strategic insight, many analysts will choose the former. Policymakers still ask the intelligence community to generate unique insight on hard problems, such as China's evolution into a world power or the prospects for economic and social development in Sub-Saharan Africa. It is probably unreasonable to assume that individuals who enjoy the fast pace of hybrid analysis will also flourish in the more measured rhythm of research, which can take months if not years to generate insights on difficult problems.

"Insight" is the new buzzword in intelligence analysis, and a number of the contributors to this volume have already suggested that this is a continuing challenge. However, it represents a long-standing desire of policymakers. Former CIA director William Colby quotes Henry Kissinger as saying: "Keep giving me things that make me think."[12] Definitions of insight are many, but a useful one is that insight is the delivery to the policymaker as customer of a new way of looking at an issue that he or she finds useful and thought provoking in fashioning policy initiatives. The trend toward having more analysts work side by side with collectors is important and in the case of the global war on terrorism critical to national security, but there is no guarantee that it will contribute significantly to the generation of the kind of analytic insight demanded by senior policymakers.

The New Analyst–Policy Spectrum

Already, the more digital and more dynamic information environment and changing analytic work practices are perturbing relations between analysts and policymakers. The findings and products of hybrid analysts and of digital analysts (i.e., those who are taking full advantage of the digital environment) are often quite different from the traditional journalistic or expertise-based commentary of analog analysts. The initial tendency was to assume that senior policymakers would not be interested in these more tactical products, but experience to date has shown that assumption to be flawed. Indeed, a new analytic spectrum is emerging that ranges from the microscopic or "forensic" focus at one end to conceptual or "sense-making" efforts at the other. On the one hand, forensic analysis, not unlike the work of criminal forensic experts, uncovers unique insights from the careful study of large amounts of often quite minute data. On the other hand, conceptual or "sense-making" analysis provides policymakers with an entire new framework for interpreting events in the Middle East, which is also highly valued. However, the expectation from policymakers today increasingly is that these conceptual insights will be informed by the sophisticated manipulation of current—often unclassified—data, not just historical knowledge. In Iraq, for example, policymakers are looking for analytic interpretations of observable data of the evolving situation there, down to the level of specific neighborhoods in Baghdad such as Sadr City, upon which to base specific decisions.

This range of analysis has probably always existed, except that instead of being viewed as a spectrum, on which all points were of roughly equal value, it was seen to be more of a hierarchy. Analysts might start their career working with basic data, but if they proved to be good enough they would graduate to strategic analysis, which was always more conceptual. It was this view that led to the recent debates in the CIA's Directorate of Intelligence, for example, as to whether "targeting" analysts deserved to be called analysts at all. With the emergence of new analytic methods, such as geospatial applications, forensic analysts have begun to deliver a much more insightful, sophisticated, and useful product to policymakers. The management of analysts, however, has not quite caught up with the implications of the spectrum. For example, the prose-writing ability of analysts is too often seen as the critical measurement of analyst performance, even though prose is often the worst medium through which to communicate the findings of forensic analysis.

This diversification in accepted analytic products should also contribute to the long-overdue demise of analytical concepts such as "current" intelligence and "finished intelligence," which arguably have never been particularly relevant distinctions to policymakers. Both terms have been so grounded in prose that writing has long been identified as the essential skill of analysis. Current intelligence has been pilloried as contributing to the many ills of analysis and has been viewed as an essentially thoughtless, mechanical production of recent reporting. This critique is exaggerated, but it does capture the problematic use of the term "current"—that the analysis of what has just happened can be devoid of insight and only needs to record the essential facts. The digital information environment now enables much more powerful and immediate analysis, and policymakers have been demanding this for a very long time.

"Finished" intelligence is not a much more useful term. It usually means that the intelligence information has been validated by some kind of organizational and hierarchical process and thus can be viewed by a policymaker or decision maker as authoritative. Certainly no one would deny that on many topics, such as the status of Iran's nuclear program, policymakers need authoritative analysis. But the use of the term "finished" implies a predictability in the tempo of international events belied by recent history. Some practitioners defend the concept of finished intelligence in order to attack new collaborative approaches to intelligence analysis. Using social software tools like MediaWiki—referred to in the intelligence community as Intellipedia—is just the beginning. Yet, critics argue that the analysis on these new platforms is not "finished," which is an excuse for not embracing or even experimenting with these new capabilities.

Although such tools have their downsides, the critics tend to ignore the positives entirely. For example, Intellipedia allows real-time collaboration among a community of experts and facilitates the kind of new work practices that the digital environment now demands (see box 15.1). In addition, such collaborative platforms and fast methods of communicating knowledge and insight are probably better suited to follow episodes such as the recent Israel/Hezbollah conflict, where understanding of what was going on evolved on a daily basis. If one examines the Internet-based Wikipedia posting on what Intellipedia does, it notes that analysts from multiple agencies have used the network to post frequent updates on recent events such as the crash of a small plane in New York City or North Korean nuclear tests.[13] The initiative to transition analysts, much less policymakers, to these new platforms will not be easy, but the speed and transparency of these new processes will win them over in the end.

BOX 15.1
Intellipedia

The Intellipedia consists of three wikis that run on JWICS (Joint Worldwide Intelligence System), SIPRNet (Secret Internet Protocol Router Network), and Intelink-U—all of which are classified and run on intranets. They are used by individuals with appropriate clearances from the sixteen agencies of the U.S. intelligence community and other national-security-related organizations, including Combatant Commands and federal departments. None are open to the public.

Intellipedia is a project of the Office of the Director of National Intelligence (ODNI) DNI CIO Intelligence Community Enterprise Services office headquartered in Fort Meade, Maryland. As of October 2006, it contained over 28,000 pages edited by 3,600 users. It includes information on the regions, people, and issues of interest to those communities. Intellipedia uses MediaWiki, the same software used by the Wikipedia free-content encyclopedia project. ODNI officials say that the project will change the culture of the U.S. intelligence community, widely blamed for failing to "connect the dots" before the attacks of September 11, 2001.

Other versions are available on the U.S. Government Secret Internet Protocol Network (SIPRNet) and the Sensitive but Unclassified Network (SBU). SBU users can access Intellipedia from remote terminals outside their workspaces via a VPN. The SIPRNet is intended to serve a similar purpose for U.S. diplomats and Department of Defense personnel who are the predominant users of this network. Open Source Intelligence users share information on the unclassified network.

Source: Wikipedia, April 2007.

Policymakers in the future also are very likely to jettison the old notion of analysis faster than the intelligence community, as the digital information environment emerges. Unfortunately, the intelligence community has been largely indifferent to this possibility, in part because it would require far-reaching change. During the last few years, and particularly during the war in Iraq, policymakers have begun to express dissatisfaction with "analysis by anecdote," even though it has long been the prevailing model. Analysis by anecdote is a natural byproduct of current collection techniques. An analyst can expect on any given day to receive a couple of dozen new anecdotes, stories, and descriptions of events relevant to a particular topic. A human intelligence (HUMINT) report might tell the story of a particular meeting. A satellite image might tell an additional story of what is happening at a particular location. And other intelligence reporting might bring to light other narratives or stories. Based on this string of classified or unclassified anecdotes, the analyst develops conclusions.

When policymakers read these conclusions, they might wonder why this analysis, based on a certain set of anecdotes, differs from something else he or she may have read or been told. Analysts may claim that their collection of anec-dotes is authoritative, but given the vagaries of collection and its serendipitous nature, that claim is not easily justified. As policymakers grapple with the need to make momentous decisions, "analysis by anecdote" seems increasingly unsat-isfying, particularly if the policymaker is aware of the powerful results possible through exploitation of all available information. The implications of this change are truly revolutionary, because in the end it should force a structural reassessment of collection practices, not just analysis.

Managing the Transition

The integration of new analytic techniques into the work of the intelligence community is already under way. In April 2007, the DNI's 100 Day Plan for integration and collaboration endorsed "the radical transformation of analysis through integration of analytic workspaces, analytic products, analytic tools, and the analytic direction of intelligence collection."[14] The first three elements speak to the need for analysts to work more as a collaborative community; the fourth addresses the growing role of analysts in assisting collection. But merely identifying elements of the new analysis in DNI policy is not sufficient to ensure a healthy and productive transition. The shift from a largely individual model of work to one that places greater emphasis upon collaboration among many represents a significant change in and challenge to the culture of the analytic community. Behavioral changes are sensitive to the reward structure of an orga-nization, which gives managers an important role in assisting the transition.

Perhaps one of the most important things managers can do is *not* to stand in the way of the naturally occurring enthusiasm for the new analysis found among the large number of recently hired analysts. As John Gannon implies in chapter 13, today's young professionals have completed an educational journey that emphasized teamwork; they are completely comfortable with cutting-edge tech-nologies. In fact, they are turned off by organizations that appear to be techno-logically naive or backward. The impressive growth of Intellipedia is testament to the new generation's enthusiasm for collaborative work.

Managers also need to recognize that their prevailing analytic model—individual analytic research and writing—was, in many ways, a function of the limited technology available until recently. Typewriters and word processors were ill suited for collaborative work. Analysts wrote papers in part because that was the only product that could be generated by the available technology. Today, managers need to be more open-minded to the potential of what amounts to revolutionary new approaches to the production of content and insight. It is their responsibility to become educated in these new techniques so they can guide intelligence officers in their application to analytic work. Technologically savvy analysts guided by expert managers will contribute more to the generation of insight than either group working on its own.

Finally, managers, who control the rewards system of the organization, have to wean their organizations away from a system that rewards individual work, writing, and specific amounts of production; they must create incentives for collaboration on difficult problems with the goal of generating insight, not just product. The intelligence community's current promotion and awards system is based on performance appraisal reports for individuals; scant attention is paid to how units or teams perform against strategic goals. Progress first must be made in setting goals for organizations, both large and small, that can be measured fairly and qualitatively, not just quantitatively. Progress in this area is an essential first step in adjusting a rewards system that perpetuates an analytic model overly dependent on the work of individual experts who are no longer capable of meeting the challenge of a multilayered and increasingly complex world.

Embracing the New Analysis

Visit any newspaper or magazine website and you will find the debate about the decline of print journalism and the need to compete with the new media. Just as our cousins in the traditional journalism business are worried about their futures, so should intelligence professionals be concerned. There should be an active debate among practitioners and users of how the "new analysis" should meet the demands of a new customer base and exploit the new technologies now available. For, when the transition to the new analysis is completed, the work of intelligence analysts will little resemble what they do today.

Although there will always be prose, there will be even more graphic demonstrations, geospatial models, interactive maps, and virtual world simulations. Just as print journalism articles are increasingly crediting multiple contributors spread across the news organization and the world for a news story, so intelligence analysis will also reflect the multiple talents of many minds and the collaborative environments powered by social networking software. We will be moving from today's nascent, even primitive Intellipedia and other wiki technologies to entirely new breakthrough platforms that we cannot yet imagine.

Old and distinct categories of analyst or collector will seem archaic. It will be harder to distinguish the reporter from the analyst, and in fact most intelligence officers will be both collector and analyst—as has long been the case in the journalism field. Insight will come from the *synthesis*, not from the dissection, of knowledge. Collaboration networks, involving both analysts and collectors, will manage large information holdings that rest on dynamic explanatory models that can be adjusted in real time to account for new developments.

As the profession of intelligence strives to become a true discipline on the order of the medical field, it cannot reject the necessity of challenging the underlying premises that might have guided its earlier development. Old theories of how to collect information, produce analysis, or deal with the customer must be questioned just as medicine jettisoned leaching patients, amputating limbs to halt infection, or removing brain lobes to control emotions. The sign of a healthy professional discipline will be the intelligence community's willingness to experiment with theories of best practices and to lead change rather than be run over by it.

Notes

1. Commission on the Intelligence Capabilities of the United States Regarding Weapons of Mass Destruction, *Report to the President of the United States* (Washington, D.C.: U.S. Government Printing Office, 2005) (hereafter, *WMD Commission Report*) 3; also available at www.wmd.gov/report.

2. Stansfield Turner, *Secrecy and Democracy: The CIA in Transition* (New York: Harper & Row, 1985), 271.

3. *WMD Commission Report*, 3.

4. Thomas Fingar, "Deputy Director of National Intelligence for Analysis Address to the Information Sharing Conference and Technology Exposition," August 21, 2006, http://dni .gov/speeches/speeches.htm.

5. Jeffrey Cooper, *Curing Analytic Pathologies: Pathways to Improved Intelligence Analysis* (Washington, D.C.: Center for the Study of Intelligence, Central Intelligence Agency, 2005).

6. Fingar, "Deputy Director of National Intelligence for Analysis Address."

7. Arika Akbar, "Eleven Charged Over Plot to Blow Up Aircraft," *Belfast Telegraph*, August 22, 2006.

8. David Ignatius, "For Hayden, Repair Work at the CIA," *Washington Post*, November 8, 2006.

9. John D. Negroponte, "The Science and Technology Challenge," remarks of the director of national intelligence at the Woodrow Wilson International Center for Scholars, September 25, 2006; available at www.wilsoncenter.org/index.cfm?fuseaction=events.

10. At the National Institutes of Health (NIH) website (http://nihroadmap.nih.gov/over view.sap), one can find the basic "collaboration" philosophy that is at work here. According to NIH: "The scale and complexity of today's biomedical research problems increasingly demands that scientists move beyond the confines of their own discipline and explore new organizational models for team science. For example, imaging research often requires radiologists, physicists, cell biologists, and computer programmers to work together in integrated teams. Many scientists will continue to pursue individual research projects; however, they will be encouraged to make changes in the way they approach the scientific enterprise. NIH wants to stimulate new ways of combining skills and disciplines in both the physical and biological sciences. The Director's Pioneer Award will encourage investigators to take on creative, unexplored avenues of research that carry a relatively high potential for failure, but also possess a greater chance for truly groundbreaking discoveries. In addition, novel partnerships, such as those between the public and private sectors, will be encouraged to accelerate the movement of scientific discoveries from the bench to the bedside."

11. Rapid analytic support and expeditionary response teams are being introduced as the first prototypes of a multidisciplinary unit of analysts equipped with the tools, tradecraft, and mission to rapidly respond to crises and emerging topics that allows analysis to drive collection. This is being modeled after Special Forces–style programs, which imbue the team members with an esprit de corps, a "get-the-job-done" attitude that stresses mission objectives over discrete job duties.

12. William Colby and Peter Forbath, *Honorable Men: My Life in the CIA* (New York: Simon & Schuster, 1978), 375.

13. *Wikipedia*, s.v. "Intellipedia," http://en.wikipedia.org/wiki/Intellipedia.

14. Office of the Director of National Intelligence, "US Intelligence Community (IC) 100 Day Plan for Integration and Collaboration," Washington, April 11, 2007; www.dni.gov/ 100-day-plan/100-day-plan.pdf.

PART SIX

New Frontiers of Analysis

HAVING DIAGNOSED PROBLEMS and identified opportunities in earlier parts of the book, the contributors to this final part provide a number of directions where the field of analysis should aim to achieve better results. One new dimension is the harnessing of technologies to enable analysts to develop more rigorous and agile methods for assessing data, sharing insights, and reaching judgments. An entirely different dimension is the expansion of analysis from what has been largely the field of foreign affairs into the politically sensitive area of domestic intelligence analysis.

The doyen of the analytic tradecraft field, Richards Heuer, offers his latest thinking on how to apply rigorous techniques, such as the Analysis of Competing Hypotheses. Building on his seminal work, *Psychology of Intelligence Analysis* (1999), he presents a practical way to employ computer techniques to simplify and speed the use of rigorous, transparent, and replicable analytic methods. His contribution to this volume and to the professionalization of analysis is simply invaluable.

Office of Naval Intelligence senior analyst Timothy Smith offers his understanding of epistemology, information technology, and knowledge management to generate new ideas for more Internet-centric warning systems that can aid our rapid learning and better forecasting of nonlinear events. This chapter is adapted from his paper, which was selected to receive one of the 2006 Director of National Intelligence Galileo Awards—which honor those presenting provocative new ways to reform the intelligence business. This chapter on warning intelligence will certainly stimulate new thinking, sketch out the new era that we are about to enter, and persuade us that we need to get there as soon as we can.

Bruce Berkowitz's examination of homeland security analysis closes part six with a serious look at how the United States must begin to grapple with the question of domestic intelligence gathering and analysis. Berkowitz has spent time in both the Central Intelligence Agency and the defense intelligence worlds and has written widely on intelligence and modern warfare. He now applies his insights into the world of analysis and to the question of how quickly the Federal Bureau of Investigation and Department of Homeland Security can develop effective analytic capabilities and what analytical issues might arise for the new domestic intelligence analyst.

CHAPTER 16

Computer-Aided Analysis of Competing Hypotheses

Richards J. Heuer Jr.

PEOPLE USE PHYSICAL TOOLS such as a hammer and saw to enhance their capacity to perform various physical tasks. People can also use simple mental tools to enhance their ability to perform mental tasks. These tools help overcome limitations in human mental machinery for perception, memory, and inference. Such limitations have been amply documented in previous works, including the author's book *Psychology of Intelligence Analysis*.[1] This chapter discusses the development and ongoing enhancement of a tool called Analysis of Competing Hypotheses (ACH), which guides and structures analysts' thinking about complex issues. This is one of a number of "thinking tools" taught to intelligence community analysts.

Many tools for overcoming recognized cognitive limitations are based on two basic principles—decomposition and externalization:

- *Decomposition* means breaking a problem down into its component parts. That is, indeed, the essence of analysis. One dictionary definition of analysis is "the separation of an intellectual or material whole into its constituent parts for individual study; the study of such constituent parts and their interrelationships in making up a whole."[2]
- *Externalization* means getting the decomposed problem out of one's head and down on paper or a computer screen in some simplified form that shows the main variables or elements of the problem and how they relate to each other.

The recommendation to compensate for limitations of working memory by decomposing and externalizing analytical problems is certainly not new. The following quote is from a letter Benjamin Franklin wrote in 1772 to the great British scientist Joseph Priestly, the discoverer of oxygen:

In the affair of so much importance to you, wherein you ask my advice, I cannot for want of sufficient premises, advise you what to determine, but if you please I will tell you how. When those difficult cases occur, they are difficult, chiefly because while we have them under consideration, all the reasons pro and con are not present to the mind at the same time, but sometimes one set present themselves, and at other times another, the first being out of sight. Hence the various purposes or inclinations that alternatively prevail, and the uncertainty that perplexes us.

To get over this, my way is to divide half a sheet of paper by a line into two columns; writing over the one Pro, and over the other Con. Then, during three or four days of consideration, I put down under the different heads short hints of the different motives, that at different times occur to me, for or against the measure.

When I have thus got them all together in one view, I endeavor to estimate their respective weights; and where I find two, one on each side, that seem equal, I strike them both out. If I find a reason pro equal to some two reasons con, I strike out the three, . . . and thus proceeding I find at length where the balance lies; and if, after a day or two of further consideration, nothing new that is of importance occurs on either side, I come to a determination accordingly.[3]

It is interesting that Franklin over two hundred years ago identified the problem of limited working memory and how it affects one's ability to make analytical judgments. Franklin also identified the solution—getting all the pros and cons out of his head and onto paper in some visible, shorthand form. The fact that this topic was part of the dialogue between such illustrious individuals reflects the type of people who use such analytical tools. These are not aids to be used by weak analysts but unneeded by the strong. Human cognitive limitations affect everyone. It is the more astute analysts who are most conscious of this and most likely to recognize the value gained by such tools.

Putting ideas into written form ensures that they will last. They will lie around for days goading you into having further thoughts. Lists are effective because they exploit people's tendency to be a bit compulsive—we want to keep adding to them. They let us get the obvious and habitual answers out of the way, so that we can add to the list by thinking of other ideas beyond those that came first to mind. One specialist in creativity has observed that "for the purpose of moving our minds, pencils can serve as crowbars"[4]—just by writing things down in ways that stimulate new associations.

Lists such as Franklin recommended are one of the simplest forms of structured analysis. An intelligence analyst might make lists of early warning indicators, alternative explanations, possible outcomes, factors a foreign leader will need to take into account when making a decision, or arguments for and against a given explanation or outcome.

Other tools for externalizing the component parts of a problem include outlines, tables, diagrams, decision trees, and matrices, with many subspecies of each. For example, diagrams include concept maps, argument maps, causal maps, influence diagrams, and flow charts. Consideration of all those tools is beyond the scope of this discussion, but the concepts of decomposition and externalization are presented here because they underlie the ACH process, which is the focus of this chapter.

Analysis of Competing Hypotheses

The component parts of ACH are evidence and arguments on the one hand and hypotheses on the other. The evidence/arguments and hypotheses are externalized in the form of a matrix in which the analyst enters information about hypotheses across the top and evidence/arguments down the side. The analyst then evaluates the consistency or inconsistency of each item of evidence or argument with each hypothesis.

The matrix helps the analyst overcome the limits of what can be maintained in working memory. The analyst can deal with each element of the problem, one at a time, without losing track of where it fits into the problem as a whole. In this way, it is possible to manage and pay attention to a larger amount of information. The matrix can also provide the focus for a systematic group analysis or discussion of the issue.

ACH offers a simple model for how to think about a complex problem when the available information is incomplete or ambiguous, as typically happens in intelligence analysis. The unique insight behind ACH is that a key element of the scientific method can and should be applied to types of intelligence problems where this method has in the past been considered inapplicable.[5] Like the scientific method, ACH proceeds by trying to refute hypotheses rather than confirm them. Unlike the scientific method, ACH cannot conduct empirical experiments to test these hypotheses. It can only test hypotheses by assembling the available intelligence reporting, open source information, and the informed logical deductions and assumptions of a knowledgeable analyst. Hence the conclusions cannot be considered "scientific," but the basic approach of seeking to refute alternative hypotheses does have significant analytical benefits. The ACH process reduces the risk of surprise by ensuring that less-likely but possible hypotheses are identified and receive full consideration.

Table 16.1 shows what an ACH matrix looks like. It shows a hypothetical analysis of Iraq's nuclear program as it may have been viewed by some analysts prior to the invasion of Iraq. There are three hypotheses: (1) Iraq's nuclear weapons development program has remained dormant since its termination after the Gulf War in 1991; (2) Iraq has begun secret efforts to reconstitute its nuclear program but is a long way from being able to create a nuclear weapon; (3) Iraq is expected to have a nuclear weapon within three years. The matrix shows just a few of many possible items of evidence. For each item, the matrix lists the type of source, rates the credibility and relevance of the evidence (high, medium, low), and assesses the consistency or inconsistency with each hypothesis.

When a list of relevant evidence is compiled in an ACH matrix, the term "evidence" is interpreted very broadly. It refers to all the factors that influence an analyst's judgment about the relative likelihood of the hypotheses. In addition to specific items of intelligence, it includes the absence of evidence that one would expect to see if a given hypothesis were true. It also includes the analyst's assumptions or logical deductions about another person, group, or country's behavior, capabilities, intentions, goals, or standard operating procedures. Assumptions and logical deductions may often generate strong preconceptions as to which hypothesis is the most likely. They often drive the analyst's final judgment, so it is important to explicitly recognize them and include them in the list of "evidence."

TABLE 16.1
Analysis of Competing Hypotheses Matrix: A Hypothetical Illustration

Evidence	Source Type	Credibility	Relevance	Hypotheses: What is the status of Iraq's nuclear weapons program?		
				1. Dormant or shut down	2. Has been started up again	3. Weapon available within this decade
1. Saddam's refusal to cooperate with UN inspectors and a major D&D program against U.S. intelligence both suggest something is being hidden.	Inference	H*	H	I	C	C
2. Saddam tried to develop a nuclear weapon prior to the 1991 Gulf War. Past behavior is the best indicator of future behavior.	Assumption	M	H	I	C	C
3. High-strength aluminum tubes imported surreptitiously are a nuclear dual-use item, which means they have both nuclear and nonnuclear uses.	Intel Reporting	H	H	C	C	C
4. Reported attempt to import yellowcake (partially refined uranium) from Niger.	HUMINT	L	M	I	C	C

Evidence	Source					
5. UN inspectors have developed no hard evidence of a reconstituted nuclear weapons program.	Liaison	M	H	C	C	I
6. U.S. intelligence has developed no hard evidence of a reconstituted nuclear weapons program through any of the collection disciplines.	Lack of intelligence reporting despite vigorous search	H	H	C	I	I
7. Senior and knowledgeable Iraqi defector has reported that Saddam Hussein has ordered WMD programs to be shut down.	HUMINT	M	H	C	I	I
8. Restarting a nuclear program would require surreptitious import of a number of prohibited items. Evidence is available only for aluminum tubes for centrifuges and yellowcake.	Inference	M	H	C	C	I
9. Major Iraqi D&D program may actually be concealing a weapons stand-down instead of a buildup due to Saddam's posture toward the Kurds, Shias, Iran, and Israel.	Contrarian hypothesis	L	H	C	I	I

(*H = high, M = medium, L = low, C = consistent, I = inconsistent)

Comparing ACH with the Intuitive Approach

ACH differs from conventional intuitive analysis in three important ways.

- It avoids the *satisficing* trap.
- It determines the *diagnosticity* of evidence.
- It forces us to *refute* weak or wrong hypotheses rather than seeking to "prove" or confirm our favorite ones.

Satisficing. Conventional intuitive analysis focuses on what we suspect is the most likely answer, then assesses whether or not the available evidence supports this answer. If it does, we pat ourselves on the back ("See, I knew it all along!") and do not look much further. This is called "satisficing"—that is, being satisfied with the first answer that seems to be supported by the evidence that is readily at hand.[6] This satisficing approach provides no stimulus for the analyst to identify and question fundamental assumptions. It bypasses the careful analysis of alternative explanations or outcomes, which should be fundamental to any complete analysis. As a result, it fails to recognize that much evidence that is seemingly supportive of the favored hypothesis is actually of limited value, because it is also consistent with one or more alternative hypotheses. Going with the first answer that seems to be supported by the evidence is efficient, because it saves time and works most of the time. It is usually also a safe approach, as the result may differ little, if at all, from the conventional wisdom. However, the analyst has made no investment in protection against surprise.

Diagnosticity. The conventional intuitive approach is to evaluate what initially appears to be the most likely hypothesis; the analyst looks for evidence to support this hypothesis. In this process, the analyst is vulnerable to bias in favor of evidence that confirms his or her initial impression. ACH requires the simultaneous analysis of multiple hypotheses. Working across the matrix, the analyst evaluates each item of evidence, one at a time, to assess whether that item is consistent or inconsistent with each of the hypotheses. This procedure determines the "diagnosticity" of the evidence.

The diagnosticity of evidence is an important concept that is, unfortunately, unfamiliar to many analysts. Evidence is diagnostic when it is inconsistent with one or more hypotheses and consistent with others. That is, it influences the analyst's judgment about the *relative* likelihood of the various hypotheses. An item of evidence that is consistent with all hypotheses has no diagnostic value. When doing an ACH analysis, it is a common experience for analysts to discover that much of the evidence supporting what they believe to be the most likely hypothesis is really not helpful, because the same evidence is also consistent with other, less likely, hypotheses.

Refuting hypotheses. Analysts typically use their knowledge and past experience to develop a tentative explanation or understanding of the situation they are analyzing. The conventional approach is to seek evidence to confirm this initial appraisal. This approach works most of the time, but it too is vulnerable to surprise. As noted above, ACH requires not only that analysts start with a full set of alternative hypotheses but also that they proceed by seeking to refute hypotheses. The most likely hypothesis is the one with the least evidence against it, not the one with the most evidence for it.

Computer-Aided ACH

The author developed the ACH methodology in the mid-1980s for a Central Intelligence Agency (CIA) training course in the analysis of deception, and it was subsequently taught in several intelligence community schools. Software to facilitate implementation and expand the capabilities of ACH has been broadly available for analyst use at CIA only since early 2006. It is now being taught throughout the intelligence community. The software was developed by the Palo Alto Research Center in consultation with the author, with funding from the Advanced Research and Development Activity Novel Intelligence from Massive Data Program and the Office of Naval Intelligence. The software is unclassified and available to the public so that it may be used in academic programs to train analysts for future employment in the intelligence or law enforcement community.[7]

Analysts find the ACH software useful for a variety of reasons. Federal Bureau of Investigation analysts like it because they see it as a great way to organize all their evidence as they proceed with an investigation. CIA analysts report that the software is user friendly, helps them use better critical thinking skills, generates a better array of alternative hypotheses, and helps account for potential deception, and because the matrix helps to depersonalize the argumentation when there are differences of opinion. Their preferred use of ACH is to gain a better understanding of the differences of opinion with other analysts or between analytical offices. The process of creating an ACH matrix requires identification of the evidence and arguments being used and how these are interpreted as either consistent or inconsistent with the various hypotheses. A review of this matrix provides a systematic basis for the identification and discussion of differences between two or more analysts. This discussion is often considered the most valuable part of the ACH process. Again, references to the matrix help depersonalize the argumentation when there are differences of opinion. These reports from ACH users support the statement in the introductory chapter of this book, that "the sharing of data, hypotheses, interpretations, and questions among analysts and other nongovernment experts is possibly where the most insightful cognition is occurring, rather than on the page of a finished assessment or a PowerPoint slide."

If discussion does not resolve differences over the matrix, it at least identifies more clearly the basis for these differences, leads to a search for other information that might resolve the differences, and enables one to track the impact of these differences on the overall analytical conclusion.

Collaborative ACH

The current version of the ACH software is designed as a standalone system for use by a single analyst. Now we have seen that analysts want to use it to facilitate group discussion and deliberation. To do so, however, they must huddle around a single computer screen, and there is no way to compare automatically matrices developed by other analysts with the same set of hypotheses and evidence.

An enhanced version of the ACH software, tentatively called Collaborative ACH, is now being developed by CIA. This will provide an excellent framework for collaboration between analysts either in the same office or working across organizational boundaries. As noted above, the cross-fertilization of ideas helps analysts avoid personal bias and generate more and better ideas. The matrix can combine inputs from analysts with different specialties. When analysts disagree, differences between matrices can be used to highlight the precise area of disagreement.

The original goal of ACH was to lead individual analysts through a structured process that changes how they think. The goal of Collaborative ACH is even more ambitious: to change how intelligence community organizations function. A primary target for change is the process for interagency coordination of intelligence products. In discussing the coordination process with the author, the former CIA deputy director for intelligence, Carmen Medina, noted that "at a coordination meeting, the *last* thing the author of a report wants to hear is a new idea." At this point in the process, positions are already locked in, and the outcome of discussions is often determined more by a strong personality or organizational influences than by informed analysis. This process is dysfunctional.

The Collaborative ACH process can help to overcome serious problems associated with the coordination process:

- It can ensure that analysis starts with a common definition of the problem, that is, the identification of alternative hypotheses (possible explanations or outcomes that need to be examined).
- It can help ensure that participating analysts from different offices and agencies are all working from the same body of evidence and arguments. Participating analysts propose items of evidence or arguments, which must then be evaluated by every other member of the group. This assures that every participating analyst has an equal opportunity to express his or her views.
- Assumptions and biases are made explicit, while differences of opinion between analysts become apparent through different ratings of the evidence. Thus differences of opinion are surfaced, discussed, and resolved to the extent possible early in the coordination process.
- When there are differences of opinion, comparison of ACH matrices provides a mechanism for tracing the origin of the differences and analyzing how much effect, if any, they have on the final conclusion.
- The ACH process also provides a framework for clear presentation of an analytical conclusion, or discussion of alternative views, at a coordination meeting or in an analytical report.

As currently planned, the Collaborative ACH program will have benefits that go beyond the simple ability to use the ACH tool to create and analyze a matrix in a collaborative process. Analysts with common interests who work in different agencies, or in different parts of the same agency, will be able to establish a common virtual workspace on Intelink, the intelligence community's shared classified network. In this virtual workspace, they will be able to work collaboratively on important issues long before they join arguments in the coordination process. They will be able to organize and access a common set of evidence concerning an issue of common concern; create, share, and compare ACH matrices; and have an interactive "chat" tool for informal communication about the matrices or any other topic or issue of interest. The same platform for online collaboration is being planned to also support other collaboration tools on Intelink.

It is sometimes said that communication is the basis for culture. If true, then opening new means for interagency communication in virtual workspaces on Intelink—where structured analytical techniques such as ACH can be used collaboratively—can be a big step toward changing the current culture of independent analytical fiefdoms. Access to this virtual workspace will be limited to registered participants in a specific project and approved observers. Observers will be able to read and ask questions or make comments or suggestions but will not be able to add or edit any item of evidence or evaluation of the evidence.

The development of Collaborative ACH will further the objective set by Thomas Fingar, the Office of the Director of National Intelligence's deputy director of intelligence for analysis: "to transform the analytic component of our community from a federation of agencies, or a collection of feudal baronies, into a community of analysts, professionals dedicated to providing the best and most timely, most accurate, most useful analytic insights to all of the customers we serve."[8] Fingar explained that collaboration is central to this, and that he always uses the word collaboration rather than cooperation: "Cooperation is something we make people do: 'Play nice in the sandbox. You will come to this coordination meeting.' That's not good enough. Collaboration must be something that people are excited about doing; do without thinking about it; do in ways that are invisible or transparent; do because they recognize it leads to better insights, more timely responses."[9] If the CIA analyst response to the current ACH software is any indication, the development of Collaborative ACH software will help achieve that goal.

Bayesian ACH

There is more than one approach to ACH. Following the publication of *Psychology of Intelligence Analysis* in 1999, other researchers began to consider the applicability of the ACH concept to their particular areas of research interest. Several research groups are pursuing Bayesian or other advanced statistical forms of ACH. Bayesian inference is a statistical procedure for quantifying uncertainty. Probabilities are based on degrees of belief rather than frequencies.[10] Hence it is an appropriate method for aggregating a series of subjective probability judgments by intelligence analysts or other subject matter experts. For Bayesian ACH, these probability judgments are about the relationship between evidence and hypotheses. The Bayesian ACH project most closely associated with the U.S. intelligence community is the Mitre Corporation project for Counter-Deception Decision Support.[11]

Bayesian ACH places greater emphasis on a more precise evaluation of the relationship between each item of evidence and each hypothesis than what might be called, by comparison, simple (or non-Bayesian) ACH. This mathematical precision is a strong plus but adds considerable complexity and makes the process less user friendly. It requires the analyst to make many more and more precise probability judgments about the relationship between each item of evidence and each hypothesis. Many Bayesian ACH analyses have multiple linked sets of hypotheses that add further to their complexity.

The Bayesian ACH approach uses these expert judgments about the evidence as inputs for calculating the probability of each hypothesis. The preparation of the matrix is substantially more time consuming than in simple ACH. It also requires the assistance of an expert in Bayesian analysis and/or other methodological procedures to train the analyst in this technique and help the analyst work through the many complex judgments that go into the matrix.

Proponents of Bayesian ACH believe that critical intelligence issues, especially an issue such as deception, are so complex that they are often beyond the cognitive ability of a human analyst to make an accurate probability assessment. To measurably and substantially improve analytic performance, these "Bayesians" model the analytical problem, with the individual analyst providing probability estimates about individual pieces of this model. The Bayesian model is then used to calculate the relative probability of each hypothesis.[12] This is in sharp contrast to simple ACH, which aspires only to provide the mainstream analyst with a useful tool for guiding the analyst's thinking in the potentially most productive channels. Simplicity, transparency, and ease of use are among its attractions.

An additional feature of the Bayesian approach is that it provides a mathematically accurate probability calculation. Whether this calculation is an accurate reflection of reality depends upon the accuracy of the analyst's judgments that go into the calculation and the appropriate adaptation of the methodology to the circumstances of the individual case. The strength of Bayesian ACH seems to be for research to learn more about how to analyze highly complex problems such as the detection of deception, plus experimental support to conventional analysts on a few selected issues. It is hoped that this research will develop insights about the analysis of such issues that can be taught to and used by mainstream analysts.

Evaluating ACH

When evaluating any analytical tool, it is useful to look at its impact on various stages of the analytic process. A simple model of how most intelligence analysts work involves four steps. When given an assignment, analysts (1) search for information, (2) assemble and organize the information in a manner designed to facilitate retrieval and analysis, (3) analyze the information to make an estimative judgment, and (4) write a report. This section looks at the impact of ACH at each stage of this process.

Search for Information

Searching for information may be the step at which ACH has the greatest impact on the analysis and makes the greatest contribution. For each hypothesis, the analyst asks, "What events should occur and what evidence should be observable if this hypothesis is correct?" And then the analyst seeks out this information. Learning and new ideas occur as analysts identify alternative hypotheses and then search for the information needed to refute rather than confirm these hypotheses. When first exposed to ACH, analysts often say it is useful because it gives them ideas they had not thought of and helps them see an issue from different perspectives.

Consideration of multiple hypotheses drives a much broader search for information than busy analysts would otherwise pursue. The focus on diagnostic information that enables the analyst to refute hypotheses casts a different perspective on what information the analyst searches for and considers most valuable. This approach can be considered an investment in reducing the risk of surprise. A couple of examples illustrate this.

India's nuclear test. Indian testing of a nuclear weapon in 1998 took the intelligence community by surprise and prompted considerable critique and introspection about U.S. intelligence performance. Shortly before the test, the intelligence community concluded that "there is no indication the Indians would test in the near term."[13] Underlying that estimate was an assumption that any preparations for a nuclear test would be observable in advance, because that is what happened several years earlier. India was preparing for a nuclear test, we observed the preparations, and we then applied enough pressure on the Indians to cause them to cancel the test.

The intelligence community assumption in 1998 that nothing had changed, and that observable test preparations would give us advance warning of any test, was never questioned. If ACH had been used, that mistake would not have happened. That is because one of the hypotheses would certainly have been that India is planning a nuclear test in the near term but will conceal preparations for the testing to avoid a repetition of what happened a couple years earlier. Consideration of this hypothesis would have required the analyst to evaluate India's motive and capability to conceal its intention. It would also have required assessing U.S. intelligence ability to see through Indian denial and deception. If that alternative hypothesis had been considered, it would have been very difficult to refute.

Iraq's nuclear weapons. It is unlikely that ACH analysis of the Iraqi nuclear program prior to the 2003 invasion of Iraq would have arrived at the correct conclusion: that the program was dormant. This is because of the history of Saddam Hussein's determination to obtain and willingness to use weapons of mass destruction (WMD), and strong memories of discovering after the 1991

Iraq war that intelligence estimates had underestimated Iraq's inventory of WMD. Analysts were determined not to underestimate the Iraqi WMD again.

However, an ACH analysis would have at least placed an important hypothesis on the table—that "Iraq is not now trying to rebuild its nuclear weapons program." If that hypothesis had been considered, it might have been unexpectedly difficult to refute. At a minimum, it would have forced analysts and policymakers to:

- Recognize that the assumptions on which the prewar national intelligence estimate was based were ten years old, and that the evidence for the nuclear program was nearly as dated.
- Scrutinize more critically the evidence that was marshaled to support the nuclear reconstitution argument (acquisition of aluminum tubes and the fabricated Niger yellowcake stories) that was not really examined closely until after the intelligence failure started to become apparent.
- Focus more attention on the testimony of Lieutenant General Hussein Kamil, Saddam's son-in-law and former manager of the Iraq WMD program who defected to Jordan in 1995.[14]

Assemble and Organize Information

The ACH software enables analysts to categorize and sort evidence in analytically useful ways. For each item of evidence or argument, the analyst enters into the matrix information on the date or time, type of source, credibility of the source, and relevance of the evidence, in addition to rating the consistency or inconsistency of the evidence with each hypothesis. Sorting the evidence by these categories makes it easy for the analyst to compare evidence from open sources with evidence from clandestine sources, compare the results of evidence from human sources versus evidence from technical sources, compare more recent evidence against older evidence, and to compare conclusions based only on hard evidence (intelligence reports) with conclusions based on soft evidence (the analyst's own assumptions and logical deductions).

Sorting and analyzing evidence by type of source can provide clues to the reliability of sources and possible deception. If all types of sources are telling a consistent story, that is a good sign. If not, the analyst needs to figure out why. Are some sources vulnerable to manipulation for the purpose of deception?

Analyze the Information

Of particular value is the ability to sort evidence by its diagnosticity. Evidence is diagnostic if it helps to distinguish the relative probability of each hypothesis. Given the goal of refuting hypotheses, only evidence that is inconsistent with one or more of the hypotheses is considered diagnostic. Sorting to bring the most diagnostic items to the top of the matrix identifies those items that appear to be driving the conclusion. It is a truism that analysts need to question their assumptions. Experience tells us that when analytical judgments turn out to be wrong, it is often because key assumptions went unchallenged and proved invalid. The problem is that analysts cannot question everything. Sorting the evidence and arguments by diagnosticity identifies those most diagnostic items that play a critical role in the conclusion. Double-checking and consideration of alternative interpretations of these items are appropriate.

The ACH software adds up the inconsistency ratings to provide a rough score for each hypothesis. The more inconsistent the evidence, the higher the score, and the less likely the hypothesis. However, this is an approximation that is no more precise than the ratings that make up that score. It does not eliminate the need for analysts to use their own good judgment. The true value of ACH is the learning process that occurs as the analyst creates the matrix, not the inconsistency score that is calculated for each hypothesis.

The inconsistency scores only tell the analyst what the analyst told the program to say through his or her selection of hypotheses and evidence and evaluation of that evidence. One purpose of the inconsistency score is to keep the analyst focused on the need to refute hypotheses, rather than confirm them, and to track progress in doing that.

Another purpose of the score is to provide an independent check on the analyst's own thinking. After completing the matrix, analysts compare the inconsistency scores with their own personal views about the hypotheses. If the relative likelihood of the hypotheses as shown by the scores matches up reasonably well with the analyst's own conclusions, this indicates that the matrix is an effective representation of that analyst's thinking. That is good. If there is a significant discrepancy between the computer-generated scores and the analyst's own thinking about the hypotheses, which happens quite often, the analyst needs to figure out why, and this is another part of the learning process. There are two principal reasons why the analyst's thinking may diverge significantly from the inconsistency scores.

If the scores in the matrix do not support what the analyst believes is the most likely hypothesis, one common explanation is that the matrix is incomplete. The analyst's thinking may be influenced by assumptions or logical deductions that have not been included in the list of evidence. In political or military analysis, for example, conclusions will often be driven by assumptions about another country's capabilities or intentions. *A principal goal of the ACH process is to identify those assumptions and other factors that drive the analyst's thinking on an issue*, so that they can then be questioned and if possible validated.

A second possibility is that the scores seem to give too much credibility to one or more of the less likely hypotheses. That will happen if the analyst has not assembled the inconsistent evidence needed to refute them. This may be because the analyst devoted insufficient attention to these hypotheses or because the evidence is simply not there. If the analyst cannot find such evidence, he or she may need to adjust their thinking to recognize that the hypothesis is more likely than previously thought.

It may seem to some readers that the ACH software could and should convert the rating of evidence/arguments in the matrix into numerical probabilities for each hypothesis rather than a simple inconsistency score. That could be done but is deliberately not done, for two main reasons:

- A much more complex rating system using Bayesian statistical inference would be required to do it accurately, and the conclusions would still be no more accurate than the analyst's subjective judgments that go into rating the evidence. As noted above, Bayesian versions of ACH with greater mathematical precision have been developed for specialized purposes, but they are less practical for broad use and are not easily understood by the typical intelligence analyst without specialized training.
- It would be too easy to misuse any simple probability calculation. The ACH software is best used as an analytical aid, not a magic answer machine. Its purpose is to help analysts structure complex problems in ways that lead them to ask questions they might not otherwise ask and see relationships they might not otherwise notice. The ultimate conclusion should come from the analyst, not a mathematical algorithm.

Write the Report

When one recognizes the importance of proceeding by eliminating rather than confirming hypotheses, it becomes apparent that any written argument for a certain judgment is incomplete unless it also discusses alternative judgments that were considered and why they were rejected.

ACH contributes only indirectly to preparation of a clearer intelligence report. The matrix will not be replicated in the report unless the report is explicitly identified as the product of an ACH analysis. However, the ACH analysis identifies the critical diagnostic evidence and arguments that lead to the analytical conclusion. It also identifies alternative conclusions and why they were rejected. That is the framework for a clear and complete report.

Conclusion

The Analysis of Competing Hypotheses software is one significant step toward bringing greater analytical rigor to the intelligence process. By no means, however, does it guarantee an accurate conclusion. It takes the analyst through an optimal analytical process and makes it easier to show how a conclusion was reached, but this does not rule out incorrect assessment of the relative weight and diagnosticity of the evidence.

When ACH reaches its full potential as a Web-based tool for interagency collaboration, it has the potential to greatly facilitate and improve the interaction between analysts and agencies on important analytical issues, improve the quality and accuracy of analysis, and reduce our vulnerability to intelligence surprise.

Notes

1. Richards J. Heuer Jr., *Psychology of Intelligence Analysis* (Washington, D.C.: Center for the Study of Intelligence, Central Intelligence Agency, 1999). A PDF version is available

at https://www.cia.gov/csi/books/19104/index.html. Also see Thomas Gilovich, Dale Griffin, and Daniel Kahneman, *Heuristics and Biases: The Psychology of Intuitive Judgment* (Cambridge: Cambridge University Press, 2002); Robyn M. Dawes, *Everyday Irrationality* (Boulder, Colo.: Westview Press, 2001); and Scott Plous, *The Psychology of Judgment and Decision Making* (New York: McGraw-Hill, 1993).

2. *American Heritage Dictionary of the English Language*, 4th ed., s.v. "Analysis."

3. Benjamin Franklin, *The Benjamin Franklin Sampler* (New York: Fawcett, 1956), cited by Ernest H. Forman and Many Ann Selly, *Decision by Objectives* (New York: World Scientific Publishing Co., 2002), chap. 3.

4. Alex Osborn, *Applied Imagination*, rev. ed. (New York: Scribner's, 1979), 202.

5. The scientific method is the systematic approach to observation, hypothesis formation, hypothesis testing, and hypothesis evaluation that forms the basis for modern science.

6. The concept of "satisficing," of seeking a satisfactory rather than an optimal solution, was developed by Herbert A. Simon and is widely used in the literature on decision analysis. See Herbert Simon, *Models of Man: Social and Rational* (New York: John Wiley & Sons, 1957). For specific research on satisficing when generating hypotheses, see Jennifer Garst, Norbert L. Kerr, Susan E. Harris, and Lori A. Sheppard, "Satisficing in Hypothesis Generation," *American Journal of Psychology* 115, no. 4 (Winter 2002): 475–500.

7. The software may be downloaded at no cost from the Palo Alto Research Center website at www2.parc.com/isstl/projects/ach/ach.html.

8. Thomas Fingar, Speech to the DNI's Information Sharing Conference and Technology Exposition, Denver, August 21, 2006; www.dni.gov/speeches/20060821_2_speech.pdf.

9. Ibid.

10. For a brief explanation of Bayesian inference, see http://en.wikipedia.org/wiki/Bayesian_probability.

11. F. J. Stech and C. Elsaesser, "Deception Detection by Analysis of Competing Hypotheses," paper presented at 2005 International Conference on Intelligence Analysis: Methods and Tools," McLean, Va., May 3–5, 2005; https://analysis.mitre.org/proceedings/Final_Papers_Files/94_Camera_Ready_Paper.pdf.

12. Christopher Elsaesser and Frank J. Stech, "Detecting Deception," in *Adversarial Reasoning: Computational Approaches to Reading the Opponent's Mind*, ed. Alexander Kott and William M. McEneaney (Boca Raton, Fla.: Chapman & Hall / CRC, 2006), 101–24.

13. Transcript of Admiral David Jeremiah's press conference on the intelligence community's failure to warn of India's nuclear tests, Central Intelligence Agency, June 2, 1998.

14. Glen Rangwala, "Briefing Notes on UNSCOM Interview of Hussein Kamil," *Iraq Watch*, February 27, 2003; http://www.iraqwatch.org/perspectives/rangwala-kamel-022703.htm.

CHAPTER 17

Predictive Warning: Teams, Networks, and Scientific Method

Timothy J. Smith

The Failing Intelligence Business Process

THE TRADITIONAL METHODOLOGY of intelligence assessment and warning is obsolete. Its inadequacy, whether for preventing surprise or guiding policy, has long been argued by Congress and a continual series of blue-ribbon commissions, and it is recognized by a small but growing cadre of reformers within the intelligence community (IC).[1] These traditional methods of synthesis, analysis, and assessment are rife with subjectivity and the risk of bias and error, and, by scientific standards, undergo insufficient analytic quality control.

The conventional process is familiar. The classic image is the production of National Intelligence Estimates (NIEs), the IC's official interagency assessments concerning threats of the highest order. NIEs subject available evidence and the multiple interpretations of the various agencies to review and formulate them into an explicit statement to support national policy and strategy decision making. However, the process begins much earlier, with endless daily intelligence assessments within each production agency. Here, all-source analysts read reports, collate and compare them, and exercise reasoned judgment to resolve discrepancies and contradictions in the reports, typically by evaluating and comparing the credibility of the respective sources. Some "ints"—for example, imagery intelligence (IMINT), signals intelligence (SIGINT), and human intelligence (HUMINT)—are deemed more credible than others. HUMINT source credibility is especially uneven. Intelligence judgments based on such comparative evaluations are then drafted for submission through agency review, followed by editing, discussion with seniors, and the resolution of contending interpretations and how best to express them. An agency then disseminates the results to its customers and IC peers.

A very similar process of ongoing debate occurs also at the national level between and among agencies, a process that culminates in authoritative NIEs, the *President's Daily Brief*, and other IC-coordinated products. Routine interagency coordination is electronic (online or "Web-enabled" in place of telephonic coordination earlier). By contrast, NIE coordination projects concern matters so vital and complex that the IC must convene together for full-scale face-to-face review, debate, and collective assessment. The NIE process "raises

266

the bar" for intelligence production. NIEs show the IC at its best, as do National Intelligence Board sessions, where the director of national intelligence and IC agency heads meet to review NIE drafts. Yet a consensus has emerged that the community's traditional best might no longer be fully adequate for national security in the post–cold war threat environment. This chapter argues that defects in long-institutionalized processes hinder the contributions of even the IC's finest minds.

It is important to emphasize that this institutional obsolescence is not unique to the IC, to the government, or even to the United States. Intelligence failure has a long history, and Americans are far from the worst offenders.[2] In fact the defects in traditional practices are inherent in standard twentieth-century bureaucratic process, across governments and even, to a significant extent, inside corporations and military services. Intelligence failure is simply one manifestation of the wider phenomenon of organizational decision failure and human error writ large.

Most of the proposed and practical reforms are becoming familiar to many observers as part and parcel of "information age business process." On the basis of these notions, this chapter examines in depth the need for modernization and, based on that, outlines a comprehensive, integrated system of structures and processes that can optimize organizational theory, scientific method, and modern technology and thereby enable the United States to produce the best possible intelligence for the twenty-first century. This proposal is designed to implement core elements of the *National Intelligence Strategy*, the 2004 Intelligence Reform and Terrorism Prevention Act, and related intelligence commissions, reform initiatives, and studies.[3] A pilot program to implement and test the proposal is certainly feasible and would demonstrate an unprecedented new capability for accurate and highly credible foresight and warning. Once mature, this new methodology and infrastructure would dramatically reduce the risk, rate, and severity of intelligence surprises and policy failures such as Pearl Harbor, the September 11, 2001, terrorist attacks, and the Iraqi civil war.

A Strategic Vision for Predictive Warning

The proposed scientific, organizational assessment methodology offers the first real predictive capability in the history of intelligence. This enhanced anticipatory power and adaptivity could be achieved through improved analysis and assessment based on current technology and today's collection capabilities with the addition of a structured but adaptive set of procedures emphasizing interagency collaboration, alternative analyses, and the rigorous testing of assumptions and assessments. All three of these elements—community-wide collaboration, expansive creative imagination, and rigorous critical reasoning—are equally vital.

Two basic premises underlie this concept. First, emerging policy on IC collaboration and information sharing (e.g., relaxed need-to-know constraints) will ensure that Web-enabled *virtual collaboration* will soon become the normal operating mode for analysts sitting at their desks producing daily intelligence across the community. Such baseline collaboration is necessary, using e-mail with Microsoft Word attachments, Intellipedia, "blogs," and similar online tools and techniques for distributed information sharing and collaboration, both "synchronous" and "asynchronous."[4] Second, such distributed collaboration will not by itself maximize the IC's predictive potential. In fact, excessive reliance on virtual collaboration might inadvertently substitute new sources of error for the current ones. Hence, the IC must simultaneously develop powerful new capabilities for "proximate," synchronous collaboration and then synthesize, from both these collaborative advances, a revolutionary new capability for IC-wide collaboration that exceeds any plans yet promulgated.

The visible centerpiece of this transformed capability would lie in the creation of a community-wide system of advanced intelligence assessment laboratories that would operate according to a formal, documented assessment methodology—specifically, scientific methodology.[5] Within these labs, interdisciplinary and interagency analytic project teams would use a wide array of methods, tools, and techniques to produce all-source finished intelligence while simultaneously advancing the state of the analytic art through experience and lessons learned. A suitable term for such "knowledge factories" might be "computational collaboratories." The director of national intelligence (DNI) might control the premier IC computational collaboratory to support national decision makers and foster interagency teaming on high-level intelligence projects such as NIEs.[6] Eventually, the IC should be netted together by a multiagency complex of such collaboratories—a "system of systems"—one in each intelligence agency (all-source and single-source), all integrated over a wide-area network at multiple levels of security. The result would be a "boundaryless" architecture of permanent, pervasive collaboration.[7]

This vision would require and propel a revolution in both the synthetic (creative-imaginative) and analytic (rigorous-critical) dimensions of intelligence assessment, as part of a major advance in the IC's analytic culture.[8] Yet because it is primarily methodological, managerial, and behavioral in nature, this solution would require only modest expenditures for technical systems development and acquisition, infrastructure, and manning levels. The new methodology would supplement standard operating procedures but transcend the routinized bureaucratic procedures and informal, intuitive reasoning that currently predominate and are prone to error.[9]

The strategic goal of this proposal is to quickly and affordably achieve substantially improved IC threat anticipation and warning. Beyond its immediate value in improving assessment within the disparate agencies of the national IC, scientific methodology, empowered by networks, would both strengthen and integrate the community, accelerate the intelligence cycle rate (the "op tempo" of our "OODA Loop"),[10] and transform the IC into a unified system of agile learning organizations with a network-centric capability optimally adapted to today's security challenges and intellectual and technological opportunities.

Current Methods and Culture

"Methodology" refers to the logic governing methods. It derives from epistemology, the theory of knowledge.[11] Methodology is applied epistemology and takes the form of an integrated theory of assessment that specifies the domain of application, the criteria of truth, the definition of evidence, and the rules for inference. Thus, although tools and techniques and even fairly basic methods proliferate in abundance, all these fall under a very small number of underlying methodologies.

Essentially two logical-factual methodologies exist for understanding the world of physical things and human behavior, one involving informal methods and the other formal methods. The informal methodology can be characterized broadly as historiography, the more or less scholarly study of qualitative evidence formulated as words and sentences in natural language. Individual scholars or analysts typically undertake this, working independently or compartmentalized under vertical chains of authority ("stovepipes") in offices within bureaucracies. Traditional intelligence assessment methodology has always been historiographical.

By definition, historiography is strictly descriptive ("graphic"). It can be applied to two time frames, both retrospective: the long-term or distant past, which is what scholars call history proper and intelligence officers call long-term analysis; or the short-term or recent past, which most would recognize as journalism or current intelligence. By its very nature, historiography cannot produce reliable inferences or assessments concerning the other important time frame: the future. Historiography cannot predict. In and of itself, it is a weak instrument for warning—necessary, as George Santayana suggested, but insufficient.

The risks associated with the misapplication of informal, intuitive, retrospective methods to problems of prediction are increasingly well understood. A growing literature in cognitive and social psychology, perceptions theory, and the history of science now describes theory and findings concerning human perception, cognitive "heuristics" (habituated rules of thumb), mental and institutional "paradigms" (belief systems), and "satisficing" (the tendency to opt for quick, seemingly adequate solutions rather than search exhaustively for utility-maximizing solutions[12]). Herbert Simon, Daniel Kahneman, and Amos Tversky, Robert Jervis, Irving Janis, and Thomas Kuhn are preeminent names in these fields.[13] *Satisficing* heuristics employ assumption-based reasoning for the sake of simplicity and efficiency and are useful under "normal" circumstances, when the risk is low. They often are optimal, in fact, especially under constraints such as time pressure. Nonetheless, haste and habit have a cost in introducing patterns of bias and error into human reasoning. Moreover, they are highly susceptible to deception and surprise, as is pointed out in chapter 8 of this volume.

Groups and organizations can fall prey to similar decision maladies, which have been addressed elsewhere in this book under the rubric "groupthink" and other forms of psychologically based analytic errors. Social dynamics can induce individuals and small groups to conform to given assumptions, stifling doubt and debate so as not to disrupt group togetherness.[14] The warning expert Cynthia Grabo has noted that "the rejection of evidence incompatible with one's own hypotheses or preconceptions, the refusal to accept or to believe that which is unpleasant or disturbing or which might upset one's superiors—these are far more common failings than most people suspect."[15] Richards Heuer, also a contributor to this volume, has summarized many of the findings from cognitive psychology and applied them to the intelligence problem in his aforementioned *Psychology of Intelligence Analysis*. The literature on intelligence and especially on deception and intelligence failure amplifies these findings.[16]

In sum, then, by their inherent nature, qualitative methodologies such as historiography are incapable of prediction and entail an excessively high risk of error when employed for that purpose—which is precisely what traditional intelligence does in the United States and other countries. The inevitable result, seen time and again, decade in and decade out, is an unnecessarily high rate of intelligence failure and surprise, with no discernable trend line of upward improvement so far. What then is required for effective anticipation and warning?

Prediction: Process and Prerequisites

The CIA has defined intelligence in relevant terms: "Reduced to its simplest terms, intelligence is knowledge and foreknowledge of the world around us—the prelude to decisions and action by U.S. policymakers."[17] Foreknowledge, conceived in a scientific, business, or intelligence sense, obviously does not imply psychic clairvoyance or deterministic "point" prediction. On the contrary, it refers to rational expectation: estimative forecasting based on available evidence and formal analytic methods.

Such estimative prediction requires both critical and creative thinking, specifically: (1) formal analytic rigor and the explication of assumptions, and (2) perception and understanding across both the depth and the breadth of a problem domain, each of which imposes its own specific methodological and practical requirements.

Critical Thinking and Analytic Depth

Critical thinking involves analyzing a problem in depth, which in turn often requires extrapolation and the projection of observed patterns and trends into the long- or short-term future based on statistics and mathematical probability. Such trend projection is typical in the related group of disciplines known as neoclassical economics, operations research, management science, and decision theory. It relies on strict deductive inference from given premises, including the precept that man is a utility-maximizing "rational actor" ("economic man"). Moreover, "man as actor" has always explicitly included both the subject of analysis (e.g., a foreign decision maker) and, implicitly, the subject performing the analysis (the analyst). Such methods, although they provide powerful tools for testing, eliminating, or justifying propositions, are only as good as their assumptions—the old "garbage in, garbage out" problem. Yet as noted above, social scientists and philosophers have revealed limitations and sources of error in human reasoning that make the selection of assumptions a "nontrivial" task subject to human error. These patterns of error not only cripple qualitative methodology; they also afflict strictly analytico-deductive methods as well, in the following ways.

First, human rationality is "bounded"—that is, limited and often biased by psychological factors involving perception, cognition, emotion, values, and personal interest.[18] Busy observers and participants often tend to form images and frame opinions rather hastily and uncritically ("leaping to conclusions" through "hasty generalization"). These perceptions produce often-implicit and inchoate mental images of the world. This subjectivity and tacit imprecision appear to be "codependent," if you will, each "enabling" the other: Comfortable biases are best defended if left camouflaged (tacit), which in turn protects them even when they are not a source of particular comfort.

Next, once observers have formed images and framed opinions, they tend to internalize them, identify with them, personalize them, and defend them against all incoming data and criticism. Thus, even sound assumptions persist and can be rendered obsolete by dynamic change in the environment. Richards Heuer and Jack Davis, among others contributing to this volume, have examined this problem, as have numerous congressional and blue-ribbon commissions.

When analysis rests on such dubious premises, even the most powerful analytico-deductive methods lack the ability not only to predict nonlinear, revolutionary discontinuities but even to identify extant and emerging trends well enough to reliably predict even evolutionary change. Until advanced models emerge,[19] the intelligence community can prevent surprise (or at least reduce the risk, rate, and severity of surprise) only if it can anticipate the innovative, asymmetric, and often devious gambits an adversary might employ. This requires a very wide span of peripheral vision that can imagine not just conventional contingencies but also plausible unprecedented ones as well—hypotheses and alternative scenarios. This breadth of imagination is a synthetic rather than an analytic function. It is what enables us to "ask the right questions" in the first place.

Creative Thinking and Synthetic Breadth

In surprises, the "ball comes in out of left field," outside the victim's span of "peripheral vision" at the time of the event, which often is narrowly focused in a given direction. Surprise thus usually comes in the form of events for which there had been previous evidence that was ignored or dismissed. In Grabo's words: "It is the history of every great warning crisis that the post-mortems have turned up numerous relevant facts or pieces of information which were available but which, for one reason or another, were not considered in making assessments at the time."[20] As noted above, social scientists have explored some of the reasons for this misdirection of attention.

However, no rules-governed procedure, algorithm, or software exists for ensuring perception, imagination, creativity, and discovery "on demand." These are stochastic, holistic, and "emergent" complex-systems phenomena, thriving through self-organized criticality at the edge of order and chaos.[21] Deterministic or reductionist analytics do not promote or proliferate hypotheses; instead, analysis *narrows* focus and *eliminates* hypotheses. Hypothesis generation is the "art" of science, the domain where intuition and imagination can and must play an indispensable role. What is required is a reliable method for stimulating and broadening such synthetic reasoning, a process the IC perhaps somewhat mis-leadingly refers to as alternative "analysis." Reliable predictive warning requires substantial improvement in synthetic methods and creative imagination.[22]

The underlying prerequisites lie in induction and abduction: the collection, collation, and ordering of data, and the process of "pattern recognition" required to infer hypotheses to explain the data and make predictions based on them.[23] Once these challenges are solved, proper task sequencing requires that this synthetic phase precede the deductive analyses described above, for it is here where alternative hypotheses emerge for subsequent testing using formal analytic methods.

Analytic-Synthetic Integration

Sound forecasting requires that both elements—synthesis and analysis, hypothesis generation and testing—be integrated into a single unified methodology to ensure that the full range of potential contingencies, including even seemingly improbable ones, are subjected to full analytic development and rigorous testing. Synthesis and analysis are complementary and, in fact, interdependent. By themselves, induction and abduction can suggest and posit a wide range of hypothetical scenarios of undetermined plausibility, but they cannot test or substantiate them in order to eliminate them or convert them into forecasts. This conversion requires formalization. In this stage, the assumptions defining the multiple alternative hypotheses are modeled for internal consistency, extrapolated into the future, and compared with known and incoming intelligence evidence. The validity of such analysis is largely a function of the range of alternative hypotheses generated in the preceding stage. What is required, then, is a continuous, total-systems feedback loop between synthetic induction and analytic deduction. This organizational learning spiral traditionally has been known as the scientific method.

Scientific Methodology: Network-Centric Prediction

Scientific methodology marries intuitive, open-minded imagination with skeptical standards of proof. Archimedes sat in a bathtub and conceived buoyancy, Newton noted the falling apple and conceived universal gravitation, and equally intuitive inspiration prompted Einstein to ask if space and time might be relative rather than absolute phenomena. But these scientists then subjected their hypotheses to rigorous mathematical formalization and both logical and factual proof, by comparing predictions deducible from the formalized theory with observable empirical data.

In fact, the entire purpose of science is to seek data and infer predictions concerning future outcomes under specified conditions. The purpose of science and the test of its utility go beyond explanation. It lies in prediction that is more accurate, precise, and hence reliable than that produced through any other method of investigation and reasoning.

Science achieves this through the union of complementary opposites in both its underlying epistemology and its methodology. Epistemologically, science unites empiricism, the doctrine that experience and observation (e.g., intelligence collection) are the basic data source for real-world fact, with rationalism, the doctrine that logical and mathematical classification and inference are the basic methods required for sound interpretation of the empirical observations (as in intelligence analysis and assessment).[24] This "rational-empirical" epistemology recognizes and exploits the power of deductive methods (logic and mathematics) to order physical facts into meaningful patterns (theories and models) and then project beyond these to make estimates about facts for which we have as yet no empirical data. This is *scientific prediction*, made possible only by the creative tension and synergy between rationalism and empiricism.

To close the rational-empirical loop, science requires that all estimates and assessments (all hypotheses and theories) be tested, both rationally for internal logical and/or mathematical coherence, and empirically for correspondence with the observable world. This testing is the essence of Francis Bacon's "experimental method." Informative results would corroborate hypotheses and justify their retention, directly contradict them suggesting their elimination, or often limit their scope of applicability through some modification. This process requires multiple alternative, competing hypotheses, because testing is a process of elimination.

"Method" applies methodology to the solution of practical problems. In science, the problem involves the quest for knowledge of the world.[25] In intelligence, the target of interest involves the capabilities and intentions of foreign actors. Scientific method implements the rational-empirical (also termed analytico-synthetic) feedback loop: Practitioners observe and measure phenomena of interest and then delineate the relationships among the data through formal theory (systems of logical and/or mathematical propositions formulated as models and algorithms). These theories or models then support the deduction of necessary observable implications. The logical formula employs hypothetical or "counterfactual" conditional propositions as premises in what reduces essentially to a standard syllogism:

Major premise (rational):   *If this theory/model is valid, and*

Minor premise (empirical):   *these data are true, then*

Conclusion: *this other observable fact must necessarily follow.*

In intelligence warning, such deduced observables are intelligence and warning (I&W) indicators—that is, known or presumed activities that correlate with a higher threat potential. If observed, one can postulate the possibility that either overt or concealed threat activity might be under way. Such inferences postulate a correlation in which the premises function as independent variables and the expected outcomes are dependent variables—deductions that must be tested, first for logico-mathematical coherence and then for correspondence with observed fact. Testing typically is conducted through laboratory experimentation in which independent variables are manipulated and their outcomes recorded and then compared with field observation (e.g., intelligence collection).

In sciences that study phenomena and systems that cannot be manipulated physically (e.g., the heavens, the Earth, the past, and mankind), scientists must substitute laboratory work and models for physical experimentation on real-world specimens. They assemble observable data from the historical record, recent or distant, but must perform all of their experiments on models. Experimentation on models is known as simulation and is conducted almost entirely on computers. This work is so important in modern science that an entire methodological subdiscipline has emerged called modeling and simulation (M&S).[26]

Practical Procedures for Network-Centric Prediction

Thinking within the "box" or paradigm of traditional intelligence "tradecraft" and vertically stove-piped bureaucracy, today's managers attempt to improve imagination by focusing on individual analysts and exhorting them to "think outside the box." The social sciences have shown, however, that this approach is likely to yield but little counterintuitive fruit.

By contrast, modern business management practice has taken a new approach, one that opens a new paradigm for broadening perception and enhancing the likelihood of discovery. This new method focuses on cross-functional *team collaboration*, which combines interdisciplinary, interdepartmental, and/or interagency experts in *Integrated Project Teams* (IPTs). Under the leadership of professional facilitators, modern IPTs use a rapidly developing suite of tools and techniques for the marshalling of available data, structured brainstorming, and the generation of plausible hypotheses concerning alternative futures and contingencies. Collaborative teaming supplies a countermeasure against groupthink, consisting of the IPT members themselves as well as the facilitator. The IPT members bring together multiple frames of reference, which skilled facilitators then elicit, fostering creative tension, fruitful conflict, cognitive dissonance, discovery, reconceptualization, and organizational learning.[27]

As noted above, current emphasis is properly placed on virtual collaboration. Distributed collaboration, however, especially if asynchronous, is fraught with implementation difficulties and can never be as dynamic, intensive, rich, or fertile as face-to-face interaction. It can commence immediately upon warning, while physical congregation requires travel; however, the difference in potential productivity and op tempo thereafter is dramatic.[28] Thus, while virtual collaboration must become the new IC "equilibrium state," it should be punctuated frequently by major lab-based projects for the production of national-level intelligence assessments, especially deep-looking and far-reaching reassessments, and for the resolution of critical controversies and the conduct of crisis- and combat-support operations. This, in turn, requires an institutional setting and infrastructure that supplement bureaucratic offices and stove-piped chains of command with a new system of horizontal integration within and across organizations and the community as a whole.

The Optimal Setting: The Computational "Collaboratory"

Unlike vertically integrated bureaucracies, laboratories are the quintessential "flat," egalitarian organizations, maximizing intercommunication while minimizing managerial friction. Computational "collaboratories" would be purpose designed to bring together analysts and methodologists for cycles of synthesis and analysis.[29] Each computational collaboratory would integrate the functions of an "electronic meeting room" for collaboration, and a "math lab" for computational analysis, and teams would perform the two activities in iterative succession to propel a spiral of discovery and learning.

These computational collaboratories would be designed to stimulate and integrate both creative "right-brain" and critical "left-brain" functions, so they should be designed in two "hemispheres." The right hemisphere would stimulate group dynamics and supply the subject matter experts with extensive access to classified and open source databases, with an ergonomic layout that encourages multilateral interchange. There, professional facilitators would coach the teams through the classic "forming, storming, norming, and performing" stages of team development while driving them at an energetic pace through problem-framing, brainstorming, and "sense-making" activities using the numerous informal and semiformal techniques intelligence methodologists and corporate facilitators have developed.[30]

The resulting mental models, scenarios, and hypotheses would then be handed over by the substantive teams to their assigned technical support group in the "math lab" or "left hemisphere" of the collaboratory for formalization in computational models and simulation testing.[31] This technical group would consist of methodologists (e.g., modelers, operations researchers, experimental designers, and statisticians) armed with the requisite logico-mathematical tools (e.g., decision theory, game theory, Bayesian statistics, evolutionary algorithms, and multi-attribute utility analysis), and simulation models (ideally systems-theoretical models).

Experimental results and findings would then be submitted back to the substantive analytic teams for the next phase of empirical review. In this stage of the cycle, facilitators would help the experts generate new hypotheses to replace those eliminated in testing. Senior substantive team leaders would determine when the cycling should be interrupted for summary assessment and reporting, based on either diminishing analytic returns or external requirements.

This process would provide an organizational learning spiral involving initial inductive synthesis, rigorous analysis, and final comprehensive synthesis and assessment. In fact, twin spirals would ensue: one involving the substantive intelligence issue under investigation and of concern therefore primarily to the intelligence analysts, and the other involving the computational-collaborative methodology itself, which must constantly undergo scrutiny and improvement by the methodologists.[32]

A suitable name for the national intelligence computational collaboratory might be the Intelligence Training, Assessment, and Simulation Center (ITASC).[33] Organizationally, analysts using the ITASC could be drawn primarily from IC production offices, not the DNI per se. The Office of the Director of National Intelligence, however, might manage the ITASC and supply a permanent staff of methodologists, technicians, and administrators who would organize and coordinate projects and agendas, facilitate the teams and perform all M&S and analysis, maintain permanent databases, and oversee the drafting of the project report (e.g., NIE).

Toward a National Intelligence Computational Collaborative Network

The ITASC and computational collaborative methodology would create an opportunity to unite the entire IC into a single enterprise or "system of systems" featuring a high degree of "boundaryless" horizontal integration. Once the ITASC has lain the groundwork, the DNI could direct and resource parallel efforts within the line agencies and commands. Some agencies have prototypes already in place, such as the Battle Lab / Innovation Center in the Defense Intelligence Agency and the Advanced Analytic Lab in the National Security Agency. Most, however, have yet to begin experimentation along these lines. Such intra-agency labs can be more austere than the national center. Each would implement interdepartmental teaming and tools-based analyses within its agency's special areas of responsibility.

Analytic labor in this national intelligence collaborative architecture would be divided according to agency charter. All, however, should function as a node in a national network integrated through the use of unified, documented scientific methodology supported by a unified family of analytic methods and a shared set of models, computational tools, and databases as well as the information technology (IT) standards and protocols required to ensure full interoperability, data exchange, and scientific replication (a "plug-and-play" capability necessary for Competitive Analysis).

Once in place, such a National Intelligence Computational Collaborative Network would enable full-spectrum network-centric intelligence. ITASC-based collaborative projects for the production of major and enduring national assessments could then be supplemented by near-real-time global interagency production of current intelligence for strategic and tactical I&W and crisis and operations support.[34] Community watch offices could undertake continuous virtual collaboration over a secure, real-time, distributed network using video teleconferencing and a unified set of IT tools and data, creating a National Operational Intelligence Watch Officers' Network (NOIWON) for the twenty-first century. IC leaders could mobilize crisis action teams in immediate response to contingencies, for action either within the ITASC or across the collaborative net. This high-intensity, high-velocity system of systems would exchange data and outputs multilaterally and also synthesize assessments through Web-enabled distributed production and dissemination. Properly implemented, the resulting whole would vastly exceed the sum of the parts, compress the intelligence cycle rate, and improve IC agility and U.S. national security response capability by an order of magnitude.

Joining Scientific Methodology and Network Centricity

Although seemingly futuristic and technologically advanced, such network centricity is now well within our technical reach and capable of overcoming pervasive and long-standing deficiencies in insight and warning. The principal challenges are more cultural and institutional than technical. To begin to build this analytic capability, the national IC must integrate horizontally in structure and function and adopt a much flatter and more integrated business model. In particular, it must:

- Tie the many agencies together into a single virtual organization through IT-enabled data sharing and advanced analytico-synthetic tools and techniques;
- bring IC analysts together to form IPTs in collaboratories that maximize imagination as well as analytic rigor;
- maximize rigor by using computational simulation models, metrics, and databases; and
- ensure that team cycles build on previous achievements by capturing all findings in these models and databases.

Such institutional transformation will both demand and drive the modernization of the IC's intellectual culture. Intelligence must progress from today's guild-based craft to a fully modern profession and graduate from today's largely intuitive, prescientific "tradecraft" to a formal interdisciplinary science of intelligence.[35]

As both Thomas Kuhn and Clayton Christensen have noted, such paradigm shifts and disruptive innovations are never easy or free from controversy. Paradigm shifts involve transitions from periods of "normal science" operating within established paradigms to "revolutionary science" that challenges the extant paradigm.[36] Disruptive innovation involves a similar shift from "sustaining" to "disruptive" technologies.[37] In both cases, innovation begins in an immature state, its future potential not at first being obvious. Extensive testing and data are required to bring it to full fruition and prove its superiority to the inevitable legions of doubters. Many potentially lucrative innovations are attacked and suppressed during this time of acute vulnerability. In intelligence reform, however, the cliché holds: "Failure is not an option." The national security stakes are just too great.

Notes

This chapter is adapted from the author's 2006 Galileo Award–winning paper, "Predictive, Network-Centric Intelligence: Toward a Total-Systems Transformation of Analysis and Assessment." The director of national intelligence holds the Galileo essay contest each year to promote innovative thinking within the IC.

1. A recent review of the history of IC reform efforts is Michael Warner and J. Kenneth McDonald, *US Intelligence Community Reform Studies since 1947* (Washington, D.C.: Center for the Study of Intelligence, Central Intelligence Agency, 2005).

2. We critique ourselves most sharply but history has shown that other governments' intelligence-based decision making often is worse—Germany, Italy, and Japan in World War II, the Soviet Union.

3. Office of the Director of National Intelligence, *The National Intelligence Strategy of the United States of America: Transformation through Innovation and Integration*, Washington, D.C., October 2005, National Intelligence Reform Act of 2004 (S.2845, 108th Congress, October 6, 2004). Two unofficial reform studies also were important influences inspiring and shaping this proposal: Edward Waltz, *Knowledge Management in the Intelligence Enterprise* (Boston: Artech House, 2003); and Deborah G. Barger, *Toward a Revolution in Intelligence Affairs*, RAND Technical Report TR-242-CMS (Santa Monica, Calif.: RAND Corporation, 2005), 47, www.rand.org/publications/TR/TR242/.

4. A previous Galileo paper proposed the use of "self-organizing" web tools such as "wikis" and "blogs" within the IC's classified network: D. Calvin Andrus, "The Wiki and the Blog: Toward a Complex Adaptive Intelligence Community," *Studies in Intelligence* 49, no. 3 (2005): 63–70. His proposal and proponency were instrumental in the creation of the current Intellipedia, a self-organizing space for analysts to share information and insights.

5. A seminal study by Isaac Ben-Israel recommended the application of scientific methodology to intelligence assessment: Isaac Ben-Israel, "Philosophy and Methodology of Intelligence: The Logic of the Estimate Process," *Intelligence and National Security* 4, no. 4 (October 1989): 660–718.

6. Pursuant to Sections 123, National Intelligence Council; 145, Office of Alternative Analysis; and 222, Independence of Intelligence, in the 2004 National Intelligence Reform Act.

7. "Boundarylessness"—in effect, horizontal integration—was one of the core tenets of chief executive Jack Welch's leadership of General Electric, a conglomerate not unlike the IC, in the 1980s and 1990s. Jack Welch, with John A. Byrne, *Jack: Straight from the Gut* (New York: Warner Business Books, 2001).

8. On "analytic culture," see Rob Johnston, *Analytic Culture in the U.S. Intelligence Community: An Ethnographic Study* (Washington, D.C.: Center for the Study of Intelligence, Central Intelligence Agency, 2005).

9. A burgeoning multidisciplinary literature addresses the problems and causes of intelligence failure. Cognitive psychology has examined the problems of bias in intuitive reasoning. The seminal application to intelligence is Richards J. Heuer, *Psychology of Intelligence Analysis* (Washington, D.C.: Center for the Study of Intelligence, Central Intelligence Agency, 1999). Seminal studies of group and governmental error include Irving L. Janis, *Groupthink: Psychological Studies of Policy Decisions and Fiascoes* (Boston: Houghton Mifflin, 1972), and Robert Jervis, *Perception and Misperception in International Politics* (Princeton, N.J.: Princeton University Press, 1976).

10. Terminology from military command and control theory: operational tempo or "op tempo" refers to the cyclic rate of C4ISR task accomplishment within and among units. The observation–orientation–decision–action (OODA) Loop was Colonel John Boyd's generalization of what we call the "intelligence cycle" or "TPED": tasking, processing, exploitation and dissemination. John Boyd, "A Discourse on Winning and Losing," unpublished briefing, www.d-n-i.net/second_level/boyd_military.htm#discourse.

11. See chapter 11 in this volume for further discussion of intelligence epistemology.

12. This is a combination of "satisfy" and "suffice," distinguished from classical utility maximization. Herbert A. Simon, "A Behavioral Model of Rational Choice," *Quarterly Journal of Economics* 54 (February 1955): 99–101. Note that satisficing often optimizes under conditions of constraint (especially temporal) and can thus provide more rational (utility-maximizing) outcomes than "paralysis by analysis."

13. The multidisciplinary literature here is vast and indispensable. Space constraints restrict full citation, but oft-cited authors include Herbert A. Simon, Daniel Kahnemann, Amos Tversky, Irving L. Janis, Allen Newell, Robert Jervis, Richard E. Nisbett, Lee Ross, Thomas Gilovich, Scott Plouse, and Thomas Kuhn.

14. Janis, *Groupthink: Psychological Studies of Policy Decisions and Fiascoes*. Such groups include organizational management teams. NIE committees are temporary ad hoc groups; members almost always remain loyal to their parent organization.

15. Cynthia Grabo, *Anticipating Surprise: Analysis for Strategic Warning* (Washington, D.C.: Joint Military Intelligence College, 2002), 39.

16. The literature here as well is substantial, but theory remains underdeveloped. Oft-cited authors include Richard Betts, Michael Handel, Ephraim Kam, James J. Wirtz, Barton Whaley, Donald C. Daniel and Katherine L. Herbig, John Gooch and Amos Perlmutter, Michael Howard, Roy Godson, Roger Hesketh and Nigel West, and Thaddeus Holt.

17. CIA Office of Public Affairs, *A Consumer's Guide to Intelligence* (Washington, D.C.: Central Intelligence Agency, 1999), vii.

18. Simon, "Behavioral Model of Rational Choice."

19. These would have to take the form of complex adaptive systems (CAS) models that produce self-organized emergence and nonlinear dynamics. The most promising models available today appear to be those based on the work of Jay Forrester; see, inter alia, *Principles of Systems* (Waltham, Mass.: Pegasus Communications, 1968/1990), and www.systemdynamics.org/. Highly sophisticated CAS models of emergence and evolutionary dynamics (e.g., agent-based models) promise even more powerful capabilities for the future.

20. Grabo, *Anticipating Surprise*, 9. Though retrospective criticism can be disparaged as "20/20 hindsight," this paper embraces the thesis argued by Bazerman and Watkins that many surprises are predictable and should have come as no surprise. Max Bazerman and Michael Watkins, *Predictable Surprises: The Disasters You Should Have Seen Coming and How to Prevent Them* (Boston: Harvard Business School Press, 2004).

21. General and complex systems theory is another discipline with a thriving literature. Good introductions include Ludwig von Bertalanffy, *General System Theory: Foundation, Development, Applications* (New York: Braziller, 1968); and Mitchell M. Waldrop, *Complexity: Life at the Edge of Order and Chaos* (New York: Simon & Schuster, 1992). The Santa Fe Institute (www.santafe.edu) and the New England Complex Systems Institute (www.necsi.org) are good sources of research information.

22. The 9/11 Commission attributed the failure to understand the gravity of the looming terrorist threat to a range of causal factors, including a "failure of imagination." The methodology proposed herein would implement the commission's call for the IC to "institutionalize imagination" through a combination of alternative analyses, "red-teaming" (i.e., role playing and simulation gaming), and "rigorous analytic methods."

23. "Abduction," a concept generally credited to Charles Sanders Peirce, refers to the formulation and selection of hypotheses. It often is characterized as "inference to the best explanation." As such it is not an alternative to induction and/or deduction. Instead, it applies both in complex sequence to formulate explanations.

24. The literature on the philosophy of science is voluminous. Two overview works can be identified as particularly influential in shaping the present proposal: Alan Cromer, *Uncommon Sense: The Heretical Nature of Science* (New York: Oxford University Press, 1993); and John Losee, *An Historical Introduction to the Philosophy of Science* (Oxford: Oxford University Press, 1972/2001).

25. In logic and scientific method, again the literature is vast and substantial. Salient authors include, in addition to Aristotle and Francis Bacon, Carl G. Hempel, Rudolf Carnap, Hans Reichenbach, R. B. Braithewaite, Ernst Nagel, Frederick Suppe, John Holland, Colin Howson and Peter Urbach, Hugh G. Gauch, David A. Schum, Paul Thagard, and Edward Waltz. This proposal has been guided in great part by the work of philosophers associated with logical positivism/empiricism, such as Carl Hempel, Hans Reichenbach, and Karl Popper.

26. E.g., see John L. Casti, *Would-Be Worlds: How Simulation Is Changing the Frontiers of Science* (Hoboken, N.J.: John Wiley & Sons, 1997); Alfred H. Hausrath, *Venture Simulation in War, Business and Politics* (New York: McGraw-Hill, 1971); and Michael Schrage,

Serious Play: How the World's Best Companies Simulate to Innovate (Boston: Harvard Business School Press, 1999).

27. For more on collaborative teaming, see Jon R. Katzenbach and Douglas K. Smith, *The Wisdom of Teams: Creating the High-Performance Organization* (Boston: Harvard Business School Press, 1993); and Warren G. Bennis and Patricia W. Biederman, *Organizing Genius: The Secrets of Creative Collaboration* (New York: Perseus Books, 1997).

28. Recent research in team performance argues for the continued importance of proximity for team performance maximization. See, inter alia, Bill Fischer and Andy Boynton, "Virtuoso Teams," *Harvard Business Review*, reprint, July–August 2005, 116–23; Martin Hoegl and Luigi Proserpio, "Team Proximity and Teamwork in Innovative Projects," *Research Policy* 33 (2004): 1153–65; and Sage Freechild, "Team Building and Team Performance Management," Phoenix Rising Coaching, 2004, www.phoenixrisingcoaching.com/documents/Article-Team BuildingandTeamPerformance.pdf.

29. This is as called for by Rob Johnston, "Integrating Methodologists into Teams of Experts," *Studies in Intelligence* 47, no. 1 (2003): 57–65; see also Johnston, *Analytic Culture in the U.S. Intelligence Community*, chap. 5.

30. Examples include Heuer's Analysis of Competing Hypotheses (ACH), in Heuer, *Psychology of Intelligence Analysis*, chap. 8; the many techniques Morgan Jones described in *The Thinker's Toolkit: 14 Powerful Techniques for Problem Solving* (New York: Three Rivers Press, 1995); and many additional group techniques discussed in the literature on team facilitation.

31. Collaborative modeling is discussed by Jac Vennix, *Team Model Building: Facilitating Team Learning Using System Dynamics* (Hoboken, N.J.: John Wiley & Sons, 1996); and by John D. W. Morecroft and John D. Sterman, eds., *Modeling for Learning Organizations* (University Park, Ill.: Productivity Press, 2000).

32. This methodology would implement "double-loop" organizational learning, as proposed by Chris Argyris and Donald Schön, *Theory in Practice: Increasing Organizational Effectiveness* (San Francisco: Jossey-Bass, 1974); and Chris Argyris and Donald Schön, *Organizational Learning: A Theory of Action Perspective* (Reading, Mass.: Addison Wesley, 1978); and the process of "socialization, externalization, combination and internalization" (SECI) proposed by Ikujiro Nonaka and Hirotaka Takeuchi in *The Knowledge Creating Company: How Japanese Companies Create the Dynamics of Innovation* (New York: Oxford University Press, 1995).

33. A name inspired by the Joint Forces Command's Joint Training, Analysis and Simulation Center (JTASC) in Suffolk, Va. By contrast with the JTASC, the ITASC would of course address foreign threats and do so across the full civil–military spectrum. Moreover, it would prioritize assessment above training.

34. The ITASC process would implement Grabo's recommendations for effective I&W found in *Anticipating Surprise: Analysis for Strategic Warning*, chap. 8, especially concerning probability judgments and impediments to warning.

35. On the need to move from guild craftsmanship to full professionalism, see Stephen Marrin, "Intelligence Analysis: Turning a Craft into a Profession," International Conference on Intelligence Analysis, May 2005; https://analysis.mitre.org/proceedings/Final_Papers_ Files/97_Camera_Ready_Paper.pdf.

36. Thomas Kuhn, *The Structure of Scientific Revolutions* (Chicago: University of Chicago Press, 1962).

37. Clayton Christensen, *The Innovator's Dilemma: When New Technologies Cause Great Firms to Fail* (Boston: Harvard Business School Press, 1997).

CHAPTER 18

Homeland Security Intelligence: Rationale, Requirements, and Current Status

Bruce Berkowitz

DOMESTIC INTELLIGENCE has a distinct, specialized mission. Its goal is to provide officials, public safety workers, and, as appropriate, the broader public with better situational awareness of potential threats within the United States. In this respect it is different from foreign intelligence, which grapples with threats outside the United States, and law enforcement, which focuses on apprehending and deterring criminals under the rules of the criminal justice system.

Historical Background

Over the years, the federal government has often engaged in domestic intelligence activities of one kind or another. It is this experience, in fact, why the idea of a domestic intelligence organization is so controversial. In some cases, officials set up ad hoc information collection operations without statutory authorization (e.g., the Richard Nixon administration's "plumbers" and "enemy's list"). In other cases, government organizations might have been acting within the legal authorities of the time, but their operations were misdirected and abusive (e.g., the Federal Bureau of Investigation's, or FBI's, surveillance of Martin Luther King in the 1960s). In yet other cases such domestic intelligence efforts were linked to larger controversies about the limits of legitimate dissent (e.g., government surveillance of various anarchists, socialists, labor organizers, student activists, draft resisters, militant environmentalists, religious groups, and political extremists on both the left and the right).

Many of these activities were revealed during the Watergate investigations of the early 1970s and the investigations of the U.S. intelligence community during the middle part of that decade. They were, to say the least, highly controversial. They also painted domestic intelligence—of almost any form—with a sinister, unsavory image. The net result was that, for almost twenty-five years, public and political sentiment ran strongly against creating organizations for either collecting or analyzing domestic intelligence.

The September 11, 2001, terrorist attacks caused many officials and other experts to reconsider these views. But even before that, some specialists were rethinking whether the United States needs an organization devoted to domestic intelligence analysis. The current discussion began to emerge in the early 1990s, as it began to appear that terrorist groups might try to target the United States directly.

U.S. allies had suffered homegrown terrorist campaigns during the 1970s and 1980s by groups like the Japanese Red Army, Italian Red Brigades, and the German Baader-Meinhof Gang. The United States itself had been largely unaffected until the first World Trade Center bombing on February 26, 1993. This seems to have been the point in time when the taboo on discussing domestic intelligence began to recede.

After this initial attack on the World Trade Center, law enforcement officials uncovered additional plots by Islamic groups to attack other targets in New York City. These incidents, and the March 20, 1995, nerve gas attack on the Tokyo subway by Aum Shinrikyo made people question whether the United States was adequately prepared. Then the bombing on April 19, 1995—just one month later—of the Alfred P. Murrah Federal Building in Oklahoma City killed 168 people and graphically illustrated the potential devastation of a terrorist strike.

A significant aspect of both the Tokyo subway attack and the Oklahoma City bombing was that the attackers, up to the time of the incident, had mainly operated within the law and thus flew under the radar of law enforcement authorities. The Aum Shinrikyo—in reality, an international cult/terrorist organization seeking weapons of mass destruction—was nominally a religious organization. The Japanese police, worried about violating its civil liberties, had deliberately avoided monitoring it.

Similarly, Timothy McVeigh and Terry Nichols, who were convicted of the Oklahoma City bombing, were also eventually linked to extremist militia, Christian identity, and survivalist groups. However, because neither had committed any serious crime before the attack, neither had appeared on the scope of any government organization. Law enforcement officials got their first lead on McVeigh when they tracked the serial number of the van that carried the bomb to a truck rental agency, and witnesses there provided a composite sketch of the renter. A state trooper happened to stop McVeigh shortly after the bombing for driving without a license plate, and this chance event, combined with the rental records, led to McVeigh's apprehension and, later, the arrest of Nichols.

This was the context when a series of government commissions and nongovernmental public interest organizations began in the mid-1990s to study the problem. Their recommendations on homeland security matters included who should conduct analysis and how and under what rules they should do it (see box 18.1).

The issue of domestic intelligence had previously surfaced when the modern intelligence community was first established in the 1940s. One of the concerns opponents to the Central Intelligence Agency (CIA) raised when it was proposed was that the new organization might become a "secret police," taking actions against U.S. citizens without restraint by the laws that control law enforcement

BOX 18.1
Recent Commissions and Reviews on Domestic Intelligence

The National Commission on Terrorism. Known as the "Bremer Commission," named after its chairman, Ambassador L. Paul Bremer, it was established by Congress in 1998 "to review the laws, regulations, directives, policies and practices for preventing and punishing international terrorism directed against the United States, assess their effectiveness, and recommend changes." The Commission issued its report in June 2000.

The U.S. Commission on National Security in the 21st Century. The "Hart–Rudman Commission," named for its cochairmen, former Senators Gary Hart (D.-Colo.) and Warren Rudman (R.-Conn.), was authorized by Congress and issued three reports during 1999–2001. It addressed a wide range of emerging national security issues, but is most often remembered for its early warning of the emerging importance of homeland security.

The Joint Inquiry of House and Senate Intelligence Committees into the Terrorist Attacks of September 11, 2001. A unique effort involving committees of both the House and the Senate, this was the first investigation into the intelligence failures connected with the September 11 attacks, including gaps in information sharing and responsibilities for monitoring developments within the United States. It issued its report in December 2002.

The Congressional Advisory Panel to Assess Domestic Response Capabilities for Terrorism Involving Weapons of Mass Destruction. Known as the "Gilmore Commission" after its chairman, former governor James Gilmore (R-Va.), it developed recommendations for Congress in annual reports from 1998 to 2003, focusing on measures for state and local governments to prepare for domestic terrorist threats.

The National Commission on Terrorist Attacks Upon the United States. Chaired by former Governor Thomas Keane (R-N.J.) and universally known as the "9/11 Commission," it issued a report in July 2004 that had the unusual status of a popular best seller. The 9/11 Commission provided a detailed account of the events leading up to the attacks, and extended the Joint Inquiry's assessment of domestic intelligence gaps.

Commission on the Intelligence Capabilities of the United States Regarding Weapons of Mass Destruction. Better known as the "WMD Commission" and cochaired by Judge Lawrence Silberman and former Senator Charles Robb, this was a direct result of the flawed intelligence that contributed to the decision by U.S. leaders to invade Iraq, and reported in March 2005. This failure led many officials to question overall U.S. capabilities to assess such threats, including domestic intelligence capabilities to monitor such threats within the United States.

Markle Task Force on National Security in the Information Age. In April 2002, the Markle Foundation, a private not-for-profit organization, assembled a panel of national security, technology, and civil liberties experts to develop recommendations for defending against terrorist attacks while also protecting civil rights. Its recommendations for an information sharing system for homeland security were explicitly incorporated into the Collins-Lieberman Intelligence Reform Bill, which eventually became the basis of the Intelligence Reform and Terrorism Prevention Act of 2004.

agencies. Accordingly, with just a few exceptions, the CIA was not allowed to turn its operational or analytic capabilities inward.

But this presented a question: If the CIA was not going to do domestic intelligence analysis, who would? The FBI was a logical candidate; of course it was already engaged in law enforcement activities against domestic and foreign terrorist organizations, and it had used analysts in a supporting role for these activities (albeit with many issues being raised in the process, as we shall see). Yet FBI leaders have been ambivalent in pursuing the domestic intelligence mission.

One reason for this reluctance was that senior FBI officials were all too aware of the domestic spying controversies of the 1970s. Few of the officials who had experienced that episode wanted to repeat it. Another reason for the reluctance was that intelligence analysis does not fit well into the law enforcement culture, which is based on responding to crimes, apprehending suspects, and obtaining convictions. There are few incentives in this model for simply collecting information that "might" eventually prove useful, which is a key component of the analytic method.

Analysis is also a frankly intellectual pursuit, and law enforcement tends to be a practical-minded culture. Historically, one could find many would-be professors in intelligence analysis organizations. One would likely find many fewer in law enforcement organizations. Analysts would pursue an MA or PhD to get ahead; special agents would pursue a JD. The kinds of questions that might mark a great analyst, such as speculating which countries might prove to be a threat five years from now, can even be illegal for a law enforcement officer to pose ("Who at the First National Bank might potentially be an embezzler next year?") As a result, analysis has historically been the proverbial redheaded stepchild at the FBI. One episode that received wide attention in 2006 was especially revealing about the prevailing mindset at the bureau..

Gary M. Bald, former assistant director of the FBI's Counterterrorism Division and the first chief of its new National Security Service (which we will discuss below), was asked in a legal deposition to explain the difference between the Sunni and Shiite strains of Islam. Bald suggested that the question was irrelevant to the FBI. "You don't need subject matter expertise," he said. "The subject matter expertise is helpful, but it isn't a prerequisite. It is certainly not what I look for in selecting an official for a position in the counterterrorism [program]."[1]

Bald was criticized for this comment, but it should be viewed in context. As a matter of principle, we *do* want police to be indifferent about a person's religious beliefs, unless they present a clear and specific threat. Besides, from a cop's perspective, a suspect's religious beliefs simply do not matter. They are irrelevant to the job at hand, which is to apprehend a suspect legally and quickly. Indeed, thinking about these factors is a distraction. So, on the street, analysis can seem like deadweight.

But from a perspective of gaining a better understanding of a potential terrorist threat to subvert or blunt an attack, the difference between Shiite and Sunni fundamentalism can be tremendously important. The sectarian affiliation of a group can suggest whether it is part of al-Qaeda (a mainly Sunni organization) or Hezbollah (an organization backed by the extremist Shiite regime in Iran). That, in turn, can provide insight into the group's resources, tactics, and goals, which can help analysts and officials anticipate threats—rather than respond.

Yet even as the FBI has been slow to perform this mission, it has also been reluctant to allow any other organization to assume responsibility for it. As FBI director Robert Mueller told the 9/11 Commission, "I do believe that creating a separate agency to collect intelligence in the United States would be a grave mistake. Splitting the law enforcement and the intelligence functions would lead both agencies fighting the war on terrorism with one hand tied behind their backs."[2]

The FBI's reaction to proposals for a separate domestic intelligence organization has been classic bureaucratic behavior. Organizations are usually reluctant to allow a new organization to undertake an activity that would overlap their own, even if they are not giving the mission a high priority. The FBI is not unique in this respect. "Turf" is a term used as frequently in discussions about bureaucracies as in discussions about lawn care.[3]

There is also a cultural element. Culture can create bureaucratic inertia, making it hard for an established organization to develop new skills, despite the best intentions of its leaders. So, for example, though FBI officials have said that terrorism is their top priority, the fact remains that the training program for new special agent recruits, which totals 701.5 hours of instruction, today still devotes only 37 hours to counterterrorism and just 1 hour to understanding Islam—but 114.5 hours to handling firearms.[4]

FBI analysts receive much more training than special agents in terrorism, but it is noteworthy that they must go to a separate facility to do so, because the main training center lacks a secure data system. It is also noteworthy that FBI analysts do not carry badges or guns—which inherently limits their stature in an organization that sees arresting criminals as its defining function. Recall, for example, how important it was to the public persona of J. Edgar Hoover that he personally participated in the 1936 arrest of Alvin Karpis.

How Is Domestic Intelligence Different?

Domestic intelligence fills a specific gap in U.S. capabilities to detect threats to the homeland. Foreign intelligence focuses on the world abroad; law enforcement focuses on criminals. Threats could stay out of the sight of both these domains, and that is the "mission space" of domestic intelligence.

Indeed, one could argue that the most serious threats to U.S. homeland security will *usually* try to occupy this space—out of sight of foreign intelligence, and outside the jurisdiction of law enforcement. Such threats do not seek to "make a statement"; rather, their objective is a successful attack against U.S. industry, infrastructure, or military installations, or to commit acts of terror that shake the resolve of U.S. citizens or alter the policy of the U.S. government. For these threats, keeping far away from law enforcement authorities is often an integral, essential part of an operational plan.

There are several differences between intelligence analysis and law enforcement. For example, the work process is different. Intelligence analysis is organized by "accounts" and aims to hypothesize and scan the range of the plausible to detect threats as early as possible. In contrast, law enforcement is organized as "cases"—the investigation of specific people or organizations connected with specific events defined by law as crimes or probable cause. The field of view of law enforcement, by its nature, is more constrained.

Also, the objective is different for each. The objective in intelligence analysis is to *alert and inform*. The ultimate objective in law enforcement is to *prove*, successfully prosecuting a case by discovering a suspect, gathering evidence, and meeting the standard required to win at trial. Whereas intelligence exists to warn *despite doubt*, law enforcement works to prove a case *beyond a reasonable doubt*.

Indeed, one of the greatest hazards in the intelligence business is confusing intelligence with evidence. Intelligence analysts must avoid becoming the effective decision-making mechanism in the policy process. That responsibility rests with elected and appointed officials. Also, intelligence, with all its inherent uncertainties, is simply not designed for that function. Intelligence always has gray areas, and it is the job of officials to make judgment calls to fill them.[5]

Law enforcement, in contrast, is designed to collect evidence, and evidence has precisely the opposite function—it *is* supposed to be the decision mechanism. When law enforcement officials collect and present enough of it to remove reasonable doubt, juries are supposed to convict (or, otherwise, acquit). This is why law enforcement officials do not go to trial unless they believe the evidence is sufficient to put this mechanism into motion.

Another difference is that intelligence and law enforcement inherently operate under different restrictions. Law enforcement can impose large costs on its targets (detention, attorney fees, loss of reputation) even when no charges are filed or a suspect is acquitted. This is one reason why law enforcement organizations must meet a higher standard before they can investigate an individual (e.g., demonstrate "probable cause").

Indeed, in some cases law enforcement officials are prohibited from doing things that private citizens or companies can do. For example, a private citizen—otherwise known as a "groupie" or "fan"—can, on a whim, compile a dossier on a Hollywood celebrity or sports star using public or commercially available data. Public interest activists often compile materials on government and corporate officials. Academic researchers may compile such files, too. U.S. law enforcement agencies usually may not, unless there is clear reason to suspect an individual of an association with illegal activity.

According to this argument, a domestic intelligence analysis organization offers a third option. Lacking law enforcement powers, such an agency could collect information with fewer risks to the civil liberties of its potential targets. Thus restrained, the potential costs to a target are reduced if it turns out that the target is innocent or misidentified.

Paradoxically, such an organization can be *more* capable in its job precisely because it *lacks* certain capabilities or authorities. Such an organization could have as much discretion in collecting information as private citizens do, and the resulting product would provide U.S. officials with better situational awareness of conditions within the United States.

Also, it is hard to create a single organization that performs two very different tasks well. Promotion opportunities and career tracks collide. Career experiences and, thus, culture are different. Different organizations simply attract different "kinds" of people, as anyone who has spent time with the Army, Navy, Air Force, and Marines—or the various agencies within the intelligence community—can attest. Each has its own personality, usually reflected in its personnel. Ideally, the culture of an organization complements its mission, and an argument can be made that domestic intelligence requires its own culture, too.

Some countries have separated domestic intelligence responsibilities from both foreign and law enforcement roles. The best known are probably Britain's MI-5 and Israel's Shabak, or Shin Bet. In Germany, the foreign intelligence service (Bundesnachtrichtendienst, BND) conducts foreign intelligence collection and analysis on terrorism, organized crime, and narcotics; the domestic intelligence agency (Bundesamt für Verfassungsschutz, BfV) collects and analyzes internal security threats from terrorists as well as right- and left-wing extremism; and the law enforcement agency (Bundeskriminalamt, BKA) investigates crimes and has arrest authorities.

Despite the similarity of their responsibilities and functions, each of these organizations has a distinctive origin, history, and features. Each was developed in the unique experience of its country and, usually, has evolved and has concentrated on a particular threat.

For example, Shabak (like other components in the Israeli intelligence community) emerged from organizations that have their roots in Israel's independence movement and conflict with neighboring states, and the fact that Israeli and Arab populations have been intermingled throughout that conflict. Also, during the past several decades, it has focused on the threat presented by the Palestinian opposition within Israel's borders, in the occupied territories, and across Israel's borders with Jordan, Syria, Lebanon, and Egypt.

Similarly, MI-5 throughout much of it history has been shaped by Britain's efforts to combat militant Irish nationalists (in addition to espionage, sabotage, and similar threats from hostile foreign governments). More recently, MI-5 has expanded and redirected its efforts to deal with transnational Islamic groups that are active in Britain, and, since the early 1990s, with foreign countries and terrorist organizations that try to illegally obtain technology to develop weapons of mass destruction.

As a result, despite the frequent calls for U.S. officials to create an "American MI-5," in reality there is no single foreign model that one could transplant into the United States, even if one wanted to. The demarcations in roles and responsibilities among foreign intelligence, domestic intelligence, and law enforcement vary from country to country and depend greatly on history, culture, the nature of the most pressing threats, and the happenstance of politics. So the best approach is to ask what capabilities the United States needs and then formulate a plan to develop them.

Activities and Methods of Domestic Intelligence Analysis

Many of the activities of the analytic component of a homeland security intelligence agency would resemble those of other analysis organizations. There would likely also be several important differences, owing to the nature of threats to homeland security, the organizations that rely on the analysis, and the constraints and opportunities that are unique to (or at least distinctly associated with) it.

Domestic intelligence begins with the assumption that officials should have at least as much information as would be available to the ordinary citizen. Like ordinary citizens, domestic intelligence services can obtain their information through a range of sources, including the direct observation of public activities, commercially available data, and data obtained from individuals and corporations on the same basis—and restrictions on use—as other consumers.

The objective of homeland security intelligence analysis is to provide effective situational awareness to relevant officials so that they can prevent attacks to the homeland. Within this general goal, specific missions include:

- The detection, identification, and analysis of social, political, technological, and military trends of concern to homeland security, and developments that could potentially result in threats to homeland security but are below the legal threshold for investigation or action by law enforcement organizations.
- The identification, monitoring, and analysis of tradecraft and technology being used by terrorists, and which may potentially be used in the future.
- The analysis of the vulnerability of targets within the United States; this analysis can often emphasize the use of commercial and other domestic information that is usually not available to either foreign intelligence or law enforcement organizations, although it is often combined with foreign intelligence and law enforcement information.
- Integrating intelligence data with information not available to law enforcement and foreign intelligence agencies to provide a comprehensive threat assessment; for example, open source data and data about specific individuals and groups within the United States, especially from the Internet, commercial databases, and proprietary data.

Law enforcement and foreign intelligence analysts, having spent most of their careers in government, are often unfamiliar with company-to-company peer agreements for handling proprietary data. Indeed, there is often the presumption that the state's requirements trump any private agreements. A specialized domestic intelligence organization could offer the opportunity to develop new, more productive relationships with commercial and private organizations that want to cooperate with the government on security but are concerned about their other responsibilities.

Recent Developments

To understand the current structure of domestic intelligence organizations (or lack thereof), it helps to keep the following factors in mind. First, both before and after September 11, 2001, the George W. Bush administration was reluctant to create new organizations for homeland security and, within that context, even more reluctant to create organizations or reallocate responsibilities for intelligence.[6] It preferred instead to make existing organizations work together more effectively. Second, the FBI, as noted, was reluctant to give up any of its responsibilities for domestic intelligence analysis. Third, the director of central intelligence was reluctant to give up any of his responsibilities for the protection—and thus control—of classified information. Fourth, organizations, positions, policies, and statutes were created in several waves between 2001 and 2006. There were often few links between these waves; each often involved a different set of players, who often disagreed on how to approach the problem. The result of all this is that there was no master designer—or master design—for the organizations currently responsible for domestic intelligence, including analysis. Rather, it is a patchwork, with gaps, inconsistencies, and ambiguities in responsibilities.

Post–September 11 Responses

Immediately after September 11, President Bush created a White House Office of Homeland Security. As support for a separate Department of Homeland Security (DHS) continued to grow in Congress during 2002, the Bush administration agreed to create such an organization. In June it proposed to consolidate several existing agencies with homeland security responsibilities into the new department. These included, among others, Customs, the Border Patrol, the Coast Guard, and the Immigration and Naturalization Service. It did *not* include any components of the National Foreign Intelligence Program[7] or the FBI.

In the negotiations that followed, Congress continued to support moving responsibilities for homeland security intelligence to the new department and giving it greater authority. The administration continued to favor a more incremental approach and generally leaving authorities and responsibilities for intelligence as they were. Disagreements over intelligence came to focus on two issues.

The first issue was whether to create a fully functional intelligence organization within DHS—the aforementioned "American MI-5." The sponsors of the legislation creating DHS favored this and wanted to establish it in the statute. The administration, along with some members of Congress, did not favor such an organization.

The second issue was over control of information. Sponsors of the legislation wanted to give ultimate decision-making authority over releasing information relevant to homeland security to the new secretary of homeland security. The

Bush administration and the leaderships of the intelligence and law enforcement communities wanted to leave this authority with the existing organizations.

Ultimately compromise was reached on both issues. Title II of the Homeland Security Act of 2002, which President Bush signed into law on November 25, 2002, established within the new DHS a new undersecretary for information analysis and infrastructure protection. The undersecretary would have responsibility for "receiving and analyzing law enforcement information, intelligence, and other information in order to understand the nature and scope of the terrorist threat to the American homeland and to detect and identify potential threats of terrorism within the United States." The undersecretary also had responsibility for "integrating relevant information, intelligence analyses, and vulnerability assessments to identify protective priorities and support protective measures."[8] The Homeland Security Act also provided for an assistant secretary for information analysis, who reported to the undersecretary.

Potentially, this structure could have been used to create an intelligence organization for homeland security intelligence analysis. However, there was significant leeway in the language, partly reflecting a desire to give the president flexibility in implementing the legislation, and partly reflecting true disagreement between Congress and the White House over how domestic intelligence analysis was to be conducted.

One could read the language in the Homeland Security Act to mean that the new department was mandated to "integrate" and "analyze" intelligence. Alternatively, one could interpret the act so that the new department was primarily to "receive" intelligence, meaning that someone else produced it. The difference is whether the DHS is a producer of intelligence or just a recipient.

The ultimate result of this phrasing was that the new department *could* create a strong, independent intelligence operation, but only if a president decides to do so. In the event, the Bush administration did not, and so while the authorities exist to create such an organization, they have not yet been fully exercised.

Similarly, the control of information was also the subject of compromise. Under the Homeland Security Act, all agencies, including intelligence organizations, were mandated to provide the secretary of homeland security with "assessments and analytical information relating to threats of terrorism." However, this would not ordinarily include " 'raw,' unprocessed data," and the secretary would have the right to receive such data only as the president provided. The president could direct intelligence agency heads to routinely give DHS access to raw intelligence, but there is no requirement for him to do so.

The Homeland Security Act reflected political reality. Congress supported creating a new, strong, autonomous organization for homeland security intelligence analysis, and the Bush administration did not. If the administration did not want such an organization, it was futile to compel it to do so, because, in the end, the executive branch would be responsible for implementation. The resulting compromise was to "kick the can down the road," so that if a future administration wanted the organization and was willing to devote the resources to it, it had the necessary authorities.

In this context, it is noteworthy that the Bush administration had some difficulty filling the position of assistant secretary for information analysis, and the post had significant turnover—three appointees in the first three years of its existence. With this much turnover (and the fact that an acting assistant secretary was occupying the post much of the time), it would be hard to expect an effective organization to emerge in any case.

Administration Initiatives

The Bush administration's preference for improving intelligence for homeland security was to realign organizations already under the authority of the FBI director and director of central intelligence, and, after intelligence reform legislation was passed, under the new director of national intelligence.

The first step was the establishment of the Terrorist Threat Integration Center (TTIC) on May 1, 2003. The TTIC was intended to serve as a national-level "fusion center" by bringing together personnel from the FBI, DHS, Defense Department, State Department, and CIA. By assigning personnel to this organization, all the participating agencies could clear each other's representatives. This had the effect of creating a single environment in which all the participants would get access to data from all federal organizations without changing underlying authorities over classification and other information controls.

Also, with the TTIC located in a single facility, each participating agency could route its data-processing network into the TTIC spaces so that TTIC analysts would have access to them. Again, this was an expediency born out of necessity; it was easier to install several computer terminals at each analyst's desk than to get all the participating organizations to adopt or recognize each other's cybersecurity standards, or (even more challenging) get them to work under a common standard. The director of the TTIC reported to the director of central intelligence.

Although the TTIC was being established in the wake of the Homeland Security Act, other developments were also under way at the FBI, which, as noted, opposed the creation of a new domestic intelligence organization. In the months following September 11, 2001, Director Mueller undertook several initiatives.

One was to move 500 field agents from criminal investigations to counterterrorist activities. At the same time, the FBI created 66 Joint Terrorism Task Forces (JTTFs) in cities throughout the country, each comprised of personnel drawn from the FBI, CIA, Defense Department, DHS, and state and local law enforcement organizations. The mission of the JTTF is to "prevent acts of terrorism, and investigate acts of terrorism in an effort to identify and prosecute those responsible." By 2005, Mueller reported to Congress that 100 JTTFs had been established.[9]

Mueller also sought to move the FBI from its traditional decentralized system, which has been dominated by the field offices, to one that has a stronger central node in which information could be integrated and analyzed more effectively. In 2001 the FBI created an Office of Intelligence in its Counterterrorism Division. In 2003 it created similar analytic organizations in the other FBI divisions, and it integrated them under a new executive assistant director for intelligence, who was made head of the Office of Intelligence, which later became the Directorate of Intelligence.

Responses to the 9/11 and WMD Commissions

In July 2004, the 9/11 Commission issued its report. The commission recommended the creation of a new national intelligence director, who would have three deputy directors, including one for domestic intelligence. This deputy director for domestic intelligence would provide strategic direction to the intelligence components of the FBI, DHS, and other domestic agencies to ensure that they worked effectively with each other and with the foreign and military components of the intelligence community. The 9/11 Commission also proposed a National Counterterrorism Center (NCTC) to enlarge the capabilities of the TTIC. The Bush administration agreed to create a director of national intelligence (DNI) (for the time being, this was the director of central intelligence) and the NCTC. It implemented these measures through an executive order on August 28, 2004. The TTIC and its approach to information fusion were transferred to the NCTC.

Then, just after the 2004 election, Congress passed the Intelligence Reform and Terrorism Prevention Act in a lame duck session. President Bush signed the bill into law on December 17. The act established a DNI (replacing the national intelligence director) and allowed the DNI to designate up to four deputies. However, it left much of the new structure of the intelligence community up to the DNI.

President Bush deferred appointing the DNI or making major changes until the WMD [weapons of mass destruction] Commission issued its report, which was not until almost four months later, on March 31, 2005. The WMD Commission made two specific recommendations that affected the organization of domestic intelligence and, as a secondary effect, ensured that there would be no new, separate agency for domestic intelligence analysis.

First, the WMD Commission recommended that the FBI create a new National Security Service (NSS), which would subsume the FBI's Counterterrorism and Counterintelligence divisions and its Directorate of Intelligence. The new NSS would be subject to the budget authorities of the DNI, which meant that he would set its budget and apportion funds to it but not oversee its day-to-day operations; these would remain with the FBI director.

Second, the WMD Commission proposed a management structure for the DNI that was significantly different from the one proposed by the 9/11 Commission. The WMD Commission recommended deputy directors for collection, strategy integration, policy and programming, and information management. Although the DNI did not adopt this approach, the WMD Commission's proposal had the effect of defusing the recommendation that had been on the table up to that time—the proposal by the 9/11 Commission to create a deputy responsible for domestic intelligence.

So, as of mid-2005, the main responsibility for domestic intelligence continued to lie within the FBI, whose leadership said it was determined to improve the bureau's capabilities. Mueller reported to Congress that, by the end of 2006, the FBI would have approximately 2,600 analysts on the job. Mueller also reported that higher-rated slots had been created for analysts to improve recruitment and retention, although it should be noted that these slots were still lower than similar positions at the analytic divisions of the established intelligence agencies.

Prospects for the Future

One of the most compelling reasons for establishing a separate organization for homeland security intelligence analysis is that it provides an opportunity for taking a different approach to intelligence. A new organization would have no established procedures, no training program, no information network, no databases, no performance standards for evaluated employees, no staff, and so on. For many senior government officials, the lack of all of these things might seem like a problem.

But for an aggressive, entrepreneurial leader, it would be a once-in-a-lifetime opportunity. With no procedures, protocols, regulations, or tenured staff, the field would be open to explore new approaches. The head of such a new service could pick and choose from approaches that seemed to work well in the past, while having a rare opportunity to try something new—and bring in people without the burden of orthodoxy.

Establishing a separate organization for domestic intelligence analysis is not only an opportunity; it is a necessity. As we have tried to show, homeland security intelligence requires a fundamentally different approach to fill the niche between foreign intelligence and law enforcement. It is a niche yet to be filled.

Notes

1. Quoted by Jeff Stein, "FBI under the Gun," *Congressional Quarterly*, May 1, 2006, 1152.

2. Testimony of Robert S. Mueller III at the Tenth Public Hearing of the National Commission on Terrorist Attacks Upon the United States, Washington, April 14, 2004.

3. See Anthony Downs, *Inside Bureaucracy* (Boston: Little, Brown, 1967). A Google search using the terms "lawn care" and "turf" yields about 660,000 entries; a search using "organizational" and "turf" yields about 809,000 entries.

4. Sari Horwitz, "Old-School Academy in Post-9/11 World," *Washington Post*, August 17, 2006.

5. See Bruce Berkowitz, "The Big Difference between Intelligence and Evidence," *Washington Post*, February 2, 2003.

6. Seth G. Jones provides a good overview of these developments. See his "Terrorism and the Battle for Homeland Security," in *Homeland Security and Terrorism*, ed. Russell Howard, James Forest, and Joanne Moore (New York: McGraw-Hill, 2006), 266–71.

7. In 2002 the National Foreign Intelligence Program (NFIP) consisted of fifteen agencies that operated under the indirect control of the director of central intelligence (DCI); in addition to the Central Intelligence Agency, which the DCI managed directly, these included the National Security Agency, National Reconnaissance Office, and intelligence components

within the armed services, and Departments of State, Treasury, and Energy, in addition to the counterintelligence arm of the Federal Bureau of Investigation. The National Intelligence Program replaced the NFIP in December 2004 under the Intelligence Reform and Terrorism Prevention Act, and the DCI was replaced by a director of national intelligence with greater authority. (The CIA is now headed by its own director, D/CIA.)

8. Quoted passages are from "Analysis for the Homeland Security Act of 2002," White House, Washington, November 25, 2002); www.whitehouse.gov/deptofhomeland/analysis/. This was, in effect, the Bush administration's official interpretation of the statute and indicated how it intended to implement it.

9. Testimony of Robert S. Mueller III, before the Senate Select Committee on Intelligence, Washington, February 16, 2005.

CONCLUSION

The Age of Analysis

ROGER Z. GEORGE AND JAMES B. BRUCE

As the twentieth century was the age of collection, so the twenty-first will be known as the age of analysis.

—Anthony Campbell, former Canadian intelligence official[1]

THE PRECEDING CHAPTERS have made the case that intelligence analysis could and should become a profession in its own right. Professionalization by itself, of course, will not heal the wounds created by recent intelligence failures. However, collectively these chapters have made the case that a more rigorous development of professional standards as well as better use of emerging new collaborative tools and techniques can improve the performance of the U.S. intelligence community (IC). We agree. However, recognizing these opportunities is not the same as taking full advantage of them. As past cases of intelligence analysis gone awry demonstrate, the same patterns of cognitive bias, unrecognized or faulty assumptions, and poor understanding of limited information have been at the heart of the analytic community's problems since the first estimates were written in the late 1940s. So what is likely to make the difference this time?

Fixing analysis seems a perennial and elusive goal. After reviewing stubbornly persistent analytical shortcomings over the years and nearly a dozen congressional inquiries, presidential commissions, and other major study efforts to address them, the recent WMD [weapons of mass destruction] Commission observed that it was "not the first to recognize the shortcomings—we trod a well-worn path. Again and again, many of the same obstacles to delivering the best possible analytical products have been identified."[2] We, too, are treading the same well-worn path here and hope that our perspectives and insights reinforce, update, and extend the others previously delivered. But our objectives in this book are broader, because we believe the new and fresh insights offered here will combine with an opportune moment in intelligence history to propel significant improvements in this vital analytical enterprise.

The news is far from all bad. As our contributors on the origins and performance of the analytic community make clear, the profession has shown that it can adjust to emerging issues and perceived analytic failures when provided with the leadership and time necessary to make those changes. And so, as John Hedley points out in chapter 1, a strong director of central intelligence like Walter

Bedell Smith working with inspired intellectual firepower like Sherman Kent could reorganize the estimates process in the 1950s to the benefit of the intelligence and policy communities. We have reached such a time as well. Where other critics may see crisis, we see an opportunity to reshape the analytic discipline by changing the way analysts are educated and trained, led and coached, and rewarded and advanced, as well as conduct their work. The results will be better analysis.

As the quotation that opens this chapter suggests, there is now perhaps an unprecedented appreciation for the importance of analysis and the resources needed to improve it are available in a way they have not been before. Also, there has been an explosion in academic attention to intelligence studies as well as interest on the part of many social scientists in applying their tools to the practice of intelligence and thereby bringing more rigor and method to advance the profession.

As teachers of graduate students who aspire to the ranks of the twenty-first century's IC, we can only admire their enthusiasm but caution them that no outside education can fully prepare them to hit the ground running and that it will take years before most can become fully capable analysts in the IC. As practitioners and teachers, we have come to appreciate the importance of developing of a lifelong learning process for intelligence analysts. IC leadership can foster this by embracing new tools and outreach programs to empower analysts to experiment and take risks in their analysis. We will also need an IC leadership that will insist on organizational learning as well as individual learning.

Professional Education

To implement changes necessary to make the analytic corps a true profession in the way Rebecca Fisher and Rob Johnston suggest in chapter 3, a major commitment is needed to common standards, knowledge building, and a "mindfulness" about the profession throughout the IC. In chapter 14, Mark Lowenthal emphasizes that "a profession is commonly defined as an occupation that requires specialized training and the mastery of specialized knowledge." The IC is taking small steps in that direction by boosting the types of training made available to its analysts. Virtually every agency is providing more specialized training in its specific field of endeavor. For example, the Central Intelligence Agency's (CIA's) Sherman Kent School for Intelligence Analysis provides a multiweek Career Analyst Program focused on giving the entry-level analyst the traditional writing and briefing tools needed to launch a successful career. It is also developing a more advanced set of training modules to help certify the analytical qualifications of those hoping to be promoted into the Senior Analytic Service. Likewise the National Defense Intelligence College performs the same function across the Defense Department's IC, even offering a master's degree in intelligence studies. Both the National Security Agency and the National Geospatial-Intelligence Agency train in their specialized schools for the study of cryptological and geospatial intelligence disciplines, and the Federal Bureau of Investigation and Department of Homeland Security are beginning to develop analyst training to equip their newly hired analysts with the necessary skills for new and emerging domestic intelligence analytical functions.

Unfortunately, even combined, these efforts do not rise to the level of being a group of truly professional educational programs that can create the collective competence needed for advancing the state of the analytic profession. CIA director Michael Hayden actually expressed surprise in 2007 that during an intelligence officer's career, he or she might take the equivalent of only a few months of training and that very few have had concentrated time away from their desks to focus on their profession and how to advance it.[3] Contrast this to the career military officer, whose twenty years in the profession will include as much as three to four years of professional military education at command and staff schools and later senior war colleges to advance one's understanding of the art of war and its relationship to national military strategy. Military education is a prerequisite for military professionalism and career development. Clearly, training and education of this caliber are a necessary—but not sufficient—condition to advance the professionalization of the analytic corps of the IC. We can take a cue from the military and realize that equivalent professional education will require a significantly greater commitment of resources.

The potential to create a more community-wide, career-long professional training program is already envisioned in the 2004 intelligence reform act that legislated a requirement to establish a National Intelligence University (NIU). To date, this embryonic effort has focused primarily on surveying the separate training programs across the community and urging "cross-registration" of students. As of this writing, the first course sponsored by the director of national intelligence (DNI) on analysis has been initiated, but it has been met with some skepticism from the other competing agency-specific training programs. Presently, the NIU is at best a nascent program—not a building with students and faculty in it—with a tiny staff and no current aspirations to become the permanent bricks-and-mortar learning institution that the term "university" is meant to convey. Instead, the NIU should look to the established National Defense University as a successful model of professional education.

Lacking a viable NIU structure, a more promising approach to the development of career-long educational opportunities would build upon the agency-specific programs to achieve a full-scale professionalization of the American analytic community. As Lowenthal notes, the DNI was given the needed authority to create a career-long, community-wide educational system that would build "one analytic culture" rather than the multitude that exist today. But to date, it remains only an idea. In chapter 13, John Gannon also makes the case for a fully resourced National Intelligence University with a professional faculty—not a largely contracted staff, as is currently the policy—where analysts would be able to learn about their history, ethics, standards, and techniques and thus raise their self-awareness, competence, and potential for professional growth in their emerging profession.

Strategic Research

One recurring theme of many contributors to this volume is the challenge of conducting analysis in a twenty-four-hour/seven-day globalized environment. If analysis is to become a profession, it must produce more than classified journalism where analysts churn out daily or even hourly situation reports by "gisting" the latest diplomatic cables, foreign news broadcasts, or clandestine reporting, even as all-source reports. A key role for analysis, as pointed out by Roger George in chapter 7, is shaping the strategic context in which policymakers must view the world; this role demands a strategic perspective, not a journalist's copy.

Yet it is just as important, as Richard Kerr notes in chapter 2, for confident judgments to rest on a solid foundation of research. We now understand as never before that when that deep knowledge is not there, analysts seem hardwired to resort—often unwittingly—to their assumptions, beliefs, and old mindsets. In chapter 12, James Bruce shows how reliance on authority and habit of thought were poor substitutes for in-depth research on WMD programs in Iraq. The WMD Commission Report has highlighted how a "current intelligence" bias distorts understanding and crowds out longer-term research—which is important not only for more accurate analysis but also for the professional development of analysts.[4] Lowenthal further notes that most commission reports and inquiries into recent failures attribute them in part to a shift away from long-term, in-depth analysis, which prevents analysts from having a broader context into which they can place new information that might then indicate an anomaly or some new emerging trend. In chapter 9, David Thomas also reinforces this point in describing a military IC that is too focused on the current and in need of developing long-term perspectives for the many global military challenges that the U.S. Armed Forces will face in the coming decades. What the profession requires, then, is a building repository of knowledge and expertise so that analytic agencies are not dependent on relatively junior analysts for reaching consequential judgments based only on a limited understanding of a particular phenomenon, simply because no analyst had spent sufficient time researching the issue very long before this latest information arrived.

Developing strategic in-depth knowledge will depend heavily on leadership decisions that acquire and protect the necessary resources for long-term research and encourage significant educational as well as experiential opportunities, such as overseas assignments, full-time language training, and greater participation in professional conferences and academic associations. Opportunities for midlevel analysts to receive additional graduate-level training and for senior analysts to take fellowship positions with outside research centers, think tanks, and major universities are few and often only reluctantly approved because managers hate to give up their most precious resources, analysts. But these kinds of opportunities offer ready-made avenues for increasing analysts' in-depth knowledge and engagement with contrasting points of view held by nongovernmental experts or those in other disciplines.

Critics—of which there are many—have a point that intelligence analysts are not always as familiar with the outside research findings that can inform intelligence analysis.[5] Some take it even further, alleging that the academic community is more published, more insightful, and more creative. However, they also miss the point that analysts are not in government service principally to become the equivalent of tenured professors or ivory tower defense thinkers entitled to dispense their wisdom at will or against all comers.[6] Analysts are principally there to serve an ever-widening set of governmental customers who have varying policy or operational agendas and both long- and short-term needs. As George illustrates, analysts are more than academics; they are the strategist's quiet partners, the ones who warn, coach, and evaluate but never decide—their role is to inform, not advocate.

Associated with the problem of developing strategic depth is the challenge of managing the open source environment. What intelligence can bring to bear on specific policy issues is often seen as the uniquely informed insights provided from a clandestine human source, an intercept, or a covertly operating website. However, those insights from classified information also necessarily rest on understanding and mastering a wealth of academic and other research openly available to analysts. Realistically, the prospect of individual analysts being able to mine all the current academic literature on terrorism or weapons proliferation or China is nil. Hence, effective methods for exploiting these rich sources need to be found. Beyond smart search engines and screening software, academic opportunities should be exploited and expanded, including "scholars in residence" (academics cleared to work inside an analytic unit for a limited time), "officers in residence" (analysts who take temporary teaching and research assignments at American universities), and fellowships permitting year or longer research efforts in nongovernmental think tanks and universities. The key will be to make such programs attractive—and to not discourage analysts from participating in them because of the insatiable current intelligence workload that overburdens most agencies.

To the extent that the profession can build its strategic depth, it will be better positioned to deal with the perennial problems of limited collection, pervasive denial, and possible deception, as well as recurring warning problems. As the noted warning specialist Cynthia Grabo explains, strategic research is critical to detecting anomalies—that is, when something out of the normal pattern appears—and putting it into a context in which the warning analyst can recognize a significant change in the offing for which policymakers might not be prepared.[7]

In this new era, strategic research probably means it is time to recast the manner in which national estimates are conceived. Lowenthal and Kerr concur in the view that National Intelligence Estimates usually are neither influential nor especially insightful in bringing new ideas to the forefront. Though considered authoritative, they are typically a restatement of what is already known or believed by the analytic community, and they seldom involve a zero-based review of intelligence, such as when a subject like Iraq and WMD are involved. Perhaps, then, some estimates need to focus on attending to the epistemological requirements, of "what we know about a subject and how we know it," as James Bruce urges in chapter 11. Too often, what passes for deep analysis may be only the latest iteration of community thinking or conventional wisdom built on previous judgments—"layering," or habit of thought—which are accepted uncritically as still true. If some estimates were consciously focused on explicating *how* we know about North Korean and Iranian nuclear programs—for example, what assumptions we are using to estimate potential weapons production, and how we might know if these hypotheses were correct or not—

policymakers would surely receive more reliable intelligence and also be more forgiving when estimates prove to be wrong. At a minimum it would remind analysts of the uncertainties under which they operate and alert collectors for the need to find and deliver both confirming and disconfirming information to test and clarify the current thinking when major policy choices are in the making.

Self-Evaluation

Commenting on the spate of presidential commissions and congressional inquiries into the September 11, 2001, terrorist attacks and the Iraq WMD case, the head of the CIA's Analysis Directorate told his workforce in 2006: "We need to be our own best critics, because if we do not do this, someone will do it for us."[8] Indeed, the lessons to be drawn from this book's focus on analytical performance issues, cognitive biases, and management challenges suggest the IC's best defenses lie in a candid self-evaluation of what it has done well and what it has not done well. This is also the essence of a learning organization. Kerr's personal reflections on performance during the cold war suggest that there is no one-time, surefire cure. Our record has both successes and failures. Those successes were usually the result of uncommon expertise, sound tradecraft, and an adequate underlying research base on which to forecast events. The failures had multiple causes. Among them were an overreliance on assumptions and overconfidence in judgments (individually through the so-called paradox of expertise, and collectively through untested conventional wisdom); a mixture of mindsets and shoddy critical thinking or a lack of creative thinking; and often a poor understanding of the weak information base on which judgments rest, and an unwitting substitution of flawed assumptions for missing information.

What distinguishes the less advertised successful forecasts and warnings—for example, the Sino–Soviet split, the Vietnam War, the 1967 Middle East War, warnings of Polish martial law or the Soviet invasion of Czechoslovakia, the breakup of Yugoslavia, the unsuccessful 1991 Moscow coup, and several serious buildups on the Indo–Pakistani border in the mid-1990s, to mention a few— might be characterized as insight based on sound expertise and careful weighing of past precedent against new information. None of these cases was solely or even partially the result of phenomenal "smoking-gun" clandestine reporting; that is, analysts still had to make hard judgments based on incomplete and sometimes conflicting information. Weak tradecraft might easily have led to the wrong conclusions: Merely assessing the order of battle in 1967 would have led to judgments predicting an Arab victory. Succumbing to political pressures, analysts might have stopped writing critical assessments on Vietnam in the 1970s. In 1990 analysts might easily have concluded that Yugoslavia could muddle through—again. Or given the growing Soviet leadership dislike of Mikhail Gorbachev, analysts might have discounted his surviving the 1991 putsch. But solid analysis prevailed, and none of those assessments was flawed.

The *lessons learned* from intelligence failures highlight what we should do less of, and the *best practices* identified in our successes highlight what to do more regularly. Both constitute vital teaching materials for professionalization. Such lessons from candid self-evaluations and postmortems should be fully incorporated into education and training programs for analysts.[9]

The Tradecraft Imperative

Similarly, a self-evaluation of the many miscalls requires a frank admission that analysts will chronically face the continuing sources of analytic error that stalk every step of the intelligence process. Among them are collection failures that overly cripple analysis; cognitive, cultural, organizational, and political biases; poor understanding of the epistemological basis of analysis; and the needed tradecraft and methodological correctives that must repudiate any complacency that sustains doing business as usual.

The case studies examined by Bruce in chapter 12 show how analytical failures have deep roots in earlier collection failures and that better analysis will result from a deeper analytic understanding of collection capabilities and limitations. Moreover, foreign denial and deception, which Bruce and Michael Bennett examine in chapter 8, can seriously degrade intelligence reliability and accuracy, especially in the vital warning function. The most promising approach to countering foreign denial and deception is developing the *prepared mind* and the *prepared organization*. These objectives should rank among the highest priorities of senior IC leadership if fully effective intelligence is a genuine national goal in the twenty-first century.

Four chapters above emphasize the crucial linkage between analytical tradecraft and intelligence judgments. This is another way of spotlighting the inescapable methodological issue of the connection between evidence and inference. Between them lie the analyst's cognitive processes and the methodological tools to navigate the cognitive shoals that will help or hinder reliable intelligence. In chapter 10, Jack Davis highlights the importance and impact of *mindset* and several kinds of bias traps; his advice on the greater use of *structured* analysis and *challenge* analysis should be heeded by managers as well as by analysts. In chapter 11, Bruce explores the epistemological roots of analytical error and explains why a more scientific approach—empowered by self-corrective mechanisms—offers the surest route to reliable intelligence. And in chapters 16 and 17, respectively, Richards Heuer and Timothy Smith demonstrate how scientifically adapted methods for intelligence can significantly improve our potential for producing reliable knowledge and foreknowledge—that is, knowledge through tested hypotheses in the Analysis of Competing Hypotheses (ACH) and foreknowledge through computer simulations and predictive network-centric warning analysis using integrated project teams and robust collaboration.

Toward a Fuller Professionalization

Recognizing these pitfalls and promises, then, a significantly enhanced analytic tradecraft and training must remind each successive generation of analysts that it can also be prone to such errors. In the past, the IC has not wanted to broadcast its own self-inflicted wounds by conveying lessons learned to the workforce. Worse, it has also been slow to acknowledge mistakes and has appeared stubbornly defensive about errors that appear obvious to virtually everyone else.[10] Sadly, in the past, the CIA, and probably other agencies as well, closely restricted the results of postmortems partly to avoid demoralizing or demonizing analysts and managers involved in the miscalls but also to prevent outside critics from using such self-evaluations against the IC. This approach has failed, however, to stem outside criticism or reduce error. Of particular importance, it has also failed to educate the workforce about performance issues. The commanding officer of the U.S. Army's Center for Lessons Learned remarked to one editor-author several years ago that "a lesson is not learned until we see changed behavior."[11] And so the past failings of intelligence analysts must lead to different behaviors—that is, much greater use of much better tradecraft than journalism methods, greater openness to the views of outside experts, and other techniques that challenge ourselves—so that a mistake made in one part of the community is not repeated in another part. Changed behavior—if for the better—is an attribute of a learning organization.

Happily, efforts in this regard are under way, but they need to be accelerated and further institutionalized throughout the community. The CIA's Product Evaluation Staff is now establishing an impressive array of evaluations that are being shared with analytic offices to highlight analytical tradecraft where it is done well or where improvement is necessary. Analysts are being encouraged to employ structured analytic techniques (previously known as Alternative Analysis) throughout the CIA's Directorate of Intelligence in ways that have not been attempted before. Similarly, the Defense Intelligence Agency has established a "Devil's Advocate" office designed to introduce more rigorous methods and to challenge conventional wisdom on critical intelligence issues. And the CIA's director of intelligence, John Kringen, embraced the necessity for self-evaluation in his own response to the Iraq WMD Commission: "We did not try to hide from the criticism or make excuses. . . . We in the Directorate of Intelligence have been intent on improving our work by addressing the commission's recommendations—and those of several other self-initiated and external reviews—head on."[12] This sentiment—indeed, commitment to self-evaluation and excellence—must become the norm and not just a short-term response to the crisis of the moment. Therefore, more efforts to showcase best practices, lessons learned, and promising new analytic techniques are needed before the analytic profession can rightly aspire to the status of the medical or legal profession. In these more mature disciplines, self-policing and peer review boards ensure the highest quality of professional performance, ethics, and standards.

A missing piece, however, in the IC's renewed interest in applying structured analytic methods is what might be called research on "what works." For the past half decade, a series of initiatives has been under way that encourage the use of Devil's Advocacy, Team A/Team B, Scenarios Development, ACH, and other structured or challenge analytic techniques. There is a widespread hope that such efforts will improve the accuracy of analytic judgments, or at a minimum make argumentation more transparent so that analysts are more self-aware of their assumptions, biases, and collection gaps. This expectation seems reasonable, yet there has been little empirical research on how applying such techniques has actually worked in practice. Some limited social science research, for example, cautions that deeper expertise is no guarantee for better accuracy in judgments.[13] Furthermore, other studies question how much experts actually know about "what works," and that some commonly accepted techniques—for example, Devil's Advocacy—may not be so helpful in opening analysts' minds to different explanations or alternative outcomes.[14] All this suggests that the profession of analysis needs to rigorously study its methods and its results to ensure that it is instilling best practices and not simply playing with the latest academic or analytic fad.

Leading—for a Change

Several contributors have remarked that criticism of failed assessments is too often laid at the feet of the analysts and not those of managers and senior leaders.[15] As Gannon notes, "leadership is vital," for if managers do not insist on and protect analytical integrity of intelligence products, no one else will. And so managers must be accountable for more than time-card certifications and the style of analytical drafts. They also must be analytical role models, particularly at a time when so many new analysts are entering the profession and require mentoring. These managers, unfortunately, have themselves been victims of the time-tested pattern of "learning on the job," so they have little formal education in leadership skills in the fashion that the military profession has developed. Moreover, as victims of too little managerial training themselves, it is hard for them to appreciate the virtue of releasing their younger wards for extended professionalization courses and further academic training or to encourage the use of new skills, which they had not been trained to employ when learning their trade.

Leadership in new modes of analysis and new work practices, as Carmen Medina suggests in chapter 15, also will require a commitment from senior IC leaders to develop better incentive structures for analysts to experiment with greater collaboration, team projects, software tools, and to reach out to nongovernmental experts in academia and perhaps overseas. Some of the chronic obstacles that analysts face in honing their analytic skills have little to do with critical thinking or tradecraft problems and more to do with administrative and security practices adopted decades ago for the battle against the Soviet Union. As Gannon notes, the IC is long overdue to reevaluate its security practices that inhibit organizations from hiring linguistically and culturally proficient "hyphenated" Americans, or reaching out to well-known experts in academia and foreign centers of excellence. As many critiques of analytic failures note, cultural bias and mirror imaging often head the list of causes for failure; yet the security practices employed for hiring and managing analysts consciously prevents them from reaching out to experts and foreigners who better understand or convey that needed sensitivity about foreign cultures. Likewise, Medina notes that more collaborative analytic techniques will require analysts to employ the power of information sharing and other knowledge-based systems, which security practices

often impede in the workplaces. Disarming the younger analysts through policies that prohibit the most commonplace technologies of personal digital assis-
tants, cellphones, and open use of the Internet for work purposes will only
discourage a "wired" generation from entering or remaining in the analytic
profession.

The sun also may be setting on the era of the "lone analyst." What new
technologies and analytic tools offer the analytic profession is a way to harness
the collective knowledge of experts across a number of disciplines and organizations to generate and test hypotheses and scan the horizon for so-called weak
signals that might become tomorrow's major intelligence issue, security threat,
or policy opportunity. The requirements of an information-driven, fast-paced
age of warfare will, as Thomas notes, demand a great deal more agility, processing power, and most important teamwork. Technology can also be the analyst's
friend and partner. As Heuer and Smith demonstrate, many promising methods
are currently available to radically improve analytic rigor, make findings transparent and testable, and encourage analysts to revisit past judgments to avoid
the inevitable consequences of major cognitive errors. For managers, then, it is
important to encourage the use of such tools and to share what is learned about
their use with others. Smith's description of the new collaborative tools available
for foresight and warning speak forcefully about the power that technology now
offers, but managers must promote, and even insist on, opportunities for analysts to employ them more routinely and systematically. This kind of experimentation is vital to understanding where future best practices will be found.

Living with Politics

For better or worse, we have left the era when intelligence was seldom in the
news or a visible part of foreign policy debates. Indeed, the trend toward making
intelligence more relevant inevitably drives it into the realm of politics. A major
theme of this book has been how to make analysis more relevant and useful to
the policy community as well as how to articulate the strengths and weaknesses
of the profession's capabilities to policymakers—all in the service of developing
realistic expectations and measures by which to judge analysis. What the practitioners, customers, and scholars of intelligence alike suggest in this book is that
the analytic profession is going to be measured by a political yardstick as well
as by a set of analytic standards. That is, analysts are of no use to their official
customers by being merely the smartest and best-informed experts on a topic.
They must address the policy needs of whoever now sits in the White House,
executive departments, and congressional offices.

How then does the profession deal with the inherent politics of analysis? A
lesson that John McLaughlin, James Steinberg, and Gregory Treverton offer on
this theme—in chapters 4, 5, and 6, respectively—is that analysts must accept
that being relevant to their policymaking customers inherently requires them to
be immersed in politics, or certainly in those key policy issues that require intelligence support. Analysts must understand the policies that decision makers are

considering as well as the risks they are running in pursuing those policies. However, analysts must at the same time remain dispassionate about their own role in assisting those decision makers in accomplishing those goals. Like the physician who lays out the likely diagnoses and prognoses under a variety of treatment plans, the analyst must let the client decide the course of action and risks he or she is most comfortable taking. In this day and age, analysts do not have the luxury of remaining disinterested in the specific problem sets that policymakers present, any more than a physician can concentrate on medical research but ignore the specific medical complaints that a patient presents.

Unprecedented partisanship in Congress will ensure that the prospect of more political controversy surrounding intelligence analysis is higher than ever before. As the contributors to this book agree, analysts must engage policymakers, address their specific needs, and even occasionally be in the room when policy decisions are made. This is perhaps a long way from where Kent first began expostulating on the proper role of analysts in the policymaking process, but it is a fact of life. Some contributors actually urge an even deeper analytic engagement in the policy realm. The former policy official Steinberg proposes a much more active involvement of intelligence representatives in the senior policy discussions to ensure that analysts understand the precise options being considered by an administration, as well as fusing intelligence and policy functions in the newly created "centers" focused on terrorism and counter-proliferation. And Bruce Berkowitz, in discussing homeland security and analysis in chapter 18, suggests that a domestic intelligence agency and its own analytic arm are likely to be needed sooner or later. It is clear that post–September 11 intelligence analysis cannot solely focus on events overseas but must answer domestic security questions as well. If these kinds of proposals are to be implemented, politics and analysis will increasingly go hand in hand.

Under these new circumstances, however, professionalism matters all the more. To guard against politicization, analysts and managers must rely even more heavily on rigorous analytical tradecraft, a tenacious defense of analytical integrity, and a willingness to raise issues that might not be on the current agenda, even if policymakers would prefer quieter support. Neither analysts nor managers can risk an attitude that policymakers "have already made up their minds, so there is no point to raising this intelligence issue." Such analytic cowardice will not protect the integrity or credibility of the profession any more than a physician saying "the patient is not interested in hearing about the diagnosis, so let's not tell him." The DNI, the director of the CIA, and other agency heads must reassert the institutional integrity of intelligence and vigorously demonstrate to policymakers what Kerr recounted to the editors: "It was never difficult to respond to political pressure by saying that 'CIA supported the president best when it provided the best and most comprehensive analysis possible.' If that analysis ran against policy, then that was the penalty of having an independent intelligence agency."[16] In the longer term, not standing up for an analytic judgment will also reduce the policy community's respect for judgments on other matters as well. Similarly, not owning up to bad judgments or playing down their significance can erode the longer-term credibility of our analysis.[17] Indeed, it is hard for the U.S. IC to present findings on Iran and North Korea these days when its credibility for rigorous tradecraft and openness to criticism on Iraq WMD has been so tarnished.[18]

As the United States enters a new century of complex, global challenges—when its predominance is by no means assured—intelligence analysis must become an even better enabler and force multiplier for U.S. national security strategies. In this sense, further professionalization of the analytic discipline is not only a self-interested necessity for the intelligence community to combat unfair and unbalanced criticism of its performance. Rather, it is a national requirement if the United States is to remain capable of maximizing its interests and influence abroad and protecting the homeland. Nothing short of the highest quality analysis will do.

Happily, the foregoing chapters suggest that appreciably improving the performance and profession of analysis is very achievable. To do so, however, our current and future leaders must commit themselves to a significant enhancement in the education of analysts, more effective analytical tradecraft, greater strategic research, more candid self-evaluation, a genuine lessons-learning capability, and enough policy engagement to ensure focused policy relevance. Effective analytical leadership will also encourage the community to be forward leaning in its use of new technologies and approaches, and to abandon the comfortable old habits and policies that stand in the way of twenty-first-century forms of collaboration and outreach. In this way, the analytic profession can come of age and perform its rightful role as the first line of defense in an increasingly dangerous world.

Notes

1. Anthony Campbell, the former chief of the Intelligence Assessments Office in the Canadian prime minister's office, addressed the issue of the intelligence–policy relationship to a U.S. National War College audience in 2002, where he laid out the idea that the huge advances in intelligence collection systems during the cold war had advanced the IC's ability to collect information, but now the challenge would be building the analytic structure that could best utilize this wealth of facts into something usable for the decision maker. See Anthony Campbell, "Intelligence Sans Frontieres: Strategic Intelligence and National Security in a Disordered World," National War College, April 15, 2002.

2. Commission on the Intelligence Capabilities of the United States Regarding Weapons of Mass Destruction, *Report to the President of the United States, March 31, 2005* (Washington, D.C.: U.S. Government Printing Office, 2005) (hereafter, *WMD Commission Report*), 389.

3. From the editors' own experience teaching at the National War College, only a handful of IC officers are able to participate in the nine-month educational programs offered at the National War College and other service war colleges where serious study of international affairs, U.S. foreign policy, and the respective roles of the armed forces, civilian policy, and intelligence communities is offered. Far too few intelligence officers are encouraged to deepen their professional studies, once they are "on the job," whereas the military continues to sponsor military officers' pursuit of advanced degrees in military science, history, or area studies.

4. *WMD Commission Report*, chap. 8, esp. 404, 420.

5. For a blistering critique of CIA performance, see Richard L. Russell, *Sharpening Strategic Intelligence: Why CIA Gets It Wrong, and What Needs to Be Done to Get It Right* (New York: Cambridge University Press, 2007). Russell, a former CIA military analyst, asserts that

the CIA discriminates against PhDs and fails to recruit nationally or internationally recognized experts into its ranks (pp. 120–22).

6. Advanced degrees and publications are, indeed, one measure of expertise but not necessarily a safeguard against cognitive or cultural bias. To be sure, CIA Sovietologists were very familiar with outside thinking and writing on the Soviet Union and had plenty of academic company in not foreseeing the ultimate demise of the communist system. Likewise, there were academic experts prior to September 11 who felt the U.S. government was hyping the terrorist threat and that, indeed, the number of significant incidents of international terrorism was falling. In one notable case, terrorism expert Larry C. Johnson wrote in the July 10, 2001, *New York Times*, "Terrorism is not the biggest security challenge confronting the United States, and it should not be portrayed that way." Larry C. Johnson, "The Declining Terrorist Threat," *New York Times*, July 10, 2001.

7. Cynthia Grabo, *Anticipating Surprise: Analysis for Strategic Warning* (Lanham, Md.: University Press of America, 2004), 9–11.

8. Speaking to an audience at "NSA-CIA Day" in March 2005, Director of Intelligence John Kringen also added that "analysis is under scrutiny."

9. *WMD Commission Report*, 425.

10. The President's (Silberman-Robb) WMD Commission faulted the Army's National Ground Intelligence Center (NGIC), the Defense Intelligence Agency's Defense HUMINT Service, and the CIA's Weapons Intelligence, Nonproliferation, and Arms Control Center (WIN-PAC) for making "such serious errors," or resisting "admitting their errors so stubbornly that questions may be fairly raised about the fundamental culture or capabilities of the organizations themselves." *WMD Commission Report*, 195–96.

11. Colonel Larry Saul, director, U.S. Center for Army Lessons Learned, interview with Roger George, February 24, 2005.

12. John A. Kringen, "How We've Improved Intelligence: Minimizing the Risk of 'Group-think'," *Washington Post*, April 3, 2006, A19.

13. See Philip E. Tetlock, *Expert Political Judgment: How Good Is It? How Can We Know?* (Princeton, N.J.: Princeton University Press, 2005). He presents evidence that experts' predictions are often no better than those of informed generalists and that most experts suffer from a hindsight bias that leads them to exaggerate their presumed record of accuracy.

14. See Steven Rieber and Neil Thomason, "Creation of a National Institute for Analytic Methods," *Studies in Intelligence* 49, no. 4 (2006): 1–9. The authors note, "Even sincere, well-informed experts with many years of collective experience are often mistaken about what are the best methods." E.g., limited research on Devil's Advocacy often shows negative, unintended results.

15. In fact, the WMD Commission singled out a failure of management, but this has received little attention beyond the usual calls for the removal of specific managers of flawed intelligence analysis to resign—hardly a long-term solution to the problem.

16. Comments provided by Richard J. Kerr to the editors in preparation for his chapter in this volume.

17. Now somewhat embarrassing in hindsight is the four-page defense of the 2002 National Intelligence Estimate (NIE), prepared by the National Intelligence Council and published in the August 13, 2003, issue of the *Washington Post*. In this "Written Statement from CIA Director Tenet," he asserts: "We stand by the judgments of the NIE as well as our analyses on Iraq's programs over the past decade. Those outside the process over the past ten years and many of those commenting today do not know, or are misrepresenting, the facts. We have a solid, well-analyzed and carefully written account in the NIE and the numerous products before it."

18. The former International Atomic Energy Agency chief and head of the Iraq Survey Group, David Kay, writing in 2005 after the Iraq WMD debacle, reflected this problem by noting that one should avoid repeating those mistakes in Iran and that "what is in doubt is the ability of the U.S. government to honestly assess Iran's nuclear status." See David Kay, "Let's Not Make the Same Mistakes in Iran," *Washington Post*, February 7, 2005.

Glossary of Analysis Terms

all-source analysis. All-source analysis is based on the best reporting available from all sources, including HUMINT (human intelligence), IMINT (imagery intelligence), SIGINT (signals intelligence), and open sources. All-source analysts are those experts able to access both classified and unclassified sources, who are not working solely with a single source of information as imagery or SIGINT analysts.

Alternative Analysis. Alternative Analysis is the term often applied to a range of structured analytic techniques used to challenge conventional thinking on an analytic problem. The word "alternative" is used to underline the importance of using various techniques—such as Devil's Advocacy, Team A/Team B, or Analysis of Competing Hypotheses—to surface "alternative" interpretations of available information.

analysis. In intelligence, analysis is a cognitive and empirical activity combining reasoning and evidence in order to produce judgments, insights, and forecasts intended to enhance understanding and reduce uncertainty for national security policymakers. Analysts prepare "finished" assessments spanning current intelligence or more strategic research issues addressing the information requirements of government officials. Analysis includes understanding and tasking collection, assessing and using open source and classified information, generating and evaluating hypotheses about events or developments, and identifying their implications for U.S. security policies.

Analysis of Competing Hypotheses (ACH). Analysis of Competing Hypotheses is a technique for identifying alternative explanations (hypotheses) for a development and evaluating all available evidence to help disconfirm, rather than confirm, these explanations. The process arrays all the data against multiple hypotheses and determines which pieces of evidence are consistent or inconsistent with each hypothesis. Analysts can quickly see that data often support multiple hypotheses and only a few will stand out as the ones that disprove a specific explanation.

analytical tradecraft. Analytical tradecraft is the term used to describe the principles and tools used by analysts to instill rigor in their thinking and prevent cognitive biases from skewing their analytic judgments. Through the use of structured analytic techniques, analysts make their argumentation and logic more transparent and subject to further investigation.

analytic assumptions. An assumption is any hypothesis that analysts have accepted to be true and which forms the basis of their assessments. The use of assumptions is part of the analytic process, but it is often difficult for analysts to identify these hypotheses in advance. Implicit assumptions can drive an analytic argument, without their ever being articulated or examined.

anchoring bias. A form of cognitive bias, anchoring occurs when a previous analysis of a subject acts to prevent analysts from reassessing their judgments and allows for only incremental change in their forecasts. In essence, the initial judgment acts as an anchor, making the final estimate closer to the original one than should be the case, given the new information available to analysts.

basic intelligence. Basic intelligence is the fundamental and factual reference material on a country or issue, which forms the foundation on which analysts can base current and estimative analysis. Examples would include economic statistics, topographic and geographic information, and documentary information on a country's form of government, rules of law, and electoral procedures and patterns. The CIA's *World Fact Book* is a product containing basic information on major countries of the world.

caveat. A caveat is a term used within the analytic community to suggest analysts are qualifying their judgments because of a problem in sourcing or in interpreting available information regarding an intelligence topic. Caveats include the use of qualifying statements, such as "we believe" or "we estimate," which indicate that analysts are reaching judgments, not stating facts.

classified intelligence. Classified intelligence information requires special, expensive, or risky methods to collect, either by technical systems or humans, which must be protected. The risk of compromising these sources and methods is given a security classification (confidential, secret, or top secret). Classified intelligence is then shared only with cleared individuals who have a "need to know" this information. Analysts use this information in written assessments, and they carefully mark these reports with the classification according to the information used.

cognitive bias. Cognitive biases are mental errors caused by unconscious and simplified information processing strategies. The human mind's natural tendency to develop patterns of thinking or "mindsets" often distorts, exaggerates, or dismisses new information in ways that produce errors in judgment or thinking. Forms of cognitive bias can include: mirror-imaging, anchoring bias, confirmation bias, and hindsight bias, to name a few.

collection gap. Analysts identify gaps in their knowledge on a subject, and these collection shortfalls become "requirements" for future collection efforts. Identifying important collection gaps not only aids collectors, but also sensitizes analysts to the need to qualify or "caveat" their judgments or set more modest levels of "confidence" in reaching their analytic conclusions.

collector. The organizations that operate a variety of technical systems or espionage units. They are part of the U.S. intelligence community and are tasked by analysts through the development of complex sets of "collection requirements." For example, the National Security Agency is the principal SIGINT collector, while the CIA's National Clandestine Service is the principal HUMINT collector.

Competitive Analysis. Competitive Analysis refers to the explicit use of competing sets of analysts or analytic units to reach judgments on the same intelligence subject. The goal is to determine whether competing analysis will uncover different sets of assumptions, use of evidence, or contrasting perspectives that would enhance analysts' understanding of an important topic. Historically, the CIA and the Defense Intelligence Agency provided competing analysis of Soviet military developments, often based on different assumptions about Soviet behavior.

confirmation bias. Confirmation bias is the human tendency to search for or interpret information in a way that confirms a preconception. Analysts will often seek out or give more weight to evidence that confirms a current hypothesis or the "conventional wisdom" while dismissing or devaluing disconfirming information.

coordination process. Many analysts or units often review an assessment because it may discuss aspects covered by more than one expert. The lead analyst or unit will coordinate its product with other experts across the agency or even with experts in other analytic agencies. This coordination process produces a "corporate" product that reflects the collective views of an agency or the entire intelligence community rather than the individual view of the principal drafter. Coordination is sometimes blamed for watering down judgments to a lowest common denominator. Conversely, coordination ensures analytical accountability, because many analysts and managers have checked sourcing, language precision, and the quality of a product.

critical thinking. Critical thinking is that mode of thinking about any subject, content, or problem in which the individual improves the quality of his or her thinking by skillfully analyzing, assessing, and reconstructing it. Critical thinking is largely self-directed, self-disciplined, self-monitored, and self-corrective thinking. It presupposes rigorous standards of excellence and mindful command of their use.

current analysis. Current analysis is reporting on developments of immediate interest that are disseminated daily or even more frequently, allowing for little time for evaluation or further research. Current analysis appears in the daily publications like the *President's Daily Brief* (*PDB*) or the *Worldwide Intelligence Report* (*WIRe*) as well as other departmental intelligence publications.

deception. Deception refers to the manipulation of intelligence by introducing false, misleading, or even true but tailored information into intelligence collection channels with the intent of influencing analytical judgments and those who use them in decision making. Deception is used in conjunction with denial (together referred to as D&D) by both state and nonstate actors to gain advantage by reducing collection effectiveness, manipulating information, or otherwise attempting to manage perceptions by targeting intelligence producers, and through them, their consumers (e.g., policymakers and war fighters). Classic intelligence failures such as Pearl Harbor, the invasion of Normandy, and the Yom Kippur War involved deception.

denial. Activities and programs by an intelligence target intended to eliminate, impair, degrade, or neutralize the effectiveness of intelligence collection against it, within and across human and technical collection disciplines. Examples of denial include communications encryption for SIGINT, camouflage and concealment for imagery, and operational security for HUMINT and all collection disciplines. Successful denial causes intelligence gaps, and the resulting missing information often degrades analysis.

departmental intelligence. Departmental intelligence is distinguished from national intelligence in that it is produced within a single department and is largely for the use of that department's senior officials. For example, the State Department's Bureau of Intelligence and Research produces departmental intelligence principally for the use of the secretary of state and other senior State Department officials, as does the Defense Intelligence Agency for the Defense Department.

Devil's Advocacy. Devil's Advocacy is an analytic technique designed to challenge a consensus view held on an intelligence topic by developing a contrary case. Such "contrarian" analysis focuses on questioning the key assumptions or the evidence used by analysts holding to the conventional wisdom. Designed more as a test of current thinking than a true alternative to it, Devil's Advocacy has been used by some intelligence agencies on those issues said to be "life or death" matters.

diagnosticity of evidence. Diagnosticity refers to the value of evidence in proving or disproving multiple hypotheses regarding an intelligence topic. If a piece of data is consistent with only one hypothesis, then it would be judged to have high "diagnosticity" for determining the strength of a hypothesis; if, on the other hand, the data can support multiple hypotheses, it is relatively unimportant and hence of little diagnostic value.

director of national intelligence. The director of national intelligence (DNI) serves as the head of the U.S. intelligence community. The DNI also acts as the principal advisor to the president, the National Security Council, and the Homeland Security Council for intelligence matters related to national security. He also oversees and directs the implementation of the National Intelligence Program.

Directorate of Intelligence (DI). The Directorate of Intelligence is the major branch of the CIA in which all-source analysis is conducted on both regional and functional topics. Within the DI, there are offices responsible for Europe/Russia, Asia, Africa and Latin America, Near East, and South Asia as well as offices responsible for analyzing transnational issues, weapons developments, proliferation, and arms control subjects.

epistemology. Epistemology is a branch of philosophy that deals with the theory, origins, and nature of knowledge. It also deals with the methods of producing knowledge and issues concerning how one knows something, including evaluating claims that something is true or false. Common epistemologies in intelligence analysis often rely on authority (the use of sources or other authoritative references), habit of thought (which is akin to anchoring bias), rationalism (i.e., the different forms of reasoning), and empiricism (the use of collected sensory data). By combining rationalism and empiricism, the epistemology of science improves analytical reliability through internal self-corrective mechanisms that are lacking in other ways of knowing.

estimative intelligence. Finished intelligence assessments that are focused on longer-term and inherently unknowable events are termed "estimative," to convey that analytic judgments rest on incomplete or sometimes nonexistent evidence. Assessments of the future actions, behavior, or military potential of known adversaries are by definition estimative. The most well-known form of estimative intelligence is the National Intelligence Estimate (NIE), which is produced by the National Intelligence Council.

fact. A fact is verified information about something that is known to exist or to have occurred, demonstrated through observation or evidence.

finished intelligence analysis. Finished analysis refers to the written assessments produced by all-source analysts, who evaluate raw intelligence reporting and prepare reports that are then disseminated to other U.S. government agencies. Examples of finished intelligence include the *President's Daily Brief*, the *National Intelligence Daily* (now called the *WIRe*), and the Defense Intelligence Agency's *Military Intelligence Digest*—all of which are produced daily. Finished analysis also includes longer-term assessments such as NIEs.

forecast. A forecast is an intelligence judgment concerning the future. In analysis, such estimative or predictive statements aim to reduce or bound uncertainty about a developing or uncertain situation and highlight the implications for policymakers. Forecasts are accompanied by probability statements—ranging, for example, from highly likely to very unlikely—or by specifying numerical "odds" that an event or outcome will or will not happen.

Groupthink. Groupthink is a concept that refers to faulty group decision making, which prevents consideration of all alternatives in the pursuit of unanimity. Groupthink occurs when small groups are highly cohesive and must reach decisions under severe time pressures. The psychologist Irving Janis developed this notion in studying U.S. decision making during the Vietnam War. It is often misapplied to analytic failures, where there might have been cognitive errors.

hindsight bias. Hindsight bias is the inclination to see past events as being more predictable and reasonable than they appeared at the time. Analysts tend to remember their own past predictions as being more accurate than they were after the fact. Analysts become biased, in effect, by knowing what has actually happened when evaluating an earlier forecast of what might occur.

HUMINT (human intelligence). HUMINT consists of collection activities to gain access to people (agents or liaison services), locations, or things (e.g., information systems) to obtain sensitive information that has implications for U.S. security interests. Examples would be information collected clandestinely by agents, obtained from foreign intelligence services of other governments ("liaison"), or more openly by diplomats and military attaches and other U.S. government officials. HUMINT is particularly valuable for analysts when assessing the plans and intentions of governments or nonstate actors.

hypothesis. A hypothesis is usually a testable theory about an intelligence topic or target, which the analyst attempts to confirm or disconfirm by examining all the evidence available. It can be a general proposition about how an adversary might be expected to behave or an explanation for why some event has occurred, which can be tested by evaluating all available information to see if those data are consistent with the hypothesis.

IMINT (imagery intelligence). Sometimes referred to as PHOTINT (photo intelligence), imagery intelligence is derived from the images collected from a variety of platforms, ranging from hand-held cameras to space-based and other overhead technical imaging systems. Imagery analysts study specific intelligence targets through the use of imaging systems and issue reports based principally on those collected images. The National Geospatial-Intelligence Agency processes and analyzes IMINT and geospatial data for use by all-source analysts and other U.S. government agencies.

insight. Insight is characterized by a clear or deep understanding of a complex situation. In analysis, insight is a new way of perceiving an issue that the policymaker finds useful and/or thought provoking in fashioning policy initiatives or in rethinking current policies.

intelligence community (IC). As of 2007, the intelligence community includes the following sixteen agencies or key elements of them: Air Force Intelligence, Army Intelligence, the Central Intelligence Agency (CIA), Coast Guard Intelligence, the Defense Intelligence Agency (DIA), the Department of Energy (DOE), the Department of Homeland Security (DHS), the State Department's Bureau of Intelligence and Research (INR), the Department of the Treasury, the Drug Enforcement

Agency (DEA), the Federal Bureau of Investigation (FBI), Marine Corps Intelligence, the National Geospatial-Intelligence Agency (NGA), the National Reconnaissance Office (NRO), the National Security Agency (NSA), and Navy Intelligence. The Director of National Intelligence (DNI) heads the IC.

intelligence failure. While there is no commonly accepted definition, failure occurs when there is a systemic or organizational inability to collect correct and accurate information in a timely fashion, or interpret this information properly and analyze it in a timely way in order to alert policymakers to a major new development. Typically, an intelligence failure is characterized by collection and analysis problems, as well as insufficient attention to bringing a warning to policymakers so they can respond appropriately.

Intelligence Reform and Terrorism Prevention Act of 2004. This legislation created the director of national intelligence and implemented many of the recommendations of the 9/11 Commission as well as other studies and commissions that focused on intelligence reform. Among the recommendations that this legislation implements were the creation of a director of national intelligence, a National Counterterrorism Center, and a National Counterproliferation Center.

interagency process. Analysts participate in many "interagency" meetings, where they present their intelligence assessments for use in policy discussions among the National Security Council, State Department, and Defense Department. Working-level "interagency" meetings are often held prior to more senior-level meetings where decisions will be made. Typically, analysts support discussions at the working level and participate in those meetings. For Deputies Committee (deputy secretary-level) or Principals Committee (secretary-level) meetings, analysts will provide briefing papers or prepare senior IC leaders who will represent the IC at those discussions.

judgment. A judgment is an analyst's conclusion characterizing a complex intelligence issue and providing a sound explanation or plausible forecast for some event or development. It rests on a critical evaluation of available evidence and a careful weighing of alternative hypotheses that might explain the event or development.

knowledge. Knowledge is justified true belief. It comprises facts, ideas, and an understanding or cognition of what is known, or the fact or condition of knowing something.

Lessons Learned. A Lessons Learned process is an approach to knowledge management whereby an organization's tacit and explicit intellectual capital is captured, validated, stored, and disseminated in order to provide all members access to the wisdom gained from past experiences. The primary goals of any Lessons Learned initiative are to develop best practices, improve training, locate expertise, and refine policies and procedures. Noteworthy Lessons Learned programs include NASA's Lessons Learned Information System and the U.S. Army's Center for Army Lessons Learned.

level of confidence. Analysts must determine how confident they are in reaching analytic judgments based on the quality of the information available and the complexity of the issue. Assigning a "low" level of confidence to a judgment may result from collection gaps, contradictory information, or the presence of deception and denial. "High" confidence may result from having very sensitive HUMINT or extremely precise technical intelligence on a military plan or a weapons system that is corroborated from multiple, independent sources.

MASINT (measurement and signature intelligence). Measurement and signature intelligence is technically derived intelligence data other than standard imagery and SIGINT. It employs a broad group of disciplines including nuclear, optical, radio frequency, acoustics, seismic, and materials sciences. Examples of MASINT are the detection of low-yield nuclear tests by seismic sensors or by collecting and analyzing the composition of air and water samples.

military analysis. Military analysis encompasses basic as well as current and estimative assessments of a foreign government's or non-state actor's military capabilities and intentions, including: order of battle, training, tactics, doctrine, strategy, and weapons systems. It also examines the entire battle space (e.g., land, sea, air, space, and cyber) as well as transportation and logistics capabilities. Other broad areas are the military production and support industries; underground facilities; military and civilian command, control, and communications systems (C3); camouflage, concealment, and deception; foreign military intelligence; and counterintelligence.

mindset. A mindset is a type of cognitive filter or lens through which information is evaluated and weighted by the analyst. Beliefs, assumptions, concepts, and information retrieved from memory form a mindset or mental model that guides perception and processing of new information. Typically, a mindset rests on a series of assumptions about the way the target of the analyst's investigation behaves. Closely related to mindset is a "mental model," which connotes a more highly developed set of ideas about a specific subject. Mindsets and mental models form quickly and become hard to change, particularly when they prove useful in forecasting future trends; once proven successful, analysts accept them uncritically despite changes in the environment that would suggest they have become outdated or inaccurate.

mirror imaging. Mirror imaging is a cognitive error that occurs when analysts presume that a foreign actor will behave much as they would in the same situation. In this sense, the analysts see their image when they observe the foreign actor. Often analysts have developed a strong expertise on a subject and believe there is a logical way to develop a weapons system, conduct a coup, or reach a decision. They will, then, presume that a foreign actor would go about these tasks as they would. Classic examples include analytic views that assumed risk-averse Soviet behavior in the Cuban missile crisis or similar Arab reluctance to start a war with Israel in 1973.

National Clandestine Service (NCS). Formerly known as the Directorate of Operations (DO), the National Clandestine Service now is responsible for directing all HUMINT operations across the U.S. government, including the FBI and Department of Defense, for conducting foreign intelligence collection and covert action abroad. The director of the NCS reports to the director of the Central Intelligence Agency. As such the NCS is the principal "collection" manager—like the National Security Agency for SIGINT—for human intelligence.

National Counterproliferation Center (NCPC). The National Counterproliferation Center was established in 2005 within the Office of the Director of National Intelligence. It coordinates intelligence support to stem the proliferation of weapons of mass destruction (WMD) and related delivery systems. It also develops long-term strategies for better collection and analysis on future WMD threats.

National Counterterrorism Center (NCTC). The National Counterterrorism Center was established in 2005 as part of the Intelligence Reform and Terrorism Prevention Act of 2004. The NCTC integrates all intelligence—both foreign and domestic—within the U.S. government pertaining to terrorism and counterterrorism. It conducts strategic operational planning and also produces intelligence analysis for key policy agencies. It is part of the Office of the Director of National Intelligence.

National Intelligence Council (NIC). The National Intelligence Council is responsible for producing National Intelligence Estimates (NIEs) for the U.S. government and for evaluating community-wide collection and production of intelligence by the intelligence community. The NIC is made up of roughly a dozen senior intelligence officers, known as national intelligence officers.

National Intelligence Daily (NID). A compilation of significant current intelligence items published six days a week by the CIA's Directorate of Intelligence in consultation with the Defense Intelligence Agency, the State Department's Bureau of Intelligence and Research, and the National Security Agency. It was provided to senior officials throughout the U.S. national security agencies and to overseas commands and diplomatic posts. In its new form, including electronic versions, the *NID* has been redesigned and named the *Worldwide Intelligence Report (WIRe).*

National Intelligence Estimate (NIE). A National Intelligence Estimate is usually a strategic assessment of the capabilities, vulnerabilities, and probable courses of action of foreign nations or nonstate actors produced at the national level as a composite of the views of analysts throughout the U.S. intelligence community (IC). It is prepared under the auspices of the National Intelligence Council, and one or more national intelligence officers will guide the drafting of the estimate. Analysts throughout the IC participate in preparing and approving the text. The NIE is then presented to the heads of the U.S. intelligence community and officially released by the director of national intelligence as the IC's most authoritative statement on an intelligence subject.

national intelligence officer (NIO). A national intelligence officer is a senior expert on either a regional area (e.g., Europe, Asia, Africa, Middle East) or a functional area (e.g., weapons of mass destruction, transnational threats, conventional military) who directs the production of NIEs on those topics. They guide and evaluate the quality of analysis in their substantive areas. NIOs represent intelligence community analysts at interagency meetings and interact regularly with senior policy officials to ensure intelligence production is directed at policy issues of importance.

"need-to-know" principle. Senior intelligence managers use this principle to determine whether intelligence will be shared with other intelligence professionals or policy officials. According to executive order, the knowledge or possession of such information shall be permitted only to persons whose official duties require such access in the interest of promoting national defense.

opportunity analysis. Opportunity analysis (sometimes referred to as action analysis) directly supports implementation of U.S. security policies by assessing the factors that could help policy planners and other decision makers to seize opportunities presented to them. While not endorsing any policy options, opportunity analysis assesses the costs and benefits of different policy actions that policymakers might consider.

order of battle (OOB). In military analysis, the order of battle identifies military units, their command structure, and the strength and disposition of personnel, equipment, and units of an organized military force on the battlefield.

OSINT (open source intelligence). Open source intelligence involves collecting information from unclassified, publicly available sources and analyzing its significance to the U.S. government. Open sources include: newspapers, magazines, radio, television and computer-based information in many foreign languages; public data found in government reports, press releases, and speeches; and professional and academic journals and conference proceedings. Increasingly, open source has focused on exploiting the Internet world of websites and bloggers. The Open Source Center is the intelligence community's primary organization responsible for the collection and analysis of open source information.

paradox of expertise. Scholars of analytic organizational cultures believe that the more expert analysts become, the more prone they are to making errors because of overconfidence in, or overreliance on, developed mental models. The paradox is that their substantive knowledge of a subject has led them to dismiss unlikely scenarios or "weak signals" of a major discontinuity.

politicization. There is no generally accepted definition of politicization, but it commonly refers to the intentional biasing of intelligence analysis to suit a particular set of political goals or agendas. Analysts can be prone to politicization if they allow their personal views to influence their analytic judgments; likewise, policymakers can "politicize" intelligence by inducing analysts to tailor their judgments to suit a policy agenda or by misrepresenting analysis as supporting their preferred policies.

***President's Daily Brief* (PDB).** The *President's Daily Brief* is a compilation of current intelligence items of high significance to national policy concerns provided daily by the Central Intelligence Agency, the Defense Intelligence Agency, and the State Department's Bureau of Intelligence and Research. A daily briefer delivers it to the president, and other briefers provide it to a select group of senior officials designated by the president as recipients. The *PDB* is constantly being refined to suit the individual needs of each president's preference for format, presentation style, and length.

Red Team Analysis. This structured analytical technique is aimed at countering cultural bias and the "mirror-imaging" problem by constructing a team of analysts who will consciously try to "think like the enemy" rather than like American intelligence analysts. The "Red Team" analysts study and then role play the key decision makers in a foreign government or perhaps a terrorist cell. They adopt the same decision-making styles, goals, or methods that an adversary might use in accomplishing its objectives. The Red Team assessments provide U.S. policymakers with an unconventional look at how their opponents might perceive a situation.

satisficing. Cognitive theorists have determined that the human brain searches for the quickest way to explain observed phenomena. Accordingly, the brain stops seeking out better explanations for some phenomenon once it finds a good enough or "satisficing" hypothesis. In decision-making situations, cognitive psychologists also have observed that groups often settle on the first satisfactory explanation for a problem and then rely upon it, despite subsequent information that might undermine the credibility of this initial hypothesis.

Scenarios Analysis (or Scenarios Development). This structured analytic technique is designed to generate multiple hypotheses about a future trend or development through the use of group-designed exercises that create alternative futures. Scenario exercises bring together experts from diverse fields and invite them to brainstorm on key factors that will shape future trends. After determining the key factors (often called "drivers"), the exercise designs three or more different futures by combining these drivers in different ways. The technique has been used extensively in private industry and other business consulting firms, but is now regularly employed by intelligence and other national security agencies.

SIGINT (signals intelligence). Interception and analysis of a target's use of technical signals and communications systems. It encompasses COMINT (communications intelligence) as well as ELINT (electromagnetic intelligence) and FISINT (foreign instrumentation or telemetry). The National Security Agency is the principal SIGINT collector in the U.S. government.

signature. Analysts rely on understanding unique "signatures" or patterns in the way a target operates, equips, or deploys military forces or weapons systems. For example, patterns of military communications can also indicate how military forces are likely to operate in the field; these signatures might indicate levels of readiness or whether operations were under way.

situation reporting. Situational reporting (commonly called "sit-reps") is analysis that is rapidly disseminated as soon as analysts prepare it, to give policymakers the most up-to-date information for a quickly developing story. "Sit-reps" typically focus on what the facts are and any immediate implications of the event. Reporting on coups, deaths of world leaders, military clashes, sudden breakdowns in order or negotiations would be the most likely topics of such reporting.

sources and methods. Sources and methods are those technical and human means of gathering information clandestinely on intelligence topics. A source can be a satellite imaging system operating high above a foreign country, a diplomat's reporting from an embassy, or a source's clandestine meeting with a case officer to report on a high-level meeting of his government. Analysts must "source" their reports and assessments by demonstrating they have a variety of reporting, preferably from very different kinds of sources and collection disciplines, and assess the validity and credibility of the reporting. Such scrutiny reduces the chances of deception or fabrication of reporting if it came from a single source.

strategic analysis. Unlike situational reporting or current analysis, strategic analysis focuses less on events than on long-term trends. It is usually performed only on subjects of enduring interest to the United States. For example, strategic analysis of foreign ballistic missile developments or of the Chinese military would be of enduring interest to policymakers, regardless of their immediate policy agendas. Strategic analysis is inherently "estimative," as there is little detailed information on trends beyond a year or more.

structured analytic techniques. Structured analytic techniques are used to provide more rigor to analytic judgments and to make them more transparent and testable. Various structured analytic techniques—such as Devil's Advocacy, Team A/Team B, Analysis of Competing Hypotheses, or Scenarios Analysis—attempt to record the logic employed by analysts in reaching judgments. By structuring the analysis according to a set of principles (e.g., listing key assumptions, evaluating the quality of information, examining multiple hypotheses, identifying collection gaps, or detecting possible deception and denial), analysts can establish more systematically their levels of confidence in judgments reached. Moreover, they can also track changes in their judgments over time and revisit conclusions that new evidence might appear to challenge.

Team A/Team B Analysis. This structured analytic technique uses separate analytic teams that contrast two or more strongly held views or competing hypotheses about an intelligence topic. Each team will develop its assessments using the available evidence after laying out their key assumptions about the topic. The value comes in arraying the two competing views side-by-side, which highlights how different premises cause analysts to reach different conclusions.

tradecraft. In analysis, tradecraft comprises the cognitive and methodological tools and techniques used by analysts to gather and organize data, interpret their meaning, and produce judgments, insights, and forecasts for policymakers and other users of finished intelligence products. An example of intelligence tradecraft is the Analysis of Competing Hypotheses. See *analytical tradecraft.*

warning analysis (strategic and tactical). Warning analysis anticipates potentially threatening or hostile activities and alerts policymakers to the possible implications should the activity occur. "Strategic" warning refers to relatively long-term developments, which provide a lengthy period of time before the event during which a policymaker can develop policies or countermeasures. "Tactical" warning refers to alerting policymakers to near-term events, for which there is little time to prepare.

***Worldwide Intelligence Report* (WIRe).** The *Worldwide Intelligence Report* has replaced the *National Intelligence Daily* (*NID*) as the CIA's current publication circulated throughout the U.S. government to senior policy officials. This is now a more web-based publication that has an electronic dissemination within Washington and overseas. It can be updated frequently throughout the day, rather than operate as a once-a-day publication like the *NID*.

worst-case analysis. Worst-case analysis occurs when analysts "assume the worst" in reaching judgments about a future event. It can occur when analysts base their analysis on assumptions that an adversary will always select a course of action aimed to create the worst problem for the United States or that the adversary's intentions are uniformly hostile toward the United States. Likewise, analysts are often accused of using such assumptions in an effort to ensure that they never fail to warn a policymaker of a possible surprise. Worst-case analysis, then, becomes a rationale for policymakers to ignore warnings that were actually far more balanced than assumed.

Contributors

Michael Bennett works as a consultant in northern Virginia. He has more than twenty years of experience in a variety of intelligence-related disciplines in both the government and the private sector and has conceived and managed projects in the areas of denial and deception, product and image security, and advanced technical collection systems. He is the coauthor of *Counterdeception Principles and Applications for National Security*.

Bruce Berkowitz is a Research Fellow at the Hoover Institution at Stanford University. His most recent government assignment was as Director, Forecasting and Evaluation, at the Department of Defense. He previously served as a CIA analyst and has published numerous books and articles about intelligence and national security affairs.

James B. Bruce is a senior political scientist at the RAND Corporation and an adjunct professor at Georgetown University in the Security Studies Program. He is a retired career CIA intelligence analyst and has served with the National Intelligence Council and in both Directorates of Intelligence and Operations and has worked extensively with other organizations in the Intelligence Community. He has taught at the National War College and has written numerous studies on intelligence and deception.

Jack Davis is a retired career CIA analyst who has written numerous articles and monographs dealing with the development and improvement of analytic methods. He is a former national intelligence officer for Latin America and served for many years as a senior instructor in the CIA's analytic training program. He continues to consult with the CIA on analytic methods.

Rebecca Fisher is a writer, researcher, and librarian whose career before joining the Intelligence Community was spent in medical libraries, including Georgetown University School of Medicine's Dahlgren Memorial Library, where she taught evidence-based medicine research techniques to medical students, faculty, and researchers. She has a particular interest in how users select and evaluate information products and how information-seeking behaviors and access to information affect life choices.

John C. Gannon is a retired career CIA intelligence analyst and adjunct professor at Georgetown University in the Security Studies Program. He has served in numerous analytic positions at the CIA, including as Deputy Director of Intelligence and as Chairman of the National Intelligence Council. He was the Staff Director on the House Select Committee on Homeland Security. He is currently Vice President for Global Analysis at BAE Systems.

Roger Z. George is currently a senior analyst with the CIA's Global Futures Partnership and an adjunct professor at Georgetown University in the Security Studies Program. He is a career CIA intelligence analyst who has served at the State and Defense Departments and has been the national intelligence officer for Europe. He has taught at the National War College and at private universities and is coeditor with Robert D. Kline of *Intelligence and the National Security Strategist: Enduring Challenges*.

John H. Hedley is a former editor of the *President's Daily Brief* and served as Chairman of the CIA's Publications Review Board. He has been the CIA Officer in Residence and an adjunct professor teaching intelligence at Georgetown University. He is a consultant for the National Intelligence Council and the CIA's Center for the Study of Intelligence, and he serves on the editorial board of the *International Journal of Intelligence and Counterintelligence*. He has written widely on intelligence issues.

Richards J. Heuer Jr. is a retired career CIA officer who served in the Directorates of Operations and Intelligence. He has written extensively on analysis, deception, counterintelligence, and personnel security. His book, *Psychology of Intelligence Analysis*, discusses the cognitive issues associated with analysis and is widely used in training analysts throughout the Intelligence Community. Most recently, he guided development of the software for Analysis of Competing Hypotheses.

Rob Johnston is an ethnographer who specializes in national security and the anthropology of work. He is the Lessons Learned Program Manager at the CIA's Center for the Study of Intelligence. He has been an Associate of the National Intelligence Council and a visiting scholar at the Sherman Kent Center, and he is the author of *Analytic Culture in the U.S. Intelligence Community: An Ethnographic Study*.

Richard J. Kerr is a former Acting Director and Deputy Director of Central Intelligence at the CIA. He spent more than thirty years as a career intelligence analyst, beginning in 1960 when he started analyzing Soviet military developments. He has held senior analytic positions at the CIA, including Office Director for East Asian Analysis and Deputy Director for Intelligence. Since his retirement in 1992, he has served on numerous high-level boards to review the quality of intelligence analysis.

Mark M. Lowenthal is President and Chief Executive Officer of the Intelligence and Security Academy and an adjunct professor of International and Public

Affairs at Columbia University. He has worked on intelligence analysis at the CIA and Department of State as well as serving as Staff Director of the House Permanent Select Committee on Intelligence. His last government post was Assistant Director of Central Intelligence for Analysis and Production. He is the author of *Intelligence: From Secrets to Policy.*

John McLaughlin is currently senior research fellow at the Paul H. Nitze School of Advanced International Studies, Johns Hopkins University. During his career at the CIA, he held numerous senior official positions, including Deputy Director of Intelligence, Chairman of the National Intelligence Council, Deputy Director of Central Intelligence, and Acting Director of Central Intelligence. He is also a frequent commentator on national news broadcasts.

Carmen A. Medina is the Director of the CIA's Center for the Study of Intelligence. Most recently, she was the Deputy Director of Intelligence. As a career CIA analyst, she has served in a number of analysis positions and has been responsible for transnational issues as well as the management of the CIA's current analysis. She has also written several articles on improving analysis.

Timothy J. Smith is a career analyst with the Office of Naval Intelligence (ONI). He has performed multiple duties in operational intelligence, warfare analysis, and modeling and simulation. He serves today as an analytic methodologist in ONI's Advanced Maritime Analysis Cell, which supports the Office of the Director of National Intelligence's policy of modernizing intelligence community integration, collaboration, and assessment methodology and tools.

James B. Steinberg served as Deputy National Security Adviser to President Bill Clinton from December 1996 to August 2000. He is also a former Director of the State Department's Policy Planning Staff and a former Deputy Assistant Secretary of State for Intelligence and Research. After leaving government, he was the Director of Foreign Policy Studies at the Brookings Institution and is now the Dean of the Lyndon B. Johnson School of Public Affairs at the University of Texas at Austin.

David Thomas is a senior intelligence officer in the Joint Warfare Support Office of the Defense Intelligence Agency (DIA) and an adjunct professor of intelligence studies at the Institute of World Politics in Washington. During his career at the DIA, he has worked on Soviet strategic military issues in the Foreign Intelligence Directorate as well as on counterintelligence and transnational warfare. He has also held assignments in the Office of the Secretary of Defense and the National Intelligence Council.

Gregory F. Treverton is Director of the RAND Corporation's Center for Global Risk and Security. He has taught at the Pardee RAND Graduate School as well as Harvard and Columbia Universities. He served on the staff of the Senate Select Committee on Intelligence and the National Security Council, and he has been the Vice Chairman of the National Intelligence Council. He has written widely on national security affairs, and his most recent book on intelligence is *Reshaping National Intelligence for an Age of Information.*

Index

Note: Page numbers followed by box, t or f indicate boxes, tables and figures in the text. Page numbers followed by n indicate endnotes.